RUSSIAN BIBLIOGRAPHY SERIES, 2

PHILIP CLENDENNING
ROGER BARTLETT

EIGHTEENTH CENTURY RUSSIA: A SELECT BIBLIOGRAPHY OF WORKS PUBLISHED SINCE 1955

Oriental Research Partners, Newtonville, 1981

ISBN 0-89250-110-3 (cloth)
ISBN 0-89250-111-1 (paper)

For a Catalogue of ORP publi-
cations, write to the Editor,
ORP, Box 158, Newtonville,
Mass. 02160

This work is #2 in our Russian
Bibliography Series.

ISBN 0-89250-110-3 (cloth) $18.00
ISBN 0-89250-111-1 (paper) $8.95

PREFACE

This bibliography seeks to provide up-to-date and representative coverage of recent writing on Russia in the eighteenth century. We have had in mind principally the undergraduate student, and the graduate starting out upon research; we hope that our work will also be of use to others. It has seemed to us that such a listing would fill a gap in existing bibliographical coverage, complementing, though not superseding, established works in the field.

As non-professional bibliographers working in an unfamiliar discipline, we are aware that we have not avoided all the pitfalls that await beginners. We have benefited from the help of a number of scholars expert in the field: Dr. David Griffiths, Prof. L. Lewitter , Dr. Isabel de Madariaga, Prof. Marc Raeff and Mr. J.S.G. Simmons read an early draft of the manuscript and made valuable suggestions. We have however sometimes neglected their advice in pursuit of our own solutions; and we are of course solely responsible for whatever errors and defects may remain. Our thanks are also due to Dr. A.G. Cross; to the staff of several libraries in Britain and the United States, notably the Bodleian Library, Oxford, Cambridge University Library, and the Widener Library, Harvard University; and especially to Ruth Parker, who typed expertly a difficult manuscript.

Philip Clendenning

Roger Bartlett

July 1980

i

INTRODUCTION

The bibliography is intended for use in undergraduate and early graduate studies, and accordingly includes material published not only in English and Russian, but also in French and German, the two European languages most useful and most accessible to American and British students of Imperial Russia. (One or two items of bibliographical value in other languages are also listed.) The contents cover separately published items, and articles in periodicals and collective works, which have appeared since 1955. Systematic coverage has been attempted to the end of 1978; for the succeeding period it has been as complete as publication schedules, our own and others', have permitted. Major journals in all four languages have been searched systematically, others consulted for particular topics or references. As far as possible we have examined personally all books listed, but this has not always been feasible, especially for very recent items.

Our aim has been to give representative coverage of recent work, and to reflect the nature and extent of scholarly interest in different areas of the general field, while at the same time maintaining a balance between these areas. It should be noted particularly that in grouping all material on cultural and intellectual developments into one section, we have not done justice to the extensive body of writing on eighteenth century language and literature. In this sphere we have tried merely to indicate the most relevant guides and reference works, and to highlight major topics.

We have usually excluded purely popular works unless (as for instance in some parts of Section 5) the absence of anything better made it seem worthwhile to mention their existence. We have included some reprints, especially those which contain new introductions or scholarly apparatus, or which make widely available older works to which we attach great importance. A small number of pre-1955 items of special interest has been included on the same basis. Doctoral dissertations accepted in Britain and North America have all been listed or referred to, together with a sprinkling from elsewhere. A final section of 'Addenda and Forthcoming Works' includes both late additions and items which we have sound reason to believe, from reliable publishers' information or from consultations with colleagues, will appear shortly. (We cannot however guarantee that all such works will appear, or will appear under the exact title listed.) An Appendix lists the eighteenth-century contents of two major pre-revolutionary Russian document collections which are of particular relevance, and which are not conveniently listed, in detail, elsewhere.

Lastly, we would emphasize that our work by no means claims to supersede existing bibliographies in the field. The student will find in the works of Berkov, Crowther, Hnik, Horak, Mayer, Terry, many items which we do not cover; and we have tried particularly

to indicate specialised bibliographies which will open up further
the different topics covered in our sections.

ARRANGEMENT

Entries have been classified into sixteen sections, which
have been further sub-divided according to the requirements of the
subject and the material involved. Sections are prefaced by brief
introductory comments. Arrangement within each section takes
account of several factors. Firstly, to facilitate use by those
unfamiliar with all the languages involved, we have divided the
material by language, English first, then French, German, Russian.
Within this division we have combined two different principles: to
proceed from the general to the particular, and from early work to
late. Thus bibliographical, survey, reference and general works
appear at the beginning of each section; the latest and the more
specialised publications tend to appear at the end.

FORM OF ENTRY

Individual volumes are normally listed under author or
(principal) editor, or failing these, under the name of the corpor-
ate body responsible for the work. There follow title; place and
date of publication; pagination (except in some cases where items
could not be examined and pagination was not established). Volume
number and edition are also shown where relevant. Reference is
given to reviews of some more important, controversial, or inacces-
sible works, and some entries have been annotated where this was
felt particularly desirable. Titles of articles are given in single
inverted commas, followed by journal title, volume or issue number
and date, and page numbers. Where an article is included in a separately published volume, the form "in:" precedes the volume editor
or title. Abbreviations have been used only for the journal titles
most frequently cited: these abbreviations are listed below. Less
common titles are given in full. Cross-references within entries
are usually given by one-word name and/or by title, followed in
brackets by the number of the entry referred to.

Russian names and titles have been transliterated in accor-
dance with a modified version of the Library of Congress system.

TABLE OF CONTENTS

ABBREVIATIONS

TITLES

AATSEEL.	*Journal of the American Association of Teachers of Slavic and Eastern European Languages. Afterwards SEEJ*
ABSEES.	*ABSEES, Soviet and East European Abstracts Series*
Acta Poloniae Hist.	*Acta Poloniae Historiae*
A. Ezh.	*Arkheograficheskii Ezhegodnik*
AHR.	*American Historical Review*
Am. Neptune.	*American Neptune*
Annales.	*Annales. Economies, Sociétés, Civilisation.*
ASEER.	*American Slavonic and East European Review. Afterwards SR.*
CalSlSt., Calif.Sl.St.	*Californian Slavic Studies*
CanAmSlSt.	*Canadian-American Slavic Studies*
Cath. Hist. Rev.	*Catholic Historical Review*
CMRS.	*Cahiers du Monde Russe et Soviétique*
Comp.St. in Soc. and Hist.	*Comparative Studies in Society and History*
CSS, CanSlSt.	*Canadian Slavic Studies. Afterwards CanAmSlSt.*
Econ.Dev.Cul.Change	*Economic Development and Cultural Change*
EEQ.	*East European Quarterly*
EHR., Econ.Hist.Rev.	*Economic History Review*
Eng. Hist. Rev.	*English Historical Review*
Et.Slav.Est.Eur.	*Etudes Slaves et Est-Européennes*
Eur.St.Rev.	*European Studies Review*
Ex. Ent. Hist.	*Explorations in Entrepreneurial History*

Ezh. A.I.	*Ezhegodnik po agrarnoi istorii Vostochnoi Evropy*
Ezh. gos. ist. muz.	*Ezhegodnik gosudarstvennogo istoricheskogo muzeia*
Ezh. ruk. otd. Push. Doma	*Ezhegodnik rukopisnogo otdeleniia Pushkinskogo Doma (Instituta russkoi literatury AN SSSR).*
Frants. Ezh.	*Frantsuzskii Ezhegodnik*
Harvard SS., Harvard Sl.St.	*Harvard Slavic Studies*
Hist.Ed.Q.	*History of Education Quarterly*
Hist. Zt.	*Historische Zeitschrift*
HJ.	*Historical Journal*
Indiana Sl.St.	*Indiana Slavic Studies*
Ist. Arkhiv.	*Istoricheskii Arkhiv*
Ist. i ist.	*Istoriia i istoriki*
Ist. SSSR.	*Istoriia SSSR*
I.Z.	*Istoricheskie Zapiski*
Izv. AN ESSR.	*Izvestiia Akademii Nauk Estonskoi SSR*
Izv. Voronezhsk. Gos.Ped. In-ta	*Izvestiia Voronezhskogo Gosudarstvennogo Pedagogicheskogo Instituta*
JbfGO.	*Jahrbücher für Geschichte Osteuropas*
JbfWirt.	*Jahrbuch für Wirtschaftsgeschichte*
JEEcH., J.Eur.Econ.Hist.	*Journal of European Economic History*
JEH., J.Econ.Hist.	*Journal of Economic History*
JES., J.Eur.Stud.	*Journal of European Studies*
JfGSLE.	*Jahrbuch für Geschichte der Sozialistischen Länder Europas*
JHI.	*Journal of the History of Ideas*
JMH.	*Journal of Modern History*
J.Russ.Stud.	*Journal of Russian Studies*

OSP.	Oxford Slavonic Papers
RES, Rev.Et.Sl.	Revue des Etudes Slaves
RH.	Russian History
RR.	Russian Review
Sb. nauch. rabot aspirantov Ist.Fak.MGU.	Sbornik nauchnykh rabot aspirantov Istoricheskogo Fakul'teta Moskovskogo Gosudarstvennogo Universiteta
Scand.Econ.Hist.Rev.	Scandinavian Economic History Review
SEEJ.	Slavonic and East European Journal
SEER.	Slavonic and East European Review
SGECRN.	Study Group on Eighteenth-Century Russia, Newsletter
SR.	Slavic Review
StGrL.	Studien zur Geschichte der russischen Literatur des 18. Jahrhunderts
Teoret. vop. fiz. i ekon. geografii	Teoreticheskie voprosy fizicheskoi i ekonomicheskoi geografii
Trans. Cam. Bibl. Soc.	Transactions of the Cambridge Bibliographical Society
Uk.Hist.	Ukrainian History
Uk.Q.	Ukrainian Quarterly
VLU(Ist.)	Vestnik Leningradskogo Gosudarstvennogo Universiteta (Istoriia)
VMU (Ist./Pravo/Filos.)	Vestnik Moskovskogo Gosudarstvennogo Universiteta (Istoriia/Pravo/Filosofiia)
Voenn. ist. Zh.	Voenno-istoricheskii Zhurnal
Vop.Ist.	Voprosy Istorii
Wm. and Mary Qtly.	William and Mary Quarterly
ZfG.	Zeitschrift für Geschichtswissenschaft
ZfO.	Zeitschrift für Ostforschung
ZfSl.	Zeitschrift für Slawistik

OTHER ABBREVIATIONS

Akad. Nauk, A.N.	Akademiia Nauk
comp.	compiler(s)
ed.	editor, edited, edition
edn.	edition
et al.	and others
J.	journal
L.	Leningrad
M.	Moscow
N.F.	Neue Folge
no., nos	number(s)
Novos.	Novosibirsk
N.S.	New Series
N.Y.	New York
Pp.	pages
Rev.	review, reviewed
St. P.	St. Petersburg
Uch. Zap.	Uchenye Zapiski
vol., vols	volume(s)

SECTION 1 - BIBLIOGRAPHY AND REFERENCE

1(a) - DIRECTORIES, GUIDES, RESEARCH AIDS

(i) GENERAL

1. BARZUN, J., GRAFF, M., The Modern Researcher. N.Y. 1977, 3rd ed. Pp. 378.

2. BEZER, C.A. (ed.), Russian and Soviet Studies: A Handbook for Graduate Students. Vol. 1: A Research Manual. Vol. 2: Financial Aid, Exchanges, Language and Travel Programs [for the Soviet Union and Eastern Europe]. Columbus, Ohio. Vol. 1: 1973. Pp. 219. Vol. 2: 1971. Pp. 122.

3. BLEJWAS, S., East Central European Studies. A Handbook for Graduate Students. Columbus, Ohio 1973. Pp. 301.

4. HILTON, R., 'Russian and Soviet Studies in France: Teaching, Research, Libraries, Archives, and Publications', *RR.*, XXXVIII, 1 (1979), 52–80.
Comprehensive account, including data on earlier guides, and addresses of institutions.

---

5. SHEPELEV, L.E., Arkhivnye razyskaniia i issledovaniia. M. 1971. Pp. 144.
Basic guide for history graduate students doing archival research in USSR.

(ii) LIBRARY AND OTHER RESOURCES: GENERAL

6. HORECKY, P., Libraries and Bibliographic Centers in the Soviet Union. 1959. Pp. 287.
Now rather out-dated.

7. RUGGLES, M., MOSTECKY, V., Russian and East European Publications in the Libraries of the United States. N.Y. 1960. Pp. 396.

8. WALKER, G., Directory of Libraries and Special Collections on Eastern Europe and the USSR. London 1971. Pp. 159.
Covers Great Britain and N. Ireland. New ed. in preparation.

9. HORECKY, P., KRAUS, D., East Central and South East Europe. A Handbook of Library and Archival Resources in North America. Santa Barbara 1976. Pp. 467.

10. BUDUROWYCZ, B., Slavic and East European Resources in Canadian Academic and Research Libraries. Ottawa 1976. Pp. 595.
English and French text.

11. GRANT, S., Scholar's Guide to Washington D.C.: Russian/ Soviet Studies. Washington D.C. 1977. Pp. 403.

---

12. KNIAZIATOVA, V.A. (comp.), Biblioteki SSSR. Spravochnik. I,
    Biblioteki RSFSR. M. 1974. Pp. 429; II, Biblioteki soiuznykh
    respublik (bez RSFSR). M. 1973. Pp. 367.

13. BAGROVA,I. IU. (ed.), Biblioteki SSSR obshchestvenno-
    politicheskogo, filologicheskogo i iskusstvovedcheskogo
    profilia. Spravochnik. M. 1969. Pp. 344.
    Directory of 1,506 Soviet libraries in human and social
    sciences.

(iii) EXCHANGES, WORK IN THE SOVIET UNION

14. BYRNES, R., Soviet-American Academic Exchanges, 1958-1975.
    Indiana 1976. Pp. 275.

15. IREX (International Research and Exchanges Board), An
    Evaluation of the Experiences of Exchange Participants 1969-70
    Through 1974-75. N.Y. 1977. Pp. 67. See also no. 2.

16. BRINE, J., 'A Reader's Guide to the Lenin Library, Moscow, and
    a Guide to Moscow Bookshops', *Solanus*, 11 (1976), 17-41.

(iv) ARCHIVES and MANUSCRIPT COLLECTIONS:
    general, and state archive repositories.

17. THOMAS, D.H., LYMAN, M.C., The New Guide to the Diplomatic
    Archives of Western Europe. Philadelphia 1975. Pp. 441.
    Revised version of 1959 edition.

18. GRIMSTED, P.K., Archives and Manuscript Repositories in the
    USSR: Moscow and Leningrad. Princeton 1972. Pp. 436.
    Essential guide. Rev: *Vop. Ist.*, 10 (1973), Brzhostovskaia,
    N., Rudel'son, K., translated in *Soviet Studies in History*,
    XV, 2 (Fall 1976), 80-98.

19. GRIMSTED, P.K., Archives and manuscript repositories in the
    USSR. Moscow and Leningrad. Supplement 1. Bibliographical
    Addenda. Zug 1976. Pp. 203.
    Rev: *CSP.*, XX, 2 (1978), 261 (Raud, C.A.).

20. GRIMSTED, P.K., 'Regional State Archives in the USSR: Some
    Notes and a Bibliography of Published Guides', *SR.*, XXVIII, 1
    (1969), 92-116.

21. GRIMSTED, P.K., Archives and Manuscript Repositories in the
    USSR: Estonia, Latvia, Lithuania and Belorussia. Princeton
    1980. Pp. 450.
    Bibliography for each institution. Correlated microfiche
    re-editions of archival finding aids and other related
    reference literature published by Inter Documentation Company,
    Zug, Switzerland.

22. PENNINGTON, A., 'Slavonic Manuscripts and their Study in
    Great Britain', *Polata knigopis'naia*, I, 1 (1978), 11-14.

23. VEDER, W., 'Slavic Manuscripts and their Study in the Netherlands', *Polata knigopis'naia*, I, 1 (1978), 39-44.

24. LESURE, M., 'Aperçu sur les fonds russes dans les archives du ministère des affaires étrangères français', *CMRS.*, IV, 3 (1963), 312-30.
Supplements his book (no.26) for consular file information.

25. SPIRIDONAKIS, B., Mémoires et documents du Ministère des Affaires Etrangères de France sur la Russie. Sherbrooke, Quebec [1965]. Pp. 160.
Rev: *RH.*, II, 2 (1975), 209 (Medlin, V.D.).

26. LESURE, M., L'histoire de la Russie aux Archives Nationales. Paris 1970. Pp. 502.

27. VODOFF, W., 'L'étude des manuscrits slaves et des slavica en France', *Polata knigopis'naia*, I, 1 (1978), 3-10.

28. CAPALDO, M., 'Les manuscrits slaves et leur étude en Italie', *Polata knigopis'naia*, I, 1 (1978), 15-38.

29. TEICH, G., Topographie der Osteuropa-Südosteuropa-und DDR-Sammlungen. München 1978. Pp. 388.
Includes bibliographies, indexes.

30. ROGOV, A., Svedeniia o nebol'shikh sobraniiakh slaviano-russkikh rukopisei v SSSR. M. 1962. Pp. 298.

31. GERASIMOVA, IU. et al. (eds), Lichnye arkhivnye fondy v gosudarstvennykh khranilishchakh SSSR. Ukazatel'. M. 1963. 2 vols. Pp. 478, 502.
Guide to personal archive holdings in state repositories, for seventeenth to twentieth centuries. Supplement announced.

32. SYRCHENKO, L., Lichnye arkhivnye fondy deiatelei russkoi literatury i iskusstva v arkhivakh SSSR. M. 1975. Pp. 166.

33. BUGANOV, V.I., 'Russkie dokumenty kontsa XV-XVIII vv. v khranilishchakh Parizha', *Vop. Ist.*, 3 (1979), 137-42.

individual institutions, Academy of Sciences

34. LEVSHIN, B.V. (otv. red.), Arkhivy Akademii Nauk Sotsialisticheskikh Stran: Bibliografiia / Die Archive der Akademien der Wissenschaften der sozialistischen Länder. Bibliographie. 1: 1917-1968, Leningrad 1971. Pp. 251. 1000 entries. 2: 1969-72, Leningrad 1975. Pp. 375, 1786 entries. USSR: vol. 1, nos 454-993; vol. 2, nos 1222-1593.

35. MURZANOVA, M.N., BOBROVA, E.I., PETROV, V.A., Istoricheskii ocherk i obzor fondov rukopisnogo otdela Biblioteki Akademii Nauk. Vypusk 1: XVIII vek. M.1956.Pp.484.

35a. KUKUSHKINA, M.(ed.), Materialy i soobshcheniia po fondam otdela rukopisnoi i redkoi knigi. vyp. 2. L.1978. Pp.352.
Article by A. Amosov (pp. 317-334) updates No.35.

36. MURZANOVA, M.N. et al. (eds), Istoricheskii ocherk i obzor
    fondov rukopisnogo otdela Biblioteki Akademii Nauk. Karty,
    plany, chertezhi, risunki i graviury. Sobraniia Petra I.
    M.-L. 1961. Pp. 288.

37. BUBNOV, N. (comp.), Opisanie rukopisnogo otdela Biblioteki
    Akademii Nauk SSSR, tom 3, vyp. 3. Istoricheskie sborniki
    XVIII-XIX vv. L. 1971. Pp. 418.

38. MALOVA, M., PANCHENKO, N., 'Obzor istoriko-literaturnykh
    arkhivnykh materialov XVIII-XX vv. postupivshikh v RO IRLI
    (PD) za 1958-61 gg', *Ezhegodnik ruk. otd. Push. Doma* (1969),
    90-114; accessions for 1962-65 in *Ezhegodnik* (1970), 108-23;
    for 1966-69, *Ezhegodnik* (1971), 106-28; for 1970-71
    Ezhegodnik (1972), 63-71.

39. VERZHBITSKII, V.G. et al. (eds); BAKST, E.I. (comp.),
    Putevoditel' po fondam lichnogo proiskhozhdeniia otdela
    pis'mennykh istochnikov Gosudarstvennogo Istoricheskogo
    Muzeia. M. 1967. Pp. 386.

40. ISTORICHESKII MUZEI, MOSKVA. Gosudarstvennyi ordena Lenina
    istoricheskii muzei. (Putevoditel'). M. 1975. Pp. 144.

41. ZHITOMIRSKAIA, S.V. (ed.), Vospominaniia i dnevniki XVIII-XX
    vv. Ukazatel' rukopisei. M. 1976. Pp. 619.
    Description of manuscript diaries and memoirs held in Lenin
    Library, Moscow. Continues E.N. Konshina's work published
    in 1951.
41a. LEVSHIN, B. Kratkii spravochnik po nauchno-otraslevym i
    memorial'nym arkhivam AN SSSR. M. 1979. Pp.252.
    Valuable guide to network of Soviet Academy of Sciences
    Archives. Updates and supplements previous guides.

1(b) - REFERENCE, ENCYCLOPEDIAS, DICTIONARIES, ATLASES

(i) GENERAL

In addition to surveys such as ZALEWSKI (47), *SR*. carries an
annual review of recent reference publications in its September
issues. For language dictionaries see (besides 43) nos. 2047-51.

42. MAICHEL, K. (comp.), SIMMONS, J.S.G. (ed.), Guide to Russian
    Reference Works. Stanford 1962-
    Outstanding annotated work. Vol. 1: General bibliographies
    and reference works; Vol. 2: History, historical sciences,
    ethnography, geography; Vol. 5: Science, medicine,
    technology.
    No more published.

43. PUSHKAREV, S. (comp.), Dictionary of Russian Historical Terms
    from The Eleventh Century to 1917. New Haven 1970. Pp. 199.
    Rev: *Uk. Q.*, XXVII, 1 (1971), 80-82.

44. ZALEWSKI, W., Guide to Selected Reference Materials: Russia
    and East Europe. Stanford 1973. Pp. 89.
    Covers holdings of Stanford Univ. Lib.

45. LOWY, G., Guide to Russian Reprints and Microfilms.
    N.Y. 1973. Pp. 364.
    Brings together scattered information about titles available.

46. SHEEHY, E.P., Guide to Reference Books. Chicago 1976, 9th ed.
    Pp. 1051.

47. ZALEWSKI, W., 'Reference Materials in Russian-Soviet Area
    Studies, 1977-78'. *RR*., (April 1979), 198-214.

48. SAMORUKOVA, N.A., Spravochnik sokrashchenii, priniatykh v
    istoricheskoi literature. M. 1964, reprinted Letchworth
    1972. Pp. 64.
    Lists the titles *and contents* of a large number of historical
    sources, especially series, which are frequently cited in
    abbreviated form.

(ii) BIOGRAPHICAL DICTIONARIES

49. ANZINER, H. et al. (comp.), Kleine Slavische Biographie.
    Wiesbaden 1958. Pp. 832.

50. KAUFMAN, I.M., Russkie biograficheskie i biobibliograficheskie
    slovari. M. 1955. Pp. 751
    1592 works listed and described. Also indexes persons
    covered in works cited.

51. MASANOV, I.F., Slovar'psevdonimov russkikh pisatelei,
    uchenykh, obshchestvennykh deiatelei. 4 vols. M. 1956-60.

52. POLOVTSOV, A A (ed.), Russkii biograficheskii slovar'. 25
    vols. St. P. 1896-1918, reprinted Kraus, Nendeln, 1964.
    The *D.N.B.* of Imperial Russia.

53. LIKHACHEV, D.S. et al. (eds), Russkie pisateli.
    Biobibliograficheskii slovar'. M. 1971. Pp. 728.
    Section II: Eighteenth century

(iii) ENCYCLOPEDIAS

The standard pre-revolutionary encyclopedia is ANDREEVSKII (ed.),
Entsiklopedicheskii Slovar', published by Brokgauz-Efron, 41
vols and 2 supplements, St. P. 1890-1907. KAUFMAN (54) and
SHMUSHKIS (55) are bibliographies.

54. KAUFMAN, I.M., Russkie entsiklopedii. M. 1960. Pp. 103.
    Covers general encyclopedias only (including Soviet works).

55. SHMUSHKIS, IA., Sovetskie entsiklopedii: ocherki istorii, voprosy metodiki. M. 1975. Pp. 191.
Information about Soviet encyclopedias; complements Kaufman (no. 54).

56. UTECHIN, S.V., Everyman's Concise Encyclopaedia of Russia. London, N.Y. 1961. Pp. 623.

57. FLORINSKY, M. (ed.), McGraw-Hill Encyclopedia of Russia and the Soviet Union. N.Y. 1961. Pp. 624.

58. PARADISE, J. et al. (eds), Great Soviet Encyclopedia: A Translation of the Third Edition. N.Y., London 1973-
Vols. 1-21 to date. Volume-by-volume translation of the *Bol'shaia Sovetskaia Ensiklopediia*. Use with caution and read review in *SR.*, XXXV, 4 (1976), 724-727 and Grimsted, P., 'Détente on the Reference Shelves?', *Wilson Library Bulletin*, (June 1975), 3-15.

59. WIECZYNSKI, J.L. (ed.), The Modern Encyclopedia of Russian and Soviet History. Gulf Breeze, Florida 1976-
18 volumes to date. Combines translations from no. 60 with original articles by Western scholars.

60. ZHUKOV, E. et al. (eds), Sovetskaia istoricheskaia entsiklopediia. 16 volumes and index. M. 1961-78.

(iv) HISTORICAL ATLASES AND ILLUSTRATED WORKS

61. CHEW, A.F., An Atlas of Russian History. Eleven centuries of changing borders. Rev. ed., New Haven 1970. Pp. 127.
39 maps.

62. GILBERT, M., Russian History Atlas. N.Y. 1972. Pp. 175.

63. KOVALEVSKY, P., Atlas historique et culturel de la Russie et du Monde Slave. Paris 1961. Pp. 216.
Pictures, maps.

1(c) - BIBLIOGRAPHIES, BIBLIOGRAPHIES OF BIBLIOGRAPHIES

(i) GENERAL

64. BESTERMANN, T., A World Bibliography of Bibliographies. 4th rev. ed., Lausanne 1965-66. 5 vols.

65. BOEHM, E., 'Bibliography: Current State and Prospects', in: LEGTERS, L. (ed.), Russia: Essays in History and Literature (Leiden 1972), pp. 152-64.

66. HORECKY, P.L. (ed.), Russia and the Soviet Union: a
    bibliographic guide to Western-Language Publications.
    Chicago 1965. Pp. 473.

67. SIMMONS, J.S.G., Russian Bibliography. Libraries and
    Archives. A Selective List of Bibliographical References
    for Students of Russian History, Literature, Political,
    Social and Philosophical Thought, Theology and Linguistics.
    Twickenham 1973. Pp. 76.
    By the doyen of western Slavic bibliographers. New edition
    in preparation.

68. BONNIERES, F. de., Guide de l'Etudiant en Russe. Paris 1977.
    Pp. 220.
    Introductory undergraduate bibliography for all fields of
    Russian studies. Works in French, English, Russian.

69. KIRPICEVA, I., Handbuch der russischen und sowjetischen
    Bibliografien. Leipzig 1962. Pp. 225.

70. KRAUSE, F. et al., Sowjetische Bibliotheks- und Buchwesen:
    Bibliographie. Berlin (E.) 1975. Pp. 293.

71. ZDOBNOV, N., Istoriia russkoi bibliografii do nachala XX
    veka. M. 1951, 2nd ed. Pp. 512.

72. ZDOBNOV, N., Sinkhronisticheskie tablitsy russkoi
    bibliografii, 1700-1928 so spiskom vazhneishikh
    bibliograficheskikh trudov. M. 1962. Pp. 191.

73. RUBAKIN, N.A., Sredi Knig. 3 vols. M. 1911-15, reprinted
    ORP., Cambridge 1973 with new introduction by A.E. Senn.
    Classic. Selective bibliography.

74. UL'IANINSKII, D., Biblioteka D.V. Ul'ianinskago:
    Bibliograficheskoe opisanie. 3 vols. M. 1912-15, reprinted
    ORP., Cambridge, 1973 with new introduction by J.S.G.
    Simmons.
    Classic. Catalogue of a library strong in bibliography,
    genealogy, heraldry and travel.

(ii) LISTINGS BY COUNTRY OR LANGUAGE

75. SCHULTHEISS, TH. (ed.), Russian Studies, 1941-1958. A
    Cumulation of the Annual Bibliographies from *The Russian
    Review*. Ann Arbor 1972. Pp. 395.
    With new author and main entry and subject index.

76. American Bibliography of Russian and East European Studies,
    1956-   Bloomington, Indiana U.P., 1957-
    Annual listing.

77. HORAK, S.M. (comp.), NEISWENDER, R. (ed.), Russia, The
    U.S.S.R. and Eastern Europe: A Bibliographic Guide to
    English-Language Publications, 1964-1974. Littleton,
    Colorado, 1978. Pp. 488, ca. 1600 entries.
    Continuation of Horecky (no. 66).

78. HNIK, T. (ed.), European Bibliography of Soviet, East
    European and Slavonic Studies, vol. 1, 1975-
    Birmingham 1977-
    Annual listing, incorporating two former national biblio-
    graphies, *Travaux et publications parus en français en
    ... sur la Russie et l'URSS* (published in *CMRS* from 1963-74)
    and *Soviet, East European and Slavonic Studies* in Britain,
    published in *ABSEES*, 1971-74; also covers German
    publications.

79. DOROTICH, D., A Bibliography of Canadian Slavists, 1951-1971.
    Saskatoon 1972. Pp. 32.

80. *Scando-Slavica*   (Copenhagen), 'List of Books and Articles
    Published by Scandinavian Slavists and Baltologists in 19-
    Annual listing.

    ────────────

81. *Cahiers du Monde Russe et Soviétique,* (École des Hautes
    Études en sciences sociales, Paris).
    Annual review of year's publications in French on Russia and
    Soviet Union. Now to be incorporated in no. 78.

82. *Revue des Études Slaves* (Paris).
    Annual compilation and bibliography of Russian literature/
    culture.

    ────────────

83. SEEMANN, K-D., SIEGMANN, F., Bibliographie der slavistischen
    Arbeiten aus den deutschsprachigen Fachzeitschriften, 1876-
    1963. Berlin- Wiesbaden 1965. Pp. 422.
    Rev: *ZfSl.*, XII (1967), 307-9 (Pohrt, H.).

84. MEYER, K., Bibliographie der Arbeiten zur osteuropäischen
    Geschichte aus den deutschsprachigen Fachzeitschriften 1858-
    1964. Berlin 1966. Pp. 314, = Bibliographische Mitteilungen
    des Osteuropa-Instituts an der Freien Universität Berlin,
    Bd. 9.

85. BAMBORSCHKE, U., Bibliographie slavistischer Arbeiten aus
    deutschsprachigen Fachzeitschriften, 1964-1973, einschlies-
    slich slavistischer Arbeiten aus deutschsprachigen nicht
    slavistischen Zeitschriften sowie slavistischen Fest-und
    Sammelschriften, 1945-1973. 2 vols in 1. Berlin 1976. Pp.736.

86. HELLMAN, M. et al. (eds), Osteuropa in der historischen
    Forschung der DDR. 2 vols. Düsseldorf 1972. Pp. 361, 406.
    Vol. 1. Darstellungen; vol. 2. Bibliographie und
    biographische Notizen.

86a. BRAND, B., Russistik in der DDR. Bibliographie zur Sprach-
    wissenschaft, Literaturwissenschaft und Methodik des Russisch
    unterrichts, 1967-1977. Berlin 1979. Pp. 338.

87. POHRT, H., Bibliographie slawistischer Publikationen aus der
    Deutschen Demokratischen Republik, 1946-1967. Berlin 1968.
    Pp. 400.
    Rev: *ZfSl.*, XV (1970), 105-7 (Gutschmidt, K.).

88. POHRT, H., Bibliographie slawistischer Publikationen aus der
    Deutschen Demokratischen Republik 1968-1972 nebst
    Nachträgen, 1946-1967. Berlin 1974. Pp. 287.
    Rev: *ZfSl.*, XIX (1974), 683-4 (Gutschmidt, K.).

89. MAHNKEN, I., POLLOK, K-H., Materialien zu einer
    slawistischen Bibliographie. Arbeiten der in Österreich,
    der Schweiz und der Bundesrepublik Deutschland tätigen
    Slawisten (1945-1963). München 1963. Pp. 257.

90. KAISER, E., HÖCHERL, A., Materialien zu einer slawischen
    Bibliographie. Arbeiten der in Österreich, der Schweiz und
    der Bundesrepublik Deutschland tätigen Slawisten (1963-1973).
    München 1973. Pp. 243.

91. RÖHLING, H., 'Bibliographie von Arbeiten zum 18.
    Jahrhundert in Ost-und Südosteuropa aus dem deutschen
    Sprachbereich', *Das Achtzehnte Jahrhundert*, red.
    W.Schmidt-Biggemann, I, 2 (1977), 26-56.
    On-going bibliography.

92. Bibliografiia Sovetskoi Bibliografii. M. 1955-
    Annual. Lists new bibliographies.

93. Ezhegodnik knigi SSSR. Sistematicheskii ukazatel'. Vol. I-
    M. 1962-
    Annual. Vol. I of each year lists works on historical
    sciences published in the year.

94. Knizhnaia Letopis', 1908
    The Russian national bibliography, appears weekly, classi-
    fied arrangement. Monthly supplement includes theses (from
    1961). Various Union Republic *Letopisi* are listed in *Bibl.
    Sov. Bibl.* (no. 92) under 'Obshchaia Bibliografiia'.

95. Letopis' zhurnal'nykh statei, M. 1926-
    Weekly listing of journal and series articles. Includes
    articles in *sborniki*.

96. Letopis' retsenzii, M. 1955-
    Bibliography of reviews.

97. Bibliografiia izdanii Akademii Nauk SSSR. Ezhegodnik.
    L. 1957-
    Annual listing of Academy of Science publications.

98. Bibliografiia kraevedcheskoi bibliografii.
    Series: 10 issues so far. See *RR.*, 4 (1977), 192
    (Zalewski, W.).

99. TIMBERLAKE, C.E., 'The Slavic Department of the Helsinki
    University Library', *SR.*, XXV, 3 (1966), 513-22.
    The microfilm library catalogue referred to is also held
    by the British Library.

100. Russian Periodicals in the Helsinki University Library; a
    checklist. Washington (Library of Congress, Processing
    Dept.), 1959. Pp. 120.

101. HORECKY, P.L., 'The Slavic and E. European resources and
    facilities of the Library of Congress', *SR.*, XXIII, 2 (1964)
    310-327.
    Also in French: *CMRS.*, III, 2 (1962), 307-22.

102. Library of Congress, Library of Congress Catalog - Books:
    Subjects. Washington 1965-
    General overview under 'Russia'; lists for example the many
    general histories of which only a few are listed here.

103. Harvard University Library. Slavic History and Literatures.
    Widener Library Shelflist. Cambridge, Mass. 1971. 4 vols.
    Pp. 837, 705, 708, 710.
    Approx. 120,000 titles. Vols 1-2: Chronological Listing;
    Vols 3-4: Author/Title Listing.

104. Harvard University, Widener Library. Finnish and Baltic
    History and Literatures. Cambridge 1972. Pp. 250.
    Widener Shelflist; Author/Title Listing. Ca. 8,600 titles.

105. New York Public Library, Dictionary Catalogue of the
    Slavonic Collection. Boston 1974. 2nd ed.
    44 vols. Authors and subjects in a single series. Includes
    some refs. to journal articles.
    Supplemented and up-dated by the rather inaccurately
    entitled Bibliographic Guide to Soviet and East
    European Studies, 1978. 3 vols. Boston 1979.

106. Bibliothèque Nationale (Paris), Catalogue général des
    livres imprimés: auteurs, collectivités- auteurs, anonymes,
    1960-69 ... 2. Caractères non Latins; 3. Caractères
    cyrilliques: russe H-R, ukrainien, biélorusse, bulgare,
    macedonien, moldave. Paris 1974. Pp. 1,149.

107. Imperial Public Library, St. Petersburg, Catalogue de la
    Section des Russica; ou, Ecrits sur la Russie en Langues
    Etrangères. St. P. 1873, reprinted Amsterdam 1964. 2 vols.

CROWTHER (113) and MEYER (114) are fundamental for W. European
scholarship on eighteenth-century Russia. ZAIONCHKOVSKII (117)
a bibliography of bibliographies, is the standard and excellent
Soviet reference work. SIMON (118) is exhaustive for its period
(works written 1917-52) but has not been brought up to date for
the eighteenth century. See also BERKOV (119), essential for its
period; MASANOV and POPOV (168-9); and for eighteenth century
publications the union catalogues and special listings (125-142).

108. International Committee of Historical Sciences, Lausanne,
     International Bibliography of Historical Sciences. 1931-

109. 'Recently Published Articles'. A separate supplement to the
     American Historical Review (AHR). Three issues annually.
     Lists new articles on history in Western-language journals
     and from principal Soviet journals.

110. ALLEN, R. (ed.), The Eighteenth Century. A Current
     Bibliography. 1926-
     Published 1926-69 by Univ. Chicago; 1970-   Univ. Iowa.
     General European coverage, some Russian material.

111. PARGELLIS, S., MEDLEY, D., Bibliography of British History.
     The Eighteenth Century 1714-1789. Oxford 1951. Pp. 642.
     Foreign affairs, pp. 34-52.

112. BROWN, L., Christie, I., Bibliography of British History
     1789-1851. Oxford 1977. Pp. 759.
     Mainly nineteenth century.

113. CROWTHER, P.A., A Bibliography of Works in English on Early
     Russian History to 1800. Oxford 1969. Pp. 236.

114. MEYER, K. (ed.), Bibliographie zur osteuropäischen Geschichte.
     Verzeichnis der zwischen 1939 und 1964 veröffentlichten
     Literatur in west-europäischen Sprachen zur osteuropäischen
     Geschichte bis 1945. Berlin 1972. Pp. 649.
     Select bibliography. Russia in the eighteenth century:
     pp. 143-70, nos. 2899-3518. Other sections also refer.

115. 'Novye knigi' and 'Stat'i v sovetskikh periodicheskikh
     izdaniiakh'.
     Regular listing of new work in each issue of *Vop. Ist.*

116. FRADKINA, Z. (ed.), Istoriia SSSR. Annotirovannyi perechen'
     russkikh bibliografii izdannykh do 1965 goda. M. 1966, 2nd
     ed. Pp. 427.
     Eighteenth century: pp.225-256.
     Special sections on Pugachev, Radishchev, P. Rumiantsev,
     Suvorov, Ushakov, Lomonosov, Pososhkov. Rev: *Vop. Ist.*, 7
     (1967) (Zaionchkovskii, P.). Largely superseded by
     Zaionchkovskii (no. 117).

117. ZAIONCHKOVSKII, P.A. (ed.), Spravochniki po istorii
     dorevoliutsionnoi Rossii. M. 1971. Pp. 415. Rev. ed. 1978.
     Pp. 615.
     Sections on encyclopedias, handbooks and special studies on
     historiography, diplomacy, cities, *gubernii*, trade, industry,
     agriculture, state administration, transport, political
     organs, science, military affairs.

118. SIMON, K.R. (ed.), DORONIN, I.P. et al.(comp.), Istoriia
     SSSR. Ukazatel' sovetskoi literatury za 1917-1952 gg.
     (Akademiia Nauk SSSR. Fundamental'naia Biblioteka
     Obshchestvennykh Nauk). 2 vols in 4. M. 1956; reprinted in
     2 vols, Kraus,Nendeln 1977.
     Fundamental for early Soviet work. Later volumes in this
     series, covering publications 1917-67, do not include work on
     the eighteenth century.

119. BERKOV, P.N. (ed.), STEPANOV, V. (comp.), Istoriia russkoi
     literatury XVIII v.: Bibliograficheskii ukazatel'. L. 1968.
     Pp. 500.
     Fundamental work for its period, going far beyond literature:
     8,216 entries. Rev: *Kritika* VI, 2 (1970), 112-117
     (Okenfuss, M.).

120. USSR COPYRIGHT AGENCY, Raboty sovetskikh istorikov za
     1970-1974 gg.: Bibliograficheskii ukazatel'. Vols I-III.
     M. 1975. Pp. 692.

121. ZAIONCHKOVSKII, P.A. (ed.), Istoriia dorevoliutsionnoi Rossii
     v dnevnikakh i vospominaniiakh. T.1: XV-XVIII veka. M. 1976.
     Pp. 301.
     First volume of new 6 volume standard work. Supplements but
     does not entirely replace S.R. Mintslov's classic bibliog-
     raphy. Rev: *SGECRN.*, 5 (1977), 70-75 (Simmons, J.S.G.).

(v) BIBLIOGRAPHIES OF FESTSCHRIFTEN, *MISCELLANIES AND ARTICLE*
     COLLECTIONS

ROTHBART (122) gives good coverage, including content listings,
for the early period dealt with. LEISTNER (123) is extremely
weak on Russian publications; his deficiencies are largely,
though not entirely, made up by the NYPL/LC *Guide* (124). A considerable number of Festschriften, and/or articles from them,
are listed at appropriate points in the present bibliography.
See also BAMBORSCHKE (no. 85).

122. ROTHBART, M., HELFENSTEIN, U. (comps), International biblio-
     graphy of historical articles in Festschriften and Miscel-
     lanies, 1880-1939. Paris 1955. Pp. 443.
     Title in French, English, German, text in French. Directed
     by H. NABHOLZ, ed. International Committee of Historical
     Sciences.

123. LEISTNER, O., International Bibliography of Festschriften.
     Osnabrück 1976. Pp. 893.

124. Guide to *Festschriften*. Published by the New York Public
Library, The Research Libraries, The Library of Congress.
Vol. 1: The Retrospective *Festschriften* Collection of the
NYPL: Materials catalogued through 1971. Boston, Mass.
1977. Pp. 597.
Vol. 2: A Dictionary Catalog of *Festschriften* in the NYPL
(1972-76) and the LC (1968-76). Boston 1977. Pp. 467.
Vol. 1 photoreproduces library cards of some 6,000 items col-
lected by NYPL over approximately 50 years to end of 1971.

*(vi) BIBLIOGRAPHIES OF WORKS PUBLISHED IN RUSSIA IN THE
EIGHTEENTH CENTURY.*

bibliographies, union catalogues. See also nos 141, 1767,
1773.

125. SOKUROVA, M., Obshchie bibliografii russkikh knig
grazhdanskoi pechati, 1708-1955. L. 1956. Pp. 283.

126. BERKOV, P. (ed.), BYKOVA, T.A., GUREVICH, M.M. (comp.),
Opisanie izdanii grazhdanskoi pechati 1708-ianvar' 1725 gg.
Svodnyi katalog. M.-L. 1955. Pp. 626.
882 entries. Appendices list (i.a.) books in foreign
languages published in Russia during the period.
Rev: *Kritika* VI, 2 (1970), 118-23 (Okenfuss, M.).

127. BERKOV, P.N. (ed.), BYKOVA, T.A., GUREVICH, M.M. (comps),
Opisanie izdanii napechatannykh kirillitsei 1689-ianvar'
1725 g. Svodnyi katalog. M.-L. 1958. Pp. 402.
215 entries. Appendices include listing for the period of
(i.a.) foreign works on Russian subjects; foreign-language
works published in Russia; addenda to Op. izd. grazhd.
pechati 1708-25 (no. 126). Rev: *Kritika* VI, 2 (1970), 118-23
(Okenfuss, M.).

128. BERKOV, P.N. (ed.), BYKOVA, T.A., GUREVICH, M.M.,
KOSINTSEVA, P.I. (comps). Opisanie izdanii napechatannykh
pri Petre I. Svodnyi katalog. Dopolneniia i prilozheniia.
L. 1972. Pp. 272.
Over 623 addenda to nos. 126-7. Takes listing of these
works to end 1727.

129. KONDAKOV, I. et al. (eds), Svodnyi katalog russkoi knigi
grazhdanskoi pechati XVIII veka, 1725-1800. Moscow. 5 vols.
1962-67, Supplement 1975.
Over 10,000 entries in all. Rev: *Kritika* VI, 2 (1970),
118-23 (Okenfuss, M.).

130. POLONSKAIA, I.M., 'Itogi raboty po sostavleniiu "Svodnogo
Kataloga russkoi knigi grazhdanskoi pechati XVIII veka"',
Trudy Gos. Biblioteki SSSR im. V.I. Lenina, XI (1969),
126-144.

131. POLONSKAIA, I.M. (comp.) Spisok razyskivaemykh izdanii, ne voshedshikh v 'Svodnyi Katalog russkoi knigi grazhdanskoi pechati XVIII veka, 1725-1800'. M. 1969. Pp. 228. Duplicated typescript. 885 entries for works known by reference but not yet (1969) located.

132. KATSPRZHAK, E.I. (ed.), ZERNOVA, A.S., KAMENEVA, T.N. (comps). Svodnyi katalog russkoi knigi kirillovskoi pechati XVIII veka. M. 1968. Pp. 567. 1491 entries. Duplicated typescript.

133. KAMENEVA, T.N., KONDAKOVA, T.I. (comps), Spisok razyskivaemykh izdanii, ne voshedshikh v 'Svodnyi Katalog russkoi knigi kirillovskoi pechati XVIII v., 1701-1800'. M. 1971. Pp. 36. Duplicated typescript. 197 items known by reference but not located by compilers of no. 132.

134. PETROV, S., Knigi grazhdanskoi pechati izdannye na Ukraine. XVIII - pervaia polovina XIX st. Katalog. Khar'kov 1971. Pp. 297. In Ukrainian. 1997 items.

135. BERKOV, P.N. (ed.), MEL'NIKOVA, N.N. (comp.), Izdaniia napechatannye v Tipografii Moskovskogo Universiteta XVIII v. M. 1966. Pp. 454. Covers works in all languages. 2758 entries.

136. BYKOVA, T. (comp.), Katalog russkoi knigi kirillovskoi pechati Peterburgskikh tipografii XVIII veka. (1715-1800). L. 1972. Pp. 178.

  library listings   (The Soviet union catalogues, above, also show Soviet library locations)

137. FESSENKO, T., Eighteenth Century Russian Publications in the Library of Congress. Washington 1961. Pp. 141. 1316 entries.

138. TYRRELL, E.P., SIMMONS, J.S.G., 'Slavonic Books of the Eighteenth Century in Cambridge Libraries', *Trans. Cambridge Bibliographical Soc*. IV, 3 (1966), 225-45.

139. KASINEC, E. (comp.), 'Eighteenth-century Russian Publications in the New York Public Library. A Preliminary Catalogue, Pt. II: The Westernization of Russia', *Bulletin New York Public Library* 9 (1971), 474-92.

140. DRAGE, C.L., 'Eighteenth-century Church Slavonic and Russian Books in United Kingdom Libraries', *Solanus* 13 (June 1978), 1-13.
_____

141. KAMENEVA, T.N. (ed.), Ukrainskie knigi kirillovskoi pechati XVII-XVIII vv. Katalog izdanii, khraniashchikhsia v Gos. Biblioteke im. V.I. Lenina. Vyp. I: 1574-1 polovine XVII v. M. 1976. Pp. 447.

142. Istoriia. Katalog izdanii XVIII v., 1725-1800. M. 1977.
     Pp. 43.
     Holdings of the State Historical Museum, Moscow.

(vii) PERIODICALS

143. SCHATOFF, M. (comp.), HALE, N. (ed.), Half a Century of
     Russian Serials, 1917-1968: Cumulative Index of Serials
     Published outside the USSR. N.Y. 1970-72.
     4 vols, listing 3700 serials.

144. HORECKY, P., CARLTON, R., The U.S.S.R. and E. Europe.
     Periodicals in Western Languages. 3rd rev. ed.
     Washington 1967. Pp. 89.
     Library of Congress holdings. 769 entries.

145. BIRKOS, A., TAMBS, C, (comp., eds), Academic Writer's
     Guide to Periodicals: II: East European and Slavic Studies.
     Kent, Ohio 1975. Pp. 572.

146. Bibliothèque Nationale (Paris), Catalogue collectif des
     périodiques conservés dans les bibliothèques de Paris et
     ... de France. Périodiques slaves en caractères
     cyrilliques. Paris 1956-65. 4 vols.

147. BRUHN, P., Gesamtverzeichnis russischer und sowjetischer
     Periodika und Serienwerke in Bibliotheken der
     Bundesrepublik Deutschland und West-Berlins. Berlin 1962-
     1976. 4 vols.

148. MASHKOVA, M., SOKUROVA, M., Obshchie bibliografii russkikh
     periodicheskikh izdanii 1703-1954, i materialy po
     statistike russkoi periodicheskoi pechati. Annotirovannyi
     ukazatel'. L. 1956. Pp. 139.

149. ANDREEVA, N.F., MASHKOVA, M.V., Russkaia periodicheskaia
     pechat'. (Obshchie i otraslevye bibliograficheskie
     ukazateli, 1703-1975). M. 1977. Pp. 183.
     Supplements but does not supersede no. 148. Rev: *Sovetskaia
     Bibliografiia,* 4 (1978), 86-90.

150. DEMENT'EV , A. et al. (eds), Russkaia periodicheskaia
     pechat'. Spravochnik. 2 vols, M. 1959. I: 1702-1894.
     Pp. 835.

151. LISOVSKII, N.M., Russkaia periodicheskaia pechat' 1703-
     1900 gg. (Bibliografiia i graficheskie tablitsy). Petrograd
     1915, reprinted ZA, Leipzig, 1965. Pp. 267, tables.

(viii) DISSERTATIONS

   Individual dissertations listed are incorporated in their
   appropriate sections. For listings of French dissertations,

1-Bibliography   15

see HILTON (4) and TERRY (152).

152. TERRY, G.M., 'A Guide to Bibliographies of Theses and
     Dissertations in the Field of Slavonic and East European
     Studies', *ABSEES*. (Oct. 1976), 'Special Section'
     pp. i-xxviii.
     Lists 148 bibliographies.

153. DOSSICK, J., Doctoral Research on Russia and the Soviet
     Union. N.Y. 1960. Pp. 248.
     Covers English-language work (N. America and U.K.). Up-dated
     by no. 154.

154. DOSSICK, J., Doctoral Research on Russia and the Soviet
     Union, 1960-1975. N.Y. 1976. Pp. 345.
     3150 titles. Continuation of no. 153. *SR*. carries in its
     December issues an annual listing of new dissertations, by
     Dossick.

155. SIMMONS, J.S.G., Theses in Slavonic Studies Approved for
     Higher Degrees by British Universities, 1907-66. *OSP.*, XIII
     (1967),and table;
     for 1967-71, *OSP.*, N.S. VI (1973), pp. 133-147
     for 1972-76, *OSP.*, N.S. X (1977), pp. 120-138.

156. JACOBS, P.M., History Theses 1901-70: Historical Research
     for Higher Degrees in the Universities of the U.K. London
     1976. Pp. 456.
     7000 entries.

157. KUEHL, W.F., Dissertations in history. An index to disser-
     tations completed in history departments of U.S. and
     Canadian Universities 1873-1960. Lexington 1965. Pp. 249.

158. XEROX UNIVERSITY MICROFILMS,   Comprehensive
     Dissertation Index 1861-1972. Ann Arbor 1973.
     37 vols. North American Dissertations. An annual index is
     also available.

159. BRUHN, P., Russika und Sowjetika unter den deutschsprachigen
     Hochschulschriften (1961-1973). Berlin 1975. Pp. 166.
     German-language dissertations.

160. DDR. 'Alphabetisches Verzeichnis der Hochschulschriften
     zum Gesamtbereich Osteuropa', in HELLMAN (no.86), II, 342-57.

161. ZAIONCHKOVSKII, P.A. et al. (eds), Doktorskie i kandidatskie
     dissertatsii, zashchishchennye v Moskovskom Gos. Un-te s
     1934 po 1954 g. Bibliograficheskii ukazatel'. M. 1956-57.
     3 vols.

162. 'Avtoreferaty dissertatsii'.
     Listed at end of *Knizhnaia Letopis'* 1955-60, of *Knizhnaia
     Letopis', Dopolnitel'nyi Vypusk*, 1960-
     The Soviet equivalent of a dissertation abstract.

163. GOS. BIBL. SSSR im. V.I. LENINA., Katalog kandidatskikh i
doktorskikh dissertatsii, postupivshikh v Biblioteku im.
V.I. Lenina i Gosudarstvennuiu Tsentral'nuiu Nauchnuiu
Meditsinskuiu Biblioteku.
Quarterly, M. 1956-

(ix) INDEXES TO JOURNAL ARTICLES AND JOURNALS

Many journals publish cumulative indexes from time to time.
MASANOV (168) is an essential reference tool; POPOV (169) surveys a number of important nineteenth-century journals though
is still incomplete; the two books by NEUSTROEV (170) are
useful, especially his *Ukazatel'* which lists the contents of
all eighteenth-century Russian journals and serials.

164. TERRY, G.M., A Subject and Name Index to Articles on the
Slavonic and East European Languages and Literatures, Music
and Theatre, Libraries and the Press, Contained in English-
Language Journals, 1920-1975. Nottingham 1976. Pp. 198.

165. TERRY, G.M., East European Languages and Literature, A
Subject and Name Index to Articles in English-Language
Journals. Oxford 1979. Pp. 275.
Ca. 10,000 entries. Covers 1900-1977. Subsumes no. 164.

166. CHARBONNEAU, L., MULLER, A., Index to the *Slavic Review* and
Predecessors; 1941-1964 inclusive. Seattle 1965. Pp. 96.

167. CLOSE, B. (comp.), *Russian Review*, Index, 1941-1971.
Stanford 1973. Pp. 219.

168. MASANOV, IU., NITKINA, N., TITOVA, Z., Ukazateli soderzhaniia
russkikh zhurnalov i prodolzhaiushchikhsia izdanii, 1755-
1970 gg. M. 1975; reprinted ORP., Newtonville, 1979 with
introduction by P.H. Clendenning. Pp. 438.
Listing of published indexes to major journals and serials,
Over 7800 cumulative indexes recorded. Reprint edition
carries addenda list of 133 titles published or scheduled
from 1971 to 1979.

169. POPOV, V., Sistematicheskii ukazatel' statei pomeshchennykh
v nizhepoimenovannykh periodicheskikh izdaniiakh s 1830 po
1884 god. St. P. 1885, reprinted Twickenham, A. Hall,
1973. Pp. 261.
Covers *Revue Britannique, Revue des Deux Mondes,
Otechestvennye Zapiski, Sovremennik, Russkii Vestnik,
Russkii Arkhiv, Vestnik Evropy, Russkaia Starina, Delo,
Slovo, Znanie, Russkaia Rech', Istoricheskii Vestnik,
Priroda i Liudi, Nabliudatel', Vsemirnyi Trud.*

170. NEUSTROEV, A.N., Istoricheskoe rozyskanie o russkikh
povremennykh izdaniakh i sbornikakh za 1703-1802 gg.
St. P. 1875, reprint Kraus, Nendeln, 1965. Pp. 878.
Later supplemented by his very important Ukazatel' k
russkim povremennym izdaniiam i sbornikam za 1703-1802 gg.
i k istoricheskomu rozyskaniiu o nikh (St. P. 1898).

171. POWELL, A., *Istoricheskie Zapiski*. Index, vols 1-90 (1937-1972). Nendeln, Liechtenstein 1976. Pp. 126.

172. *Istoricheskie Zapiski*. Ukazatel' soderzhaniia, vols 1-100, in vol.100 (1977), 375-407.

173. Zhurnal *Istoriia SSSR*, 1957-1976 gg. Bibliograficheskii Ukazatel'. M.1978. Pp. 100.

174. POWELL, A., *Voprosy Istorii* - Author Index 1945-1975. Nendeln 1977.
12,000 authors, and book reviews.

175. POWELL, A., *Voprosy Istorii* - Subject Index 1945-1975, 3 vols. Nendeln 1977.
36,000 subject entries.

2(a) - HISTORIOGRAPHY

MAZOUR (179, 182) has been the standard Western authority;
VERNADSKY (183) is the latest significant Western contribution,
TIKHOMIROV (190) the standard Soviet account. For the
eighteenth century PESHTICH (199) is unrivalled. TATISHCHEV,
PESHTICH, DOBRUSHKIN (204-206) treat one of the major
historiographical achievements of the period.

176. STEARNS, P.N. (ed.), A Century for Debate: 1789-1914.
     Problems in the Interpretation of European History. N.Y.
     1969. Pp. 511.

177. BLACK, C. (ed.), Rewriting Russian History. Soviet
     Interpretations of Russia's Past. N.Y. 1956. Pp. 413; 2nd
     ed. 1962. Pp. 431.
     Includes essay on treatment of Peter I.

178. TILLETT, L., The Great Friendship: Soviet Historians on the
     Non-Russian Nationalities. Chapel Hill 1969. Pp. 468.

179. MAZOUR, A.G., The Writing of History in the Soviet Union.
     Stanford 1971. Pp. 383.

180. WHITE, J.D., 'M.N. Pokrovsky and the Origins of Soviet
     Historiography', Glasgow Ph.D., 1972.

181. BARBER, J.D., 'The Bolshevization of Soviet Historiography,
     1928-1932', Cambridge Ph.D., 1972.

182. MAZOUR, A.G., Modern Russian Historiography. Westport, Conn.
     1975. 2nd rev. ed. Pp. 224.

183. VERNADSKY, G., Russian Historiography. A History. Belmont
     Mass. 1977. Pp. 385.
     Includes sections on 18th century scholarship, historio-
     graphy of the Russian Orthodox church.

184. BARON, S., HEER, N. (eds), Windows on the Russian Past:
     Essays on Soviet Historiography Since Stalin. Columbus 1977.
     Pp. 177. Rev: *SEER.*, 56, 3 (1978), 452-4 (Dukes, P.).

185. ENTEEN, G., The Soviet Scholar-Bureaucrat. M.N.Pokrovskii
     and the Society of Marxist Historians. Pennsylvania State
     U.P. 1978. Pp. 236.

186. GEYER, D., 'Gegenwartsfragen der sowjetischen
     Geschichtswissenschaft', *Vierteljahrshefte für
     Zeitgeschichte,* 15 (1967), 109-120.

187. RAAB, H., 'Die Entwicklung des Historismus in der russischen
     Literatur des 18. und des beginnenden 19. Jahrhunderts',
     StGrL., 4 (1970), 455-480.

188. KRAPP, B., 'Zur Geschichte Russlands und der UdSSR',
     Geschichte in Wissenschaft und Unterricht, 24 (Oct. 1973),
     615-42.

189. ROBEL, G., HALM, H., Alieni de Russia. 3 vols. Vol. I:
     München 1977. Vols 2-3 forthcoming.
     3-volume project describing all reports and works by
     foreigners about Russia up to 1855.

190. TIKHOMIROV, M.N., NECHKINA, M. et al. (eds), Ocherki istorii
     istoricheskoi nauki v SSSR. M. 1955-66. 4 vols. Pp. 692,
     861, 830, 851.

     Soviet historians and their work:

191. ALATORTSEVA, A.I., ALEKSEEVA, G.D. (comp.), NECHKINA, M.V.,
     GORODETSKII, E.N. (eds), 50 let sovetskoi istoricheskoi
     nauki. Khronika nauchnoi zhizni 1917-1967. M. 1971.
     Pp. 526.
     Chronicle of important events in historians' world.
     Personal and geographical name, but no subject, index.

192. DRUZHININ, N.M. et al. (eds), Sovetskaia istoricheskaia
     nauka ot XX - XXII s'ezdu KPSS. Vol. I: Russia. M. 1963.
     Pp. 627.
     Essays on different areas, and bibliography of publications
     1956-61.

193. CHEREPNIN, L., '50 let sovetskoi istoricheskoi nauki i
     nekotorye itogi izucheniia feodal'noi epokhi istorii Rossii',
     Ist. SSSR, 6 (1967) 77-99.

194. NECHKINA, M.V., 'O periodizatsii istorii sovetskoi
     istoricheskoi nauki', *Ist. SSSR* 1 (1960), 77-91.
     See same author's article on results of ensuing discussion
     in *Ist. SSSR*, 2 (1962), 57-78

195. DOROSHENKO, V.V., 'Zametki o novoi literature po istorii
     feodal'noi Rossii', *Ist. SSSR*, 5 (1968), 147-169.

     Soviet views of Western historians:

196. PASHUTO, V.T., CHEREPNIN, L.G., SHTRANGE, M.M., Kritika
     burzhuaznykh kontseptsii istorii Rossii perioda feodalizma.
     M. 1962. Pp. 430.
     Useful collection of essays.

197. FEIGINA, A., 'Petrovskaia epokha v rabotakh istorikov
     kapitalisticheskikh stran', *Ist. SSSR*, 4 (1972), 185-93.

198. MIRONOV, B.N., 'Nekotorye skhemy istorii SSSR v sovremennoi
     anglo-amerikanskoi burzhuaznoi istoriografii', in:
     VAINSHTEIN, O.L. et al. (eds), Kritika noveishei
     burzhuaznoi istoriografii. Sb. statei (L. 1976), pp. 56-86.
     = Institut Istorii AN SSSR, Leningradskoe otdelenie, *Trudy*,
     vyp. 15. Vyp. 10 (1967) bears the same title.

199. PESHTICH, S.L., Russkaia istoriografiia XVIII veka. 3 parts.
L. 1961-1971. Pp. 276, 344, 173.
Part I: Short historiographical sketch. Historical
knowledge in Russia ca.1650-ca.1750. Works of Mankiev,
Polikarpov, B.Kurakin, Huyssen, Shafirov, Prokopovich,
Gallart. 'Gistoriia Sveiskoi Voiny'. Military, civil,
diplomatic history in early eighteenth-century works.
Tatishchev's source studies for 'Istoriia Rossiiskaia'.
Part II: History and historical knowledge in Russia in second
half of eighteenth-century. Tatishchev, Lomonosov, Müller,
Schlözer, Emin, Catherine II, Rychkov. Beginnings of
bourgeois historiography: Krestinin, Chulkov.
Part III: Shcherbatov, Boltin, minor figures. Particular
historical problems and local history in works 1750-1800.

200. KRANDIEVSKII, S., Ocherki po istoriografii ekonomicheskoi
istorii XVII-XIX vv. Khar'kov 1964. Pp. 305.

201. PUTNYN, E., Istoki russkoi istoriografii antichnosti -
M.V. Lomonosov, A.N. Radishchev. Saratov 1968. Pp. 134.

202. SAKHAROV, A.M., 'Iz istorii istoricheskoi mysli v Rossii
nachala XVIII v.', *VMU(Ist)*, 3 (1972), 70-86.

203 ALPATOV, M., Russkaia istoricheskaia mysl' i zapadnaia
Evropa. XVII-pervaia chetvert' XVIII v. M. 1976. Pp. 454.
Rev: *AHR.*, 82, 1 (1978), 230 (O'Brien. C.B.).

204. TATISHCHEV, V.N., Istoriia Rossiiskaia. (Podgotovili k
pechati M.P. Iroshnikov, A.N. Savel'eva, pod red. A.I.
Andreeva, S.N. Valka, M.N. Tikhomirova). 7 vols. M.-L. 1962-
68.
Rev: vols. 1-4: *Vop. Ist.*, 10 (1965), 149-52 (Kopanev, A).

205. PESHTICH, S.L., 'Neobkhodimoe dopolnenie k novomu izdaniiu
"Istorii Rossiiskoi" V.N. Tatishcheva', in: Problemy istorii
feodal'noi Rossii. Sb. statei k 60-letiiu prof. V.V.
Mavrodina (no. 220), pp. 215-222.
Discusses unreliability of Tatishchev's use of sources.

206. DOBRUSHKIN, E., '"Istoriia Rossiiskaia" V.N. Tatishcheva i
polemika I.N. Boltina i M.M. Shcherbatova', in: N. PAVLENKO,
et al. (eds), *Istochnikovedenie otechestvennoi istorii*, vyp.
I (Moscow 1973), pp. 101-119.

2(b) - ACCOUNTS AND BIBLIOGRAPHIES OF SOME INDIVIDUAL SCHOLARS

Works of senior Soviet scholars may be listed in the series
Materialy k biobibliografii uchenykh SSSR. Many *Festschriften*
also include lists of works: some are given below. See also
for BESKROVNYI, no. 1306; CHEREPNIN, 612, 615; IATSUNSKII, 614;

POKROVSKII, 180, 185, 287; VON RAUCH, 1743; WINTER, 1737.

general listings, Soviet

207. NECHKINA, M. (ed.), Istoriia istoricheskoi nauki v SSSR.
Dooktiabr'skii period. Bibliografiia. M. 1965. Pp. 704.
Lists historians, eighteenth-twentieth centuries, and
studies on them. Volume announced for Soviet period (1979).

208. KRAINEVA, N., PRONINA, P. (comps), Trudy Instituta Istorii
Akademii Nauk SSSR, 1936-1965 gg. Bibliografiia. M. 1968.
4 vols in 2. Pp. 280, 291, 340, 347.

Alekseev

209. NESMEIANOV, A.N. (ed.), Mikhail Pavlovich Alekseev.
M. 1972. Pp. 127.
Series *Materialy k biobibliografii uchenykh SSSR*.

210. BUSHMIN, A.S. et al.(eds), Stravnitel'noe izuchenie
literatur. Sb. statei. K 80-letiiu akad. M.P. Alekseeva.
L. 1976. Pp. 562.
Pp. 555-8: 'Bibliografiia trudov M.P. Alekseeva, 1972-75 gg'.

Berkov

211. BERKOV, P., Literary Contacts between Russia and the West
since the Fourteenth Century. Collected Studies of P.N.
Berkov in Russian, French, German, Italian. London 1973.
Various pagination.

212. BLINDER, R.A., MASHKOVA, V.M. (comps), P.N. Berkov,
Izbrannoe: trudy po knigovedeniiu i bibliografovedeniiu.
M. 1978. Pp. 263.
Bibliography, pp. 247-57, includes lists of published works.

Bogoslovskii

213. CHEREPNIN, L.V., 'Akademik Mikhail M. Bogoslovskii', *I.Z.*,
vol. 93 (1973), 223-71.

Druzhinin

214. IVANOV, L.M. et al. (eds), Problemy sotsial'no-
ekonomicheskoi istorii Rossii. Sb. statei. K 85-letiiu so
dnia rozhdeniia akad. N.M. Druzhinina. M. 1971. Pp. 373.
'Spisok nauchnykh trudov akad. Druzhinina za 1965-70 gg.'
Up-dates list in previous Festschrift.
Latest(90th-birthday) collection, ed. L.V. CHEREPNIN,
appeared M. 1976.

Firsov

215. ERMOLAEV, I., LITVIN, A., Professor N.N. Firsov. Ocherk
zhizni i deiatel'nosti. Kazan' 1976. Pp. 100.
Life, works of specialist in eighteenth century economic
history and middle Volga region.

Kafengauz

216. CHEREPNIN, L.V., 'B.B. Kafengauz kak istorik', *A. Ezh.* (1970), 195-201.

217. 'Spisok trudov B.B. Kafengauza i retsenzii na nikh', in: DRUZHININ (ed.) (no. 439), pp. 508-18.

Kliuchevskii

218. NECHKINA, M.V., Vasilii Osipovich Kliuchevskii: istoriia zhizni i tvorchestva. M. 1974. Pp. 635.

Liashchenko

219. KIKTENKO, T.P., SKOKAN, E.I. (comps), VIRNYK, D.F. (ed.), Petr Ivanovich Liashchenko, 1876-1955. Bibliograficheskii ukazatel'. Kiev 1961. Pp. 58.

Mavrodin

220. SHAPIRO, A.L. (ed.), Problemy istorii feodal'noi Rossii. Sb. statei k 60-letiiu prof. V.V. Mavrodina. L. 1971. Pp. 271. 'Spisok nauchnykh trudov V.V. Mavrodina', pp. 257-67.

221. PETROVA, V.A. (comp.), 'Spisok nauchnykh trudov V.V. Mavrodina', in: EZHOV (ed.) (no. 616), pp. 190-94.

Sacke

222. UNGER, M., 'Georg Sacke. 2 Januar 1902 - 27 April 1945', *Wissenschaftliche Zeitschrift* der Karl Marx Universität, Leipzig, *Gesellschafts-und Sprachwissenschaftliche Reihe,* Jg. 26 (1977), Heft 4, 379-381 List of works, pp. 380-81

Tarle

223. SHERTER, S.R., 'The Soviet System and the Historian: E.V. Tarle (1875-1955) as Case Study', Wayne State Ph.D., 1968.

224. HOESCH, E., E.V. Tarle (1875-1955) und seine Stellung in der Sowjetischen Geschichtswissenschaft. Wiesbaden 1964. Pp. 172.

225. 'Bibliografiia pechatnykh trudov akad. E.V. Tarle', in his: Sochineniia, ed. ERUSALIMSKII, A.S. et al., 12 vols (M. 1957-62), XII, 486-521.

Troitskii

226. IUKHT, A., 'O nauchnom nasledii S.M. Troitskogo' and 'Spisok nauchnykh trudov S.M. Troitskogo', *I.Z.*, 98 (1977), 314-66.

Valk

227. AFFERICA, J., 'Sigismund Natanovich Valk, 1887-1975', *SR.*,
XXXIV, 4 (1975), 804-11.
Dean of Leningrad historians. List of works in no. 236,
pp. 504-13.

Vernadsky

228. FERGUSON, A., 'Bibliography of the Works of George
Vernadsky', in: FERGUSON, A.D., LEVIN, A. (eds), Essays in
Russian History. A Collection Dedicated to George Vernadsky
(Hamden, Conn. 1964), pp. xi-xxv.

Comprehensive(posthumous) listing and discussion in no. 183.

2(c) - SOURCES AND THEIR USE: ISTOCHNIKOVEDENIE

229. *Arkheograficheskii Ezhegodnik*, 1957-
Bibliographies published up to 1967.

230. NOVOSEL'SKII, A.A. (ed.), Problemy istochnikovedeniia.
M. 1941-
12 volumes to date.

231. TIKHOMIROV, M.N., Istochnikovedenie SSSR. Vyp. I: S
drevneishikh vremen do kontsa XVIII v. M. 1962. Pp. 495.
Sections III and IV cover eighteenth century. Systematic
discussion of archival and published sources.

232. KOVAL'CHENKO, I.D. (ed.), Istochnikovedenie istorii SSSR.
M. 1973. Pp. 559.
Essays on law, legislation, state administration
(Beliavskii); political collections and publicists
(Beliavskii); economic-geographical and statistical descrip-
tions (Milov); periodicals (Dmitriev); memoirs, diaries,
mss. (Beliavskii). Written for advanced history students
in USSR.

233. IATSUNSKII, V.K., 'O vyiavlenii i publikatsii istochnikov po
sotsial'no-ekonomicheskoi istorii Rossii XVIII-XIX vekov',
A. Ezh.(1957), 169-189.

234. SHERMAN, I.L., Russkie istoricheskie istochniki X-XVIII v.
Khar'kov 1959. Pp. 250.

235. KUZ'MINA, V.D., Speranskii, M.N. Rukopisnye sborniki XVIII v.
M. 1963. Pp. 266.
Speranskii's works.

236. NOSOV, N.E. et al. (eds), Issledovaniia po otechestvennomu
istochnikovedeniiu. Sb. statei posviashchennykh 75-letiiu
S.N. Valka. M. 1964. Pp. 519.

237. PUSHKAREV, L.N., 'Opredelenie istoricheskogo istochnika v russkoi istoriografii XVIII-XIX vv', *A. Ezh.* (1966), 75-86.

238. ALPATOV, M.A., 'Petrovskie "Vedomosti" kak istochnik po istorii Zapadnoi Evropy', *A. Ezh.* (1967), 119-131.

239. FLOROVSKII, A., 'Iz materialov po istorii Rossii epokhi Petra I v cheshskikh arkhivakh', *A. Ezh.* (1967), 236-241.

240. NIKOLAEVA, A., Voprosy istoriografii russkogo istochnikovedeniia XVIII-XX vekov. M. 1970. Pp. 83.

241. KNIAZEVSKAIA, T. et al. (eds), Problemy rukopisnoi i pechatnoi knigi. M. 1976. Pp. 362.
Grammars of eighteenth century (Kondakov); Novikov's library (Slukhovsky); Mss and books (Kozhin).

242. PUSHKAREV, L., Klassifikatsiia russkikh pis'mennykh istochnikov po otechestvennoi istorii. M. 1975. Pp. 282.
Rev: *Kritika*, XIII, 2 (1977), 111-129 (Kasinec, E.).

243. VESELOVSKII, S., Trudy po istochnikovedeniiu i istorii Rossii perioda feodalizma. M. 1978. Pp. 650.

244. NOVOSEL'SKII, A.A., PUSHKAREV, L.N. (eds), Redkie istochniki po istorii Rossii. M. 1977. 2 parts. Pp. 163, 186.

HISTORIES OF RUSSIA

SOLOV'EV (245, 267) is an unsurpassed source of facts. KORNILOV
and MILIUKOV (246, 247) represent liberal historiography of the
late nineteenth- early twentieth centuries; 284 is another standard pre-revolutionary work. Nos. 248-57 are representative
modern academic histories. FLORINSKY (248), now rather old,
presents an avowedly personal view but gives a full factual
account. RIASANOVSKY and DUKES (257, 255) seek especially to
indicate varying approaches to topics treated, DUKES giving
prominence to Soviet views. PIPES (280), SZAMUELY (281),
BILLINGTON (274) are important studies which develop particular
interpretations. Standard Soviet histories are DRUZHININ (269)
and NECHKINA (270); HOFFMANN (260) gives a useful overview. The
best separate account of the eighteenth century, and somewhat
revisionist, is RAEFF (289).

245. SOLOV'IEV, S.M., History of Russia from the Earliest Times.
     Gulf Breeze, Florida. 1976-
     Translation of no.267. Breaks off in 1770s. Divided into
     projected 50 vols., each with a new introduction but many
     without Solov'iev's footnotes and additional comments.
     3 vols published to date.

246. KORNILOV, A., Modern Russian History from the Age of
     Catherine the Great to the End of the Nineteenth Century.
     Trans. by Kaun, A.S. N.Y. 1943, reprinted N.Y. 1970.
     2 vols. Pp. 310, 284.

247. MILIUKOV, P. (et al.), History of Russia. N.Y. 1968-9.
     3 vols: Pp. 362, 315, 415.
     Trans. from French edition of 1932-3. Rev: *RR.*, 29, 2
     (1970), 210-213.

248. FLORINSKY, M., Russia, A History and An Interpretation. 2
     vols. Latest edition 1970. Pp. 1511.

249. BROMLEY, J.S. et al. (eds), The New Cambridge Modern History,
     VI (Cambridge 1970),chap. XXI, 716-740 (M.S. Anderson); VII
     (1957), chap. XIV, 318-338 (I. Young); VIII (1965), chap. XI,
     306-32 (I. Young); IX (1965), chap. XVIII, 495-524 (J.M.K.
     Vyvyan).
     Russian history 1688-1830.

250. SMIRNOV, I.I. (ed.), A Short History of the USSR. 2 vols.
     M. 1965. Pp. 334, 413.
     Soviet version. See no. 2640 for newer edition.

251. HARCAVE, S., Russia, A History. Philadelphia 1968, 6th ed.
Pp. 787.

252. CLARKSON, J., A History of Russia. N.Y. 1969, 2nd ed.
Pp. 928.

253. GREY, I., The Horizon History of Russia. N.Y. 1970. Pp.416.

254. KIRCHNER, W., A History of Russia. N.Y. 1972, 5th ed.
Pp. 403.

255. DUKES, P., A History of Russia: Medieval, Modern and
Contemporary. London-N.Y. 1974. Pp. 361.

256. DMYTRYSHYN, B., A History of Russia. N.Y. 1977. Pp. 640.

257. RIASANOVSKY, N., A History of Russia. Oxford 1977, 3rd ed.
Pp. 782.

258. MATHIAS, P., POSTAN, N.M., Cambridge Economic History of
Europe, VII, The Industrial Economies, 2: The United States,
Japan and Russia. Cambridge 1978. Pp. 639.
Chap. VII, 308-415: O. Crisp, Labour and Industrialization in
Russia. Chap. VIII, 416-493, M.C. Kaser, Russian
Entrepreneurship. Include material on the eighteenth century.

259. BESANÇON, A., BLANC, S. et al., L'Empire russe de 1762 à
1855. Paris 1966. Pp. 352.

260. HOFFMANN, P., 'Gesamtdarstellungen zur Geschichte der UdSSR',
ZfG., XXV, 4 (1977), 466-9.
Review article of Russian general histories of the USSR;
starts with eighteenth- and nineteenth-century classics, but
concentrates on Soviet presentations from Pokrovskii onwards

261. WITTRAM, R., 'Das russische Imperium und sein
Gestaltwandel', Historische Zeitschrift, 187 (1959), 563-593.

262. MIRSKIJ, D., Russland. Von der Vorgeschichte bis zur
Oktoberrevolution (trans. from English (London 1931-1952) by
W. Wagmuth). München 1967. Pp. 489.

263. SETHE, P., Russische Geschichte. Frankfurt 1968. Pp. 171.

264. RIMSCHA, H. von, Geschichte Russlands. Darmstadt 1972.
Pp. 694.

265. GOEHRKE, C., HELLMAN, M., LORENZ, R., Russland. Frankfurt
1973. Pp. 382.
Rev: Hist. Zeitschrift, 223 (1976), 136-8 (Birth, E.).

266. ZERNACK, K. (ed.), Handbuch der Geschichte Russlands. Vol.I.
Stuttgart 1976.
Several more volumes forthcoming

267. SOLOV'EV, S.M., Istoriia Rossii s drevneishikh vremen, ed.
CHEREPNIN, L., 15 vols. M. 1959-66.
Classic of nineteenth-century scholarship. Breaks off in
1770s. English translation, no.245.

268. KLIUCHEVSKII, V.O., Sochineniia. 8 vols. M. 1956-8.
Another classic. Some parts available in English translation.

269. DRUZHININ, N.M. et al. (eds), Ocherki istorii SSSR. Period
feodalizma. (1) Rossiia v pervoi chetverti XVIII v. M. 1954.
Pp. 814. (2) Rossiia vo vtoroi chetverti XVIII v. M. 1957.
Pp. 866. (3) Rossiia vo vtoroi polovine XVIII v. M. 1956.
Pp. 894. Maps and charts.
A standard Soviet account, by collective including most major
Soviet historians.

270. NECHKINA, M. et al. (eds), Istoriia SSSR s drevneishikh
vremen do nashikh dnei. III: Prevrashchenie Rossii v velikuiu
derzhavu. Narodnye dvizheniia XVII-XVIII vv. M. 1967. Pp.747.
Complete work, by collective of authors, planned in 12 vols.
Vol. 3 covers the eighteenth century. Rev: *Ist. SSSR*, 1,
(1968), 146-50 (Murav'ev, A.).

271. PASHUTO, V.T. (ed.), Illiustrirovannaia istoriia SSSR.
M. 1977. Pp. 462.

SURVEYS OF PARTICULAR FIELDS AND THEMES

272. DVORNIK, F., The Slavs in European History and Civilization.
New Brunswick, N.J. 1962. Pp. 688.
Review and 'Festive Profile' of F. Dvornik by L. Nemec in
Cath. Hist. Rev., LIX, 2 (1973), 185-225.

273. ANDERSON, T., Russian Political Thought. An Introduction.
Ithaca (N.Y.) 1967. Pp. 444.
From Kievan Russia to present.

274. BILLINGTON, J.H., The Icon and the Axe: An Interpretative
History of Russian Culture. N.Y. 1967. Pp. 786.

275. RICE, T.T., Czars and Czarinas of Russia. N.Y. 1968.
Pp. 320, maps and prints.

276. BERGAMINI, J.D., The Tragic Dynasty. A History of the
Romanovs. London 1970. Pp. 512.

277. PORTAL, R., The Slavs. A Cultural and Historical Survey of
the Slavonic Peoples. N.Y. 1970. Pp. 508. Illustrations
and maps.
Rev: *SR.*, XXX, 2 (1971), 378-9. Poor translation of French
edition.

278. DUKES, P., The Emergence of the Superpowers. A Short
Comparative History of the U.S.A. and the U.S.S.R. London
1970. Pp. 155.

279. SEIDEN, J., 'The Mongol Impact on Russia from the 13th Century to the Present: Mongol Contributions to the Political Institutions of Moscovy, Imperial Russia, and the Soviet State', Georgetown Ph.D., 1971.

280. PIPES, R., Russia under the Old Regime. N.Y. 1974. Pp. 361.

    (Translated into Russian , Kembridzh 1980. Pp. 425).
    Rev: *SR.*, XXXIV, 4 (1975) (Treadgold, D.).
        CanAmSlSt.,XIV, 1 (1980), 74–87. (Szeftel, M.).

281. SZAMUELY, T., The Russian Tradition. N.Y. 1975. Pp. 443.

282. LAW, D.A., Russian Civilization. N.Y. 1975. Pp. 490.

283. AUTY, R., OBOLENSKY, D. (eds), Companion to Russian Studies. Vol. 1: An Introduction to Russian History. Cambridge, England 1976. Pp. 403.
    Essay and bibliography on eighteenth century by M. Raeff (291).
    Vol. 2: An Introduction to Russian Language and Literature. Camb. 1977. Pp. 300.

    Vol. 3: An Introduction to Russian Art and Architecture. Oxford 1980.

284. MILIUKOV, P.M., Outlines of Russian Culture (Trans. by Wieczynski, J.L.). 3 parts. Gulf Breeze, Florida 1976–77.

ANTHOLOGIES, ESSAYS

285. BLINOFF, M. (comp.), Life and Thought in Old Russia. Pennsylvania State U.P. 1961. Pp. 222.
    Anthology, fifteenth to nineteenth centuries. Rev: *SEER.*, 41 (1962-3), 265-6 (Malnik, B.).

286. RIHA, T. (ed.), Readings in Russian Civilization. 3 vols in 1. Chicago 1964. Pp. 801.
    Paperback edition in 3 separate volumes.

287. POKROVSKII, M.N., Russia in World History: Selected Essays by M.N. Pokrovskii. Ed. SZPORLUK, R. Ann Arbor 1970. Pp. 241.

288. CHERNIAVSKY, M. (ed.), The Structure of Russian History: Interpretative Essays. N.Y. 1970. Pp. 436.
    Includes relevant essays by M. Cherniavsky, A. Kahan (2), M. Raeff, H.L. Roberts.

289. RAEFF, M., Imperial Russia, 1682-1825; The Coming of Age of Modern Russia. N.Y. 1971. Pp. 176.
Rev: *RR.*, 30, 4 (1971), 394-5.

290. LENTIN, A., Russia in the Eighteenth Century: From Peter the Great to Catherine the Great (1696-1796). London-N.Y. 1973. Pp. 139.

291. RAEFF, M., 'Peter I to Nicholas I', in: AUTY-OBOLENSKY (283), I, 121-195.

292. DUKES, P., 'Russia and the Eighteenth-Century Revolution', *History*, LVI, 188 (1971), 371-386.

The only major project on eighteenth-century documents still in
progress is the long-lived 'Pis'ma i bumagi Petra Velikogo'
(301-302). Contents-listing of two other major Russian documentary publications will be found in the Appendix. VERNADSKY-
PUSHKAREV (293) gives the fullest selection in English, although
often in excerpt. DUKES (295) gives some longer items, including several earlier documents as background. For other editions
of the Nakaz see nos. 517, 1703. RAEFF (296) is focussed
primarily on the nineteenth and twentieth centuries.

293. VERNADSKY, G., PUSHKAREV, S. et al. (comps and eds), A Source
  Book for Russian History from Early Times to 1917. 3 vols.
  New Haven 1972. Vol. 2: Peter the Great to Nicholas I.
  Pp. 884.
  138 items on eighteenth century. Rev: *SR.*, XXXIII, 2 (1974),
  336-8.

294. DMYTRYSHYN, B., Imperial Russia. A Source Book, 1700-1917.
  London-N.Y. 1967; 2nd ed. Hinsdale, Ill. 1974. Pp. 497.
  30 items on eighteenth century. Companion volume on
  'Medieval Russia'.

295. DUKES, P. (comp. and ed.), Russia under Catherine the Great.
  Vol. I: Select Documents. II: Catherine the Great's
  Instruction (Nakaz) to the Legislative Commission, 1767.
  Newtonville 1977-8. Pp. 176, 128.
  I: 19 items, with introductions, including Table of Ranks,
  1762 Manifesto to Nobility, 1775 Provincial Statute, 1785
  Noble Charter, documents on Pugachev, writings of Tatishchev,
  Catherine, Desnitskii, Polenov, Rychkov.
  II: Previously unpublished contemporary translation of the
  Nakaz, with introduction.

296. RAEFF, M., Plans for Political Reform in Imperial Russia,
  1730-1905. Englewood Cliffs, N.J. 1966. Pp. 159.
  Eighteenth century: 1730 crisis, 1763 Council proposal.

297. NOVOSEL'SKII, A.A., KAFENGAUZ, B.B. (eds), Materialy po
  istorii SSSR. Vypusk 5: Dokumenty po istorii XVIII v.
  M. 1957. Pp. 878.
  Sections on brick production, Ukrainian metallurgy, non-
  agricultural villages, Iakut agriculture, risings of 1707-9
  and 1773-5; 1727 list of manufactures; Tatishchev and
  Russkaia Pravda; diary of pomeshchik Annenkov. Introduction,
  notes, to each section

298. BELIAVSKII, M.T. (comp.), Dvorianskaia Imperiia XVIII Veka.
  (Osnovnye zakonodatel'nye akty). M. 1960. Pp. 224.
  19 documents *in extenso,* a few abridgements; including mani-
  festos on nobility (1762 and 1785), secularization (1764),
  land survey (1765), towns (1785), statutes on provincial
  administration (1775), police and welfare (1782).

299. BESKROVNYI, L.G., KAFENGAUZ, B.B. (eds), BELIAVSKII, M.T.,
      PAVLENKO, N.I. (comps), Khrestomatiia po istorii SSSR.
      XVIII Vek. M. 1963. Pp. 787.
      181 items. Rev: *Vop. Ist.*, 12 (1963), 27-9 (Troitskii S.M.).

300. MAVRODIN, V.V. et al. (eds), Sb. dokumentov po istorii SSSR
      dlia seminarskikh i prakticheskikh zaniatii (period
      feodalizma). M. 1970-73. 5 vols. V: XVIII v.

301. Pis'ma i bumagi Imperatora Petra Velikogo. Tom XII, vypusk
      2: Iun' - dekabr' 1712. M. 1977. Pp. 631.
      Latest issue of a venerable and important series, which
      began publication in 1888. See no. 302.

302. POD'IAPOL'SKAIA, E., 'Ob istorii i nauchnom znachenii
      izdaniia "Pis'ma i bumagi imperatora Petra Velikogo"', *A. Ezh.*
      (1972), 56-70.

SECTION 5 - GENERAL HISTORY, WORKS BY PERIOD

5(a) - PETER THE GREAT

ANDERSON (310) provides the best introduction, superseding
SUMNER (304) which is still valuable. The standard, and outstanding, account is WITTRAM (336). Soviet biographies of
rulers are rare: PAVLENKO (344) is well done. RAEFF (312) and
DMYTRYSHIN (313) are particularly useful selections. See also
nos 501, 2641. MASSIE(309) is the latest popular book.

303. PAVLOVA-SIL'VANSKAIA, M.P., 'Annotirovannaia bibliografiia
inostrannoi literatury o Petre I (1947-1970 gg.)'
in: PAVLENKO (no. 343).
Bibliography of non-Russian literature on Peter 1947-70: 158
titles. Continues list covering foreign literature to 1947
given in ANDREEV, A.I. (ed.), Petr Velikii. Sb. Statei.
M.-L. 1947.

304. SUMNER, B., Peter the Great and the Expansion of Russia.
London 1956. Pp. 216.

305. KLIUCHEVSKII, V., Peter the Great. Trans. by L. Archibald.
N.Y. 1958. Pp. 282.
Translation of nineteenth century classic (see no. 268).

306. GREY, I., Peter the Great, Emperor of All Russia. London
1962. Pp. 505.

307. OLIVA, L.J., Peter the Great. Englewood Cliffs, N.J. 1970.
Pp. 181.

308. PUTNAM, P., Peter the Revolutionary Tsar. N.Y. 1973.
Pp. 269.

309. MASSIE, R., Peter the Great. New York 1980. Pp. 924.

310. ANDERSON, M.S., Peter the Great. London 1978. Pp. 207.

311. OLIVA, L.J. (ed.), Russia in the Era of Peter the Great.
Englewood Cliffs, N.J. 1969. Pp. 184.
Readings.

312. RAEFF, M. (comp.), Peter the Great Reforms Russia. Boston,
2nd ed., 1972. Pp. 199
Readings. First ed., 1963, entitled: Peter the Great,
Reformer or Revolutionary?

313. DMYTRYSHIN, B., Modernization of Russia under Peter I and
Catherine II. N.Y. 1974. Pp. 157.
Documents.

314. BLANC, S., 'The Economic Policy of Peter the Great',
in: BLACKWELL (no. 564), pp. 21-49.

315. LEWITTER, L., 'Peter the Great, Poland and the Westernization of Russia', *JHI.*, XIX, 4 (1958), 493-506.

316. BENSON, S., 'The Role of Western Political Thought in Petrine Russia', *CanAmSlSt.*, VIII, 2 (1974), 254-74.

317. MERGUERIAN, B.J., 'Political Ideas in Russia during the Period of Peter the Great (1682-1730)', Harvard Ph.D., 1971.

318. WARNER, R.H., 'The Kožuchovo Campaign of 1694, or the Conquest of Moscow by Preobraženskoe', *JbfGO.*, XII, 4 (1965), 487-96.

319. ZGUTA, R., 'Peter I's "Most Drunken Synod of Fools and Jesters"', *JbfGO.*, XXI, 1 (1973), 18-21.

320. CRACRAFT, J., 'Some Dreams of Peter the Great: A Biographical Note', *CanAmSlSt.*, VIII, 2 (1974), 173-98.

321. WORTMAN, R., 'Peter the Great and Court Procedure', *CanAmSlSt.*, VIII, 2 (1974), 303-11.

322. ANDERSON, M.S., 'The Court of Peter the Great' in: DICKENS, A.G. (ed.), The Courts of Europe: Politics, Patronage and Royalty 1400-1800. N.Y. 1977. Pp. 355; 342 illustrations.

323. KROLL, M. (trans. and ed.), Letters from Liselotte; Elizabeth Charlotte, Princesse Palatine and Duchess of Orleans, "Madame", 1652-1722. London 1970. Pp. 269. Peter at Versailles.

324. SUBTELNY, O., 'Peter I's "Testament", a Reassessment"', *SR.*, XXXIII, 4 (1974), 663-78.

325. BLAMBERG, M.O., 'The Publicists of Peter the Great' Indiana Ph.D., 1974.

326. McNALLY, R., 'Chaadaev's Evaluation of Peter the Great', *ASEER.*, 1 (1964), 31-44.

327. CRACRAFT, J., 'The Tercentenary of Peter the Great in Russia', *CanAmSlSt.*, VIII, 2 (1974), 319-27.

---

328. VALLOTTON, H., Pierre le Grand. Paris 1958. Pp. 550.

329. REAU, L., Pierre le Grand. Paris 1960. Pp. 198.

330. PORTAL, T., Pierre le Grand. Paris 1961. Pp. 312.

331. BLANC, S., Pierre le Grand. Paris 1974. Pp. 128. Selection of documents and readings.

332. VILLARDEAU, S. de, MAZON, A. (eds), 'Abrégé de la vie du
     comte Tolstoy', in: *Analecta Slavica*, A Slavonic Miscellany
     for Prof. Bruno Becker   (Amsterdam 1955), pp. 19-35.
     Peter's collaborator.

333. BLANC, S., 'Histoire d'une phobie: le Testament de Pierre le
     Grand', *CMRS.*, III (1962), 122-139.

334. BABKINE, A. (ed.), 'Les lettres de Russie du Général Pierre
     Lefort', *CanAmSlSt.*, X, 1 (1976) 47-73. See also no. 350.

335. NIVAT, G., 'La genèse d'un roman historique soviétique:
     "Pierre le Grand" d'Alexis Tolstoi', *CMRS.*, II, 1 (1961),
     37-56.

336. WITTRAM, R., Peter I. Czar und Kaiser. Göttingen 1964.
     2 vols. Pp. 490, 646.
     Rev: *JbfGO.*, XIII, 2 (1965), 161-73 (Geyer, D.), and 1783.
     The standard full-length biography. Preceded by an excel-
     lent short preliminary study (1954).

337. GOEDEKE, H. (comp.), Peter der Grosse und seine Zeit.
     Ausstellung zum 300. Geburtstag 20 Dez. 1972-6 März 1973.
     Marburg 1973. Pp. 59, illustrations.

338. KAFENGAUZ, B.B., 'Die wirtschaftliche Entwicklung Russlands
     im ersten viertel des 18. Jhdts und die Reformen Peters I',
     in: WINTER, E. (ed.), E.W. Von Tschirnhaus (no. 1759),
     pp. 223-233.

339. SOMMER, E.F., 'Der junge Tsar Peter in der Moskauer
     Deutschen Sloboda', *JbfGO.*, N.F.V., 1/2 (1957), 67-105.

340. WITTRAM, R., 'Peter des grossen erste Reise in den Westen',
     JbfGO., N.R.III, 4 (1955), 373-403.

341. HOFFMANN, P., 'Die Zeit Peters I in der Darstellung der
     sowjetischen Historiographie', *JfGSLE.*, XVI, 2 (1972),
     187-24.
     Survey of Soviet writing on early eighteenth century.

342. BAGGER, H., Peter den Stores Reformer. En
     Forskningsoversigt. Aarhus 1979. Pp. 120.
     'Peter the Great's Reforms. A Survey of Research'. Good
     bibliography.

343. PAVLENKO, N.I., NIKIFOROV, L., VOLKOV, M. (eds), Rossiia v
     period reform Petra I. M. 1973. Pp. 384.
     Includes articles on international relations: Peter's social
     and political views; social origins of Russian army
     officers; government circles of Petrine period; serf dues
     and taxes; Astrakhan' rising; Russian engravings; biblio-
     graphy of foreign works on Peter (no. 303).

344. PAVLENKO, N.I., Petr Pervyi. M. 1975. Pp. 382.
     Latest Soviet biography, by outstanding scholar.

345. KLIUCHEVSKII, V.O., 'Petr Velikii sredi svoikh sotrudnikov', in: Sochineniia (no. 268), VIII, 314-50.

346. KOZLOV, O., 'Delo Tsarevicha Alekseia', *Vop. Ist.*, 9 (1969), 214-220.

347. NIKOLAEVA, M., '"Testament" Petra I tsarevichu Alekseiu', in: *XVIII Vek*, IX, 1974, 93-111.

348. PAVLENKO, N.I., 'Tri tak nazyvaemykh zaveshchaniia Petra I', *Vop. Ist.*, 2 (1979), 129-44.

349. BABKIN, A. (ed. and intro.), 'Pis'ma Frantsa i Petra Lefortov o "Velikom Posol'stve"', *Vop. Ist.*, 4 (1976), 120-132.
Material from Geneva archives. Cp. no. 334.

5(b) - 1725-1762

Modern coverage of this period is altogether inadequate, with the exception of the 1730 crisis: a measure of the situation is the fact that the works of K. Waliszewski and R. Nisbet Bain, pioneering biographers from the turn of the century, have all been recently reprinted (they have not been listed here). More recent biographies are all popular, with the exception of LEONARD (371) and FLEISCHHACKER (372). LIPSKI (364-5), SCHMIDT (366), KEEP (368), RAEFF (370) are useful studies of particular questions. TROITSKII (352) is important. Some individual figures and fields of this period are covered in other sections. See also 249. 634-5.

GENERAL.

350. LONGWORTH, P., The Three Empresses: Catherine I, Anne and Elizabeth of Russia. N.Y. 1972. Pp. 242.

351. KOZLOV, O., 'K voprosu o politicheskoi bor'be v Rossii v pervoi polovine XVIII v.', *Ezh.gos.ist.muz.*, (1965-6), 119-128.

352. TROITSKII, S.M., 'Istoriografiia "dvortsovykh perevorotov" v Rossii XVIII v.', *Vop. Ist.*, 2 (1966), 38-53.

CATHERINE I, PETER II, 1730

353. YANOV, A., 'The Drama of the Time of Troubles, 1725-30', *CanAmSlSt.*, XII, 1 (1978), 1-59. See also XII, 4, 593.

354. LABELLE. D., 'The Failure of the Dvorianstvo to Establish a Government of Limited Representation in 1730'. Ph.D. dissertation, Chicago 1961.

Peter the Great (in wax by K. Rastrelli)

Catherine I

355. RAEFF, M., 'The Succession Crisis of 1730', in: RAEFF (296), pp. 41-52.

356. RANSEL, D.L., 'Political Perceptions of the Russian Nobility. The Constitutional Crisis of 1730', *Laurentian University Review*, IV, 3 (1971-2), 20-38.

357. DUKES, P., MEEHAN-WATERS, B., 'A neglected Account of the Succession Crisis of 1730: James Keith's Memoir', *CanAmSlSt.*, XII, 1 (1978), 170-83. See also XII no.4, 593.

358. CRACRAFT, James, 'The Succession Crisis of 1730: A View from the Inside', *CanAmSlSt.*, XII,1 (1978), 60-85. See also XII no. 4, 593.

359. ZIEGLER, C. (ed.), La première Catherine, seconde femme de Pierre le Grand: notes et anecdotes ... d'après un manuscrit inédit du 18. siècle. Paris 1956. Pp. 121.

360. PROTASOV, G.A., '"Konditsii" 1730 g. i ikh prodolzhenie', *Uchenye Zapiski Tambovskogo Gos. Ped. In-ta*, vyp. XV (1957), 215-31.

361. PROTASOV, G.A., 'Zapiska Tatishcheva o "proizvol'nom rassuzhdenii" dvorianstva v sobytiiakh 1730 g.', *Problemy Istochnikovedeniia*, XI (1963), 237-65.

362. PROTASOV, G.A., 'Sushchestvoval li "politicheskii plan" D.M. Golitsyna? (K istorii Rossii XVIII v.)', *Istochnikovedcheskie raboty* (Tambovsk. ped. in-ta), vyp. 3 (1973), 90-107.

ANNA IVANOVNA

363. CURTIS, M., A Forgotten Empress: Anna Ivanovna and her Era. N.Y. 1974. Pp. 335.

364. LIPSKI, A., 'Some aspects of Russia's Westernization during the reign of Anna Ivanovna, 1730-40', *ASEER.*, XVIII (1959), 1-11.

365. LIPSKI, A., 'A Re-examination of the "Dark Era" of Anna Ioannovna', *ASEER.*, XXV, 3 (1965), 477-88.

366. SCHMIDT, S., 'La politique intérieure du tsarisme au milieu du XVIIIe siècle', *Annales*, XXI, 1 (1966), 95-110. Volynskii's and Shuvalov's projects described.

367. KIRILOV, I.K., Tsvetushchee Sostoianie Vserossiiskogo Gosudarstva. Ed. RYBAKOV, V.A. et al. M. 1977. Pp. 443. Reprint of classic 1727-37 description of Russia which includes much statistical material. Introduction (pp. 24) covers Kirilov's distinguished career in state service.

ELIZABETH PETROVNA. See also nos 350-1, 366.

368. KEEP, J.L.H., 'The Secret Chancellery, the Guards and the Dynastic Crisis of 1740-1741', *Forschungen zur Osteuropäischen Geschichte*, XXV (1978), 169-93.

369. OLIVIER, D., Elisabeth de Russie. Paris 1962. Pp. 381.

PETER III

370. RAEFF, M., 'The Domestic Policies of Peter III and his Overthrow', *AHR.*, LXXXV, 5 (1970), 1289-1310.

371. LEONARD, C.S., 'A Study of the Reign of Peter III of Russia', Indiana Ph.D., 1976.

372. FLEISCHHACKER, H., 'Porträt Peters III', *JbfGO.*, V (1957), 127-189.

5(c) - 1762-1801

CATHERINE II

Despite a vast number of biographies, there is still no satis-factory overall account; MADARIAGA (2643) will go far to fill this gap. Recent doctoral research has also examined Catherine's life and personality (376-8). The best introduction to Catherine as ruler is RAEFF (382). GRIFFITHS (383) is a stimu-lating defence against the traditional charges of hypocrisy levelled by, for example, PORTAL (390). Catherine's memoirs (384, 394), originally in French, are a significant though tainted source. See also no. 551.

   biographical studies

373. GREY, I., Catherine the Great. Autocrat and Empress of all Russia. London 1961. Philadelphia 1962. Pp. 254.
     Rev: *SR.*, XXII, 1 (1963), 141-2.

374. OLDENBOURG, Z., Catherine the Great (trans. from French by Anne Carter). N.Y. 1965. Pp. 378.
     Rev: *RR.*, 24 (1965), 418-9.

375. TROYAT, H., Catherine the Great. Translated from the French by E. Read. London 1979. Pp. 512.

376. PETSSCHAUER, P., 'The Education and Development of an Enlightened Absolutist: The Youth of Catherine the Great 1729-1762', New York Ph.D., 1969.

377. PETSSCHAUER, P., 'Catherine the Great's Conversion of 1744', *JbfGO.*, XX, 2 (1972), 179-193.

378. PERMENTER, H.R., 'The Personality and Cultural Interests of the Empress Catherine II as revealed in her Correspondence with Friedrich Melchior Grimm', Texas Ph.D., 1969.

379. GOOCH, G.P., Catherine the Great and other Studies. London-N.Y. 1954;, rep. Hamden, Conn. 1966. Pp. 292.

380. TARLE, E.V., 'Angliiskii posol i Ekaterina v 1756-7 gg.', in: Sochineniia, ed. ERUSALIMSKII, A.S., et al., 12 vols (M. 1957-62), IV, 471-80.

Catherine as ruler:

381. OLIVA, L. JAY, Catherine the Great. Englewood Cliffs 1971. Pp. 184.

382. RAEFF, M. (ed.), Catherine the Great: A Profile. N.Y. 1972. Pp. 331.

383. GRIFFITHS, D., 'Catherine II: The Republican Empress', *JbfGO.*, XXI, 3 (1973), 323-44.

general:

384. |Catherine II|, The Memoirs of Catherine the Great. Ed. MAROGER, D., trans. from the French by M. Budberg. London 1955. Pp. 400.

385. RAEFF, M., 'Random Notes on the Reign of Catherine II in the Light of Recent Literature', *JbfGO.*, XIX, 4 (1971), 541-56.

386. ALEXANDER, J., 'Some Recent American Publications on the Reign of Catherine the Great', *CanAmSlSt.*, VII, 1 (1973), 112-18.

387. RANSEL, D., 'The Memoirs of Count Münnich', *SR.*, XXX, 4 (1971), 843-52.

388. MEEHAN-WATERS, B., 'Catherine the Great and the Problem of Female Rule', *RR.*, 34, 3 (1975), 293-308.

389. RASMUSSEN, K., 'Catherine II and the Image of Peter I', *SR.*, XXXVII, 1 (1978), 51-69.

390. PORTAL, R., Sous le masque du libéralisme: Cathérine de Russie. Paris 1965. Pp. 295.

391. GAXOTTE, P., et al., Cathérine de Russie. Paris 1966. Pp. 287. Includes essay by R. Portal.

392. TROYAT, H., Catherine la Grande. Paris 1977. Pp. 544.

393. JESSEN, H. (comp.), Katherine II von Russland im Spiegel der Zeitgenossen. Düsseldorf 1970. Pp. 439.

394. FLEISCHHACKER, H. (ed. and intro.), Katharina II in ihren Memoiren. Frankfurt a/M. 1972. Pp. 468.
Rev: ZfSl., XXI (1976), 428 (Donnert, E.).

395. FLEISCHHACKER, H., Mit Feder und Zepter. Katharina II als Autorin. Stuttgart 1978. Pp. 208
Rev: ZfSl. XXIV (1979), 599-600 (Donnert, E.).

PAUL I.

The standard older work is no. 406; 402 is an important new study.

396. ALMEDINGEN, E., So Dark A Stream: A Study of the Emperor Paul I of Russia, 1754-1801. London 1959. Pp. 240.

397. McGREW, R.E., 'A political portrait of Paul I from the Austrian and English diplomatic archives', JbfGO., N.F. XVIII, 4 (1970), 503-29.

398. PAPMEHL, K. (ed.), 'Letters by L.K. Pitt, British Chaplain in St. Petersburg, on the Person and Policies of Emperor Paul', CanAmSlSt., VII, 1 (1973), 85-106.
This number of CanAmSlSt. is a Special Issue on Paul I.

399. KEEP, J., 'Paul I and the Militarization of Government', CanAmSlSt., VII, 1 (1973), 1-15.

400. WARNER, R.H., 'The Political Opposition to Tsar Paul I', New York Ph.D., 1977.

401. KENNEY, J.J., 'Lord Whitworth and the Conspiracy Against Tsar Paul I: The New Evidence of the Kent Archive', SR., XXXVI, 2 (1977), 205-219.

402. RAGSDALE, H. (ed.), Paul I: A Reassessment of His Life and Reign. Pittsburg 1978 (UCIS Series in Russian and E. European Studies, 2). Pp. 185.

403. GRUNWALD, de C., L'assassinat de Paul 1er. Paris 1960. Pp. 206.

404. ZUBOW, V., Zar Paul I: Mensch und Schicksal. Stuttgart 1963. Pp. 315.

405. SCHARF, C., 'Staatsauffassung und Regierungsprogram eines aufgeklärten Selbstherrschers: Die Instruktion des Grossfürsten Paul von 1788', in: SCHULIN, E. (ed.), Gedenkschrift Martin Göhring: Studien zur europäischen Geschichte (Wiesbaden 1968), pp. 91-106.

406. KLOCHKOV, M., Ocherki pravitel'stvennoi deiatel'nosti vremeni Pavla I. Petrograd 1916, reprinted Cambridge 1973. Pp. 628.

407. OKUN', S.B., 'Dvortsovyi perevorot 1801 goda v
dorevoliutsionnoi literature', *Vop. Ist.*, 11 (1973), 34-52.

407a. OKUN'. S.B., PAINA, E.S., 'Ukaz ot 5 aprelia 1797 g. i ego
evoliutsiia. (K istorii ukaza o trekhdnevnoi barshchine)',
in: NOSOV (no. 236), pp. 283-98.

SECTION 6 - POLITICAL HISTORY

6(a) - THE REGIME: ABSOLUTISM

For works on individual rulers and episodes see Section 5; studies of individual statesmen are largely recorded in Sections 5 and 11. CRUMMEY (408) and TORKE (422) survey the recent Soviet debate on the nature of Russian absolutism, a few contributions to which are listed as nos 439-443. DRUZHININ (439), a most important collection, restarted the Soviet debate. BRUUN (409) and GAGLIARDO (410) are useful general discussions, offering fact and interpretation; KRIEGER (411) is more theoretical. RAEFF (414) offers an important new perspective, sympathetic to the lines explored by GEYER (431-432). RANSEL (418) is an important discussion of the mechanisms of absolute government. Nos 423-4 are symposia devoted to the general subject of absolutism. See also no. 2327.

408. CRUMMEY, R., 'Russian Absolutism and the Nobility', *JMH.*, 49, 3 (1977), 456-68.
Review article on the Soviet debate. Excellent bibliography in footnotes.

409. BRUUN, G., The Enlightened Despots. N.Y.1967. 2nd ed. Pp.120.

410. GAGLIARDO, J.G., Enlightened Despotism. N.Y. 1967. Pp. 118.

411. KRIEGER, L., An Essay on the Theory of Enlightened Despotism. Chicago 1975. Pp. 115.

412. WITTFOGEL, K.A., 'Russia and the East: A Comparison and Contrast', *SR.*, 22 (1963), 627-43, 656-62.

413. RIASANOVSKY, N.V., 'Oriental Despotism and Russia', *SR.*, 22 (1963), 644-9.

414. RAEFF, M., 'The Well-Ordered Police State and the Development of Modernity in Seventeenth-and Eighteenth-Century Europe: An Attempt at a Comparative Approach', *AHR.*, 80, 5 (1975), 1221-44.

415. VENTURI, F., 'From Scotland to Russia: An Eighteenth Century Debate on Feudalism', in: CROSS (ed.), *Proceedings* (no. 1794), pp. 2-25.

416. KAPLAN, F., 'Tatiščev and Kantemir, Two Eighteenth-Century Exponents of a Russian Bureaucratic Style of Thought', *JbfGO.*, XIII, 4 (1965), 497-510.

417. RANSEL, D., 'Nikita Panin's Imperial Council Project and the Struggle of Hierarchy Groups at the Court of Catherine II', *CanAmSlSt.*, IV, 3 (1970), 443-63.

418. RANSEL, D.L., The Politics of Catherinian Russia: The Panin Party. New Haven-London 1975. Pp. 327.
Based on Ph.D. thesis, Yale 1969.

419. RASMUSSEN, K.M., 'Catherine II and Peter I: The Idea of a Just Monarch, The Evolution of An Attitude in Catherinian Russia', UC Berkeley Ph.D., 1973.

420. SZEFTEL, M., 'La monarchie absolue dans l'Etat moscovite et l'Empire russe (fin XVe siècle - 1905)', *Recueils de la Société Jean Bodin*, 22 (1969), 727-57. Reprinted in SZEFTEL, M., Russian Institutions and Culture up to Peter the Great (London 1975), pp. 727-57 .
Overview.

421. ANDERSON, P., L'Etat absolutiste: ses origines et ses voies. 2 vols. Paris 1978. Pp. 203, 409. Vol. II: L'Europe de l'Est.
Trans. from English.

422. TORKE, H.-J., 'Die neuere Sowjethistoriographie zum Problem des russischen Absolutismus', *Forschungen zur osteuropäischen Geschichte*, 20 (1973), 113-33.

423. HUBATSCH, W. (ed.), Das Zeitalter des Absolutismus:1600-1789. 4 Aufl. Braunschweig 1975. Pp. 276.

424. ARETIN, K.O., FREIHERR von (ed.), Der Aufgeklärte Absolutismus. Cologne 1974. Pp. 390.
Essays include no. 426. Rev: *HJ.*,XVIII, 2 (1975), 401-8 (Behrens, B.), and no. 427 (Fuchs, P.).

425. LEHMANN, H., 'Zum Wandel des Absolutismusbegriffs in der Historiographie der BRD', *ZfG.*, XXII (1974), 3-27.
Mostly on German absolutism.

426. HOFFMANN, P., 'Entwicklungsetappen und Besonderheiten des Absolutismus in Russland', in: ARETIN (no. 424).

427. FUCHS, P., 'Der Absolutismus als Forschungsproblem. Zwei neue Bestandsaufnahmen', *Hist. Zt.*, 220, 3 (1975), 642-48. Review article on ARETIN (no.424).

428. ALEXEIEV, N., 'Beiträge zur Geschichte des russischen Absolutismus im 18. Jahrhundert', *JbfGO.*, 6 (1958), 7-81.

429. GLASENAPP, I.von, Staat, Gesellschaft und Opposition in Russland im Zeitalter Katharinas der Grossen. München 1964. Pp. 223.
Rev: *JbfGO.*, XIV, 1 (1966), 119-20 (McConnell,A.).
Chap. V compares living standards and mortality rates in Russia and Western Europe.

430. DONNERT, E., HOFFMAN, P., 'Zur Frage der wirtschaftlichen und sozialen Grundlage des Absolutismus in Russland', *ZfG.*, XIV (1966), 758-65.

431. GEYER, D., '"Gesellschaft" als staatliche Veranstaltung.
Bemerkungen zur Sozialgeschichte der russischen
Staatsverwaltung im 18. Jhdt.', *JbfGO.*, N.F. XIV,1 (1966), 21-50.

432. GEYER, D., 'Staatsaufbau und Sozialverfassung. Probleme des
russischen Absolutismus am Ende des 18. Jahrhunderts',
CMRS., VII, 3 (1966), 366-77.

433. KUETTLER, W., 'Gesellschaftliche Voraussetzungen und
Entwicklungstyp des Absolutismus in Russland', *JbfGSLE.*,
13, 2 (1969), 71-108.

434. HOFFMANN, P., 'Aukflärung, Absolutismus, aufgeklärter
Absolutismus in Russland', *Studien zur Geschichte der
russischen Literatur des XVIII Jhdts*, 4 (1970), 9-40.

435. DONNERT, E., 'Aufgeklärter Absolutismus und Agrarfrage in
Russland in der zweiten Hälfte des 18. Jahrhunderts', *ZfG.*,
XX (1972), 974-86.

436. DONNERT, E., 'Zur Gesellschaftspolitik und Staatsräson des
aufgeklärten Absolutismus in Russland unter Katharina II',
JfGSLE., XVIII, 2 (1974), 147-70.

437. DONNERT, E., 'Zur bürgerlichen Ideologie der russischen
Gesellschaft in der zweiten Hälfte des 18. Jahrhunderts',
ZfG., XXII, 7 (1974), 730-41.

438. DONNERT, E., Politische Ideologie der russischen
Gesellschaft zu Beginn der Regierungszeit Katherinas II,
Berlin (E.) 1976. Pp. 206.
Reproduces his articles almost verbatim.

───────────────

439. DRUZHININ, N.M. (ed.), Absoliutizm v Rossii. M. 1964.
Pp. 519.
Festschrift for B.B. Kafengauz. 14 essays in the origins,
nature of absolutism: structure of absolutist government;
policies towards nationalities; *mestnichestvo, zemskie
sobory* and absolutism; reflections of absolutism in
eighteenth century. Seminal for the Soviet debate.

440. DRUZHININ, N.M., 'Prosveshchennyi absoliutizm v Rossii',
in: DRUZHININ (no. 439), pp. 428-59.

441. PAVLENKO, N.I., 'Idei absoliutizma v zakonodatel'stve XVIII
v.', in: DRUZHININ (no. 439), pp. 389-427.

442. FEDOSOV, I.A., 'Sotsial'naia sushchnost' i evoliutsiia
rossiiskogo absoliutizma (XVIII- pervaia polovina XIX v.),
Vop. Ist., 7 (1971), 46-65.

443. OKUN' S.B., 'K voprosu o sushchnosti russkogo absoliutizma
(vtoraia polovina XVIII - nach. XIX v.), *Problemy
otechestvennoi i vseobshchei istorii*, vyp. 2 (1973), 110-17.

444. GRATSIANSKII, P.S., 'Russkie prosvetiteli 60-80kh gg.
XVIII v. o proiskhozhdenii i sushchnosti gosudarstva',
Problemy gosudarstva i prava na sovremennom etape, vyp. 8
(1974), 40-46.

445. PETROVA, V.A., 'Politicheskaia bor'ba vokrug senatskoi
reformy 1763 goda', *VLU(Ist.),* 14 (1967), 63-75.

446. SAFONOV, M.M., 'Konstitutsionnyi proekt N.I. Panina - D.I.
Fonvizina', *Vspomogatel'nye istoricheskie distsipliny,*
6 (1974) (Leningradsk. otd. Arkheogr. Komissii AN SSSR),
281-94.

6(b) - GOVERNMENT AND ADMINISTRATION: INSTITUTIONS OF CENTRAL
     AND LOCAL GOVERNMENT, THE BUREAUCRACY

While there are several good reference works on the government
apparatus (447-451), government institutions as such have been
studied less in recent years than their personnel, the bureaucracy. LE DONNE's work (458-60, 533), part of a larger study,
combines both aspects. ORLOVSKY (473) and RAEFF (474) give
comprehensive overviews of recent work. The various studies of
TROITSKII (226; 472; 490-3) are fundamental to this field as a
whole. Apart from no. 455, financial matters are dealt with
in Section 7.

   *REFERENCE WORKS ON GOVERNMENT, PERSONNEL AND
   INSTITUTIONS*

447 AMBURGER, E., Geschichte der Behördenorganisation
Russlands von Peter dem Grossen bis 1917. Leyden 1966.
Pp. 630
Unique.
_____

448. CHERNOV, A.V., Gosudarstvennye uchrezhdeniia Rossii v
XVIII v. (Zakonodatel'nye materialy). Spravochnoe posobie.
M. 1960. Pp. 579.
Lists decrees involving or affecting each institution.

449. EROSHKIN, N.P., Istoriia gosudarstvennykh uchrezhdenii
dorevoliutsionnoi Rossii. M. 1960. Pp. 395. 2nd ed.
M. 1968. Pp. 368.

450. STESHENKO, L.A., SOFRONENKO, K.A., Gosudarstvennyi stroi
Rossii v pervoi chetverti XVIII v. M. 1973. Pp. 119.

451. ZAIONCHKOVSKII, P.A., Pravitel'stvennyi apparat
samoderzhavnoi Rossii v XIX veke. M. 1978. Pp. 288.
Refers to eighteenth century.

452. POULSEN, T.M., 'The Provinces of Russia: Changing Patterns with Regional Allocation of Authority, 1708-1762', Wisconsin Ph.D., 1963.

453. LINCOLN, W.B., 'The Russian State and its Cities: A Search for Effective Municipal Government 1786-1842', *JbfGO.*, XVII, 4 (1969), 531-41.

454. JONES, R.E., 'Catherine II and the Provincial Reform of 1775: A Question of Motivation', *CanAmSlSt.*, IV, 3 (1970), 497-512.

455. DURAN, J.A., 'The Reform of Financial Administration in Russia during the Reign of Catherine II', *CanAmSlSt.*, IV, 3 (1970), 485-96.

456. ARMSTRONG, J.A., 'Old Regime Governors: Bureaucratic and Patrimonial Attributes', *Comp. St. in Soc. and Hist.*, XIV, 1 (1972), 2-29.
Comparison of France 1661-1789 and Russia 1762-1881. In error on Russian nobility. See same author in *Revue Internat. des Sciences Administratives*, 38, 1 (1972), 21-40.

457. RAEFF, M., 'The Empress and the Vinerian Professor: Catherine II's Projects of Government Reforms and Blackstone's Commentaries', *OSP.*, N.S. VII (1974), 18-41.

458. LE DONNE, J.P., 'Appointments to the Russian Senate, 1762-1796', *CMRS.*, XVI, 1 (1975), 27-56.

459. LE DONNE, J.P., 'The Evolution of the Governor's Office, 1727-64', *CanAmSlSt.*, XII, 1 (1978), 86-115.

460. LE DONNE, J.P., 'Catherine's governors and governors-general, 1763-1796', *CMRS.*, XX, 1 (1979), 15-42.

461. SCOTT, F.D., Sweden: The Nation's History. Minneapolis 1977. Pp. 654. Peter I's use of Swedish models.

462. SZEFTEL, M., 'La participation des assemblées populaires dans le gouvernement central de la Russie depuis l'époque Kiévienne jusqu' à la fin du XVIIIe siècle', *Recueils de la Société Jean Bodin*, 25 (1965), 339-65, reprinted in SZEFTEL (no. 420), pp. 339-65.

463. PUTTKAMER, E. von, 'Einflüsse schwedischen Rechts auf die Reformen Peters des Grossen', *Zeitschrift für ausländisches öffentliches Recht und Völkerrecht*, XIX (1958), 369-84.

464. FILIPPOV, A. et al. (eds), Istoriia Pravitel'stvuiushchego Senata za dvesti let, 1711-1911. St. P. 1911, reprinted 1973. 5 vols.
Eighteenth century: vols 1-2.

465. VODARSKII, IA. E., 'Iz istorii sozdaniia Glavnogo Magistrata', in: USTIUGOV (ed.) (no. 604), pp. 101-113.

466. STESHENKO, L., 'Obrazovanie kollegii iustitsii (1719-1725)', *VMU(Pravo)*, 6 (1966), 63-69.

467. STESHENKO, L., 'Fiskaly i prokurory v sisteme gosudarstvennykh organov Rossii pervoi chetverti XVIII v.', *VMU(Pravo)*, 2 (1966), 51-58.

468. BOGOSLOVSKII, M., Oblastnaia reforma Petra Velikogo, provintsiia 1719-1727 gg. M. 1902, reprinted 1970, 2 vols. Pp. 522, 45.

469. ZHELUDKOV, V.F., 'Vvedenie gubernskoi reformy 1775 g.', in: MAVRODIN (no. 843), pp. 161-90.

470. PAVLOVA-SILVANSKAIA, M., 'Sozdanie v 1775 godu soslovnykh sudov dlia krest'ian', *VMU(Ist.)*, 3 (1963), 69-74.

471. RAFIENKO, L.S., 'Instruktsiia sibirskomu gubernatoru 1741 g.', *A.Ezh.* (1973), 58-67.

472. TROITSKII, S.M., 'Ob ispol'zovanii opyta Shvetsii pri provedenii administrativnykh reform v Rossii v pervoi chetverti XVIII v.', *Vop.Ist.*, 2 (1977), 67-75.

BUREAUCRACY AND ADMINISTRATION

473. ORLOVSKY, D., 'Recent Studies on the Russian Bureaucracy', *RR.*, 35, 4 (1976), 448-68.

474. RAEFF, M., 'The Bureaucratic Phenomena of Imperial Russia, 1700-1905', *AHR.*, 84, 2 (1979), 399-411. Review article on recent and forthcoming work.

475. RAEFF, M., 'The Russian Autocracy and its Officials', *Harvard Slavic Studies*, IV (1957), 77-92.

476. CLARKSON, J., 'Some Notes on Bureaucracy, Aristocracy, and Autocracy in Russia, 1500-1800', in: RITTER, G. (ed.), Entstehung und Wandel der modernen Gesellschaft (Berlin 1970), pp. 187-220.

477. BROWN, P.B., 'Early Modern Russian Bureaucracy: The Evolution of the Chancellery System from Ivan III to Peter the Great'. Chicago Ph.D., 1977.

478. KEEP, J., 'Light and Shade in the History of Russian Administration', *CanAmSlSt.*, VI, 1 (1972), 1-9. Comment by H.-J. Torke in *ibid.*, pp. 10-13.

479. TORKE, H.-J., 'Continuity and Change in the Relations between Bureaucracy and Society in Russia, 1613-1861', *CanAmSlSt.*, V (1971), 457-76.

480. YANEY, G., The Systemization of Russian Government: Social
Evolution in the Domestic Administration of Imperial Russia,
1711-1905. Urbana 1973. Pp. 430.
Rev: no. 481.

481. KEEP, J., 'Programming the Past: Imperial Russian
Bureaucracy and Society under the Scrutiny of Mr. George
Yaney', *CanAmSlSt.*, VIII, 4 (1974), 569-81.
Review of Yaney (no. 480).

482. RANSEL, D., 'Bureaucracy and Patronage: The View from an
Eighteenth Century Russian Letter Writer', in: JAHER, F.C.
(ed.), The Rich and Well Born and the Powerful: Elites and
Upper Classes in History (Urbana 1973).

483. BENNETT, H., 'Evolution of the meaning of *chin*: an introduction to the Russian institution of rank ordering and niche
assignment from the time of Peter the Great's Table of Ranks
to the Bolshevik revolution', *Calif. Sl. St.* (1978).

484. HASSELL, J.E., 'Implementation of the Russian Table of Ranks
During the Eighteenth Century', *SR.*, XXIX, 2 (1970), 283-96.

485. FEINSHTEIN, S.C., 'V.N. Tatishchev and The Development of
the Concept of State Service in Petrine and Post-Petrine
Russia', New York Ph.D., 1971.

486. HASSELL, J.E., 'The Vicissitudes of Russian Administrative
Reform 1762-1801', Cornell Ph.D., 1967.

487. BLANC, S., 'La pratique de l'administration russe dans la
première moitié du XVIII s.', *Revue d'histoire moderne et
contemporaine*, X, 1 (1963), 45-64.

488. DEMIDOVA, N.F., 'Biurokratizatsiia gosudarstvennogo
apparata absoliutizma v XVII-XVIII v.', in: DRUZHININ
(no. 439), pp. 206-42.

489. TROITSKII, S.M., 'Sotsial'nyi sostav i chislennost'
biurokratii Rossii v seredine XVIII v.', *I.Z.*, vol. 89,
295-353.

490. TROITSKII, S.M., 'Materialy perepisi chinovnikov v 1754-
1756 gg. kak istochnik po sotsial'no-politicheskoi i
kulturnoi istorii Rossii XVIII v.', *A. Ezh.* (1967), 132-48.

491. TROITSKII, S.M., 'Iz istorii sozdanii Tabeli o rangakh',
Ist. SSSR., 1 (1974), 98-111.

492. TROITSKII, S.M., Russkii absoliutizm i dvorianstvo v XVIII
v. (formirovanie biurokratii). M. 1974. Pp. 396.
Rev: *Vop. Ist.*, 1 (1976), 154-7 (Aleksandrov, V.A.);
Kritika XII, 1 (1976), 26-41 (Meehan-Waters, B).

493. SHEPELEV, L.E., Otmennenye istoriei.Chiny, zvaniia i tituly
v Rossiiskoi Imperii. Sistema voennykh, grazhdanskikh i
pridvornykh chinov, zvanii i titulov ... L. 1977. Pp. 153.

BUTLER (495, 497, 501, 517) has made a significant contribution to the rather patchy recent writing in this field. The Commission of 1767-68 continues to attract much scholarly attention (510-518), though Western research has tended to ignore earlier eighteenth-century codification attempts. 517 gives a full bibliographical history of Catherine's *Nakaz* The two English texts, published by DUKES and REDDAWAY, are listed as nos 295 and 1703 respectively. DUKES' study of the nobility (638) also deals with the 1767 Commission.

GENERAL

494. SZEFTEL, M., 'Russia (before 1917)', in: GILISSEN, J. (ed.), Bibliographical Introduction to Legal History and Ethnology (Brussels 1966), vol. D", section 9. Pp. 58.
Comprehensive source for research on legal history including the peasantry.

495. BUTLER, W.E., Russian and Soviet Law. An annotated catalogue of reference works, legislation, court reports, serials and monographs on Russian and Soviet law (including international law). Zug 1976. Pp. 122.
The 1100 works described are all available on microfiche.

496. KSENSOVA, T., Iuridicheskaia Literatura. Annotirovannyi ukazatel' otechestvennoi bibliograficheskoi literatury i posobii, izd. v 1831-1970 gg. M. 1972. Pp. 144.

497. BUTLER, W.E. (ed.), Russian Law: Historical and Political Perspectives. Leiden 1977. Pp. 266.
Essays, incl. nos 504, 675.

498. YANEY, G., 'Law, Society and the Domestic Regime in Russia, In Historical Perspective', *American Political Science Review*, LIX, (1965), 379-90.

499. WORTMAN, R., The Development of a Russian Legal Consciousness. Chicago 1976. Pp. 345.
Mainly nineteenth century.

500. HAMMER, D.P., 'Russian and Roman Law', *ASEER.*, XVI, 1 (1957), 1-13.

501. BUTLER, W.E. (intro.), P.P. Shafirov, A Discourse Concerning The Just Causes of The War Between Sweden and Russia: 1700-1721. Dobbs Ferry, N.Y. 1973 [Pp. 289].
Facsimile reproduction of Russian and English texts.

502. VENTURI, F., 'Cesare Beccaria and Legal Reform', in: WOOLF, S. (ed.), Italy and the Enlightenment. Studies in a Cosmopolitan Century (London 1972), pp. 154-64.

503. CIZOVA, T., 'Beccaria in Russia, *SEER.*, XL, 95 (1961-2), 384-408.

504. BROWN, A.H., 'The Father of Russian Jurisprudence: The Legal Thought of S.E. Desnitskii', in: BUTLER (no. 497), pp. 117-141.

505. LEONTOVICH, F., Literatura istorii russkago pravo. Warsaw 1902; reprinted 1973. Pp. 597.
Good bibliography.

506. GRABAR', V.E., Materialy k istorii literatury mezhdunarodnogo pravo v Rossii, 1647-1917. M. 1958. Pp. 491.
Eighteenth century: pp. 38-176.

507. GRATSIANSKII, P., Politicheskaia i pravovaia mysl' Rossii vtoroi poloviny XVIII veka. M. 1978.

508. GRATSIANSKII, P., Desnitskii. M. 1978. Pp. 109.

509. BELIK, A.P. (ed.), V.F. Malinovskii. Izbrannye obshchestvenno-politicheskie sochineniia. M. 1958. Pp. 169.
Malinovskii (1765-1814), a *prosvetitel'*, wrote a number of tracts at the end of the eighteenth- beginning of the nineteenth centuries.

LEGISLATIVE PROJECTS AND COMMISSIONS; CATHERINE II'S NAKAZ

510. AUGUSTINE, W.R., 'The Economic Attitudes and Opinions Expressed by the Russian Nobility in the Great Commission of 1767', Columbia Ph.D., 1969.

511. GIVENS, R.D., 'Supplication and Reform in the Instructions of the Nobility', *CanAmSlSt.*, XI, 4 (1977), 483-502.

512. DANIEL, W.L., 'Russian Attitudes Toward Modernization: The Merchant - Nobility Conflict in the Legislative Commission, 1767-1774', North Carolina Ph.D., 1973.

513. DANIEL, W.L., 'The Merchants' View of the Social Order in Russia as revealed in the Town *Nakazy* from *Moskovskaia Guberniia* to Catherine's Legislative Commission', *CanAmSlSt.*, XI, 4 (1977), 503-522.

514. SINTON, J.W., 'The Instruction from Kazan Guberniia at the Legislative Commission of 1767', Indiana Ph.D., 1968.

515. MORRISON, K., 'Catherine II's Legislative Commission. An Administrative Interpretation', *CanAmSlSt.*, IV, 3 (1970), 464-84.

515a. VAN LARE, D. H., ' Tula Province in the Eighteenth Century: The Deputy Instructions to the Legislative Commission of 1767 as a Source for Local History', Ph.D., Kansas 1978.

516. PAPMEHL, K.A., 'The Problem of Civil Liberties in the Records of the "Great Commission"', *SEER.*, 42, 2 (1963-4), 274-91.

517. BUTLER, W.E., 'The *Nakaz* of Catherine the Great', *American Book Collector* XVI, 5 (1966), 1-10.
Bibliographical history of the *Nakaz*.

518. RANSEL, D., 'Catherine II's Instruction to the Commission on Laws: an Attack on Gentry Liberals?', *SEER.*, L, 118 (1972), 10-28.

519. DMYTRYSHYN, B., 'The Economic Content of the 1767 Nakaz of Catherine II', *ASEER.*, 19 (1960), 1-9.

520. BROWN, A.H., 'S.E. Desnitsky, Adam Smith and the Nakaz of Catherine II', *OSP.*, N.S., VII (1974), 42-59.

521. COQUIN, F.-X., La Grande Commission Legislative (1767-1768): Les Cahiers de Doléances urbaines. Paris-Louvain 1971. Pp. 258.

522. KNABE, B., 'Die Struktur der russischen Posadgemeinden und der katalog der Beschwerden und Forderungen der Kaufmannschaft (1762-67)', *Forschungen zur osteuropäischen Geschichte* 22, 1975. Pp. 396.
Rev: *SR.*, 38, 1 (1979), 107-8 (Rieber, A.J.).

523. MAN'KOV, A.G., 'Ispol'zovanie v Rossii shvedskogo zakonodatel'stva pri sostavlenii proekta ulozheniia 1720-1725 gg.', in: Istoricheskie sviazi Skandinavii i Rossii IX-XX vv. (L. 1970), pp. 112-26.

524. MAN'KOV, A.G., 'Proekt Ulozheniia Rossiiskogo Gosudarstva 1720-1725 gg.', in: Problemy istorii feodal'noi Rossii. Sb. statei k 60-letiiu prof. V.V. Mavrodina (no. 220), pp. 157-66.

525. MAN'KOV, A.G., 'Krepostnoe zakonodatel'stvo v Rossii pervoi poloviny XVIII v. (po materialam proekta Ulozheniia 1720-1725 gg.)', *Ezh. A.I.* (1971), 146-55.

526. SOFRONENKO, K., Malorossiikii prikaz Russkogo gosudarstva vtoroi pol. XVII i nachala XVIII veka. M. 1960. Pp. 177.

527. RUBINSHTEIN, N.L., 'Ulozhennaia Kommissiia 1754-1766 gg. i ee proekt novogo ulozheniia "o sostoianii poddannykh voobshche"' *I.Z.*, vol. 38, 208-251.

528. NEDOSEKIN, V.I., 'K diskussii po krest'ianskomu voprosu v Rossii nakanune vosstaniia Pugacheva', *Izv. Voronezhskogo Gos. Pedagogich. In-ta*, 63 (1967), 326-46.

529. KURMACHEVA, M., 'Problemy obrazovaniia v Ulozhennoi Komissii 1767 g.', in: PAVLENKO (ed.) (no. 661), pp. 240-264.

530. OMEL'CHENKO, O., 'Politicheskaia teoriia v "Nakaze Kommissii o sostavlenii proekta novogo ulozheniia" Ekateriny II', *VMU(Ist.)*, 1 (1977), 77–92.

531. BELIAVSKII, M.T., 'Vopros o krepostnom prave i polozhenii krest'ian v "Nakaze" Ekateriny II', *VMU(Ist.)*, 6 (1963), 44–64.

JUDICIARY, POLICE, PENAL SYSTEM

532. HINGLEY, R., The Russian Secret Police: Muscovite, Imperial Russian and Soviet Political Security Operations. N.Y. 1970. Pp. 313.
Brief look at the eighteenth century; emphasis on Soviet period.

533. LE DONNE, J.P., 'The Provincial and Local Police under Catherine the Great, 1775–1796', *CanAmSlSt.*, IV, 3 (1970), 513–28.

533a. LE DONNE, J.P.,'The Judicial Reform of 1775 in Central Russia', *JbfGO.*, N.F. 21 (1973), 29–45.

---

534. KAISER, F.B., Die Russische Justizreform von 1864: Zur Geschichte der Russischen Justiz von Katharina II bis 1917. Leiden 1972. Pp. 552.
Includes systematic description of pre-reform legal system, which was based on 1775 provincial reform and 1785 Charter to Towns.

---

535. GOLIKOVA, N.V., 'Organy politicheskogo syska i ikh razvitie v XVII–XVIII v.', in: DRUZHININ (no. 439), pp. 255–58.

536. SIZIKOV, M.I., 'Uchrezhdeniia reguliarnoi politsii Rossii pervoi poloviny XVIII v. i ikh arhivy v nastoiashchee vremia', *Vspomogatel'nye istoricheskie distsipliny* (Ural'sk. Un-t.), Sb. 1 (1974), 24–31.

537. SIZIKOV, M.I., 'O pozitivnykh funktsiiakh reguliarnoi politsii Rossii v pervoi chetverti XVIII v.', *Sb. aspirantskikh rabot Sverdlovskskogo iuridicheskogo un-ta*, vyp. 14 (1972), 131–38.

538. GOLIKOVA, N., Politicheskie protsessy pri Petre I, po materialam Preobrazhenskogo Prikaza. M. 1957. Pp. 338.

539. GERNET, M., Istoriia tsarskoi tiurmy. 5 vols. 2nd ed. M. 1951–6; 3rd ed. 1962–5. Vol. I: 1762–1825. Pp. 327.

540. DVORIANOV, V.N., V sibirskoi dal'nei storone. (Ocherki istorii tsarskoi katorgi i ssylki. 60-e gody XVIII v.–1917 g.) Minsk 1971. Pp. 374.

541. GORIUSHKIN, L.M. et al. (eds), Ssylka i katorga v Sibiri XVIII–nachalo XX vv. Novosibirsk 1975. Pp. 302.
Rev: *ZfG.*, XXV (1977), 602–3 (Thomas, L.).

7(a) - GENERAL

The 'traditional' areas of Russian social and economic history
are covered in succeeding sub-sections. RANSEL (550), ATKINSON
(549), ALEXANDER (552) exemplify new directions in Western
scholarship. KAHAN (553) is characteristically stimulating;
KLIBANOV (556) and RODIN (557) also cover unfamiliar ground.
Russia's economic development has continued to generate controversy in journals and miscellanies, monitored and reported by,
for example, BARON (566) and GOEHRKE ˙ (586). See also 200,
258, 338.

GUIDES AND BIBLIOGRAPHIES

542. KAHAN, A., 'Quantitative Data for the Study of Russian
History' in: LORWIN, V.R. and PRICE, J.M. (eds), The
Dimensions of the Past (New Haven 1972), pp. 361-430.

543. KAZMER, D.R. and V., Russian Economic History: A Guide to
Information Sources. Detroit 1977. Pp. 520.
Rev: *SEER.*, 57, 1 (1979), 147-8 (Crisp, O.).

544. SIVOLGIN, V.E., Politicheskaia ekonomiia. Istoriia
ekonomicheskoi mysli. Annotirovannyi ukazatel'
otechestvennykh bibliograficheskikh posobii, izdannyh v
1812-1972 gg. M. 1974. Pp. 68.
Rev: *Bib. Sov. Bib.*, 4 (1974), 35.

545. MASHIKHIN, E., SIMCHERA, V., Statisticheskie publikatsii
v SSSR: bibliograficheskii ukazatel' 1918-1972. M. 1975.
Pp. 279.

546. INSTITUTE OF SCIENTIFIC INFORMATION IN SOCIAL SCIENCES
(INION),
Ekonomicheskaia istoriia: Ukazatel' Sovetskoi literatury
1973-77 gg. M. 1978- 5 vols planned, 3 to date.
Continues series of 2 previous bibliographies, for 1960-69
(M. 1970, 5 vols) and 1969-73 (M. 1974, 5 vols); bibliogra-
phies issued in connection with International Congress of
Economic History. Effectively a selective cumulation of
monthly *Novaia sovietskaia literatura po obshchestvennym
naukam: Ekonomika.*

SOCIAL HISTORY

547. BLACK, C.E., 'The Nature of Imperial Russian Society',
ASEER., 20 (1961), 565-82.

548. BECKER, C., '"Raznochintsy": the Development of the Word
and The Concept', *ASEER.*, 18 (1959), 63-74.

549. ATKINSON, D., 'Society and the Sexes in the Russian Past',
in: ATKINSON, D., DALLIN, A., LAPIDUS, G. (eds), Women in
Russia (Stanford 1977), pp. 3-36.
From earliest times. Little on eighteenth century.

550. RANSEL, D. (ed.), The Family in Imperial Russia: New Lines
of Historical Research. Illinois U.P. 1978. Pp. 342.
Conference proceedings.
'Annotated Bibliography', pp. 305-36.

551. KOCHAN, M., Life in Russia under Catherine the Great.
London-N.Y. 1960. Pp. 182.
Lavishly illustrated introduction.

552. ALEXANDER, J.T., 'Medical Professionals and Public Health in
"Doldrums" Russia (1725-62)', *CanAmSlSt.*, XII, 1 (1978),
116-35.
See 'Addenda and Corrigenda', *ibid.*, XII, 4, 593; and
Section 12(i).

553. KAHAN, A., 'The Costs of Westernization in Russia: the
Gentry and the Economy in the Eighteenth Century', in:
CHERNIAVSKY, M. (ed.), The Structure of Russian History
(no. 288), pp. 224-250.
Reprinted from *SR.*, XXV, 1 (1965), 40-66.

554. GESEMAN, W., Die Entdeckung der unteren Volksschichten
durch die russische Literatur. Zur Dialektik eines
literarischen Motivs von Kantemir bis Belinskij. Wiesbaden
1972. Pp. 315.

555. SANNINSKII, B., 'Kto takie raznochintsy?', *Vop. Literatury*,
4 (1977), 232-240.

556. KLIBANOV, A.I., Narodnaia sotsial'naia utopiia v Rossii.
Period feodalizma. M. 1977. Pp. 335. Vyp 2. M. 1978.
Pp. 342.

557. RODIN, F.N., Burlachestvo v Rossii (XVI-XIX vv). Istoriko-
sotsiologicheskii ocherk. M. 1975. Pp. 245.

ECONOMIC, AND ECONOMIC THOUGHT

558. PASHKOV, A.I. (ed.), A History of Russian Economic Thought,
Ninth through Nineteenth Centuries. Trans.and ed. LETICHE,
J.M. Berkeley 1964. Pp. 690.

559. GERSCHENKRON, A., Economic Backwardness in Historical
Perspective. A Book of Essays. N.Y. 1965 - Cambridge,
Mass. 1966. Pp. 456.

560. GERSCHENKRON, A., Europe in the Russian Mirror: Four
Lectures in Economic History. Cambridge, Eng. 1970.
Pp. 158.

561. MITCHELL, B.R., European Historical Statistics, 1750-1970.
N.Y. 1975. Pp. 811.
Some reference to Russia in the eighteenth century - better
for nineteenth century. New edition announced.

562. BAYKOV, A., 'The Economic Development of Russia', *Econ.
Hist. Rev.* (Series 2), 7 (1954-5), 137-49.
Mid-eighteenth century onwards.

563. CRISP, O., 'The Economic History of Pre-Reform Russia',
SEER., LI, 125 (1973), 582-593.

564. BLACKWELL, W.L. (ed.), Russian Economic Development from
Peter the Great to Stalin. N.Y. 1974. Pp. 460.
Reprinting and translation of essays, including Peter the
Great (Blanc, no. 315), iron industry (Iatsunskii).

565. HELLIE, R., 'The Foundations of Russian Capitalism', *SR.*,
1 (1967), 148-54.

566. BARON, S.H., 'The Weber Thesis and the Failure of Capitalist
Development in Early Modern Russia', *JbfGO.*, N.F., XVIII, 3
(1970), 321-336.
Mainly seventeenth century focus.

567. BARON, S.H., 'The Transition from Feudalism to Capitalism in
Russia. A Major Soviet Controversy', *A.H.R.*, 77, 3 (1972),
715-29.

568. KAHAN, A., 'Continuity in Economic Activity and Policy
during the Post-Petrine Period in Russia', *J. Econ. Hist.*,
25 (1965), 61-85.

569. KAHAN, A., 'A proposed mercantilist code in the Russian iron
industry, 1734-36', *Explorations in Entrepreneurial History*,
2nd series, II, 2 (1965), 75-89.
Review of documents.

570. CLENDENNING, P.H., 'Eighteenth Century Russian Translations
of Western Economic Works', *J. Eur. Econ. Hist.*, I, 3
(1972), 745-753.

571. ROBINSON, E., 'The Transference of British Technology to
Russia 1760-1820: A Preliminary Enquiry', in: RADCLIFFE, B.
(ed.), Great Britain and her World, 1750-1914: Essays in
Honour of W.O.Henderson (Manchester 1975), pp. 1-26.

572. BROWN, J.H., 'The Publication and Distribution of the *Trudy*
of the Free Economic Society, 1765-1796', *RR.*, 36, 3 (1977),
341-351.

573. O'BRIEN, C.B., 'Ivan Pososhkov: Russian Critic of
Mercantilist Principles', *ASEER.*, 14 (1955), 503-11.

574. LEWITTER, L.R., 'Ivan T. Pososhkov (1652-1726) and "The
Spirit of Capitalism"', *SEER.*, LI, 125 (1973), 524-553.

575. TAYLOR, N.W., 'Adam Smith's First Russian Disciple',
     SEER., XLV, 105 (1967), 425-38.

576. BROWN, A.H., 'Adam Smith's First Russian Followers',
     in: SKINNER, A.S. and WILSON, T. (eds), Essays on Adam
     Smith (Oxford 1975), pp. 247-73.

577. CLENDENNING, P.H., 'William Gomm. A Case Study of the
     Foreign Entrepreneur in Eighteenth Century Russia', *J. Eur.*
     Econ. Hist., VI, 3 (1977), 533-48.

578. McGREW, R.E., 'Dilemmas of Development: Baron Heinrich
     Friedrich Storch (1766-1835) on the Growth of Imperial
     Russia', *JbfGO.*, N.F., 24, 1 (1976), 31-71.

579. BRAUDEL, F. and GRUBER, A. (eds), La Russie et l'Europe,
     XVIe-XXe siècles. Paris 1970. Pp. 430.
     Also in Russian: Franko-russkie ekonomicheskie sviazi, red.
     Brodel, F., M. 1970. Eighteenth-century items include
     eighteenth-century Russia in Turkish archives; John Law
     and Russia; Shcherbatov; Tatishchev and mercantilism;
     Russian trade in 1784.

580. BLANC, S., 'A propos de la politique économique de Pierre
     le Grand', *CMRS.*, III, 1 (1962), 122-139.
     Translated in nos. 314, 564.

581. CONFINO, M., 'Les enquêtes économiques de la Société libre
     d'économie de Saint Petersburg, 1765-1820', *Revue*
     Historique, 227, 1 (1962), 155-180.

582. CHAMBRE, H., 'Pososhkov et le mercantilisme', *CMRS.*, IV,
     3 (1963), 335-365.

583. TROITSKII, S.M., 'Le "système" de John Law et ses
     continuateurs russes', in: BRAUDEL (no. 579), pp. 31-67.

584. GEYER, D. (ed.), Wirtschaft und Gesellschaft im
     vorrevolutionären Russland. Köln 1975. Pp. 412.
     Rev: *Hist. Zt.*, 223 (1976), 386-8 (Hecker, H.).

585. HOFFMANN, P. and LEMKE, H. (eds), Genesis und Entwicklung
     des Kapitalismus in Russland. Berlin 1973. Pp. 267.
     Articles by Soviet and East German scholars - seventeenth
     and eighteenth centuries.

586. GOEHRKE, C., 'Zum gegenwärtigen Stand der
     Feudalismusdiskussion in der Sowjetunion', *JbfGO.*, 22, 2
     (1974), 214-47.

587. AMBURGER, E., 'Der fremde Unternehmer in Russland bis zur
     Oktoberrevolution im J. 1917', *Tradition: Zeitschrift für*
     Firmengeschichte und Unternehmerbiographie, 4 (1957),
     337-56.

588. AMBURGER, E., Die Anwerbung ausländischer Fachkräfte für die
     Wirtschaft Russlands vom 15. bis ins 19 Jhdt. Wiesbaden
     1968. Pp. 220.

589. BUCK, H.R., 'Die wirtschaftlichen Voraussetzungen des
     russischen Machtaufstieges unter Peter I', *Saeculum*, XIX, 1
     (1968), 224-249.

590. DONNERT, E., 'Zur Gesellschaftsauffassung Dmitrij Golicyns',
     Jbf. Wirt., 2 (1973), 121-130.
     Ideas on reform, economic and social thought 1770-1800.

591. DONNERT, E., 'A. Ja. Polenov und die russischen
     Preisschriften der Petersburger Freien Ökonomischen
     Gesellschaft der Jahre 1766-1768', *JfGSLE.*, XVII, 2 (1973),
     195-208.

592. DONNERT, E., 'Zum Wirken der Petersburger Freien
     Ökonomischen Gesellschaft in der zweiten Hälfte des 18 Jhdts'
     JfGSLE., XVIII, 1 (1973), 161-187.

593. AMBURGER, E., 'Die Gründung gelehrter Gesellschaften in
     Russland unter Katharina II', in: ISCHREYT, H., red.,
     Wissenschaftspolitik in Mittel- und Osteuropa.
     Wissenschaftliche Gesellschaften, Akademien und Hochschulen
     im 18. und beginnenden 19. Jhdt. (Berlin 1977), pp. 259-270.

594. STRUMILIN, S.G., Ocherki ekonomicheskoi istorii Rossii i
     SSSR. M. 1966. Pp. 513.

595. KHROMOV, P.A., Ekonomicheskoe razvitie Rossii: Ocherki
     ekonomiki Rossii s drevneishikh vremen do Velikoi
     Oktiabr'skoi Revoliutsii. M. 1967. Pp. 535.

596. MAVRODIN, V.V., Ekonomicheskii rost Rossii, vnutrenniaia i
     vneshniaia politika tsarizma v kontse XVII - pervoi polovine
     XVIII veka: lektsii. M. 1957. Pp. 67.

597. DULOV, A.V., 'Prirodnye usloviia i razvitie
     proizvoditel'nykh sil Rossii v XVIII-seredine XIX veka',
     Vop. Ist., 1 (1979), 38-53.

598. NECHKINA, M.V., 'O "voskhodiashchei" i "niskhodiashchei"
     stadiiakh feodal'noi formatsii', *Vop. Ist.*, 7 (1958),
     86-108.
     Started a discussion among Soviet historians on periodiza-
     tion of 'feudal formation' in Russia: see further articles
     in *Vop. Ist.*, 1, 9, 11 (1959), 8 (1962), 12 (1963).

599. BESKROVNYI, L.G. et al. (eds), K voprosu o pervonachal'nom
     nakoplenii v Rossii (XVII-XVIII vv.). Sbornik statei.
     M. 1958. Pp. 540.
     Includes essays on hired labour and the spread of serfdom.

600. POLIANSKII, F.A., Pervonachal'noe nakoplenie kapitala v
     Rossii. M. 1958. Pp. 416.

601. PAVLENKO, N.I., '0 nekotorykh storonakh pervonachal'nogo nakopleniia v Rossii', *I.Z.*, vol. 62 (1958), 170-197.

602. IATSUNSKII, V.K., 'Osnovnye etapy genezisa kapitalizma v Rossii', *Ist. SSSR.*, 5 (1958), 59-91.

603. MAVRODIN, V.V. (ed.), Voprosy genezisa kapitalizma v Rossii. Sb. statei. L. 1960. Pp. 239.
Essays on differentiation of peasantry, evolution of nobility and autocracy; labour force and entrepreneurship; trade and tariffs; national debt; the capitalist town; genesis of capitalism.

604. USTIUGOV, N. (ed.), Voprosy sotsial'no-ekonomicheskoi istorii i istochnikovedeniia perioda feodalizma v Rossii; Sb. statei k 70-letiiu A.A. Novosel'skogo. M. 1961. Pp. 366.

605. VALK, S.N. et al. (eds), Issledovaniia po istorii feodal'no-krepostnicheskoi Rossii. Sb. statei. M.-L. 1964. Pp. 209.
Articles on military and labour history; Petersburg artillery works 1700-1750; Archangel fair; internal trade in early eighteenth century.

606. BULYGIN, I.A. et al., 'Nachal'nyi etap genezisa kapitalizma v Rossii', *Vop. Ist.*, 10 (1966), 65-90.

607. PAVLENKO, N.I., 'Spornye voprosy genezisa kapitalizma v Rossii', *Vop. Ist.*, 11 (1966), 81-102.
Continuation of discussion started by no. 606.

608. NOSOV, N. (ed.), Vnutrenniaia politika tsarizma (seredina XVI-nachalo XX v.). L. 1967. Pp. 401.
Essays include: government and Petersburg workers 1700-1750.

609. SHUNKOV, V.I. et al. (eds), Perekhod ot feodalizma k kapitalizmu v Rossii. Materialy vsesoiuznoi diskussii. M. 1969. Pp. 413.
Essays: part of ongoing debate. See Baron (no. 567).

610. CHEREPNIN, L.V. et al. (eds), Aktual'nye problemy istorii Rossii epokhi feodalizma. Sb. statei. M. 1970. Pp. 467.

611. SKAZKIN, S. et al. (eds), Problemy genezisa kapitalizma; k Mezhdurarodnomu Kongressu ekonomich. istorii v Leningrade, v 1970 g. Sb. statei. M. 1970. Pp. 523.
Essays summarising the principal views on periodization of modern Russian history.

612. PASHUTO, V.T. et al. (eds), Feodal'naia Rossiia vo vsemirno-istoricheskom protsesse. Sb. statei, posviashchennyi L.V. Cherepninu. M. 1972. Pp. 439.
Essays: see especially those listed here, nos. 1043, 1148, 1149, 1151, 1626. 'Spisok nauchnykh trudov L.V. Cherepnina', pp. 7-28

613. KRUTIKOV, V.I. et al. (eds), Voprosy ekonomicheskoi i
     sotsial'noi istorii Rossii XVIII-XIX vv. Tula 1973.
     Pp. 69.

614. IATSUNSKII, V.K., Sotsial'no-ekonomicheskaia istoriia
     Rossii XVIII-XIX vv. Izbrannye trudy. M. 1973. Pp. 302.
     Posthumous collection of his essays, mainly on nineteenth
     century topics. Includes list of his works.

615. PASHUTO, V.T. (ed.), Obshchestvo i gosudarstvo feodal'noi
     Rossii. Sb. statei posviashchennyi 70-letiiu akad. L.V.
     Cherepnina. M. 1975. Pp. 351.
     Essays include urban reform of 1775; class structure and
     development; New Russia; the land commune; Tatishchev;
     'Third Estate' project in 1760s; Ivan Trevogin; Sweden and
     Russian 'collegii'. List of Cherepnin's works, pp. 344-47.

616. EZHOV, B. (ed.), Iz istorii feodal'noi Rossii: St. i ocherki.
     K 70-letiiu rozhdeniia Prof. V.V. Mavrodina. L. 1978.
     Pp. 198.
     Essays: Social and economic aspects of feudalism; agricul-
     tural development of Russia; bibliography of Mavrodin's
     works (no. 221). Previous Mavrodin Festschrift: no. 220.

617. PTUKHA, M.V., Ocherki po istorii statistiki v SSSR, 2 vols,
     M. 1955, 1959. Pp. 472, 476. Vol.1: Statisticheskaia
     mysl' v Rossii (do kontsa XVIII v.)
     Rev: *Vop. Ist.*, 12 (1956), 151-3 (Iatsunskii, V.K.).

618. GOZULOV, A., Ocherki istorii otechestvennoi statistiki.
     M. 1972. Pp. 312.
     Describes statistical publications in historical perspec-
     tive; bibliography.

619. KARATAEV, N., Ekonomicheskie nauki v Moskovskom Universitete
     1755-1955. M. 1956. Pp. 341.

620. KARATAEV, N., Ocherki po istorii ekonomicheskikh nauk v
     Rossii XVIII veka. M. 1960. Pp. 290.

621. KOVALEV, V.P., 'O dvizhenii ekonomicheskoi mysli v russkoi
     periodike kontsa XVIII-pervoi poloviny XIX veka',
     VLU(Ist.), 14 (1974), 92-100.

622. STRUMILIN, S.G., 'K voprosu ob ekonomike petrovskoi epokhi'
     in: Poltava. Sb. statei (no. 1324), pp. 179-189.
     Attacks Miliukov thesis that Russian people could not afford
     Petrine reforms.

623. PAVLENKO, N.I., 'Torgovo-promyshlennaia politika pravitel'-
     stva Rossii v pervoi chetverti XVIII veka', *Ist. SSSR.*, 2
     (1978), 49-69.

624. SHMIDT, S., 'Proekt P.L. Shuvalova 1754 g., "O raznykh
     gosudarstvennoi pol'zy sposobakh"', *Ist. Arkhiv.*, 6 (1962),
     100-119.

625. TARLE, E., 'Byla li Ekaterininskaia Rossiia otstaloiu
     stranoiu?', reprinted in Sochinenia, ed. ERUSALIMSKII, A.S.
     et al. (12 vols. M. 1957-62), IV, 441-68.
     Famous article which started a long debate.

626. ORESHKIN, V.V., Vol'noe Ekonomicheskoi Obshchestvo v Rossii,
     1765-1917. Istoriko-ekonomicheskii ocherk. M. 1963.
     Pp. 195.

627. PETROVA, V.A., 'Ustav Vol'nogo Ekonomicheskogo Obshchestva
     i M.V. Lomonosov', in: SHAPIRO, A.L. (ed.), Problemy
     feodal'noi Rossii. Sb. statei k 60-letiiu Prof. V.V.
     Mavrodina (no. 220), pp. 223-34.

628. PETROVA, V.A., 'Vol'noe Ekonomicheskoe Obshchestvo i Krest'
     ianskaia Voina 1773-75 gg. v Rossii', in: Problemy
     otechestvennoi i vseobshchei istorii, sb. statei. Vyp.3,
     red. EZHOV, V.A. (L. 1976), pp. 69-72.

7(b) - THE NOBILITY

The standard older work, ROMANOVICH-SLAVATINSKII, has been
reprinted (655). Among newer studies RAEFF (629) offers a
re-interpretation taken further by JONES (641); see reviews of
RAEFF (639; 650; 659) and for a rejection PIPES (280). Among
recent Soviet writers TROITSKII is outstanding (492; 658-60;
see 226). PAVLENKO (661) is also important. Recent French
publications (646-8) provide valuable general reference tools.
See also Section 7(c), especially BLUM (667) and CONFINO
(677-80).

629. RAEFF, M., Origins of the Russian Intelligentsia: The
     Eighteenth-Century Nobility. N.Y. 1966. Pp. 248.

630. BELOFF, M., 'Russia', in: GOODWIN, M. (ed.), The European
     Nobility in the Eighteenth Century. 2nd ed. (London 1967),
     pp. 172-189.
     Takes up the interpretation of G. Sacke.

631. AUGUSTINE, W.R., 'Notes toward a Portrait of the
     Eighteenth-Century Nobility', *CanAmSlSt.*, IV, 3 (1970),
     373-425.

632. LEITSCH, W., 'The Russian Nobility in the Eighteenth
     Century', *EEQ.*, XI, 3 (1977), 317-340.

633. CRUMMEY, R., 'Peter and the Boiar Aristocracy, 1689-1700'
     CanAmSlSt., VIII, 2 (1974), 274-88.

634. MEEHAN-WATERS, B.M., 'The Russian Generalitet of 1730:
     Towards a Definition of Aristocracy', Rochester Ph.D., 1970.
     Book in preparation.

635. MEEHAN-WATERS, B., 'The Muscovite noble origins of the Russians in the Generalitet of 1730', *CMRS.*, XII, 1-2 (1971), 28-75.

636. MEEHAN-WATERS, B., 'The Russian Aristocracy and the Reforms of Peter the Great', *CanAmSlSt.*, VIII, 2 (1974), 288-303.

637. MEEHAN-WATERS, B., 'Elite Politics and Autocratic Power', in: CROSS (ed.), *Proceedings* (no. 1794), pp. 229-46.

638. DUKES, P., Catherine the Great and the Russian Nobility. Cambridge, England 1967. Pp. 269.

639. BUSHKOFF, L., 'State, Society and the Eighteenth-Century Russian Nobility', *CanSlSt.*, III, 1 (1969), 121-7. Review of Raeff, *Origins* (629) and Dukes, *Catherine* (638).

640. JONES, R.E., 'The Russian Gentry and the Provincial Reform of 1775', Cornell Ph.D., 1968.

641. JONES, R.E., The Emancipation of the Russian Nobility, 1762-1785. Princeton 1973. Pp. 326.

642. GIVENS, R., 'Servitors or Seignors: The Nobility and the Eighteenth Century Russian State'. U.Cal.Berkeley Ph.D.1975.

643. CORNELL, N.W., 'The Role of the Nobility in Agricultural Change in Russia during the Reign of Catherine II', Illinois Ph.D., 1972.

644. GRIFFITHS, D., KAMENDROVSKY, V., 'The Fate of the Trading Nobility Controversy in Russia: A Chapter in the Relationship Between Catherine II and the Russian Nobility', *JbfGO.*, 26, 2 (1978), 198-221.

645. WILLIAMSON, D., The Counts Bobrinsky. A Genealogy. Edgware 1962. Pp. 43.

646. IKONNIKOV, N.F. (ed.), La Noblesse de Russie. Eléments pour servir à la réconstitution des régistres généalogiques de la noblesse d'après les actes et documents disponibles complétés grâce au concours dévoué des nobles russes. 2nd ed., 26 fascicles. Paris 1957-66.

647. SCHAKOVSKOY, D., Société et Noblesse Russe. T.1: A-Aplečeev. Rennes 1978. Pp. 340. Continuation of N.F. Ikonnikov, La Noblesse de Russie (no.646).Vol. 2 due 1979, series on-going.

648. GMELINE, P. DE, Dictionnaire de la Noblesse Russe. Paris 1978. Pp. 999.

649. LARAN, M., 'Nobles et paysans en Russie: de "l'age d'or" du servage à son abolition, 1762-1861', *Annales*, XXI, 1 (1966), 111-140.

650. CONFINO, M., 'Histoire et psychologie. A propos de la noblesse russe au XVIII s', *Annales*, XXVI, 6 (1967), 1163-1205.
A review article on Raeff, *Origins* (629).

651. RUFFMANN, K.-H., 'Der russische Adel als Sondertypus der europäischer Adelswelt', *JbfGO.*, N.F. 9, 2 (1961), 161-78.

652. KLUXEN, K., ROOS, H., BIRTSCH, G., ed. and intro., VIERHAUS, R., publisher. Der Adel vor der Revolution. Zur sozialen und politischen Funktion des Adels im vorrevolutionären Europa. Göttingen 1971. Pp. 95.

653. DONNERT, E., 'Zur politischen Ideologie der russischen Adelsaristokratie in der zweiten Hälfte des 18. Jhdts', *ZfSl.*, XVIII (1973), 588-96.

654. REXHAUSER, R., 'Besitzverhältnisse des russichen Adels im 18. Jahrhundert. Historische Fragen, methodische Probleme'. Phil. Diss. Erlangen, 1971.

655. ROMANOVICH-SLAVATINSKII, A.V., Dvorianstvo v Rossii ot nachala XVIII veka do otmeny krepostnogo prava. 1st ed., St. P. 1870, reprinted 1968. Pp. 564.
2nd ed. (Kiev 1912) is preferable.

656. KARNOVICH, E.P., Zamechatel'nye bogatstva chastnykh lits v Rossii. St. P. 1874, reprinted 1964. Pp. 380.

657. SHEPUKOVA, N.M., 'Ob izmenenii razmerov dushevladeniia pomeshchikov Evropeiskoi Rossii v pervoi chetverti XVIII - pervoi polovine XIX vv.', *Ezh. A.I.* (1963), 388-419.

658. KABUZAN, V., TROITSKII, S.M., 'Izmeneniia v chislennosti, udel'nom vese i razmeshchenii dvorianstva v Rossii v 1782-1858 gg.', *Ist. SSSR.*, 4 (1971), 153-169.

659. TROITSKII, S.M., 'Russkoe dvorianstvo XVIII v. v izobrazhenii amerikanskogo istorika', *Ist. SSSR.*, 5 (1970), 205-212.
Discussion of Raeff, *Origins* (no. 629).

660. TROITSKII, S.M., 'K probleme konsolidatsii dvorianstva Rossii v XVIII v.', *Materialy po istorii sel'skogo khoziaistva i krest'ianstva SSSR.*, VIII (M. 1974), pp. 128-151.

661. PAVLENKO, N., Dvorianstvo i krepostnoi stroi Rossii XVI-XVIII vv. Sb. statei pamiati A.A. Novosel'skogo. M. 1975. Pp. 345.
Includes nos. 529, 662-4, 694, 709.

662. INDOVA, E.I., 'K voprosu o dvorianskoi sobstvennosti v
Rossii v pozdnii feodal'nyi period', in: PAVLENKO (no. 661),
pp. 272-91.

663. POD'IAPOL'SKAIA, E., 'K voprosu o formirovanii dvorianskoi
intelligentsii v pervoi chetverti XVIII v.', in: PAVLENKO
(no. 661), pp. 181-9.

664. PAVLENKO, N.I., 'O rostovshchichestve dvorian v XVIII v.
(k postanovke voprosa)', in: PAVLENKO (no. 661), pp. 265-
271.

7(c) - PEASANTS AND PEASANT INSTITUTIONS; LANDLORDS; SERFDOM

This section includes work on the peasant commune (683-4,
724-31) and the peasant question (674-5, 733a-743), as well as
on serfdom and the rural economy. More technical agricultural
questions are dealt with in Section 7(g). The standard general
work is BLUM (668); his most recent book (669) offers a useful
comparative account of peasant emancipation across Europe.
CONFINO's work (677-80,909-10), is most important. The fundamental
Russian study on the peasantry remains SEMEVSKII (686); Soviet
scholars have however produced numerous valuable monographs, in
addition to the proceedings of the Symposium on Agrarian History
of E. Europe, published in *Ezh. A.I.* and latterly in volumes on
N. Russia (722, 731-3, 915).

665. PETROVICH, M., 'The Peasant in 19th-C. Historiography',
in: VUCINICH, W. (ed.), The Peasant in Nineteenth-Century
Russia (Stanford 1968), pp. 191-230.
Nineteenth-century writing on all periods.

666. KOSLOW, J., The Despised and the Damned: The Russian
Peasant through the Ages. N.Y. 1972. Pp.174.

667. BLUM, J., 'The Rise of Serfdom in Eastern Europe', *AHR.*, 62
(1956-7), 807-36.

668. BLUM, J., Lord and Peasant in Russia from the Ninth to the
Nineteenth Century. Princeton 1961. Pp. 656.
Rev: *JEH.*, 24 (1964), 53-59 (Gerschenkron, A.); *SR.*, 21
(1962), 527-529 (Szeftel, M.).

669. BLUM, J., The End of the Old Order in Rural Europe.
Princeton 1978. Pp. 505.

670. AKSAKOV, S.T., Chronicles of A Russian Family, trans. Beverley, M.C., intro. Mirsky, D.S. London-N.Y. 1960. Pp. 398.
Abridged translation of *Semeinaia Khronika*, including classic recreation of eighteenth-century rural life in Orenburg province. Earlier full translation by J. Duff has now been reprinted (3 vols, with differing titles, 1978).

671. KAHAN, A., 'Notes on Serfdom in Western and Eastern Europe', *JEH.*, XXXIII, 1 (1973), 86-99.

672. ESPER, T., 'The odnodvortsy and the Russian Nobility', *SEER.*, XLV, 104 (1967), 124-34.

673. DOMAR, E.D., 'The Causes of Slavery and Serfdom: A Hypothesis', *JEH.*, XXX, 1 (1970), 18-32.
Prompted by Kliuchevskii's account of the development of serfdom in Russia. Not restricted to eighteenth century.

674. MADARIAGA, I. de, 'Catherine II and the Serfs: A Reconsideration of some Problems', *SEER.*, LII, 126 (1974), 34-62.

675. DUKES, P., 'Catherine II's Enlightened Absolutism and the Problem of Serfdom', in: BUTLER (no. 497), pp. 93-115.

676. DROUJININA, E.I., 'Les rapports agraires en Russie aux XVIIe et XVIIIe siècles', in: Le village en France et en URSS: des origines à nos jours. Colloque franco-soviétique organisé à Toulouse du 24 au 29 mai 1971 (Toulouse 1975), pp. 209-23.

677. CONFINO, M., 'La politique de tutelle des seigneurs russes envers leurs paysans vers la fin du XVIII s.', *Revue des Etudes Slaves*, 37 (1960), 39-70.

678. CONFINO, M., 'Le paysan russe jugé par la noblesse au XVIII siècle', *Revue des Etudes Slaves*, 38 (1961), 51-63.

679. CONFINO, M., 'Seigneurs et intendants en Russie aux XVIII-XIX siècles', *Revue des Etudes Slaves*, 41 (1962), 61-91.

680. CONFINO, M., Domaines et seigneurs en Russie vers la fin du XVIII siècle. Etude de structures agraires et de mentalités économiques. Paris 1963. Pp. 311.
Based on Works of the Free Economic Society.

681. INDOVA, E.I., 'Les activités commerciales de la paysannerie dans les villages de la région de Moscou (1700-1750)', *CMRS.*, V, 2 (1964), 206-228.

682. KERBLAY, B.H., L'Isba d'hier et d'aujourd'hui: L'Evolution de l'habitation rurale en URSS. Lausanne 1973. Pp. 249.

683. GOEHRKE, C., Die Theorien über Entstehung und Entwicklung
     des 'Mir'. Wiesbaden 1964. Pp. 215.
     Schriften der Arbeitsgemeinschaft für Osteuropaforschung
     der Universität Münster.

684. GOEHRKE, C., 'Neues zum Mir', in: Oestliches Europa:
     Spiegel der Geschichte. Festschrift für M. Hellmann
     (Wiesbaden 1977), pp. 17-34.

685. KAHK, J., 'Der Bauer in der Literatur und im wirklichen
     Leben. Die progressiven baltischen Schriftsteller und ihr
     Held', in: BERINDEI, D. et al (hrsg.), Der Bauer Mittel-
     und Osteuropas im sozioökonomischen Wandel des 18. u. 19
     Jhdts. Beiträge zu seiner Lage und deren Widerspiegelung
     in der zeitgenössischen Publizistik und Literatur (Köln/
     Wien 1973), pp. 351-365.
     Rev: *JbfGO.*, N.F. 23 (1975), 545-7 (Scheibert, P.).

686. SEMEVSKII, V.I., Krest'iane v tsarstvovanie imperatritsy
     Ekateriny II. St. P., 2nd ed., 1903, reprint announced
     with new introduction by J. LeDonne. Newtonville 1981. 2 v.
     Pp. 1400.
     Classic account. On Semevskii see Petrovich (no. 665).

687. FEDOROV, V.A., Pomeshchich'i krest'iane tsentral'no-
     promyshlennogo raiona Rossii kontsa XVIII - pervoi poloviny
     XIX v. M. 1974. Pp. 308.
     Rev: *RR.*, 35, 2 (1976), 194-5; *Vop. Ist.*, 1 (1978), 161-3
     (Krutikov, V.I.).

688. TIKHONOV, IU., Pomeshchich'i krest'iane v Rossii.
     Feodal'naia renta v XVIII-nachale XVIII vv. M. 1974.
     Pp. 335.
     Rev: *AHR.*, 83, 1 (1978), 229-30 (Hellie, R.); *Vop. Ist.*,
     9 (1975), 171-3 (Man'kov, A.C.).

689. POKHILEVICH, D.L., Krest'iane Belorussii i Litvy vo vtoroi
     polovine XVIII v. Vilnius 1966. Pp. 215. Cp. no. 2404.

690. KOZLOVSKII, P.G., Krest'iane Belorussii vo vtoroi polovine
     XVII-XVIII vv. (Po materialam magnatskikh votchin). Minsk
     1969. Pp. 203.

691. VOLKOV, S.I., Krest'iane dvortsovykh vladenii podmoskov'ia
     v seredine XVIII v. M. 1959. Pp. 262.

692. INDOVA, E.I., Dvortsovoe khoziaistvo v Rossii; pervaia
     polovina XVIII v. M. 1964. Pp. 352.

693. BULYGIN, I.A., Monastyrskie krest'iane Rossii v pervoi
     chetverti XVIII v. M. 1977. Pp. 327.

694. BULYGIN, I.A., 'Osobaia kategoriia feodal'no-zavisimykh
     krest-ian v pervoi polovine XVIII v. (Iz istorii
     sekuliarizatsii tserkovnykh vladenii)', in: PAVLENKO (no.
     661), pp. 190-212.

695. KOMISSARENKO, A.I., 'Polovnichestvo na Viatke v pervoi polovine XVIII v.', *Ezh. A.I.* (1966), 242-9.

696. KONDRASHENKOV, A., 'Sel'skoe khoziaistvo pripisnykh krest'ian Zaural'ia v XVIII v.', *Ezh. A.I.* (1966), 249-58.

697. VAGINA, P.A., 'O nekotorykh prichinakh otmeny instituta pripisnykh krest'ian v kontse XVIII v.', *Ezh. A.I.* (1968), 148-52.

698. BALAGUROV, IA. A., Pripisnye krest'iane Karelii v XVII - XIX vv. Petrozavodsk 1962. Pp. 350.

699. PROTORCHINA, V.M., 'K istorii voronezhskikh odnodvortsev v XVIII v.', *Izvestiia Voronezhskogo gos. ped. instituta*, (1956), 107-131.

700. TKACHEVA, N., 'Iz istorii odnodvortsev v XVIII v.', *Ezh. A.I.* (1970), 133-141.

701. RABINOVICH, M.D., 'Odnodvortsy v pervoi polovine XVIII v.', *Ezh. A.I.* (1971), 137-45.

702. SHEPUKOVA, N.M., 'Izmenenie udel'nogo vesa chastnovladel'-cheskogo krest'ianstva v sostave naseleniia Evropeiskoi Rossii (XVIII-pervaia polovina XIX vv.)', *Vop. Ist.*, 12 (1959), 123-36.

703. SHEPUKOVA, N.M.,'Podvornaia perepis' 1710 g. i chislennost' russkogo krest'ianstva v Sibiri', *Ezh. A.I.* (1966), 227-233.

704. TIKHONOV, IU., 'Krest'ianskoe khoziaistvo Tsentral'noi Rossii pervoi chetverti XVIII v. (1716)', *Ist. SSSR*, 4 (1971), 169-178.

705. SHAPIRO, A.L., 'Razvitie rynochnykh otnoshenii i krepostnichestvo v russkoi derevne v pervoi polovine XVIII v.', *Ezh. A.I.* (1961), 207-217.

706. RAZORENOVA, N.B., 'Zemledel'cheskoe khoziaistvo beglykh krest'ian v srednem Povolzh'e v pervoi treti XVIII v.', *VMU(Ist).*, 5 (1975), 34-52.

707. SHABANOVA, A., 'Biudzhety krest'ianskikh khoziastv Aleksandro-Svirskoi votchiny v seredine XVIII veka (Iz opyta sostavleniia krest'ianskikh biudzhetov)', *Ezh. A.I.* (1970), 104-113.

708. BULYGIN, I.A., Polozhenie krest'ian i tovarnoe proizvodstvo v Rossii, vtoraia polovina XVIII v. M. 1966. Pp. 212.
On materials of votchina of A.I. Polianskii, Penza.

709. ZAOZERSKAIA, E.I., 'Pomeshchik Zhukov i ego khoziaistvo' in: PAVLENKO (no. 661), pp. 213-226.

710. OSHANINA, E.N., 'Khoziaistvo pomeshchikov Pazukhinykh v XVII-XVIII vekakh', *Vop. Ist.*, 7 (1956), 84-92.

711. TROITSKII, S.M., 'O vliianii fiskal'noi sisteme na polozhenie krest'ian Rossii v XVII-XVIII vv.', *Ezh. A.I.* (1963), 283-95.

712. TROITSKII, S.M., 'Raionirovanie form feodal'noi renty v krupnoi votchine Rossii v pervoi chetverti XVIII v. (po arkhivu kn. A. Menshikova)', *Ezh. A.I.* (1968), 116-126.

713. KOVAL'CHENKO, I., MILOV, L., 'Ob intensivnosti obrochnoi ekspluatatsii krest'ian Tsentral'noi Rossii v kontse XVIII-pervoi polovine XIX v.', *Ist. SSSR.*, 4 (1966), 55-80. Comment by RYNDZIUNSKII, P., in *Ist. SSSR.*, 6 (1966), 44-65.

714. MELESHKO, V.I., 'Sotsial'no-ekonomicheskoe polozhenie krest'ian v krichevskom starostve v kontse XVII- pervoi polovine XVIII v.', *Ezh. A.I.* (1968), 94-102.

715. RUBINSHTEIN, N.L., 'O razlozhenii krest'ianstva i tak nazyvaemom pervonachal'nom nakoplenii v Rossii', *Vop. Ist.*, 8 (1961), 61-85.

716. INDOVA, E.I. et al., 'Burzhuaznoe rassloenie krest'ianstva v Rossii XVII-XVIII vv.', *Ist. SSSR.*, 3 (1962), 80-105.

717. VOLKOV, M., TROITSKII, S.M., 'O burzhuaznom rassloenii krest'ian i skladyvanii rynka naemnoi rabochei sily v Rossii v pervoi polovine XVIII v.', *Ist. SSSR.*, 4 (1965), 86-105.

718. KAZANTSEV, B.N., 'Zakonodatel'stvo russkogo tsarizma po regulirovaniiu krest'ianskogo otkhoda v XVII-XIX vv.', *Vop. Ist.*, 6 (1970), 20-31.

719. FEDOROV, V.A., 'Krest'ianin-otkhodnik v Moskve (konets XVIII- pervaia polovina XIX v.)', in: TANTN (ed.), *Russkii Gorod* (no. 776), I, pp. 165-80.

720. TOMSINSKII, S., 'Torgovlia i podriadnichestvo krest'ian Priural'ia v 1720-1740-kh godakh', *Ist. SSSR.*, 2 (1965), 146-153.

721. SERBINA, K., Krest'ianskaia zhelezodelatel'naia promyshlennost' severo-zapadnoi Rossii XVI- pervoi poloviny XIX v. L. 1971. Pp. 263.

722. KAMKIN, A.A., 'Poriadnye krest'ian-polovnikov pomorskikh uezdov v XVI-XIX vv.', in: Agrarnaia istoriia Evropeiskogo Severa SSSR (no. 915), pp. 104-107.

723. GROMYKO, M.M., Trudovye traditsii russkikh krest'ian Sibiri (XVIII - pervaia pol. XIX v.). M. 1975. Pp. 351. Rev: *Ist. SSSR.*, 6 (1976), 189-90 (Boiarshinova, Z.).

724. DANILOV, V.P., 'K voprosu o kharaktere i znachenii
krest'ianskoi pozemel'noi obshchiny v Rossii', in:
Problemy sotsial'no-ekonomicheskoi istorii Rossii. Sb.
statei k 85-letiiu akademika N.M. Druzhinina (no. 214),
pp. 341-59.

725. ALEKSANDROV, V.A., Sel'skaia obshchina v Rossii (XVII-
nachalo XIX vv.). M. 1976. Pp. 323.

726. PUSHKAREV, S.J., Krest'ianskaia pozemel'no-peredel'naia
obshchina v Rossii. Newtonville 1976. Pp. 155.
Reprints original Parts I and II (Prague 1939-41), with
new Part III, introduction by M. Raeff and additional bibliography of works by David A.J. Macey.

727. BAKLANOVA, E.N., Krest'ianskii dvor i obshchina na
russkom severe. Konets XVII- nachalo XVIII v. M. 1976.
Pp. 221. Rev: *Ist. SSSR.*, 4 (1978), 175-8.

728. GORIUSHKIN, L. (ed.), Krest'ianskaia obshchina v Sibiri
XVII-nachale XX v. Novosibirsk 1977. Pp. 283.

729. VDOVINA, L.N., 'Zemel'nye peredely v krest'ianskoi
obshchine v 20-50-e gody XVIII veka', *Ist. SSSR.*, 4
(1973), 140-154.

730. INKIN, V., 'Dvorishche i sel'skaia obshchina v selakh
voloshskogo prava Golitskogo podgor'ia XVI-XVIII vv. po
materialam Samborskoi ekonomiki', *Ezh. A.I.* (1966), 113-
128.

731. KOLESNIKOV, P.A. et al. (eds), Ezhegodnik po agrarnoi
istorii. Vypusk 6: Problemy istorii russkoi obshchiny.
Voprosy agrarnoi istorii evropeiskogo severa SSSR.
Vologda 1976. Pp. 150.

732. IANIN, V. et al. (eds), Materialy XV sessii simpoziuma po
problemam agrarnoi istorii, vypusk II. Vologda 1976.
Pp. 168.

733. IANIN, V. (ed.), Problemy agrarnoi istorii. 2 parts.
Minsk 1978. Pp. 167, 182.

733a. SEMEVSKII, V.I., Krest'ianskii vopros v Rossii v XVIII i
pervoi polovine XIX vv. St. P. 1888. Reprinted 1971.
2 vols in 1. Pp. 1350.

734. ALEFIRENKO, P., Krest'ianskoe dvizhenie i krest'ianskii
vopros v Rossii v 30-50 kh godakh XVIII veka. M. 1958.
Pp. 422.
Rev: *Vop. Ist.*, 7 (1959) (Troitskii, S.); *Ist. SSSR.*, 3
(1959), 193-5 (Kafengauz, B.B.).

735. KOGAN, E.S., Ocherki istorii krepostnogo khoziaistva po
materialam votchin Kurakinykh 2-i poloviny XVIII veka.
M. 1960. Pp.126.

736. MAN'KOV, A., Razvitie krepostnogo prava v Rossii vo vtoroi polovine XVII v. M.-L. 1962. Pp. 422.
Rev: *Vop. Ist.*, 9 (1963), 116-8 (Zadera,A.G., Pronshtein, A.P.). Includes measures of Peter I.

737. BELIAVSKII, M.T., Krest'ianskii vopros v Rossii nakanune vosstaniia E.I. Pugacheva. Formirovanie antikrepostnicheskoi mysli. M. 1965. Pp. 382.
Rev: *Ist. SSSR.*, 3 (1968), 101-110 (Pavlenko, N.I.).
See also no. 528.

738. BELIAVSKII, M.T., LOONE, L., 'Dokumenty ob obsuzhdenii krest'ianskogo voprosa v Vol'nom Ekonomicheskom Obshchestve v 1767-68 gg.', *A. Ezh.* (1960), 345-66.

739. BELIAVSKII, M.T., 'Obsuzhdenie krest'ianskogo voprosa nakanune krest'ianskoi voiny pod predvoditel'stvom E.I. Pugacheva.(Konkurs Vol'nogo Ekon. Obshchestva v' 1766-1768 gg.)', *Ezh. A.I.* (1960), pp. 307-318.

740. KUZ'MINA, M.P., 'V.N.Tatishchev o krest'ianstve' in: Voprosy ekonomicheskoi istorii i ekonomicheskoi geografii. Sb. statei (Sverdlovsk 1964), pp. 218-227.

741. KOGAN, E.S., 'Proekt vykupa krest'ian (Rostovskaia votchina kn. Kurakinykh konets XVIII v.)', *Ezh. gos. ist. muz.* (1965-6), 150-170.

742. KOMISSARENKO, A.I., 'Proekt vvedeniia lichnoi krepostnoi zavisimosti ekonomicheskikh krest'ian v Rossii v pervye gody posle sekuliarizatsii tserkovnykh imushchestv (60-e gody XVIII veka)', *Ezh. A.I.* (1970), 95-104.

743. GOLIKOVA, N.B., 'Torgovlia krepostnymi bez zemli v 20-kh godakh XVIII v.', *I.Z.*, 90 (1972), 303-331.

7(d) - COSSACKS

LONGWORTH (744) is the best - and very readable - English-language account, giving an overall history. COLOBUTSKII (751, 752) treats the Zaporozhian and Black Sea hosts, ROZNER (750) the Iaik, PRONSHTEIN (746-49) the Don.

744. LONGWORTH, P., The Cossacks. London 1969. Pp. 409.
Rev: *SR.*, XXXI, 4 (1972) 870-75; rebuttal, *SR.*, XXXIII, 4 (1974), 411-16.
Good bibliography.

745. GLASKOW, Gen. W., History of the Cossacks. N.Y. 1972. Pp. 163.
Rev: *RR.*, XXXII, 2 (1973), 205-7

746. PRONSHTEIN, A.P., 'Obzor materialov po istorii donskogo kazachestva XVIII-XIX vv., khraniashchiesia v Gos. Arkhive Rostovskoi Oblasti', *A. Ezh.* (1957), 228-42.

747. PRONSHTEIN, A.P., 'Usilenie krepostnogo gneta na Donu v XVIII v.', *Vop. Ist.*, 6 (1955), 56-66.

748. PRONSHTEIN, A.P., 'O voinskoi sluzhbe donskikh kazakov v XVIII v.', *A. Ezh.* (1965), 369-75.

749. PRONSHTEIN, A.P. (ed.), Zemlia Donskaia v XVIII v. Rostov n/D. 1965. Pp. 374.
Rev: *Vop. Ist.*, 5 (1963), 116-8 (Rozner, I.G.).

750. ROZNER, I.G., Iaik pered burei. M. 1966. Pp. 208. See also no. 892.

751. GOLOBUTSKII, V.A., Chernomorskoe Kazachestvo. Kiev 1956. Pp. 414.

752. GOLOBUTSKII, V.A., Zaporozhskoe Kazachestvo. Kiev 1957. Pp. 461.

752a. GORDEEV, A., Istoriia Kazakov v 4 tomakh. Paris 1968-71. III (1970): Ot Petra Velikogo do 1914 g. Pp. 290.

752b. GOLOBUTSKII, V.A., 'Zaporozhskaia Sech'', *Vop. Ist.*, 12 (1970), 93-106.

752c. CHEKMENEV, S.A., 'Sotsial'nye otnosheniia i klassovaia bor'-ba kazachestva i krest'ianstva v Predkavkaz'e v kontse XVIII-pervoi polovine XIX v.', *Ezh. A.I.* (1971), 177-85.

7(e) – MERCHANTS, OTHER URBAN SOCIAL GROUPS

There is no satisfactory general account of the Russian merchantry. BILL (753) is quite inadequate; KAUFMANN-ROCHARD (762) is good but focuses on the pre-Petrine period. See also GRIFFITHS (644, 2649), and nos. 997, 1017, 1100, 2651.

MERCHANTS

753. BILL, V.T., The Forgotten Class: the Russian Bourgeoisie from the Earliest Beginnings to 1900. N.Y. 1959. Pp. 229. Rev: *ASEER.*, 19 (1960), 111-113 (Berlin, M.).

754. LAUBER, J.M., 'The Merchant-Gentry Conflict in 18th Century Russia', Iowa Ph.D., 1967.

755. BARON, S.H., 'Who were the Gosti?', *Calif. Slav. St.*, VII
     (1974), 1-40.
     Mainly seventeenth- early eighteenth centuries.

756. BARON, S.H., 'The Fate of the *gosti* in the reign of Peter
     the Great', *CMRS.*, XIV, 4 (1973), 488-512.

757. SZEFTEL, M., 'The Legal Condition of the Foreign Merchants
     in Muscovy', Recueils de la Société Jean Bodin, *Les Grandes
     Escales*, XXXIII, 2e partie (1972), 335-8.

758. DANIEL, W., 'The Merchantry and the Problem of Social Order
     in the Russian State: Catherine II's Commission on Commerce',
     SEER., LV, 2 (1977), 185-203.

759. JONES, R.E., 'Jacob Sievers, Enlightened Reform, and the
     Development of a 'Third Estate' in Russia', *RR.*, 36, 4 (1977)
     424-438.

760. PORTAL, R., 'Aux origines d'une bourgeoisie industrielle en
     Russie', *Revue d'histoire moderne et contemporaine*, VIII
     (1961), 35-60.

761. BLANC, S., 'Aux origines de la bourgeoisie russe', *CMRS.*, 5
     (1964), 294-301.

762. KAUFMANN-ROCHARD, J., Origines d'une bourgeoisie russe (XVI
     et XVII s.). Marchands de Moscovie. Paris 1969. Pp. 307.
     Mainly pre-eighteenth century.

763. KELLENBENZ, H., 'Marchands en Russie aux XVIIe et XVIIIe
     siècles', *CMRS.*, XI, 4 (1970), 576-620; XII, 1-2 (1971),
     76-109.

764. KOSHMAN, L.V., 'Russkaia doreformennaia burzhuaziia.
     Postanovka voprosa i istoriografiia problemy', *Ist. SSSR.*, 6
     (1974), 77-94.

765. VOEIKOV, M.IA., 'Formirovanie gorodskoi burzhuazii v Rossii
     XVII-XVIII vv.', in: SHUNKOV (no. 787), pp. 193-198.

766. VARTENOV, G., 'Moskovskoe i inogorodnoe kupechestvo vo
     vtoroi polovine XVIII veka', in: STEPANOV, N.N. (ed.),
     Voprosy istorii SSSR XVI-XVIII vv.. Sbornik statei
     (L. 1955), pp. 272-90.

767. PAVLENKO, N.I., 'Iz istorii sotsial'no-ekonomicheskikh
     trebovanii russkoi burzhuazii vo vtoroi polovine XVIII v.',
     I.Z., vol. 59 (1957), 328-344.

768. KLOKMAN, IU., 'Torgovo-promyshlennaia deiatelnost'
     naseleniia ostashkovskoi slobody v seredine XVIII v.', in:
     BESKROVNYI, L. (ed.), K voprosu o pervonachal'nom nakoplenii
     v Rossii (XVII-XVIII vv.) (no. 599), pp. 376-403.

769. INDOVA, E.I., 'Rol' dvortsovoi derevni pervoi poloviny
XVIII v. v formirovanii russkogo kupechestva', *I.Z.*, vol.
68 (1961), 189-210.

770. PAVLENKO, N.I., 'Odvorianivanie russkoi burzhuazii v
XVIII v.', *Ist. SSSR.*, 2 (1961), 71-87.

771. GROMYKO, M.M., 'K kharakteristike sotsial'noi psikhologii
sibirskogo kupechestva XVIII v.', *Ist. SSSR.*, 3 (1971),
58-71.

772. AKSENOV, A.I., Moskovskoe kupechestvo v XVIII v. (Opyt
genealogicheskogo issledovaniia). Avtoreferat kandidatskoi
dissertatsii. M. 1974.

773. KOZINTSEVA, P.I., 'Predlozheniia "Rossiiskikh kuptsov
Sankt-Peterburgskikh zhitelei" - istochnik dlia
ekonomicheskoi istorii vtoroi chetverti XVIII v.', in:
NOSOV, N. (ed.), Issledovaniia po otechestvennomu
istochnikovedeniiu (no. 236), pp. 304-7.

774. PAVLENKO, N.I. (ed.), Zhurnal ili zapiska zhizni i
prikliuchenii Ivana A. Tolchenova. M. 1974. Pp. 468.
Unique journal of Tver' merchant at the end of the
eighteenth century.

7(f) - URBAN HISTORY

Urban history has emerged from obscurity in the past ten years,
with new interest among Western and Soviet scholars. HAMM (778)
provides a number of stimulating essays; ROZMAN (779) traces
the city's role in the early stages of modernization. MORRISON
(781) charts thoroughly the growth of urban population through
peasant immigration. See also KNABE (522), based on the classic of KIZEVETTER (794), and the notable work of HITTLE (2651).
Among Soviet scholars, RYNDZIUNSKII, KLOKMAN, IANIN are
valuable (782-6, 792). VODARSKII (790) is good on local history
and urbanization, though the main focus is the nineteenth century. VIL'KOV (800, 801) includes a good bibliography in footnotes. Works on towns of particular regions, 783, 796-802;
Moscow and St. Petersburg: 803-818. See also nos. 196, 992.

775. BARON, S.H., 'The Town in "Feudal" Russia', *SR.*, XXVIII, 1
(1969), 116-123.
Review of *Goroda feodal'noi Rossii* (no. 787).

776. GUTKIND, E., Urban Development in Eastern Europe: Bulgaria,
Romania, and the USSR. N.Y. 1972. Pp. 457, 250 illustra-
tions.
Vol. 8 of author's 'International History of City
Development', N.Y. 1964-72.

777. JONES, R.E., 'Urban Planning and The Development of Provincial Towns in Russia During the Reign of Catherine II', in: GARRARD (no. 1595), pp. 321-344.

778. HAMM, M.F. (ed.), The City in Russian History. Lexington, Kt. 1976. Pp. 350. Maps.

779. ROZMAN, G., Urban Networks in Russia 1750-1800, and Pre-Modern Periodization. Princeton 1976. Pp. 337.

779a. HAUMANN, H., ' Die russische Stadt in der Geschichte', *JfGOst.*, XXVII, 4(1979), 481-98.

780. HITTLE, J.M., 'Catherinian Reform, Social Change and the Decline of the *Posad* Community', in: ROWNEY, D.K., ORCHARD, G.E. (eds), Russian and Slavic History (Columbus 1977), pp. 274-301.

781. MORRISON, D., '"Trading Peasants" and Urbanization in Eighteenth Century Russia: The Central Industrial Region', Columbia Ph.D., 1979.

782. RYNDZIUNSKII, P.G., Gorodskoe grazhdanstvo doreformennoi Rossii. M. 1958. Pp. 588.
Standard work, covering end eighteenth- first half nineteenth centuries.

783. KLOKMAN, IU., Ocherki sotsial'no-ekonomicheskoi istorii gorodov severo-zapada Rossii v seredine XVIII v. M. 1960. Pp. 221.
Rev: *Kritika*, I, 1 (1964), 16-22 (Hittle, J.).

784. KLOKMAN, IU. P., 'Russkii gorod XVIII v. i evoliutsiia gorodskogo stroia Zapadnoi Evropy', in: PASHUTO (no. 612), pp. 69-80.

785. KLOKMAN, IU. P., 'Gorod v zakonodatel'stve russkogo absoliutizma vo vtoroi polovine XVIII v.', in: DRUZHININ (no. 439), pp. 320-354.

786. KLOKMAN, IU. P., Sotsial'no-ekonomicheskaia istoriia russkogo goroda. Vtoraia polovina XVIII v. M. 1967. Pp. 333.
Rev: *JbfGO.*, N.F. 16, 7 (1968), 129-32 (Geyer, D.).

787. SHUNKOV, V.I. (ed.), Goroda feodal'noi Rossii. Sb. statei pamiati N.V. Ustiugova. M. 1966. Pp. 563.
Rev: Baron, S. (no. 775); *Ist. SSSR.*, 3 (1967), 156-61 (Sakharov, A.).
Valuable-contains over 30 essays on 18th Century.

788. MILOV, L.V., 'O tak nazyvaemykh agrarnykh gorodakh Rossii XVIII veka'. *Vop. Ist.*, 6 (1968), 54-64.

789. RYNDZIUNSKII, P.G., 'Osnovnye faktory gorodoobrazovaniia v Rossii vtoroi poloviny XVIII veka', in: IANIN (ed.) (no. 792), I, pp. 105-27.
Also as separate mimeographed text, M. 1972.

790. VODARSKII, IA., Promyshlennye seleniia tsentral'noi Rossii v period genezisa i razvitiia kapitalizma. M. 1972. Pp. 256. Rev: *Vop. Ist.*, 4 (1973), 147-9 (Fedorov, V.A.).

791. KABUZAN, V., PULLAT, R., 'Obzor statisticheskikh istochnikov o chislennosti i sostave gorodskogo naseleniia Rossii XVIII - nachala XIX vv. (1719-1917 gg.)', *Izv. A.N.E.S.S.R. (obshchestv. nauki)*, 24, 2 (1975), 150-70. Résumés in English and Estonian. See also no. 1404.

792. IANIN, V.L. (ed.), Russkii gorod (Istoriko-metodologicheskii sbornik). Vyp. I: M. 1976. Pp. 296. Vyp. II: M. 1979. Pp. 295.

793. LAVROV, V., Razvitie planirovochnoi struktury istoricheski slozhivshikhsia gorodov. M. 1977. Pp. 175. Illustrations.

794. KIZEVETTER, A.A., Posadskaia obshchina v Rossii XVIII stoletiia. M. 1903, reprinted Newtonville 1978. Pp. 803. New introduction and updated bibliography by G. Rozman.

795. RABINOVICH, M., Ocherki etnografii russkogo feodal'nogo goroda. M. 1978. Pp. 328.

796. VEKOV, M., 'Goroda Tverskoi provintsii v pervoi chetverti XVIII v.', in: NAROCHNITSKII (ed.) (no, 1383), pp. 143-163.

797. MESKHIA, M.A., Goroda i gorodskoi stroi feodal'noi Gruzii (XVII-XVIII vv.). Tbilisi 1959. Pp. 440. Rev: *Vop. Ist.*, 6 (1962), 145-8 (Beriashvili, T. et al.).

798. TRON'KO, P.T., 'Proshloe i nastoiashchee Ukrainy v istorii ee gorodov i sel', *Vop. Ist.*, 1 (1971), 69-80. Review of large series on Ukrainian towns (no. 2590).

799. GRITSKEVICH, A., Chastnovladel'cheskie goroda Belorussii v XVI-XVIII vv. Minsk 1975. Pp. 248. Rev: *Vop. Ist.*, 4 (1977), 157-60 (Kulakovskii, V.M.).

800. VILKOV, O.N. (ed.), Goroda Sibiri: Ekonomika, upravlenie i kul'tura gorodov Sibiri v dosovetskii period. Novos. 1974. Pp. 300. Rev: *SGECRN.*, 4 (1976), 70-73 (Jones, W.G.).

801. VIL'KOV, O.N. (ed.), Istoriia gorodov Sibiridosovetskogo perioda (XVII-nachala XX v.). Novos. 1977. Pp. 301. Sequel to no. 800; see also nos. 2550-54.

802. TODOROV, N., Balkanskii gorod XV-XIX vekov. Sotsial'no-ekonomicheskoe i demograficheskoe razvitie. M. 1976. Pp. 516.

802a. RABINOVICH, M., Ocherki etnografii russkogo feodal'nogo goroda. Gorozhane, ikh obshchestvennyi i domashnii byt. M. 1978. Pp. 320.

On Moscow, BERTON (803) is disappointing, with much potted and confused historical comment. ILYIN (804) is a superb picture album. IATSUNSKII (806) is the standard Soviet account, with an extensive bibliography. KADUSHKIN (805) is part of an on-going series and will be essential when completed. For St Petersburg BATER (810) is outstanding. KOMELOVA (817) is valuable for reproductions of engravings by the eighteenth-century artist Makhaev. VIATKIN (813) is the standard multi-volume account and provides a good survey of development.

(i) Moscow

803. BERTON, K., Moscow, An Architectural History. London 1977. Pp. 256. 85 b/w. illustrations.

804. ILYIN, M., Architectural Monuments of Moscow, Eighteenth-first third of Nineteenth Century. M. 1975. 2 vols. I: pp. 114; 104 plates. II: pp. 356; 322 plates.

805. KADUSHKIN, N. (comp.), MASLOV, I. (ed.), Istoriia Moskvy. Ukazatel' literatury. Ch. 1: Po leninskim mestam Moskvy i Podmoskov'ia. M. 1974. Pp. 418.

806. IATSUNSKII, V. et al. (eds), Istoriia Moskvy v shesti tomakh. M. 1953-57. 6 vols in 8. Bibliography, charts and maps.

807. SNEGIREV, V.L., Moskovskie slobody. Ocherki po istorii moskovskogo posada XIV-XVIII vv. M. 1956. Pp. 238. Includes the Foreign (German) Quarter.

808. ROGOV, A., 'Pamiatniki svetskoi arkhitektury Moskvy XVIII v.', *Ist. SSSR.*, 4 (1968), 154-61.

809. SYTIN, P.V., Istoriia planirovki i zastroiki Moskvy. 3 vols. M. 1972. Vol. 2 covers eighteenth century.

(ii) St. Petersburg

810. BATER, J., St. Petersburg: Industrialization and Change. London 1976. Pp. 411. Based on Ph.D. thesis, London 1969.

811. MUNRO, G.E., 'The Development of St. Petersburg as an Urban Center during the Reign of Catherine II (1762-1796)', North Carolina Ph.D., 1973.

812. PISHVANOVA, V.I., GLUSHKOV, T. (comps), Istoriia Leningrada. Katalog rukopisei. L. 1954. Pp. 124. Manuscripts in the Saltykov-Shchedin Library.

813. VIATKIN, M.P. (ed.), Ocherki istorii Leningrada, 6 vols. Leningrad 1955-70. I: Period feodalizma (1703-1861 gg). Pp. 896.

814. LUPPOV, S.P., Istoriia stroitel'stva Peterburga v pervoi chetverti XVIII veka. M. 1957. Pp. 190.

815. PETROV. G., Kronshtadt. Rasskaz ob istorii goroda ot ego osnovaniia do nashikh dnei. L. 1971. Pp. 390.

816. KOSHKAROVA, L. (comp.), Gravirovannye i litografirovannye vidy Peterburga-Leningrada v sobranii Gosudarstvennoi Publichnoi Biblioteki im. M. Saltykova-Shchedrina. Katalog. L. 1965. Pp. 433 Catalogue of engravings.

817. KOMELOVA, G.N. (comp.). Vidy Peterburga i ego okrestnostei serediny XVIII veka po risunkam Makhaeva. Graviury. L. 1968. Pp. 93. 87 illustrations. Eng./Russ. captions.

818. GOROD glazami khudozhnikov. Peterburg-Petrograd-Leningrad v proizvedeniakh zhivopisi i grafiki. Al'bom. L. 1978. Pp. 396. 283 illustrations.

7(g) - SOCIAL MOVEMENTS AND POPULAR REVOLTS

The main focus here is on Pugachev, although earlier events have been well covered by Soviet scholarship. ALEXANDER'S two books (822, 824) give a scholarly account; RAEFF and LONGWORTH (823, 825) are useful shorter discussions. MAVRODIN, the doyen of Soviet Pugachev specialists, has produced studies both on the background of the revolt (845-6) and on the revolt itself (886-7). CHEREPNIN (879) is a stimulating collection of essays with valuable bibliography in Russian and Western languages. General works: 819, 820, 838, 842-7; peasant protest: 837, 844, 847-50, 854-68; regional accounts: 858-66; urban risings: 869-72; pretenders: 827, 873-5; peasant wars: 820-31, 834-41, 876-903. See also 2327.

819. AVRICH, P., Russian Rebels, 1600-1800. N.Y. 1972. Pp. 309.

820. ALEXANDER, J.T., 'Recent Soviet Historiography on the Pugachev Revolt: A Review Article', CanAmSlSt., IV, 3 (1970), 602-617.

821. ALEXANDER, J.T., 'Western views of the Pugachev rebellion', SEER., XLVIII, 113 (1970), 520-536.

822. ALEXANDER, J.T., Autocratic Politics in a National Crisis: The Imperial Russian Government and Pugachev's Revolt, 1773-1775. Bloomington 1969. Pp. 345. Based on Ph.D., thesis, Indiana 1966.

823. RAEFF, M., 'Pugachev's Revolt' in: FOSTER, R. and GREENE, J. (eds), Preconditions of Revolution in Early Modern Europe (Baltimore 1970), pp. 161-202.

824. ALEXANDER, J.T., Emperor of the Cossacks: Pugachev and the Frontier Jacquerie of 1773-1775. Lawrence, Kansas 1973. Pp. 245.
First general book-length study in English.

825. LONGWORTH, P., 'The Pugachev Revolt: The Last Great Cossack Peasant Rising', in: LANDSBERGER, H.A. (ed.), Rural Protest: Peasant Movements and Social Change (London 1974), pp. 194-256.
An earlier version: *J. Eur. Stud.*, III (1973), 1-35.

826. LONGWORTH, P., 'The Subversive Legend of Sten'ka Razin', *Russia/Rossiia* (Torino), 2 (1975), 17-40.

827. LONGWORTH, P., 'The Pretender Phenomenon in Eighteenth-Century Russia', *Past and Present*, 66 (Feb. 1975), 61-83.

828. LONGWORTH, P., 'Peasant Leadership and the Pugachev Revolt', *J. Peasant Studies*, II, 2 (1975), 183-205.

829. LONGWORTH, P., 'Popular Protest in England and Russia: Some Comparisons and Suggestions', in: CROSS (ed.) (no. 1794). pp. 263-278.

830. SPIRO, P., 'The British Perception of Russian Domestic Conditions during the Pugachev Rebellion', in: CROSS (ed.) (no. 1794), pp. 247-262.

831. DUKES, P., 'Towards a Comparison of the Jacobite and Pugachev Movements', in: CROSS (ed.) (no. 1794), pp. 279-92.

832. BENNIGSEN, A., 'Un mouvement populaire au Caucase au XVIIIe siècle. La "Guerre Sainte" du sheikh Mansur (1785-1791), page mal connue et controversée des relations russo-turques', *CMRS.*, V, 2 (1964), 159-205.

833. EECKAUTE, D., 'Les brigands en Russie du XVIIe au XIXe siècle', *Revue d'Histoire Moderne et Contemporaine*, XII (1965), 161-202.

834. PASCAL, P., La révolte de Pougatchëv. Paris 1971. Pp. 274.

835. HOFFMANN, P., 'Der Bauernkrieg in Russland 1773-75 unter der Führung Emel'jan Pugačevs. Bericht über die sowjetische Jubiläums-literatur', *ZfG.*, XXIII (1975), 1318-21.
Lists 24 titles.

836. PETERS, D., Politische und gesellschaftliche Vorstellungen in der Aufstandsbewegung unter Pugačev (1773-1775). Berlin 1973. Pp. 364. (Forschungen zur Osteuropäischen Geschichte, Bd. 17.).

837. HEITZ, G. et al. (hrsg.), Der Bauer im Klassenkampf.
Studien zur Geschichte des deutschen Bauernkrieges und der
bäuerlichen Klassenkämpfe im Spätfeudalismus. Berlin 1975.
Pp. 608.
Rev: *ZfG.*, XXIV (1976), 945-7 (Schildbauer, J.). Includes
200-anniversary article on Pugachev by Mavrodin.

838. DONNERT, E., 'Soziale Bewegungen und
gesellschaftspolitisches Denken in Russland in der zweiten
Hälfte des 18. Jhdts', *ZfG.*, XXIV (1976), 879-888.

839. HOFFMAN, P., SCHUTZLER, H., 'Der Pugačev-Aufstand in
zeitgenössischen deutschen Berichten', *JfGSLE.*, VI (1962),
337-365.

840. ROZNER, I., 'Deutsche Teilnehmer am Bauernkrieg unter der
Führung Pugačevs', *Ost und West* (no. 1737), pp. 417-26.

841. TATARINCEV, A.G., 'Zum Widerhall des Pugačev-Aufstandes im
Saratower Gebiet. Aus der Geschichte der deutschen
Kolonisation in der zweiten Hälfte des 18. Jhdts', *Zt. für
Slawistik* XIII (1968), 196-206.

842. KIRILLOV, V.I., 'Noveishaia sovetskaia literatura o
krest'ianskikh i gorodskikh dvizheniiakh v Rossii (XI-
XVIII vv.)', *Vop. Ist.*, 3 (1965), 127-140.
Covers 1957-64, with reference to surveys of earlier
literature. Bibliography 1953-73 in no. 879.

843. BERNADSKII, V.N., 'Ocherki iz istorii klassovoi bor'by i
obshchestvenno-politicheskoi mysli Rossii v tretei chetverti
XVIII v.', L. 1962 =Leningradskii Gos. Ped. In-t im.
Gertsena, *Uchenye Zapiski* (istoriia), 229 (1962)
ed. V.V. MAVRODIN, 3-160.

844. INDOVA, E., PREOBRAZHENSKII, A.A., TIKHONOV, IU.,
'Klassovaia bor'ba krest'ianstva i stanovlenie burzhuaznykh
otnoshenii v Rossii (vtoraia polovina XVII-XVIII v.)', *Vop.
Ist.*, 12 (1964), 27-53.
See also *Vop. Ist.*, 1 (1965), 'Vstrechi v redaktsii', for
discussion. Claims that class struggle brought greater
peasant participation in economy.

845. MAVRODIN, V.V., Klassovaia bor'ba i obshchestvenno-
politicheskaia mysl' v Rossii v XVIII v. (1725-1773 gg.).
Kurs lektsii. L. 1964. Pp. 195.

846. MAVRODIN, V.V., Klassovaia bor'ba i obshchestvenno-
politicheskaia mysl' v Rossii v XVIII v. (1773-1790 gg.).
Kurs lektsii. L. 1975. Pp. 214.
Sequel to no. 845.

847. NOSOV, N.E. et al. (eds), Krest'ianstvo i klassovaia bor'ba
v feodal'noi Rossii. Sb. statei pamiati I.I. Smirnova.
L. 1967. Pp. 456.

848. RUBINSHTEIN, N.L., 'Krest'ianskoe dvizhenie v Rossii vo
vtoroi polovine XVIII veka', *Vop. Ist.*, 11 (1956), 34-51.

849. VALK, S.N. (ed.), KUDRIAVTSEVA, S.I. et al. (comp.),
Krest'ianskoe dvizhenie v Rossii 1796-1825. Sb. dokumentov.
M. 1961. Pp. 1048.
Rev: *Vop. Ist.*, 5 (1963), 120-2 (Parusov, A.I.); gives
additional bibliography.

850. PROKHOROV, M.F., 'Opyt sostavleniia svodnykh tablits
vystuplenii pomeshchich'ikh krest'ian Rossii 1760-1773 gg.
(po materialam fondov mestnykh uchrezhdenii Moskovskoi
gubernii)', *A. Ezh.* (1972), 126-34.

851. PREOBRAZHENSKII, A.A., 'Klassovaia bor'ba ural'skikh
krest'ian i masterovykh liudei v nachale XVIII v', *I.Z.*,
vol. 58 (1956), 246-272.

852. VAGINA, P., 'O kharaktere volnenii masterovykh ural'skikh
zavodov v poslednei chetverti XVIII v.', *Ist. SSSR.*, 1
(1965), 132-9.

853. ZAOZERSKAIA, E. (ed.), Volneniia rabotnykh liudei i
pripisnykh krest'ian na metallurgicheskikh zavodakh Rossii
v pervoi polovine XVIII v. Sbornik dokumentov. M. 1975.
Vyp. 1-3. Pp. 559.

854. GESSEN, V.IU., 'Napadenie beglykh krest'ian na pomeshchich'i
votchiny v 20-30kh godakh XVIII v.', *Vop. Ist.*, 12 (1954),
103-110.

855. BONDAREVSKAIA, T.P., 'Beglye krest'iane srednego
Povolzh'ia v seredine XVIII v.', in: NOSOV (ed.) (no. 847),
pp. 305 399.

856. MAMSIK, T., Pobegi kak sotsial'noe iavlenie. Pripisnaia
derevnia Zapadnoi Sibiri 1740-1800. M. 1978. Pp. 206.

857. KOSACHEVSKAIA, E.M., 'Narodnyi mstitel' Semen Garkusha',
in: EZHOV (no. 616), pp. 141-8.

858. CHEREVAN', A.S., 'Sovmestnaia bor'ba ukrainskikh i russkikh
krest'ian protiv feodal'nogo gneta v 60-70 godakh XVIII v.',
Vop. Ist., 12 (1953), 29-41.
Pugachev in the Ukraine.

859. GOLOBUTSKII, V., 'Gaidamatskoe dvizhenie na Zaporozh'e vo
vremia "Koliivshchiny" i krest'ianskogo vosstaniia pod
predvoditel'stvom E.I. Pugacheva', *I.Z.*, vol. 55 (1956),
310-343.

860. POLIAKOV, IU., 'V.V. Krestinin i obshchestvennaia bor'ba v
Arkhangel'skom posade v 60-90-kh godakh XVIII v.', *Ist.
SSSR.*, 2 (1958), 78-102.

861. BUKALOVA, V.M., 'Antifeodal'naia bor'ba kabardinskikh krest'ian vo vtoroi polovine XVIII veka', *Vop. Ist.*, 6 (1961), 75-84.

862. KAKHK, IU. IU., Krest'ianskoe dvizhenie i krest'ianskii vopros v Estonii v kontse XVIII i pervoi chetverti XIX veka. Tallin 1962. Pp. 476.
Rev: *Vop. Ist.*, 10 (1963), 147-9 (Kruus, Kh.).

863. DRAKOKHRUST, E.I., 'Antifeodal'noe vystuplenie krest'ian promyslovykh sel vladeniia Kochubeev v Novgorod-Severskom namestnichestve (1795 g.), *Ezh. gos. ist. muz.* (1965-66), 106-118.

864. KOZLOVSKII, P., 'Klassovaia bor'ba krest'ian v magnatskikh votchinakh Belorussii vo vtoroi polovine XVIII v.', *Ezh. A.I.* (1966), 268-280.

865. SHABANOVA, A., 'Klassovaia bor'ba krest'ian v votchine Aleksandro-Svirskogo monastyria nakanune sekuliarizatsii (50e-nachalo 60-kh godov XVIII veka)', *VLU(Ist).*, 14 (1966), 50-60.

866. SHABANOVA, A.M., 'Bor'ba krest'ian Aleksandro-Svirskoi votchiny v pervoi polovine XVIII v.', *Ezh. A.I.* (1971), 156-60.

867. BALAGUROV, IA.A., Kizhskoe vosstanie 1769-1771. Petrozavodsk 1969. Pp. 95.
Revised and abridged edition of 1951 original.

868. BALAGUROV, IA.A., Kizhskoe vosstanie 1769-1771: dokumenty. Petrozavodsk 1977. Pp. 127.

869. BUGANOV, V.I., Moskovskie vosstaniia kontsa XVII veka. M. 1969. Pp. 440.
Risings of 1682 and 1698. Rev: *Vop. Ist.*, 1 (1971), 156-9 (Volkov, M.).

870. BUGANOV, V.I. (ed.), Vosstanie v Moskve 1682 goda. Sb. dokumentov. M. 1976. Pp. 346.
See also discussion with N.I. Pavlenko, *Ist. SSSR.*, 2 (1971), 3 (1973).

871. CHERNOV, A.V., 'Astrakhanskoe vosstanie 1705-1706 gg.', *I.Z.*, vol. 64 (1958), 186-216.

872. GOLIKOVA, N.B., Astrakhanskoe vosstanie 1705-1706 gg. M. 1975. Pp. 327.
Rev: *Vop. Ist.*, 11 (1976), 161-3 (Chistiakova, E.V.).

873. TROITSKII, S.M., 'Samozvantsy v Rossii XVII-XVIII vv.', *Vop. Ist.*, 3 (1969), 134-146.

874. RAZORENOVA, N.V., 'Iz istorii samozvanstva v Rossii 30-kh godov XVIII v.', *VMU(Ist.)*, 6 (1974), 54-67.

875. FREIDENBERG, M.M., 'Stepan Malyi iz Chernogorii', *Vop.
Ist.*, 10 (1975), 118–32.

876. MAVRODIN, V.V., 'Sovetskaia istoricheskaia literatura o
krest'ianskikh voinakh v Rossii XVII-XVIII vv.', *Vop. Ist.*,
5 (1961), 24–47.

877. SHAPIRO, A.L., 'Ob istoricheskoi roli krest'ianskikh voin
XVII-XVIII v Rossii', *Ist. SSSR.*, 5 (1965), 61–80.

878. SMIRNOV, I.I. et al. (eds), Krest'ianskie voiny v Rossii
XVII-XVIII vv. L. 1966. Pp. 328.
Smirnov on Bolotnikov; Man'kov on Razin; Pod'iapol'skaia
on Bulavin; Mavrodin on Pugachev.

879. CHEREPNIN, L.V. et al. (eds), Krest'ianskie voiny v Rossii
XVII-XVIII vekov: problemy, poiski, resheniia. M. 1974.
Pp. 447.
Collection of essays. Valuable bibliography of work on
Pugachev and peasant war in Russian and other languages,
1953-1973 (pp. 400-444).

880. POD'IAPOL'SKAIA, E.P., Vosstanie Bulavina, 1707-1709.
M. 1962. Pp. 216.
Rev: *Vop. Ist.*, 12 (1963), 124-7 (Buganov, V.I.; Lebedev,
V.I.); *JbfGO.*, N.F. XIII, 3 (1965), 457-8.

881. LEBEDEV, V.I., Bulavinskoe vosstanie, 1707-1708. M. 1967.
Pp. 153.

882. OVCHINNIKOV, P.V. (ed. and intro.), 'Sledstvie i sud nad
E.I. Pugachevym', *Vop. Ist.* (1966), no. 3, 125-38; no. 4,
111-126; no. 5, 107-121; no. 7, 92-109; no. 9, 137-149.
Documents.

883. INDOVA, E. (ed.), Krest'ianskaia voina 1773-1775 gg. v
Rossii. Dokumenty. M. 1973. Pp. 440.

884. OVCHINNIKOV, P.V. et al. (eds), Dokumenty stavki E.I.
Pugacheva, povstancheskikh vlastei i uchrezhdenii, 1773-
1774 gg. M. 1975.
570 documents. Full details of previous documentary publications on Pugachev.

885. NAZAROV, V., RAKHMATULLIN, M., 'Novye sborniki dokumentov
o krest'ianskoi voine 1773-5 gg. v Rossii' *Ist. SSSR.*, 1
(1977), 164-183.

886. MAVRODIN, V.V. (ed.), Krest'ianskaia voina v Rossii v
1773-1775 godakh. Vosstanie Pugacheva. 3 vols.
Leningrad 1961-1970. I: 587; II: 512; III: 488.
The standard Soviet account.

887. MAVRODIN, V.V. et al., Pugachev i ego spodvizhniki.
M. 1965. Pp. 140.

888. ANDRUSHENKO, A.I., Krest'ianskaia voina 1773-1775 gg.
na Iaike, v Priural'e, na Urale i v Sibiri. M. 1969.
Pp. 360.

889. RAKHMATULLIN, M.A., 'Krest'ianskaia voina v Rossii 1773-
1775 godov', *Ist. SSSR.*, 6 (1973), 35-53.

890. BELIAVSKII, M.T., 'Krest'ianskaia voina 1773-1775 i ee
osobennosti, *VMU(Ist.)*, 4 (1974), 64-77.

891. BELIAVSKII, M.T., 'Pervii etap krest'ianskoi voiny 1773-
1775 godov i ego osobennosti', *Ist. SSSR.*, 1 (1975), 60-9.

892. ROZNER, I.G., Kazachestvo v krest'ianskoi voine 1773-75 gg.
L'vov 1966. Pp. 200.

893. MARTYNOV, M.N., 'Satkinskii zavod vo vremia vosstaniia
Emel'iana Pugacheva', *I.Z.*, vol. 58 (1956), 208-245.

894. MARTYNOV, M.N., 'Voskresenskii zavod v krest'ianskoi voine
1773-1775 gg.', *I.Z.*, vol. 80 (1967), 287-304.

895. SEMENIUK, G.I., 'Politika tsarizma v Kazakhstane do
nachala Krest'ianskoi voiny 1773-1775 gg. (Tsarizm i
feodal'naia verkhushka Kazakhskogo obshchestva)',
in: NOSOV (no. 847), pp. 414-446.

896. MAVRODIN, V.V., 'Ob uchastii kolonistov Povolzh'ia v
vosstanii Pugachova', in: NOSOV (no. 847), pp. 400-414.
Earlier German version in *JfGSLE.*, 7 (1963), 189-99.

897. OVCHINNIKOV, P.V., '"Nemetskii" ukaz E.I. Pugacheva', *Vop.
Ist.*, 12 (1969), 133-141.

898. RUBINSHTEIN, E.I., 'Otkliki pugachevskogo dvizheniia v
kaluzhskom krae', *Ezh. A.I.* (1971), 161-66.

899. BELIKOV, T.I., Uchastie kalmykov v krest'ianskoi voine pod
rukovodstvom E.I. Pugacheva. (1773-1775 gg.). Elista
1971. Pp.167.
Rev: *Vop. Ist.*, 4 (1974), 141-2.

900. ALISHEV, S.KH., Tatary Srednego Povolzh'ia v pugachevskom
vosstanii. Kazan' 1973. Pp. 215.

901. ALEKSANDROV, A.A. (comp.), Krest'ianskaia voina pod
predvoditel'stvom Emel'iana Pugacheva v Udmurtii. Sbornik
dokumentov. Izhevsk 1974. Pp. 355.

902. KURMACHEVA, M.D., Krest'ianskaia voina 1773-75 gg. v
Nizhegorodskom krae. Gor'kii 1975. Pp. 126.

903. NESTEROV, V. (ed.), Krest'ianskaia voina pod predvoditel'-
stvom E. Pugacheva v Chuvashii. Sb. dokumentov. Cheboksary
1972. Pp.528.

CONFINO (910) is an outstanding investigation of peasant agriculture and the attitudes to it of peasant and lord.
LIASHCHENKO (916) is a re-issue of an older established work.
RUBINSHTEIN (918) is thorough, with some exceptions, and
valuable, as is MILOV (920). Survey and historiographic works:
904, 913-18; land holding, surveying, use: 907, 919-932;
productivity, techniques: 918, 933-39; regional studies: 939-56.

RUSSIAN AGRICULTURE, LANDHOLDING AND LAND-USE

904. BLUM, J., 'Russian Agriculture in the last 150 Years of
Serfdom', *Agricultural History*, 34 (1960), 3-12.

905. DREW, R.F., 'The Emergence of an Agricultural Policy for
Siberia in the 17th and 18th Centuries', *Agricultural
History*, 33 (1959), 29-39.

906. KAHAN, A., 'Natural Calamities and Their Effect Upon Food
Supply in Russia. (An Introduction to a Catalogue)',
JbfGO., N.S., XVI, 3 (1968), 353-77.
Appendix A, the catalogue of 'Recorded Natural Calamities
Affecting Agriculture and Food Supply in Russia', covers
period 867-1965. Nineteen entries for the eighteenth
century.

907. EECKAUTE, D., 'La mensuration générale des terres en Russie
dans la deuxième moitié du XVIIIe s.', *CMRS.*, V, 3 (1964),
320-8.

908. EECKAUTE, D., 'La législation des forêts au XVIIIe s.',
CMRS., IX, 2 (1968), 194-208.

909. CONFINO, M., 'La comptabilité des domaines privés en
Russie', *Revue d'histoire moderne et contemporaine*, VIII
(1961), 31-40.

910. CONFINO, M., Systèmes agraires et progrès agricole:
l'assolement triennal en Russie aux XVIIIe-XIXe siècles.
The Hague-Paris 1969. Pp. 495.
Rev: no. 911.

911. REGEMORTER, J.L. van, 'Systèmes agraires et progrès
agricole en Russie au XVIIIe siècle', *Annales*, XXVI, 1
(1971), 40-5.
Review of Confino (no. 910).

912. SACKE, G., 'Das Problem des Grundbesitzes in der
Regierungszeit Katherinas II', *JfGSLE.*, V (1961), 201-33.

913. IATSUNSKII, V.K., 'Osnovnye momenty istorii sel'-
skokhoziaistvennogo proizvodstva v Rossii s XVI v. do
1917 g.', *Ezh. A.I.* (1964), 44-64.

914. VORONINA, E., 'Rol' sel'skokhoziaistvennykh kultur v agrarnom progresse Rossii v razlichnye istoricheskie periody', *Ezh. A.I.* (1968), 189-96.

915. KOLESNIKOV, P.A. et al. (eds), Voprosy agrarnoi istorii Evropeiskogo Severa SSSR. Vologda 1970. Vyp. 3: Agrarnaia istoriia Evropeiskogo Severa SSSR. Pp. 608.

916. LIASHCHENKO, P.I., Ocherki agrarnoi evoliutsii Rossii. M. 1971. 2 vols in 3.

917. IANIN, V.L. et al. (eds), Sovetskaia istoriografiia agrarnoi istorii SSSR do 1917 g. Kishinev 1978. Pp. 262. Some material on the eighteenth century.

918. RUBINSHTEIN, N.L., Sel'skoe khoziaistvo Rossii vo vtoroi polovine XVIII v. M. 1957. Pp. 494
Rev: *Vop. Ist.*, 6 (1958), (Sivkov, K.)

919. MILOV, L.V., 'O variantakh "Ekonomicheskikh primechanii" vtoroi poloviny XVIII v.', *Ist. SSSR.*, 2 (1957), 96-121.

920. MILOV, L.V., Issledovanie ob 'Ekonomicheskikh Primechaniiakh' k General'nomu Mezhevaniiu. K istorii russkogo krest'ianstva i sel'skogo khoziaistva vtoroi poloviny XVIII v. M. 1965. Pp. 312.

921. PREOBRAZHENSKII, A.A., 'Struktura zemel'noi sobstvennosti v Rossii XVII-XVIII vv.', *Ezh. A.I.* (1966), 128-36

922. IASMAN, Z., 'Popytki vvedeniia uluchshennykh sel'-skokhoziaistvennykh orudii v pomeshchich'ikh khoziaistvakh', *Ezh. A.I.* (1965), 246-55.

923. SIVKOV, K.V., 'Novye iavleniia v tekhnike i organizatsii sel'skogo khoziaistva Rossii vo vtoroi polovine XVIII v.', *Ezh. A.I.* (1969), 153-62.

924. IASMAN, Z.D., 'Vozniknovenie sel'skokhoziaistvennogo mashinostroeniia v krepostnoi Rossii', *Vop. Ist.*, 3 (1972), 38-50.

925. KOLOTINSKAIA, E.N., Pravovye osnovy zemel'nogo kadastra v Rossii. M. 1968. Pp. 270.
Chapter on eighteenth century.

926. SOBOLEV, S.S., 'Iz istorii zemel'nogo kadastra v Rossii' in: Materialy po istorii sel'skogo khoziaistva i krest'-ianstva SSSR, Sb. VII (M. 1969), pp. 163-189.

927. KOPYL, I.F., 'Iz istorii russkoi agronomii XVIII v. (I.M. Komov o zemledelii)', in: Materialy po istorii sel'-skogo khoziaistva i krest'ianstva SSSR, Sb. VII (M. 1969), pp. 84-98.

928. INDOVA, E.I., 'Voprosy zemledeliia v "Trudakh Vol'nogo ekonomicheskogo obshchestva" vo vtoroi polovine XVIII veka', *Ezh. A.I.* (1970), 114-23.

929. KRUTIKOV, V.I., 'Dushevladenie i zemlevladenie pomeshchikov Tul'skoi gubernii v XVIII - nachale XX vv.', *Ezh. A.I.* (1971), 186-94.

930. KOVAL'CHENKO, I.D., 'Nekotorye voprosy genezisa kapitalizma v krest'ianskom khoziaistve Rossii', *Ist. SSSR.*, 6 (1972), 65-87.

931. ZHIDKOV, G.P., Kabinetskoe zemlevladenie 1747-1917 gg. Novos. 1973. Pp. 264.
Rev: *Vop. Ist.*, 4 (1975), Ryndziunskii, P.

932. PREOBRAZHENSKII, A.A., 'Ob evoliutsii feodal'noi zemel'noi sobstvennosti v Rossii XVII - nachala XIX vv.', *Vop. Ist.*, 5 (1977), 46-62.

933. LEKHNOVICH, V.S., 'K istorii kul'tury kartofelia v Rossii', in: Materialy po istorii sel'skogo khoziaistva v SSSR, Sb. II (M.-L. 1956), pp. 258-401.

934. KOLESNIKOV, P., 'Dinamika posevov i urozhainosti na zemliakh vologodskoi gubernii v XVII-XIX vv.', *Ezh. A.I.* (1964), 240-8.

935. INDOVA, E.I., 'Urozhai v tsentral'noi Rossii za 150 let (XVII-XVIII vv.)', *Ezh. A.I.* (1965), 141-55.

936. PROKOF'EVA, L., 'Urozhainost' zernovykh kul'tur belozerskogo kraia v pervoi polovine XVIII v.', *Ezh. A.I.* (1968), 127-32.

937. MILOV, L.V., 'O proizvoditel'nosti truda v zemledelii Rossii v seredine XVIII v.', *I.Z.*, vol. 83 (1969), 244-58.

938. INDOVA, E.I., 'Zemledel'cheskaia praktika v tsentral'noi Rossii XVIII v.', in: Materialy po istorii sel'skogo khoziaistva i krest'ianstva SSSR, Sb. VII (M. 1969), pp. 32-44.

939. SHABANOVA, A., 'O roli podseki v zemledel'cheskom khoziaistve krest'ian Prisvir'ia v kontse XVII-pervoi polovine XVIII vv.', *VLU(Ist.)*, 2 (1968), 56-66.

940. STRODS, KH., '"Zheleznyi inventar'" i ego rol' v sotsial'-no-ekonomicheskom razvitii Latvii vo vtoroi polovine XVIII i pervoi polovine XIX vv.', *Ezh. A.I.* (1966), 337-47.

941. STRODS, KH., 'Klimat, pochva i sel'skoe khoziastvo v Latvii (konets XVIII-pervaia polovina XIX veka)', *Ezh. A.I.*, (1970), 124-39.

942. STRODS, KH., 'Latyshskii krest'ianin i sel'-
skokhoziaistvennaia tekhnika (konets XVIII-pervaia polovina
XIX v.)', in: CHEREPNIN, L. (ed.), Iz istorii ekonomicheskoi
i obshchestvennoi zhizni Rossii. Sb. st. k 90-letiiu N.M.
Druzhinina (M. 1976), pp. 93-104.

943. VAKHTRE, S., 'O vliianii klimaticheskikh uslovii na
urozhai v Estonii v XVIII-XIX vv.', *Ezh. A.I.*(1968), 203-8.

944. KAKHK, IU., TARVEL, E., 'Agrarnaia istoriia Estonii - itogi
i zadachi issledovaniia', *Ist. SSSR*, 1 (1971), 58-74.

945. BARANOVICH, A.I., Magnatskoe khoziaistvo na iuge Volyni v
XVIII v. M. 1955. Pp. 182.
Rev: *Vop. Ist.*, 5 (1956), 176-8 (Diadichenko, V.).

946. MELESHKO, V.I., 'Rynochnye sviazi sel'skogo khoziaistva
vostochnoi Belorussii vo vtoroi polovine XVII i v XVIII vv.',
Ezh. A.I. (1966), 193-206.

947. KARPACHEV, A., 'Zemskoe zemlevladenie gorozhan v Belorussii
XVII-XVIII vv.', *Ezh. A.I.* (1966), 206-17.

948. POKHILEVICH, D., CHUGAI, V., 'Korolevskie lesa Belorussii i
Litvy vo vtoroi polovine XVIII v. (proizvodstvo, naselenie)'
Ezh. A.I. (1966), 361-74.

949. KOZLOVSKII, P.G., Magnatskoe khoziaistvo Belorussii vo
vtoroi polovine XVIIIv. (Tsentral'nyi i zapadnye zony).
Minsk 1974. Pp. 182.

950. MELESHKO, V.I., Ocherki agrarnoi istorii vostochnoi
Belorussii (vtoraia polovina XVII-XVIII vv.). Minsk 1975.
Pp.

951. MARKINA, V.A., Magnatskoe pomest'e pravoberezhnoi Ukrainy
vtoroi poloviny XVIII v. (sotsial'no-ekonomicheskoe
razvitie). Kiev 1961. Pp. 232.

952. NEDOSEKIN, V.I., 'Chetvertnoe zemlepol'zovanie odnodvortsev
iuga Rossii v XVIII v.', *Trudy Voronezhskogo Gos. Un-ta*
53, 1 (1960), 28-45.

953. SEKIRINSKII, S.A., 'Nekotorye cherty razvitiia sel'skogo
khoziaistva Kryma i prilegaiushchikh k nemu zemel' iuzhnoi
Ukrainy v kontse XVII-pervoi polovine XIX vv.', *Ezh. A.I.*
(1960), 403-17

954. BOROVOI, S. et al., 'O nekotorykh zakonomernostiakh
razvitiia agrarnykh otnoshenii v iuzhnykh koloniziruemykh
okrainakh evropeiskoi Rossii (1750-1850)', *Ezh. A.I.* (1968),
7-19.

955. DRAGNEV, D., Sel'skoe khoziaistvo feodal'noi Moldavii
(konets XVII-nachalo XIX vv.). Kishinev 1975. Pp. 287.

956. KONDRASHENKOV, A., 'K voprosu o roli "desiatinnoi pashni" v razvitii zemledeliia v Zaural'e i zapadnoi Sibiri v XVIII v.', *Ezh. A.I.*(1965), 177-84.

7(i) - INDUSTRY, CRAFTS AND LABOUR

FALKUS (960) and the Cambridge Economic History of Europe (258) provide general introductions. IATSUNSKII (981) is useful on the late eighteenth and early nineteenth centuries. ISAEV (978) gives valuable statistical information; POLIANSKII is weak on the nature of manufactures (971-2) but strong on crafts (975). On labour, PANKRATOVA (1004), VALK (1013), SEMENOVA (1014) are excellent. The structure of industry: 970-981; heavy industry, 981-993; other branches 994-1003; labour, 1004-1014, 810, 959.

957. GREGORY, P., 'Russian Industrialization and Economic Growth. Results and Perspectives of Western Research', *JbfGO.*, XXV, 2 (1977), 200-218.
Not only eighteenth century, but gives a convenient overview of the subject.

958. TUGAN-BARANOVSKII, M., The Russian Factory in the 19th Century. Homewood, Illinois 1970. Pp. 474.
English translation of T-B's classic *Russkaia fabrika v proshlom i nastoiashchem*. Long introduction on eighteenth century, though now dated.

959. TURIN, S.P., From Peter the Great to Lenin: A History of the Russian Labour Movement. London 1935, reprinted 1968. Pp. 220.

960. FALKUS, M.E., The Industrialization of Russia, 1700-1914. London 1972. Pp. 96.

961. GOLDMANN, M., 'The Relocation and Growth of the Pre-Revolutionary Russian Ferrous Metal Industry', *Ex. Ent. Hist.*, IX (1956), 19-36.
Seventeenth century onwards.

962. KAHAN, A., 'Entrepreneurship in the early development of iron manufacturing in Russia', *Econ. Dev. Cul. Change*, X, 4 (1962), 395-422.

963. KAHAN, A., 'The "Hereditary Workers" thesis and the development of a factory labour force in 18th and 19th century Russia', in: ANDERSON, C.A., BOWMAN, M.J. (eds), Education and Economic Development (Chicago 1965),pp. 291-98.

964. KAHAN, A.,'A proposed Mercantilist Code in the Russian Iron Industry, 1734-1736', *Ex. Ent. Hist.*, 2nd series, II, 2 (1965), 75-89.

965. ALEXANDER, J.T., 'Catherine II, Bubonic Plague and the Problem of Industry in Moscow', *AHR.*, LXXIX, 3 (1974), 637-671.

966. CONFINO, M., 'Maîtres de forges et ouvriers dans les usines métallurgiques de l'Oural aux XVIIIe-XIXe siècles', *CMRS.*, I, 2 (1960), 239-285.

967. ZAOZERSKAIA, E., 'Le salariat dans les manufactures textiles russes au XVIIIe siècle', *CMRS.*, VI, 2 (1965), 189-223.

968. PAVLENKO, N.I., 'Zum Problem der Struktur der russischen Manufaktur im 17-19 Jhdt.', *JfGSLE.*, XIII, 2 (1969), 109-120.

969. WIDERA, B., 'Anfänge der industriellen Grossproduktion und Verbreitung der Lohnarbeit unter den Facharbeitern Russlands im 17. und 18. Jahrhundert', in: HOFFMAN, P., LEMKE, H. (eds), Genesis und Entwicklung des Kapitalismus in Russland (no. 585), pp. 96-128.

970. PORTAL', R., 'Razvitie novoi promyshlennosti v Rossii v XVIII v.', *I.Z.*, vol. 55 (1956), 360-365.

971. POLIANSKII, F.IA., Ekonomicheskii stroi manufaktury v Rossii XVIII veka. M. 1956. Pp. 452.
Rev: *Vop. Ist.*,4 (1957), 150-156 (Vilenskaia, E.S.).

972. POLIANSKII, F.IA., 'Ekonomicheskii stroi manufaktury v Rossii XVIII veka', *Vop. Ist.*, 6 (1956), 74-87.
Part of ongoing discussion.

973. MIKHAILOV, P.I., 'O vozniknovenii kapitalisticheskoi manufaktury v Rossii', *Vop. Ist.*, 2 (1957), 75-84.
Mainly textiles, eighteenth to early nineteenth century.

974. KARPACHEV, A.M., 'O sotsial'no-ekonomicheskoi sushchnosti votchinnoi manufaktury (po materialam belorusskikh manufaktur vtoroi poloviny XVIII veka)', *Vop. Ist.*, 8 (1957), 100-117.
Part of a discussion. Belorussia at this time was part of Poland and 'had not yet undergone the active influence of the more developed Russian economy'.

975. POLIANSKII, F.IA., Gorodskoe remeslo i manufaktura v Rossii v XVIII veke. M. 1960. Pp. 199.

976. RAZGON, A.M., 'Melkotovarnoe proizvodstvo vo vtoroi polovine XVIII v. i genezis kapitalisticheskoi manufaktury', *Ist. SSSR.*, 1 (1960), 63-82.

977. RYBAKOV, IU., 'Programma i organizatsiia sbora svedenii po promyshlennoi statistike Rossii XVIII–XIX vekov. (Vedomosti fabrik i zavodov)', *A. Ezh.* (1964), 107–117.
Became a book on nineteenth-century statistics.

978. ISAEV, G.S., Rol' tekstil'noi promyshlennosti v genezise i razvitii kapitalizma v Rossii, 1760–1860. L. 1970. Pp. 322.

979. INDOVA, E.I., 'O rossiiskikh manufakturakh vtoroi poloviny XVIII v.', in: NAROCHNITSKII (no.1383), pp. 248–345.
Prints official list of Russian factories and manufacturers, 1775.

980. NOSOV, N.E. (ed.), Remeslo i manufaktura v Rossii, Finliandii, Pribaltike. Materialy II Sovietsko-finskogo simpoziuma po sotsial'no-ekonomicheskoi istorii, 13–14 dek. 1972. L. 1975. Pp. 199.
Title, summaries, table of contents also in Finnish and German.

981. IATSUNSKII, V.K., 'Krupnaia promyshlennost' Rossii v 1790–1860 gg.', in: ROZHKOVA, M. (ed.), Ocherki ekonomicheskoi istorii Rossii pervoi poloviny XIX v. (M. 1959), pp. 118–220.

982. PAVLENKO, N.I., Istoriia metallurgii v Rossii XVIII veka. Zavody i zavodovladel'tsy. M. 1962. Pp. 564.
Rev: *Vop. Ist.*, 12 (1963) (Ustiugov, N.V.).

983. STRUMILIN, S.G., Istoriia chernoi metallurgii v SSSR. |Izbrannye proizvedeniia|. M. 1967. Pp. 441.

984. KOZLOV, A.G. et al. (eds), Gornozavodskaia promyshlennost' Urala na rubezhe XVIII–XIX vv. Sbornik dokumental'nykh materialov. Sverdlovsk 1956. Pp. 297.

985. PAVLENKO, N.I., 'O proiskhozhdenii kapitalov, vlozhennykh v metallurgiiu Rossii XVIII v.', *I.Z.*, vol. 62 (1958), 170–197.

986. PREOBRAZHENSKII, A.A., 'Iz istorii pervykh chastnykh zavodov na Urale v nachale XVIII v', *I.Z.*, vol. 63 (1958), 156–179.

987. BALAGUROV, IA.A., Olonetskie gornye zavody v doreformennyi period. Petrozavodsk 1958. Pp. 211.

988. NEDOSEKIN, V.I., 'Metallurgicheskaia promyshlennost' chernozemnogo tsentra Rossii XVIII veka', *Izv. Voronezhsk. Gos. Ped. In-ta*, XXXI (1960).

989. PAVLENKO, N.I., 'Instruktsii zavodskim prikazchikam A.N. Demidova', *Ist. Arkhiv.*, 5 (1962), 148–160.

990. KAZANTSEV, R., Na starom ural'skom zavode. Perm 1966.
Pp. 124.
Includes eighteenth-century steam engine building.

991. ZAOZERSKAIA, E.I., U istokov krupnogo proizvodstva v
russkoi promyshlennosti XVI-XVIII vv. K voprosu o genezise
kapitalizma v Rossii. M. 1970. Pp. 474.

992. CHERKASOVA, A.S., 'Gornozavodskaia manufaktura i protsess
gorodoobrazovaniia v Rossii XVIII v.', I.Z., vol. 93
(1973), 293-308.

993. KOZYREVA, Z.P., MOLCHANOV, V.N. et al. (eds), Istoriia
Tul'skogo oruzheinogo zavoda, 1712-1972. M. 1973.
Pp. 494.
Rev: Vop. Ist., no. 5 (1974), 152-4 (Tumanov, A.S.).
Emphasis on later period.

994. LUK'IANOV, P., Istoriia khimicheskikh promyslov i
khimicheskoi promyshlennosti Rossii do kontsa XIX v. 6
vols. M.-L. 1946-65.

995. PAZHITNOV, K.A., Ocherki istorii tekstil'noi
promyshlennosti dorevoliutsionnoi Rossii. Sherstianaia
promyshlennost'. M. 1955. Pp. 247.
Pp. 9-29 on eighteenth century.

996. PAZHITNOV, K., Ocherki istorii tekstil'noi promyshlennosti
dorevoliutsionnoi Rossii. Khlopchatobumazhnaia, l'no-pen'-
kovaia i shelkovaia promyshlennost'. M. 1958. Pp. 423.
Companion volume to no. 995.

997. DANILOVA, L., 'Melkaia promyshlennost' i promysly v russkom
gorode vo vtoroi polovine XVII-nachale XVIII v.', Ist.
SSSR., 3 (1957), 87-111.

998. VOLKOV, M., 'Kupecheskie kozhevennye predpriatiia pervoi
chetverti XVIII v.', Ist. SSSR., 1 (1966), 138-151.

999. TSEITLIN, M., Ocherki razvitiia lesozagotovok i
lesopileniia v Rossii. M. 1968. Pp. 295.

1000. SERBINA, K.N., Krest'ianskaia zhelezodelatel'naia
promyshlennost' severo-zapada Rossii XVI-pervoi poloviny
XIX vv. L. 1971. Pp. 264.
Rev: Vop. Ist., 8 (1973), 157-9 (Kolesnikov, P.A.).

1001. EFREMOVA, I. et al. (comps), Istoriia fabrik i zavodov
Gor'kovskoi oblasti. Ukazatel' literatury. Gor'kii 1974.
Pp. 386.

1002. RUBINSHTEIN, E.I., Polotnianaia i bumazhnaia manufaktura
Goncharovykh vo vtoroi polovine XVIII v. M. 1975. Pp. 166.

1002a. VOLKOV, M., Ocherki istorii promyslov Rossii vtoraia
pol. XVII-pervaia pol. XVIII v. Vinokurennoe proizvodstvo. M. 1979. Pp. 335.

1003. VOLKOV, M., 'Promyshlennost' sela Pavlova v nachale
      XVIII v.', *I.Z.*, 99 (1977), 357-374.

1004. PANKRATOVA, A.M., Formirovanie proletariata v Rossii
      (XVII-XVIII vv.). M. 1963. Pp. 489.
      Rev: *JbfGO.*, N.F., XIV, 1 (1966), 117-9 (Von Laue, T.).

1005. VORONOV, N.V., 'O rynke rabochei sily v Rossii v XVIII
      veke. (Po materialam kirpichnoi promyshlennosti)', *Vop.
      Ist.*, 3 (1955), 90-99.

1006. PAVLENKO, N.I., 'Naemnyi trud v metallurgicheskoi
      promyshlennosti Rossii vo vtoroi polovine XVIII veka',
      Vop. Ist., 6 (1958), 41-58.

1007. RUBINSHTEIN, E.I., 'Rabochaia sila na possessionnoi
      manufakture Goncharovykh vo vtoroi polovine XVIII v.',
      Ist. SSSR., 1 (1958), 160-176.

1008. ZAOZERSKAIA, E.I., Rabochaia sila i klassovaia bor'ba na
      tekstil'nykh manufakturakh v 20-60 XVIII v. M. 1960.
      Pp. 449.

1009. KARPENKO, Z., 'Formirovanie rabochikh kadrov v gornozavod-
      skoi promyshlennosti zapadnoi Sibiri (1725-1860 gg.)',
      I.Z., vol. 69 (1961), 222-252.

1010. ARTEMENKOV, M.N., 'Naemnye rabochie moskovskikh manufaktur
      v 40-70-kh godakh XVIII v.', *Ist. SSSR.*, 2 (1964), 133-44.

1011. GOLIKOVA, N.B., 'Iz istorii formirovaniia kadrov naemnykh
      rabotnikov v pervoi chetverti XVIII v.', *Ist. SSSR.*, 1
      (1965), 75-93.

1012. GOLIKOVA, N.B., Naemnyi trud v gorodakh Povolzh'ia v pervoi
      chetverti XVIII veka. M. 1965. Pp. 174.

1013. VALK, S.N. et al. (eds), Istoriia rabochikh Leningrada,
      1703-1965. 2 vols. L. 1972. Pp. 556, 460.
      Rev: *SR.*, XXXIII, 3 (1974), 522-7 (Zelnik, R.).

1014. SEMENOVA, L.N., Rabochie Peterburga v pervoi polovine
      XVIII v. L. 1974. Pp. 214.
      Rev: *SGECRN*, 3 (1975), 57-61 (Hollingsworth, B.).

SYMONS (1015) is disappointing: in general, transportation is a neglected field (see also 1028-9). KOVAL'CHENKO (1020) is an impressive piece of scholarship which opened new perspectives.

1015. SYMONS, L., WHITE, C.I. (eds), Russian Transport: An Historical and Geographical Survey. London 1975. Pp. 192. Eighteenth-century merchant marine and river transport. Mostly on nineteenth and twentieth centuries, however.

1016. DREW, R.F., 'The Siberian Fair, 1600-1750', *SEER.*, 39 (1960-1), 423-39.

1017. AMBURGER, E., 'Zur Geschichte des Grosshandels in Russland: die Gosti', *Vierteljahrschrift für Sozial- und Wirtschaftsgeschichte* 46, 2 (1959), 248-261.

1018. KAFENGAUZ, B.B., Ocherki vnutrennego rynka Rossii pervoi poloviny XVIII v. M. 1958. Pp. 356.

1019. STRUMILIN, S.G., 'O vnutrennem rynke Rossii XVI-XVIII vv. (po povodu knigi B.B. Kafengauza)', *Ist. SSSR.*, 3 (1959), 75-87.

1020. KOVAL'CHENKO, I.S., MILOV, L., Vserossiiskii agrarnyi rynok XVIII-nachalo XX veka. M. 1974. Pp. 412. Cp. their article in *Ist. SSSR.*, 1 (1969), 27-57. Rev: *Vop. Ist.* 9 (1975), 164-70 (Kakhk I., Ryndziunskii, P.).

1021. BASHARIN, G.P., 'Rynok Iakutii kontsa XVIII - pervoi poloviny XIX vv.', *I.Z.*, vol. 55 (1956), 289-309.

1022. SHUL'GA, I.G., 'K voprosu o razvitii vserossiiskogo rynka vo vtoroi polovine XVIII veka (po materialam levoberezhnoi Ukrainy)', *Vop. Ist.*, 10 (1958), 35-45.

1023. VOLKOV, V.M., 'Iz istorii bor'by za ukrainskii rynok vo vtoroi chetverti XVIII v.', *VMU(Ist.)*, 1 (1961), 43-58.

1024. TROITSKII, S.M., 'Ustiuzhskii khlebnyi rynok v pervoi chetverti XVIII v.', *Ezh. A.I.* (1966), 234-42.

1025. VARTENOV, G.L., 'Gorodskie iarmarki tsentral'noi chasti evropeiskoi Rossii vo vtoroi polovine XVIII v.' *Uchenye Zapiski Leningradsk. Gos. Ped. In-ta*, 194 (1958), 137-68.

1026. VARTENOV, G.L., 'Kupechestvo i torguiushchee krest'ianstvo tsentral'noi chasti evropeiskoi Rossii vo 2-oi polovine XVIII v.', in: MAVRODIN (ed.) (no. 843), pp. 161-80.

1027. ALEKSANDROV, V., 'Nachalo Irbitskoi iarmarki', *Ist. SSSR.*, 6 (1974), 36-57.

1028. MAL'TSEVA, N.A. (ed.), BUNINA, F.I. et al. (comps).
Materialy po istorii sviazi v Rossii, XVIII-nachalo XX vv.
Obzor dokumental'nykh materialov. L. 1966. Pp. 335.

1029. ISTOMINA, E.G., 'Vyshnevolotskii vodnyi put' vo vtoroi
polovine XVIII-nachale XIX v.', in: NAROCHNITSKII (no.
1383), pp. 193-206.

7(k) – CURRENCY, FINANCE, BANKING, TAXATION, PRICES.

SPASKII's work, available in English and Russian (1030, 1037),
is complemented by DIACHKOV (1038). The works of TROITSKII on
state budget and finances (1051-54) and of MIRONOV on prices
(1044-49) are essential contributions, though the latter's
failure to allow for the Amsterdam market must be made good
from R ILEY (2652).

1030. SPASSKY, I.G., The Russian Monetary System. A historico-
numismatic survey. Rev. ed., Amsterdam 1967. Pp. 256.
Illustrated. Trans. from third Russian ed. M. 1962.

1031. HARRIS, R.P., A Guidebook of Russian Coins, 1725-1970.
Santa Cruz 1971. Pp. 160.

1032. BREKKE, B., The Copper Coinage of Imperial Russia, 1700-
1917. Malmo 1977. Pp.296.
Highly informative account.

1032a. LE DONNE, J., ' Indirect Taxes in Catherine's Russia: The
Salt Code of 1781', *JbfGO.*, N.F. 23 (1975), 161-91.

See also his article on the liquor monopoly in
the above journal,(1976),pp. 173-207.

1033. CROSS, A.G., 'The Sutherland Affair and its Aftermath',
SEER., L, 119 (1972), 257-275.
Sutherland was court banker to Catherine II.

1034. McGREW, R., 'The Politics of Absolutism: Paul I and the
Bank of Assistance for the Nobility', *CanAmSlSt.*, VII, I
(1973), 15-39.

1035. BUIST, M.G., At Spes Non Fracta. Hope and Co., 1770-1817:
merchant bankers and diplomats at work. The Hague 1974.
Pp. 716.
Dutch loans to Russia 1780-1800.

1036. MICHAILOVITCH, G., Grand Duc., Monnaies de l'Empire de
Russie 1725-1894. Trans. by Tacké, N. Boston 1973.
Reprint of 1916 French edition, with new foreword. Pp. 657.
Rev: *CanAmSlSt.*, V, 1 (1975), 116.

1037. SPASSKII, I.G., Russkaia monetnaia sistema; istoriko-
numismaticheskii ocherk. 4th rev. ed. L. 1970. Pp. 255.

1038. DIACHKOV, A., UZDENIKOV, V., Monety Rossii i SSSR. M. 1978.
Pp. 650.

1039. KLIUCHEVSKII, V.O., 'Russkii rubl' XVI-XVIII v. v ego
otnoshenii k nyneshnemu', in: Sochineniia (no. 268), VII
(M. 1959), pp. 170-236.

1040. TROITSKII, S.M., 'Iz istorii russkogo rublia', *Vop. Ist.*,
1 (1961), 59-75.
Five-hundred-year survey shows that coinage in hands of
ruling classes is a powerful weapon of exploitation.

1041. BOROVOI, S.IA., Kredit i banki v Rossii, seredina XVII v.-
1861 g. M.-L. 1958. Pp. 288.

1042. BOROVOI, S.IA., 'Voprosy kreditovaniia torgovli i
promyshlennosti v ekonomicheskoi politike Rossii XVIII v.',
I.Z., vol. 33, 92-122.

1043. PAVLOVA-SIL'VANSKAIA, M., 'O kharaktere innostrannykh
zaimov v Rossii vo vtoroi polovine XVIII v.', in: PASHUTO
(no. 612), pp. 81-91.

1044. MIRONOV, B.N., 'Dvizhenie tsen rzhi v Rossii v XVIII v.',
Ezh. A.I. (1965), 156-63.

1045. MIRONOV, B.N., 'O metodike obrabotki istochnikov po istorii
tsen. K issledovaniiu problemy obrazovaniia
vserossiiskogo natsional'nogo rynka', *A. Ezh.* (1968), 154-
65.

1046. MIRONOV, B.N., 'O dostovernosti vedomostei o khlebnykh
tsenakh XVIII v.', in: Vspomogatel'nye istoricheskie
distsipliny, vyp. 2 (1969), pp. 249-62.

1047. MIRONOV, B.N., 'Statisticheskaia obrabotka otvetov na
senatskie ankety 1767 g., o prichinakh rosta khlebnykh
tsen', in: Materialy i metody v istoricheskikh
issledovaniiakh (M. 1971).

1048. MIRONOV, B.N., '"Revoliutsiia tsen" v Rossii v XVIII veke',
Vop. Ist., I (1971), 49-61.

1049. MIRONOV, B.N., 'Dvizhenie khlebnykh tsen v Rossii v 1801-
1914 gg.', *Vop. Ist.*, 2 (1975), 45-57.

1050. ANISIMOV, E., 'Materialy Komissii D.M. Golitsyna o podati
(1727-1730 gg.)', *I.Z.*, vol. 91 (1973), 338-352.

1051. TROITSKII, S.M., 'Istochniki dokhodov v biudzhete Rossii v
seredine XVIII v. (20-60e gody)', *Ist. SSSR.*, 3 (1957),
176-198.

1052. TROITSKII, S.M., 'Iz istorii finansov v Rossii v seredine
XVIII v.', *Ist. Arkhiv.*, 2 (1957), 122-35.

1053. TROITSKII, S.M., 'Iz istorii sostavleniia biudzheta v
Rossii v seredine XVIII v.', *I.Z.*, vol. 78 (1965), 181-203.

1054. TROITSKII, S.M., Finansovaia politika russkogo absoliutizma
v XVIII veke. M. 1966. Pp. 275.
Rev: *Kritika*, III, 2 (1967), 1-10 (Okenfuss, M.); *Vop.
Ist.*, 7 (1968), 158-60 (Demidova, N.F.).

7(l) - FOREIGN TRADE, INTERNAL AND EXTERNAL TARIFFS

EHRMAN (1058) and WILLIAMS (1059) give a good view of British
trade generally, but are weak on Russia. TROITSKII (1098-99)
broadens the picture of Russian government attitudes (the old
standard on this, by Firsov, has been reprinted), while his and
other studies of individual ports and markets (1102-07, 1116,
1118) have filled in much concrete detail. VOLKOV (1124) deals
with an important and neglected aspect of Anglo-Russian commercial relations, for which CLENDENNING (1070-1) provides the
background. On tariffs LODYZHENSKII (1121) is still the best.

FOREIGN TRADE

1055. KIRCHNER, W., Commercial Relations Between Russia and
Europe, 1400 to 1800: Collected Essays. Bloomington 1966.
Pp. 332.
Several items on eighteen century including French-Russian
trade.

1056. KELLENBENZ, H., 'The Economic Significance of the
Archangel Route (from the late 16th to the late 18th
Century)', *JEEcH.*, II, 3 (1973), 541-581.

1057. KAHAN, A., 'Observations on Petrine Foreign Trade',
CanAmSlSt., VIII, 2 (1974), 222-237.

1058. EHRMAN, J., The British Government and Commercial
Negotiations with Europe, 1783-1793. Cambridge, England
1962. Pp. 231.

1059. WILLIAMS, Judith B., British Commercial Policy and Trade
Expansion, 1750-1850; with a bibliographical chapter by
David M. Williams. Oxford 1972. Pp. 514.

1060. HUNT, N., 'The Russia Company and the Government, 1730-
1742', *OSP.*, VII (1957), 27-65.

1061. HILDEBRAND, K., 'Foreign Markets for Swedish Iron in the
Eighteenth Century', *Scand. Econ. Hist. Rev.*, VI, 1 (1958),
3-52.

1062. PRICE, J., 'The Tobacco Venture to Russia: Enterprise,
Politics and Diplomacy in the Quest for a Northern Market
for English Colonial Tobacco, 1676-1722', *Transactions of
the American Philosophical Society*, N.S., LI, Pt. 1 (1961),
1-118.

1063. ÅSTRÖM, S.E., From Stockholm to St. Petersburg: commercial
factors in the political relations between England and
Sweden 1675-1700. Helsinki 1962. Pp. 146.

1064. ÅSTRÖM, S.E., From Cloth to Iron: The Anglo-Baltic trade in
the late 17th Century. 2 vols. Helsingfors 1963-5.
Overlaps to 1710; good bibliography.

1065. KIRBY, D.G., 'The Balance of the North and Baltic Trade:
George Mackenzie's Relation, August 1715', *SEER.*, LIV, 3
(1976), 429-451.

1066. MACMILLAN, D.S., 'The Scottish-Russian Trade: Its
Development, Fluctuations,and Difficulties, 1750-1796',
CanAmSlSt., IV, 3 (1970), 426-442.

1067. MACMILLAN, D.S., 'The Russia Company of London in the
Eighteenth Century: The Effective survival of a "Regulated"
Chartered Company', *The Guildhall Miscellany*, IV (February-
April 1973), 222-235.

1068. MACMILLAN, D.S., 'Paul's "Retributive Measures" of 1800
Against Britain: The Final Turning-Point in British
Commercial Attitudes towards Russia', *CanAmSlSt.*, VII, 1
(1973), 68-78.

1069. MACMILLAN, D.S., 'Problems in the Scottish Trade with Russia
in the Eighteenth Century: A Study in Mercantile
Frustration', in: CROSS (ed.), *Proceedings* (no. 1794),
pp. 164-181.

1070. CLENDENNING, P.H., 'The Anglo-Russian Commercial Treaty of
1766', Cambridge Ph.D., 1976.

1071. CLENDENNING, P.H., 'The Background and Negotiations for the
Anglo-Russian Commercial Treaty of 1766', in: CROSS (ed.),
Proceedings (no. 1794), pp. 145-64.

1072. HAUTA, K., European and American Tar in the English Market
during the 18th and 19th Centuries. Helsinki 1963.
Pp. 180.

1073. DURIE, A.J., 'Linen, Flax and Iron: The British Linen
Company and the Baltic', *SGECRN.*, 3 (1975), 29-40.

1074. KAHAN, A., 'Eighteenth-Century Russian-British Trade.
Russia's Contribution to the Industrial Revolution in Great
Britain', in: CROSS (ed.), *Proceedings* (no. 1794),
pp. 181-190.

1075. FOX, F., 'French-Russian Commercial Relations in the
Eighteenth Century and The French-Russian Commercial Treaty
of 1787', Delaware Ph.D., 1966. See also nos. 1212,1217.

1076. FOX, F., 'A view of French-Russian Trade Relations in the
Eighteenth Century: The Ms. Le Gendre', *JbfGO.*, N.F., XVI,
4 (1968), 481-98.

1077. FREDERICHSON, J.W., 'American Shipping in the Trade with
Northern Europe, 1783-1880', *Scand. Econ. Hist. Rev.*, IV, 2
(1956), 110-25.

1078. CROSBY, A.W., 'The Beginnings of Trade Between the United
States and Russia', *Am. Neptune*, 21 (1961), 207-15.

1079. CROSBY, A.W., America, Russia, Hemp and Napoleon.
(American trade with Russia and the Baltic 1783-1812).
Columbus, Ohio 1965. Pp. 320.
Based on Boston Ph.D., 1961.

1080. RASCH, A.A., 'American Trade in the Baltic, 1783-1807',
Scand. Econ. Hist. Rev., XIII (1965), 44-49.

1081. SAUL, N.E., 'Beginnings of American-Russian Trade, 1763-
1766', *Wm. and Mary Qtly.*, 3rd Series (1969), 596-600.

1082. BOLKHOVITINOV, N.N., 'Russo-American Trade Relations
during the U.S. War of Independence', *Vop. Ist.*, 1 (1975),
49-57, trans. in *Soviet Studies in History*, XIV, 3
(1975-6), 29-45.

1083. KNOPPERS, J., Dutch Trade with Russia from the time of
Peter I to Alexander I: A Quantitative Study in Eighteenth
Century Shipping. Montreal 1976. 3 vols.
Tables, charts. Rev: *CanAmSlSt.*, XII (1978),185-6 (Unger,R.).

1084. HERLIHY, P.A.M., 'Russian Grain and Mediterranean Markets
1774-1861', Pennsylvania Ph.D., 1963.

1085. HERLIHY, P.A.M., 'Russian Wheat and the Port of Livorno,
1794-1861', *JEEcH.*, V, 1 (1976), 45-68.

1086. SLADKOVSKII, M., History of Economic Relations Between
Russia and China. Trans. from the Russian by M. Roublev.
Jerusalem 1966. Pp. 299. See nos. 1119, 1206.

1087. WHEELER, M.E., 'The Origins of the Russian-American
Company', *JbfGO.*, XIV, 4 (1966), 485-494.
Corrects Okun"s account.

1088. FERRIER, R.W., 'The Armenians and the East India Company in
Persia in the Seventeenth and Early Eighteenth Centuries',
Econ. Hist. Rev., Second Series, XXVI, 1 (1973), 38-62.
Persian-Russian trade. Material based on Cambridge Ph.D.,
1971.

7-Foreign trade/tariffs   97

1089.   JEANNIN, P., 'Les comptes du Sund comme source pour la
        construction d'indices généraux de l'activité économique
        en Europe (XVI-XVIIIe siècles)', *Revue Historique*, 231
        (1964), 55-102, 307-340.

1090.   CADOT, M., REGEMORTER, J.L. van, 'Le commerce extérieur de
        la Russie en 1784, d'après le journal de voyage de Baert
        du Hollant', *CMRS.*, X, 2 (1969), 371-91.

1091.   GIROD DE L'AIN, G., 'Le commerce de Marseille avec la
        Russie à la fin du XVIII s.', *Marseille (revue municipale)*
        série 3, no. 89 (1972), 7-13.

1092.   REYCHMAN, J., 'Le commerce polonais en Mer Noire au XVIIIe
        siècle par le port de Kherson', *CMRS.*, VII, 1 (1966),
        234-8.

1093.   MIKHOV, N.V., Contributions à l'Histoire du Commerce de la
        Turquie et de la Bulgarie, vol. 6: Auteurs Français,
        Allemands et Anglais. Sofia 1970. Pp. 573.
        24 essays on eighteenth century Balkan economy and trade
        with Europe.

1093a. AMBURGER, E., 'Russische Handelsagenten und
        Handelslehrlinge im Auslande. Missglückte Versuche aus der
        Mitte des 18. Jahrhunderts', *JbfGO.*, N.F., XIV, 1 (1966),
        161-66.

1094.   AMBURGER, E., 'Das neuzeitliche Narva als Wirtschaftsfaktor
        zwischen Russland und Estland', *JbfGO.*, N.F., XV, 1 (1967),
        197-208.

1095.   ELIAS, O.H., 'Revaler Handelsschiffahrt im 18-ten
        Jahrhundert', *JbfGO.*, N.F., XV, 1 (1967), 16-28.

1096.   ETZOLD, G., Seehandel und Kaufleute in Reval nach dem
        Frieden von Nystad bis zur Mitte des 18. Jahrhunderts.
        Marburg/Lahn 1975. Pp. 245.

1097.   ELSINGER, F., Die Juchtenlederherstellung im Wandel der
        Zeiten. 7 vols, Wien 1975.
        Vol. 6: Austro-Russian leather trade 1775-1800.

1098.   TROITSKII, S.M., 'Novyi istochnik po istorii
        ekonomicheskoi mysli v Rossii v seredine XVIII v.
        "Rassuzhdenie o rossiiskoi kommertsii" sekretaria Senata
        F.I. Sukina)', *A. Ezh.* (1966), 425-436.

1099.   TROITSKII, S.M., 'Zapiska senatora N.E. Murav'eva o
        razvitii kommertsii i putei soobshcheniia v Rossii (60-e
        gody XVIII v.)', in: NAROCHNITSKII (no. 1383), pp. 234-247.

1100.   RUBINSHTEIN, N.L., 'Vneshniaia torgovlia Rossii i russkoe
        kupechestvo vo vtoroi polovine XVIII v.', *I.Z.*, vol. 54,
        (1955), 343-361.

1101. KOZINTSEVA, R.I., 'Uchastie kazny vo vneshnei torgovle
Rossii v pervoi chetverti XVIII v.', *I.Z.*, vol. 91 (1973),
267-337.

1102. TROITSKII, S.M., 'Rynok Arkhangel'ska v pervoi chetverti
XVIII v.', *Trudy Istoriko-Arkhivnogo Instituta*, vyp. 9
(1956).

1103. REPIN, N.N., 'Iz istorii torgovykh sviazei Rossii so
stranami zapadnoi Evropy cherez Arkhangel'ska v pervoi
chetverti XVIII v.', *Sb. nauchnykh rabot aspirantov Ist.
Fak. MGU* (1970), 196-215.

1104. REPIN, N.N., 'K voprosu o sviazi vneshnego i vnutrennego
rynka Rossii vo vtoroi polovine XVII-pervoi chetverti
XVIII v. (po materialam Arkhangel'skogo porta)', *VMU(Ist.)*,
6 (1970), 56-72.

1105. KOZINTSEVA, R., 'Vneshnetorgovyi oborot Arkhangel'gorodskoi
iarmarki i ee rol' v razvitii vserossiiskogo rynka',
in: Issledovaniia po istorii feodal'no-krepostnoi Rossii
(no. 605), pp. 116-63.

1106. MIRONOV, B.N., 'K voprosu o roli russkogo kupechestva vo
vneshnei torgovle Peterburga i Arkhangel'ska vo vtoroi
polovine XVIII-nachale XIX veka', *Ist. SSSR.*, 6 (1973),
129-141.

1107. MIRONOV, B.N., 'Eksport russkogo khleba vo vtoroi polovine
XVIII-nachale XIX v.', *I.Z.*, vol. 93 (1974), 149-188.

1108. ATTMAN, A., NAROCHNITSKII, A. (eds), Ekonomicheskie sviazi
mezhdu Rossiei i Shvetsiei v XVIII v. M. 1978. Pp. 296.

1109. BIRON, A. (ed.), Ekonomicheskie svyazi Pribaltiki s
Rossiei. Sbornik statei. Riga 1968. Pp. 284.
Foreign trade and agricultural development. Baltic river
trade routes.

1110. STRODS, KH., 'Vliianie torgovoi politiki Rossiiskoi imperii
na razvitie sel'kogo khoziaistva Latvii v XVIII veke',
in: BIRON (no. 1109), pp. 146-172.

1111. KOMISSARENKO, A., SHARKOVA, I., 'Dokumenty ob ustanovlenii
priamykh russko-ital'ianskikh torgovykh sviazei v seredine
XVIII veka', *Sovetskie arkhivy*, 2 (1972), 89-100.

1112. KOMISSARENKO, A., SHARKOVA, I., 'K istorii russko-ital'-
ianskoi torgovli v 40-50 kh godakh XVIII v.', *I.Z.*, vol. 98
(1977), 313-330.

1113. KUKANOVA, N.G., Ocherki po istorii russko-iranskikh
torgovykh otnoshenii v XVII-pervoi polovine XIX veka.
Saransk 1977. Pp. 284.
Best account available.

1114. MARKOVA, O.P., 'Russko-iranskaia torgovlia v poslednie desiatletiia XVIII veka', *Uchenye zapiski Instituta Vostokovedeniia* (Baku), I (1959), 103-115.

1115. IUKHT, A.I., 'Torgovlia Rossii s Zakavkaz'em i Persiei vo vtoroi chetverti XVIII veka', *Ist. SSSR.*,1 (1961), 131-146.

1116. IUKHT, A.I., 'Torgovye sviazi Astrakhani v 20-kh gg. XVIII v.', in: NAROCHNITSKII (no. 1383), pp. 177-92.

1117. ANTONOVA, K.A. (ed.), Russko-indiiskie otnosheniia v XVIII veke. Sb. dokumentov. M. 1965. Pp. 654. Mainly economic relations through Persia, based on Astrakhan customs records.

1118. MATVIEVSKII, P.E., 'O roli Orenburga v russko-indiiskoi torgovle v XVIII v.', *Ist. SSSR.*, 3 (1969), 98-111.

1119. SLADKOVSKII, M.I., Ocherki ekonomicheskikh otnoshenii SSSR s Kitaem. M. 1957. Pp. 455. See also nos.1206, 1086.

1120. VILKOV, O.N., 'Kitaiskie tovary na Tobol'skom rynke v XVIII v.', *Ist. SSSR.*, 1 (1958), 105-124.

INTERNAL AND EXTERNAL TARIFFS

1121. LODYZHENSKII, K., Istoriia russkogo tamozhennogo tarifa. St. P., 1886, reprinted ORP.,Cambridge, Eng. 1972. Pp. 410. Rev: *SEER.*, 57, 1 (1979), 153-4 (Crisp, O.).

1122. KAFENGAUZ, B.B., 'Tamozhennye knigi XVIII veka', *A. Ezh.*, (1957), 127-137.

1123. KOSINTSEVA, R., 'Ot tamozhennogo tarifa 1724 g. k tarifu 1731 g.', in: MAVRODIN (no. 603), pp. 182-216.

1124. VOLKOV, M.I., 'Tamozhennaia reforma 1753-1757 gg.', *I.Z.*, vol. 71 (1973), 134-157.

1125. KOPYLOV, A., 'Iz istorii tamozhennogo dela v Sibiri', *A. Ezh.* (1964), 350-371.

Recent coverage of topics in this area has been rather patchy.
See also sections on military history, foreign trade, cultural
relations, local and regional history. Arrangement is by countries or regions, with chronological sequence by subject within
each sub-section.

GENERAL   See also no. 501.

1126. ISRAEL, F.L. (ed.), Major Peace Treaties of Modern History,
1645-1967. N.Y. 1967. 4 vols.

1127. ANDERSON, M.S., 'Eighteenth Century Theories of the Balance
of Power', in: HATTON, R., ANDERSON, M.S. (eds), Studies in
Diplomatic History; Essays in memory of D.B. Horn   (London
1970), pp. 183-195.

1128. BOHLEN, A., 'Changes in Russian Diplomacy under Peter the
Great', *CMRS.*, VII, 3 (1966), 341-58.

1129. BUTLER, W.E., 'Anglo-Russian Diplomacy and the Law of
Nations', in: CROSS (ed.), *Proceedings* (no. 1794), pp. 296-
305.

1130. KAPLAN, H.H., Russia and the outbreak of the Seven Years'
War. Berkeley 1968. Pp. 165.
Traditional diplomatic approach.

1131. GRIFFITHS, D.M., 'Russian Court Politics and the Question
of an Expansionist Foreign Policy under Catherine II,
1762-1783', Cornell Ph.D., 1967.

1132. GRIFFITHS, D.M., 'The Rise and Fall of the Northern
System: Court Politics and Foreign Policy in the First Half
of Catherine II's Reign', *CanAmSlSt.*, IV, 3 (1970), 547-69.

1133. RAGSDALE, H. (ed.), 'Documents on the Foreign Policy of
Paul I from the Former Prussian Archives', *CanAmSlSt.*,
VII, 1 (1973), 106-112.

1134. SAUL, N.E., Russia and the Mediterranean, 1797-1807.
Chicago-London 1970. Pp. 268.
Based on Ph.D. dissertation, Columbia 1965.

1135. GRIMSTED, P.K., The Foreign Ministers of Alexander I:
Political Attitudes and the Conduct of Russian Diplomacy,
1801-1825. Berkeley 1969. Pp. 367.

1136. THADDEN, R. von, et al. (eds), Das Vergangene und die
Geschichte.Festschrift für R. Wittram. Göttingen 1973.
Pp. 472.

1137. AMBURGER, E., 'Das Personal des russischen auswärtigen Dienstes unter Peter I', in: THADDEN (no. 1136), pp. 298-311.

1138. STASZEWSKI, J., 'Die Mission des Fürsten Boris Kurakin nach Rom im Jahre 1707', in: *Ost und West* (no. 1737), pp. 200-214.

1139. KLUETING, H., 'Graf Ostermann - Ein Westfale als verantwortlicher Leiter der russischen Aussenpolitik in den Jahren 1725 bis 1741' *Westfälische Zeitschrift*, 126/7 (1976), I Abtg., 61-90. (See also 1529-1531).

1140. KLUETING, H., 'Die Projekte des Jacob Pistorius aus Mecklenburg und die Politik des Grafen Ostermann', *JbfGO.*, XXV, 1 (1977), 52-66.

1141. DONNERT, E., 'Zur aussenpolitischen Ideologie der russischen Gesellschaft in der zweiten Halfte des 18. Jhdts', *ZfSl.*, XIX (1974), 70-3.

1142. RAHBEK-SCHMIDT, K., 'Wie ist Panins Plan zu einem Nordischen System entstanden?', *ZfSl.*, II (1957), 406-22.

1143. GROMYKO, A.A. et al. (eds), Diplomaticheskii slovar'. M. 1971-3. 3 vols. Pp. 611, 590, 719.

1144. GROMYKO, A.A. et al. (eds), Istoriia diplomatii. 2nd ed. 5 vols. M. 1959-74.
Eighteenth century: Vol. I, 319-458.

1145. BESKROVNYI, L. et al. (eds), Mezhdunarodnye sviazi Rossii v XVII-XVIII vv.: Ekonomika, Politika i Kul'tura. Sb. statei. M. 1966. Pp. 506.
Essays: Russia and China (Skachkov); A.L. Schlözer in Russia (Cherepnin); German-Russian relations and South Ukraine (Druzhinina); Russian-Swedish trade in 1720s (Nekrasov); Holland and Peter I (Winter); French-Russian cultural relations (Baklanova); Rousseau in Russia (Shtrange); Russian-Hungarian relations in early 1700s (Pereni); Russian-Hungarian economic and cultural relations (Stern); Russia and Bosphorus, 1711-14 (Krylov); Russia and USA (Startsev); Russia and Japan (Konstantinov).

1146. FEIGINA, S.A., Alandskii kongress. Vneshniaia politika Rossii v kontse Severnoi Voiny. M. 1959. Pp. 546.
Rev: *Vop. Ist.*, 7 (1962), 135-7 (Stanislavskaia, A.M.).

1147. NIKIFOROV, L.A., Vneshniaia politika Rossii v poslednie gody Severnoi Voiny. Nishtadskii mir. M. 1959. Pp. 496.

1148. SHASKOL'SKII, I.P., 'Vazhnaia predposylka bor'by Rossii za Baltiku v XVII-nachale XXIII v.', in: PASHUTO (no. 612) pp. 368-73.

1149. NEKRASOV, G.A., 'Mezhdunarodnoe priznanie rossiiskogo velikoderzhaviia v XVIII v.', in: PASHUTO (no. 612), pp. 381-8.

1150. NEKRASOV, G.A., Rol' Rossii v evropeiskoi mezhdunarodnoi politike 1725-39 gg. M. 1976. Pp. 319.
Rev: *AHR.*, 83, 1 (1978), 230-1 (Ransel, D.).

1151. TROITSKII, S.M., 'Russkie diplomaty v seredine XVIII v.', in: PASHUTO (no. 612), pp. 398-406.

1152. FRUMENKOV, G.G., 'Rossiia i semiletniaia voina 1756-1763 gg.', *Vop. Ist.*, 9 (1971), 107-19.

AMERICA

1153. GADDIS, J.L., Russia, the Soviet Union, and the United States: An Interpretative History. N.Y. 1978. Pp. 309.
Rev: *RH.*, V, 2 (1978), 243-4 (Gilbert, D.).

1154. GRIFFITHS, D.M., 'Soviet Views of Early Russian-American Relations', *Proceedings of the American Philosophical Society*, 116, 2 (1972), 148-56.
Bibliographic survey of Soviet writings on the American Revolution.

1155. BOLKHOVITINOV, N.N., trans. and ed. SMITH, C.J., Russia and the American Revolution. Tallahassee, Fla. 1976. Pp. 277. Translation of no. 1847. See nos. 1839-40.

1156. GRIFFITHS, D.M., 'Catherine the Great, the British Opposition and the American Revolution', in: KAPLAN, L.S. (ed.), The American Revolution and 'A Candid World' (Kent, Ohio 1977), pp. 85-110.

1157. GRIFFITHS, D.M., 'Nikita Panin, Russian Diplomacy, and the American Revolution', *SR.*, XXVIII, 1 (1969), 1-24.

1158. GRIFFITHS, D.M., 'An American Contribution to the Armed Neutrality of 1780', *RR.*, 30, 2 (1971), 164-173.

1159. GRIFFITHS, D.M., 'American Commercial Diplomacy in Russia, 1780-1783', *William and Mary Quarterly*, 3rd series, XXVII, 3 (1970), 379-410.

1160. FURAEV, V.K., 'Sovetskaia istoriografiia otnoshenii mezhdu SSSR i SShA', *Amerikanskii Ezhegodnik* (1972), 156-178.

1161. BOLKHOVITINOV, N., Stanovlenie russko-amerikanskikh otnoshenii 1775-1815. M. 1966. Pp. 639.
Rev: *Vop. Ist.*, 6 (1968), 182-4 (Fursenko, A.). See no. 1839.

1162. BOLKHOVITINOV, N. (comp.), 'Novye dokumenty o mirnom posrednichestve Rossii v voine SShA za nezavisimost' (1780-81)', *Amer. Ezh.* (1975), 231-45.

AUSTRIA AND PRUSSIA

1163. FLOROVSKII, A.V., 'Russo-Austrian Conflicts in the Early 18th Century', *SEER.*, XLVII, 107 (1969), 94-114.

1164. ROIDER, K.A., The Reluctant Ally: Austria's Policy in the Austro-Turkish War, 1737-1739. Baton Rouge 1972. Pp. 198. Based on Ph.D. dissertation, Stanford 1970.

1165. ROIDER, K.A., 'Kaunitz, Joseph II and the Turkish War', *SEER.*, LIV, 4 (1976), 583-557.

1166. McGILL, W.J., 'The Roots of Policy: Kaunitz in Vienna and Versailles, 1749-1753', *JMH.*, 43, 2 (1971), 228-245.

1167. BATZEL, J.C., 'Austria and The First Three Treaties of Versailles, 1755-1758', Brown Ph.D., 1974.

1168. SCOTT, H., 'Frederick II, the Ottoman Empire and the Origins of the Russo-Prussian Alliance of April 1764', *European Studies Review,* VII, 2 (1977), 153-75.

1169. MADARIAGA, I. de, 'The Secret Austro-Russian Treaty of 1781', *SEER.*, XXXVIII, 90 (1959), 114-45.

1170. FLOROVSKII, A., 'Versuche einer russisch-österreichischen Annäherung in den ersten Jahren des Nordischen Krieges (1702-1705)', *JfGSLE.*, X (1967), 253-271.

1171. STRIBRNY, W., Die Russland-Politik Friedrichs des Grossen 1764-86. Würzburg 1966. Pp. 248.

1172. WINTER, E., 'Grundlagen der österreichischen Russland-politik am Ende des 18. Jhdt.', *ZfSl.*, IV (1959), 94-110.

1173. FLOROVSKII, A.V., Ot Poltavy do Pruta; iz istorii russko-avstriiskikh otnoshenii v 1709-1711 gg. K 85-oi godovshchine so dnia rozhdeniia prof. Antoniia Vasilievicha Florovskogo (1884-1968)/ From Poltava to Prut. To the 85th Anniversary of the Birth of Prof. Antonii Vasilevitsch Florovskii (1884-1968). Prague 1971. Pp. 139. Table of contents and summary in English. = *Acta Universitatis Carolinae. Philosophica et historica. Monographia 30,* 1969 (sic). Posthumous publication of F.'s last monographic study. Introduction gives biographical sketch, footnotes list 5 articles on Russo-Austrian relations under Peter I, including no. 1170.

1174. MURRAY, J.J., George I, the Baltic and the Whig Split in 1717; a study in diplomacy and propaganda. London-Chicago 1969. Pp. 366.
Northern War.

1175. MAKAY, D., 'The Struggle for Control of George I's Northern Policy, 1718-19', *JMH.*, 45, 3 (1973), 367-387.

1176. ROBERTS, M., Macartney in Russia (*Eng. Hist. Rev.*, Supplement no. 7). London 1974. Pp. 81.

1177. MADARIAGA, I. de., Britain, Russia and the Armed Neutrality of 1780: Sir James Harris' Mission to St. Petersburg during the American Revolution. London-New Haven 1962. Pp. 496.
Based on Ph.D. dissertation, London.

1178. GRIFFITHS, D.M., 'Catherine II, George III, and the British Opposition', in CROSS (ed.), *Proceedings* (no. 1794), pp. 306-320.

1179. MARCUM, J.W., 'Vorontsov and Pitt: The Russian Assessment of a British Statesman, 1785-1792', *Rocky Mountain Soc. Sci. Journal*, X, 2 (1973), 49-56.

1180. RUFFMANN, K.-H., 'England und der russische Zaren-titel', *JbfGO.*, N.F. III (1955), 217-24.

1181. MEDIGER, W., Mecklenburg, Russland und England-Hannover 1706-1721. Ein Beitrag zur Geschichte des Nordischen Krieges. 2 vols. Hildesheim 1967. Pp. 221, 480.
Vol. 1 contains only notes, bibliography, index.
Quellen und Darstellungen zur Geschichte Niedersachsens, Bd. 70.

1182. RODZINSKAIA, I., 'Russko-angliiskie otnosheniia v shestidesiatykh godakh XVIII v.', *Trudy Moskovskogo Gosudarstvennogo Istoriko-Arkhivnogo Instituta*, 21 (1965), 241-69.

1183. RODZINSKAIA, I., 'Istochniki po istorii russko-angliiskikh otnoshenii 1760-1770 gg.', *Trudy Moskovskogo Gosudarstvennogo Istoriko-Arkhivnogo Instituta*, 24 (1966), 134-158.

1184. STANISLAVSKAIA, A.M., Russko-angliiskie otnosheniia i problemy Sredizemnomor'ia (1798-1807). M. 1962. Pp. 504.
Rev: *Vop. Ist.*, 10 (1963), 149-51 (Sirotkin, V.G.).
Complements Saul (no. 1134).

1185. ATKIN, M., Russia and Iran, 1780-1828. Minneapolis 1980.

1186. GALOIAN, G., Rossiia i narody Zakarkaz'ia. Ocherki politicheskoi istorii ikh vzaimootnoshenii s drevneishikh vremen do pobedy Vel. Okt. Sots. Rev. M. 1976. Pp. 455.

1187. MARKOVA, O.P., Rossiia, Zakavkaz'e i mezhdunarodnye otnosheniia v XVIII v. M. 1966. Pp. 322.
Rev: *JbfGO.*,N.F., XV, 2 (1967), 283-4 (Pierce, R.).

1188. KUMYKOV, T. (ed.), Kabardino-russkie otnosheniia v XVI-XVIII vv. M. 1957. 2 vols. Pp. 477, 423.

1189. IKHILOV, M.M.,et al. (eds), Russko-dagestanskie otnosheniia XVII-pervoi chetverti XVIII vv.; dokumenty i materialy. Dagestanskoe knizh. izd-vo, 1958. Pp. 334.
Volume for 'XVIII - nachalo XIX veka' announced for 1978.

1190. BUSHUEV, P.P., Posol'stvo Artemiia Volynskogo v Iran v 1715-1718 gg. M. 1978. Pp. 288.

1191. ALIEV, F.,Missiia russkogo poslannika A.P. Volynskogo v Azerbaidzhan (1716-1718). M. 1979.

1192. PLOSKIKH, V., Pervye kirgizsko -russkie posol'skie sviazi, 1784-1827 gg. Frunze 1970. Pp. 114.

1193. PAICHADZE, G., Russko-gruzinskie politicheskie otnosheniia v pervoi polovine XVIII v. Tbilisi 1970. Pp. 280.

1194. VOSKANIAN, V. (ed.), Armiano-russkie otnosheniia. Sbornik dokumentov.
3 vols to date. Vol 3: Armiano-russkie otnoshenie vo vtorom tridtsatiletii XVIII veka. Erevan 1978. Pp. 409.

CHINA

1195. SCHWARTZ, H., Tsars, Mandarins, and Commissars: A History of Chinese-Russian Relations. N.Y. 1973. Pp. 300.

1196. KIRBY, E.S., Russian Studies of China. Progress and Problems of Soviet Sinology. Toronto-London 1975. Pp. 209.

1197. MALYSHEV, A.N., 'Russia's Early Relations With China: 1619-1792', Colorado Ph.D., 1967.

1198. MANCALL, M., Russia and China. Their Diplomatic Relations to 1728. Cambridge 1971. Pp. 396. Based on Ph.D. dissertation, Harvard 1963.

1199. FOUST, C., Muscovite and Mandarin: Russia's Trade with China and its Setting, 1727-1805. Chapel Hill 1969. Pp.424.

1200. SCOTT, G.A.K., 'The Formation of the Turkestan Frontier between Russia and China in the 18th Century', Oxford D.Phil., 1972.

1201. WIDMER, E., The Russian Ecclesiastical Mission in Peking during the Eighteenth Century. Cambridge, Mass. 1976. Pp. 262.

1202. MARTIN, H., Chinakunde in der Sowjetunion nach sowjetischen Quellen. Hamburg 1972. Pp. 210.

1203. STARY, G., Chinas erste Gesandte in Russland. Wiesbaden 1976. Pp. 231.
1733 Chinese ambassador in St. P.

1204. SKACHKOV, P., Ocherki istorii russkogo kitaevedeniia. M. 1977. Pp. 504.

1205. DUMAN, L.I. et al. (eds), Russko-kitaiskie otnosheniia, 1689-1916; ofitsial'nye dokumenty. M. 1958. Pp. 136.

1206. SLADKOVSKII, M.I., Istoriia torgovo-ekonomicheskikh otnoshenii narodov Rossii s Kitaem. (do 1917 g.). M. 1974. Pp. 369.
Bibliography: pp. 357-363. See also no. 1119.

1207. KURDIUKOVA, I., 'Iz istorii russko-kitaiskikh otnoshenii (1695-1720 gg.)', *Ist. Arkhiv*, 3 (1975), 174-84.

1208. GUREVICH, B., 'Vtorzhenie Tsinskoi imperii v Tsentral'nuiu Aziiu vo vtoroi polovine XVIII veka i politika Rossii', *Ist. SSSR.*, 2 (1973), 98-114.

1209. GUREVICH, B.P., MOISEEV, V.A., 'Vzaimootnosheniia tsinskogo Kitaia i Rossii s Dzhungarskim Khanstvom v XVII-XVIII vv. i kitaiskaia istoriografiia', *Vop. Ist.*, 3 (1979), 43-55.

1210. GUBER, A.A. (ed.), Politika evropeiskikh derzhav v iugo-vostochnoi Azii (1760-1860). Dokumenty i materialy. M. 1962. Pp. 654.
French/Russian text.

FRANCE AND FRENCH REVOLUTION

On Peter I's visit to France see also nos. 323, 2260; on the French Revolution, 1458, 1463, 2349, 2366, 2369.

1211. OLIVA, L.J., Misalliance: A Study of French Policy in Russia During the Seven Years' War. N.Y. 1964. Pp. 218.
Based on Ph.D. dissertation, Syracuse 1961.
Rev: *JbfGO.*, N.F., 14, 1 (1966), 443-4 (Mediger, W.).

1212. FOX, F., 'Negotiating with the Russians: Ambassador Ségur's Mission to Saint-Petersburg, 1784-1789', *French Historical Studies*, VII, 1 (1971), 47-72. See no. 2626.

1213. MARCUM, J., 'Catherine II and the French Revolution: A Reappraisal', *CSP.*, XVI, 2 (1974), 187-202.

1214. RAGSDALE, H., 'A Continental System in 1801: Paul I and Bonaparte', *JMH.*, 42, 1 (1970), 70-89.

1215. RAGSDALE, H., 'Was Paul Bonaparte's Fool?: The Evidence of the Danish and Swedish Archives', *CanAmSlSt.*, VII, 1 (1973), 52-68.

1216. SAVANT, J., 'Louis XVI et l'alliance russe', *La Nouvelle Revue des Deux Mondes* (Dec. 1975), 306-324.

1217. REGEMORTER, J.L. van, 'Commerce et politique. Préparation et négotiation du traité franco-russe de 1787', *CMRS.*, IV, 3 (1962), 230-57. See also nos. 1075-6.

1218. SHTRANGE, M.M., La révolution française et la société russe. Traduit du russe par Jean Champenois. M. 1960. Pp. 227. Translation of no. 1221.

1219. LIUBLINSKAIA, A.D. (ed.), Russkii diplomat vo Frantsii (Zapiski Andreia Matveeva). L. 1972. Pp. 296. Foreign policy of Peter I.

1220. MARKOVA, O.P., 'O neitral'noi sisteme i franko-russkikh otnosheniiakh (vtoraia polovina XVIII v.), *Ist. SSSR.*, 6 (1970), 42-55.

1221. SHTRANGE, M.M., Russkoe obshchestvo i frantsuzskaia revoliutsiia 1789-1794. M. 1956. Pp. 205. Cp. no. 1218. An earlier essay on same subject, *I.Z.*, vol. 39, 98-120.

1222. DZHEDZHULA, K.E., Rossiia i velikaia frantsuzskaia burzhuaznaia revoliutsiia kontsa XVIII veka. Kiev 1972. Pp. 452. Rev: *Kritika*, X, 1 (1973), 37-49 (Okenfuss, M.).

1223. KURMACHEVA, M.D., 'Russkaia burzhuaznaia istoriografiia o vlianii velikoi frantsuzskoi revoliutsii na politiku Ekateriny II', in: PASHUTO (no. 612), pp. 423-32.

JAPAN

1224. LENSEN, C., The Russian Push Towards Japan. Russo-Japanese Relations, 1697-1875. Princeton 1959. Pp. 553.

1224a. GRIVNIN, V. (comp.), Bibliografiia Iaponii: literatura, izdannaia v Rossii s 1734 po 1917 g. M. 1965. Pp. 378.

1225. FAINBERG, E. IA., Russko-iaponskie otnosheniia v 1697–
1875 gg. M. 1960. Pp. 314.
Rev. *Vop. Ist.*, 3 (1963), 132-3 (Stadnichenko, A.).

1226. PREOBRAZHENSKII, A., 'Pervoe russkoe posol'stvo v Iaponiiu',
Ist. Arkhiv, 4 (1961), 113–148.

POLAND

1227. DAVIES, N., Poland: Past and Present. A Select Bibliography
of Works in English. Newtonville 1977. Pp. 220.
Gives full listing for eighteenth century.

1228. LEWITTER, L., 'Russia, Poland and the Baltic 1697-1721',
HJ., XI, 1 (1968), 3-34.

1229. LEWITTER, L., 'Poland, Russia and the Treaty of Vienna of
5 January 1719', *HJ.*, XIII (1970), 3-30.

1230. DZIEWANOWSKI, M.K., 'King Stanislaw Leśzczynśki: Some
Remarks and Question Marks; and a Rejoinder', *JbfGO.*, N.F.
16 (1968), 104-116, 557-558.
Footnotes include recent works on Leśzczynśki.

1231. KAPLAN, H.H., 'The First Partition of the Polish-Lithuanian
Commonwealth, 1762-1773', Columbia Ph.D., 1960.

1232. TOPOLSKI, J., 'Reflections on the First Partition of Poland
(1772)', *Acta Poloniae Hist.*, 27 (1973), 89-104.

1233. STONE, D., Polish politics and national reform 1775-88.
Boulder 1976. Pp. 122.

1234. ŁOJEK, J., 'Catherine II's Armed Intervention in Poland:
Origins of the Political Decisions at the Russian Court in
1791 and 1792', *CanAmSlSt.*, IV, 3 (1970), 570-593.

1235. WANDYCZ, P., The Partitioned Lands of Poland 1795-1918.
Seattle 1974. Pp.431.

1236. ŁOJEK, J. (ed.), 'La politique de la Russie envers la
Pologne pendant le premier partage d'après un document
secret de la cour russe de 1772', *CanAmSlSt.*, VIII, 1
(1974), 116-136.

1237. ZERNACK, K., 'Stanislaus August Poniatowski. Probleme
einer politischen Biographie', *JbfGO.*, N.F., XV, 3 (1967),
371-92.

1238. JABLONOWSKI, H., 'Die erste Teilung Polens', in: id.,
Russland, Polen und Deutschland: Gesammelte Aufsätze
(Köln-Wien 1972), pp. 222-61.

1239. ARTAMONOV, V., 'Pol'sko-russkie otnosheniia 1710-1714 gg.',
in: KOROLIUK, V. (ed.), Voprosy istoriografii i
istochnikovedeniia slaviano-germanskikh otnoshenii
(M. 1973), pp. 230-246.

SPAIN AND SPANISH AMERICA

1240. PIERCE, R.A., 'Source Materials for a Project on Russian
Colonization in South America (1735-1737)', *California
Slavic Studies*, 1 (1960), 182-196.
Interesting abortive episode.

1241. TAMBS, L.A., 'Anglo-Russian enterprise against Hispanic
South America, 1732-1737', *SEER.*, XLVIII, 112 (1970),
357-373.

1242. HULL, A.H., 'Spanish and Russian Rivalry in the North
Pacific Regions of the New World, 1760-1812', Alabama Ph.D.
thesis, 1966.

1243. SCHOP SOLER, A.M., Die spanish-russischen Beziehungen im 18.
Jahrhundert. Wiesbaden 1970. Pp. 264.
Rev: *Ist. SSSR.*, 6 (1973), 207-9 (Dodolev, M.A.).

1244. SLEZKIN, L.IU., 'Positsiia Rossii v otnoshenii ispanskoi
Ameriki na rubezhe XVIII-XIX vekov', *Vop. Ist.*, 6 (1963),
47-59. 1780s-1813.

1245. BEKAREV, A.D. et al. (eds), Rossiisko-kubinskie i
sovetsko-kubinskie sviazi, XVIII-XX vv. M. 1975. Pp. 352.
Rev: *Vop. Ist.*, no. 4 (1977), 160-2 (Belovolov, IU.G.).
Eighteenth-century contacts were visitors Karzhavin and
Lakier.

SWEDEN AND THE BALTIC

- *SWEDEN*. See also 'Great Northern War' and no. 461.

1246. ROBERTS, M. (ed.), Sweden's Age of Greatness, 1632-1718.
London 1973. Pp. 314.
'Problems in Focus' series.

1247. HATTON, R., OAKLEY, S., 'The Rise and Fall of Sweden,
1611-1721', in: WELLS, P. (ed.), European History 1500-
1700 (London 1976), pp. 135-50.

1248. HATTON, R., Charles XII of Sweden. London 1968. Pp. 656.

1249. BARTON, H.A., 'Russia and the Problem of Sweden-Finland,
1721-1809', *EEQ.*, V, 4 (1972), 431-455.

1250. METCALF, M.F., Russia, England and Swedish Party Politics, 1762-1766. The Interplay Between Great Power Diplomacy and Domestic Policies During Sweden's Age of Liberty. Stockholm-New Jersey 1977. Pp. 278.
Rev: *SEER.*, LVII, 1 (1979), 128-9 (Christie, I.R.); *SR.*, XXXVIII, 2 (1979), 297 (Ransel, D.).

1251. ROBERTS, M., Essays in Swedish History. London 1967. Pp. 358.
Includes Russo-Swedish relations in 1770's.

1252. MISIUNAS, R.J., 'Russia and Sweden 1772-1778', Yale Ph.D., 1971.

1253. BARTON, H.A., 'Gustav III of Sweden and the East Baltic 1771-1792', *J. Baltic Studies*, VII, 1 (Spring 1976), 13-30.

1254. NEKRASOV, G.A., 'Torgovo-ekonomicheskie otnosheniia Rossii so Shvetsiei v 20-30 godakh XVIII v.', in: BESKROVNYI (no. 1145), pp. 259-90.

1255. NEKRASOV, G.A., 'Istoricheskie "ekskursy" g-na B. Sigbana v russko-shvedskie otnosheniia XVIII v. i real'nye fakty istorii', *Ist. SSSR.*, 3 (1962), 192-209.
Polemic over Swedish-Russian relations in the eighteenth century.

1256. TARLE, E., Severnaia voina i shvedskoe nashestvie na Rossiiu. M. 1958. Pp. 478. Reprinted in Tarle's *Sobranie Sochinenii* (M. 1957-62), vol. X; and trans. into French: no. 1319.

1257. NIKOFOROV, L.A., 'Vopros o posrednichestve Frantsii mezhdu Rossiei i Shvetsiei v kontse severnoi voiny', *Ist. SSSR.*, 6 (1958), 124-140.

1258. NEKRASOV, G.A., Russko-shvedskie otnosheniia i politika velikikh derzhav v 1721-1726 gg. M. 1964. Pp. 227.

   - *BALTIC*

1259. ROBERTS, M., 'Great Britain, Denmark, and Russia, 1763-1770', in: HATTON, R., ANDERSON, M.S. (eds), Studies in Diplomatic History: Essays in Memory of D.B. Horn (London 1970), pp. 256-268.

1260. MEDIGER, W., 'Russland und die Ostsee im 18. Jahrhundert', in: Senatskommission für das Studium des Deutschtums im Osten an der Rheinischen Fr.-Whms-Uni., Bonn, hrsg., Der Ostseeraum im Blickfeld der deutschen Geschichte (Köln 1970), pp. 141-65.

1261. MENKE, C.F., 'Die wirtschaftlichen und politischen Beziehungen der Hansestädte zu Russland im 18. und frühen 19. Jhdt.', Phil. Diss., Göttingen 1959

1262. VOGRIN, V.E., 'Zakliuchenie russko-datskogo soiuznogo dogovora 1709 g.', *I.Z.*, vol. 93 (1973), 309-327.

TURKEY, THE CRIMEA, THE BALKANS · See also nos. 2418-9.

1263. SVERCHEVSKAIA, A. (comp.), Bibliografiia Turtsii, 1713-1917. M. 1961. Pp. 265. 5078 items.

1264. OGNEVA, A.IU., 'Literatura po balkanskim problemam, vyshedshaia v SSSR (1970-72)', in: Mezhdunarodnye otnosheniia na Balkanakh (M. 1974), pp. 322-329.

1265. GEORGIEV, V.G. et al., Vostochnyi vopros vo vneshnei politike Rossii konets XVIII-nachalo XX v. M. 1978. Bibliography pp. 411-425.

1266. COOK, M. (ed.), A History of the Ottoman Empire to 1730. Cambridge, Eng. 1977. Pp. 246.

1267. SHAW, S.J., History of The Ottoman Empire and Modern Turkey. Cambridge, Eng. 1976-7. 2 vols. Vol.I: Empire of the Gazis ... 1280-1808. Pp. 351.

1268. SUBTELNY, O.M., 'The Unwilling Allies: The Relation of Hetman Pylyp Orlyk with the Crimean Khanate and the Ottoman Porte, 1710-1742', Harvard Ph.D., 1973.

1269. SUBTELNY, O.M., 'Great Power Politics in E. Europe and the Ukrainian Emigrés, 1709-42', *CanAmSlSt.*, XII, 1 (1978), 136-53.

1270. ANDERSON, M.S. (ed.), The Great Powers and the Near East, 1774-1923 (Documents in Modern History Series). London 1970. Pp. 182. Section I, 9-21, The Rise of Russian Power and the French Invasion of Egypt, covers 1774-1799.

1271. ANDERSON, M.S., 'The Great Powers and the Annexation of the Crimea, 1783-4', *SEER.*, XXXVII, 88 (1958), 17-41.

1272. FISHER, A., The Russian Annexation of the Crimea 1772-1783. Cambridge 1970. Pp. 180. Based on Columbia Ph.D. thesis, 1967.

1273. ITZKOWITZ, N., MOTE, M., Mubadele. An Ottoman-Russian Exchange of Ambassadors. Chicago 1970. Pp. 261. Annotated edition of two diaries kept by the Russian and Ottoman ambassadors, 1775-6.

1274. WIECZYNSKI, J.L., 'The Myth of Kuchuk-Kainardja in American Histories of Russia', *Middle Eastern Studies*, IV, no. 4 (1968), 376-379.

1275. DAVISON, R.H., 'Russian Skill and Turkish Imbecility: The Treaty of Küchük Kainardji Reconsidered', *SR.*, XXXV, 3 (1976), 463-483.

1276. KRAMER, G., McGREW, R., 'Potemkin, the Porte, and the Road to Tsargrad: The Shumla Negotiations, 1789-1790', *CanAmSlSt.*, VIII, 4 (1974), 467-488.

1277. BENNIGSEN, A., 'Peter the Great, the Ottoman Empire, and the Caucasus', *CanAmSlSt.*, VIII, 2 (1974), 311-19.

1278. McKNIGHT, J.L., 'Admiral Ushakov and the Ionian Republic: The Genesis of Russia's First Balkan Satellite', Wisconsin Ph.D., 1965.

1279. CVETKOVA, B., 'Analyse d'un document ottoman concernant les relations entre la Russie et les terres balkaniques au début du XVIIIe siècle', *CMRS.*, IX, 1 (1968), 65-9.

1280. VEINSTEIN, G., 'Missionaires jésuites et agents français en Crimée au début du XVIIIe siècle', *CMRS.*, X, 3-4 (1969), 414-458.

1281. GÖKBILGIN, Ö., DESAIVE, D., 'Le Khanat de Crimée et les campagnes militaires de l'Empire ottomane, fin du XVIIe - début du XVIIIe siècle, 1687-1736', *CMRS.*, XI, 1 (1970), 110-117.

1282. VEINSTEIN, G., 'Les Tartars de Crimée et la seconde élection de Stanislas Leśzczyński', *CMRS.*, XI, 1 (1970), 24-92.

1283. HOESCH, E., 'Das sogenannte 'griechische Projekt' Katherinas II', *JbfGO.*, N.F., XII, 1 (1964), 168-206. A revisionist view. Cp. no. 1287.

1284. ORESHKOVA, S., Russko-turetskie otnosheniia v nachale XVIII v. M. 1971. Pp. 205. Rev: *Kritika*, XVIII, 1 (1972), 1-12 (Subtelny, O.).

1285. KRYLOVA, T.K., 'Russkaia diplomatiia na Bosfore v nachale XVIII v. (1700-1709)', *I.Z.*, vol. 65 (1959), 249-277.

1286. DRUZHININA, E.I., Kiuchuk-Kainardzhiiskii mir 1774 goda (ego podgotovka i zakliuchenie). M. 1955. Pp. 366.

1287. MARKOVA, O.P., 'O proiskhozhdenii tak nazyvaemogo grecheskogo proekta (80-e gody XVIII v.)', *Ist. SSSR.*, 4 (1958), 52-78.

1288. STANISLAVSKAIA, A.M., 'Rossiia i Gretsiia v kontse XVIII-nachale XIX v.', *Ist. SSSR.*, 1 (1960), 59-76.

1289. ARSH, G.L., Eteristskoe dvizhenie v Rossii. Osvoboditel'
naia bor'ba grecheskogo naroda v nachale XIX v. i russko-
grecheskie sviazi. M. 1970. Pp. 370.
Greek independence movement. Some references to eighteenth
century. See also the English work of R. Clogg (London
1976).

1290. GROSUL, IA. (ed.), Istoricheskie sviazi narodov SSSR i
Rumynii v XV-nachale XVIII v. Dokumenty i materialy.
M. 1965-70. 3 vols.
Danubian principalities (Moldavia & Wallachia). Relations
1408-1711.

1291. SEMENOVA, L.E., Russko-voloshskie otnosheniia v kontse
XVII-nachale XVIII v. M. 1969. Pp. 165.

1292. ARSH, G.L., 'Russko-albanskie sviazi v period russko-
turetskoi voiny 1787-1791 gg.', *I.Z.*, 63 (1958), 259-268.

OTHER.   See also no. 1145.

1293. DRUHE, D.N., Russo-Indian Relations, 1466-1917. N.Y. 1970.
Pp. 333.
Good bibliography.

SECTION 9 - MILITARY AND NAVAL HISTORY

9(a) - *Military: General*

There is no comprehensive English-language account. The standard work on the eighteenth century is BESKROVNYI (1305), the
leading Soviet authority in the field. ANDOLENKO (1299) covers
the Imperial period, concentrating on operations. URLANIS
(1315) is an interesting study of a neglected subject.

1294. LYONS, M., The Russian Imperial Army: a Bibliography of
Regimental Histories and Related Works. Stanford 1968.
Pp. 188.

1295. JONES, D. (ed.), Russian and Soviet Military Encyclopedia.
Gulf Breeze, Florida 1977-. Vols 1-4 by end 1980.
Trans. of the Soviet military encyclopaedia (no. 1302)
with additional articles commissioned for this publication.

1296. NIKOLAIEFF, A.M., 'Peter the Great as a Military Leader',
Army Quarterly and Defence Journal, 80 (1960), 78-86.

1297. HELLIE, R., 'The Petrine Army: Continuity, Change, and
Impact', *CanAmSlSt.*, VIII, 2 (1974), 237-254.

1298. MAVRODIN, V.V. (comp. and intro.), Fine Arms from Tula,
Eighteenth and Nineteenth Centuries. L. 1977. Pp. 149.
64 pp. of colour plates.
Hermitage collection.

1299. ANDOLENKO, S., Histoire de l'Armée Russe. Paris 1967.
Pp. 476.

1300. LEVASHEVA, Z.P., Bibliografiia russkoi voennoi bibliografii.
M. 1950. Reprinted Cambridge 1972. Pp. 58.
Covers period before 1917.

1301. KAVTARADZE, A., 'Voennye entsiklopedicheskie slovari i
entsiklopedii dorevoliutsionnoi Rossii (1724-1915 gg.)',
Voen. ist. zhurnal, 1 (1973), 103-8.

1302. KIR'IAN, M. et al. (eds), Sovetskaia voennaia entsiklopediia v 8tt., M. 1976-.
6 vols to date.

1303. BESKROVNYI, L.G., Ocherki po istochnikovedeniiu voennoi
istorii Rossii. M. 1957. Pp. 452.

1304. BESKROVNYI, L.G., Ocherki voennoi istoriografii Rossii.
M. 1962. Pp. 320.

1305. BESKROVNYI, L.G., Russkaia armiia i flot v XVIII v.
M. 1958. Pp. 643.
Rev: *Ist. SSSR.*, 1 (1960), 169-171 (Strokov, A.).

1306. SHUNKOV, V. (ed.), Voprosy voennoi istorii Rossii XVIII i
pervoi poloviny XIX vv. M. 1969. Pp. 445.
Festschrift for Beskrovnyi. Essays include bibliography of
military works by Beskrovnyi; military in eighteenth-
century; Russian and Soviet historiography; military
thought, war literature; Northern War and nobles; Osterman
in Sweden, 1719; Shuvalov and War School, 1755; maps and
Pugachev; soldiers' songs.

1307. SOTNIKOV, A.A. (ed.), Voenno-istoricheskii muzei artillerii,
inzhenernykh voisk i voisk sviazi. Kratkii putevoditel'.
L. 1968, 6th ed. Pp. 270, illustrations.

1308. VOLKOV, E., 'Iz istorii zarozhdeniia i razvitiia voenno-
morskoi literatury v Rossii', *Voen. ist. zhurnal*, 7 (1971),
87-91.

1309. RABINOVICH, M.D., 'Strel'tsy v pervoi chetverti XVIII v.',
I.Z., vol. 58 (1956), 273-305.

1310. LESHCHINSKII, L.M., Voennye pobedy i polkovodtsy russkogo
naroda vtoroi poloviny XVIII v. M. 1959. Pp. 224.

1311. AVTOKRATOV, V.N., 'Pervye komissariatskie organy russkoi
reguliarnoi armii (1700-1710 gg.)', *I.Z.*, vol. 68 (1961),
163-188.

1312. ZOLOTAREV, B.V., 'K voprosu o nachale artilleriiskogo i
inzhenernogo obrazovaniia v Rossii', in: Problemy istorii
feodal'noi Rossii. Sb. statei k 60-letiiu prof. V.V.
Mavrodina (no. 220), pp. 195-206.

1313. PRUDNIKOV, IU., 'Komplektovanie ofitserskogo korpusa
russkoi armii v 1774-1804 gg.', *VMU(Ist.)*, 2 (1972), 61-73.

1314. BELIKOV, T.I., Uchastie Kalmykov v voinakh Rossii v XVII,
XVIII i pervoi chetverti XIX vv. Elista 1960. Pp. 142.

1315. URLANIS, V.TS., Voiny i narodonaselenie Evropy. Liudskie
poteri vooruzhennykh sil evropeiskikh stran v voinakh
XVII-XX vv. (Istoriko-statisticheskoe issledovanie).
M. 1960. Pp. 567.
Rev: *Vop. Ist.*, 5 (1962), 147-9 (Pokshishevskii, V.).

The war has been neglected for the most part in Western
literature, though HATTON'S biography (1248) puts Charles XII
in a favourable light. The old standard is TARLE (1319 is a
translation of the Russian original); the latest study is by
SHUTOI (1323, 1328). The 250th anniversary of Poltava produced a considerable response, particularly two important
collections (1324, 1326). PORFIR'EV (1327) is a technical
account. ROZENBETSKAIA (1321) is a catalogue of Leningrad
holdings. See also nos. 1146-48, 1174, 1181, 1256-57.

1316. JACKSON, W.G.F., Seven Roads to Muscovy. London 1957, N.Y.
      1958. Pp. 334.
      Essays include invasion of Russia by Charles XII.
      Rev: *RR.*, 18 (1959), 348-9 (Raeff, M.).

1317. TOKARZEWSKI-KAREZEWICZ, Prince J., 'The Battle of Poltava',
      Ukrainian Review (London), 6, no. 2 (1959), 13-20, and no.
      3, 49-67.

1318. ANDRUSIAK, N., 'From Muscovy to Russia: the Battle of
      Poltava, 1709', *Ukrainian Quarterly*, 18 (1962), 167-74.

1319. TARLE, E.V. (trans. by Champenois, J.), La guerre du Nord
      et l'invasion suédoise en Russie. 2 vols. M. (Progress)
      1966. Pp. 327, 419.

1320. ANNERS, E., Das Karolinsche Militärstrafrecht und die
      Kriegsartikel Peters des Grossen. Upsala 1961. Pp. 212.

1321. ROZENBETSKAIA, E. (comp.), Katalog arkhivnykh dokumentov
      po Severnoi voine 1700-1721 gg. L. 1959. Pp. 433.

1322. GOL'DENBERG, L.A., 'Kratkii obzor kartograficheskikh
      istochnikov XVIII veka po istorii severnoi voiny (1700-
      1721 gg.)', *Vop. Ist.*, 11 (1959), 143-52.
      Archival holdings.

1323. SHUTOI, V.E., Bor'ba narodnykh mass protiv nashestviia
      armii Karla XII, 1700-1709. M. 1958. Pp. 447.

1324. BESKROVNYI, L.G. et al. (eds), Poltava. K 250-letiiu
      poltavskogo srazheniia. M. 1959. Pp. 459.
      Rev: *ZfG.*, VIII (1960), 1510-11 (Hoffmann, P.).

1325. BESKROVNYI, L.G., 'Poltavskaia pobeda', *Vop. Ist.*, 12
      (1959), 41-57.
      Anniversary article and shows it, but useful. Full
      bibliography in footnotes.

1326. GREKOV, M.V., KOROLIUK, V.D. (eds), Poltavskaia pobeda.
      Iz istorii mezhdunarodnykh otnoshenii nakanune i posle
      Poltavy. M. 1959. Pp. 265.
      Rev: *ZfG.*, VIII (1960), 1510-11 (Hoffman, P.).

1327. PORFIR'EV, E.I., Poltavskoe srazhenie 27 iiunia 1709 g.
M. 1959. Pp. 110.
Rev: *ZfG.*, VIII (1960), 1510-11 (Hoffman, P.).

1328. SHUTOI, V.E., Severnaia voina (1700-1721 gg.). M. 1970.
Pp. 160.

*9(c) - Other Military Campaigns (Seven Years War, wars with Persia,
Turkey, Austria, France)*

1329. LONGWORTH, P., The Art of Victory: the Life and
Achievements of Generalissimo Suvorov, 1729-1800. London
1965. Pp. 350.
Rev: *SEER.*, XLV (1967), 250-51 (Squire, P.S.).

1330. DUFFY, C., The Army of Maria Theresa. The Armed Forces of
Imperial Austria, 1740-1780. Newton Abbott 1977.
Pp. 256.
Refers to Russia.

1331. AKDES NIMET KURAT, 'Der Prutfeldzug und der Prutfrieden
von 1711', *JbfGO.*, N.F., X, 1 (1962), 13-66.
Summary of larger, exhaustive Turkish work

1332. GROEHLER, O., Die Kriege Friedrichs II. Berlin 1968. Pp.256.

1333. BANGERT, D.E., Die russisch-oesterreichische militärische
Zusammenarbeit im Siebenjährigen Kriege in den Jahren
1758-59. Boppard am Rhein 1971. Pp. 430.
Rev: *ZfG.*, XXI (1973), 617-8 (Mittenzwei, I.).

1334. NOSTITZ, F.A. von., Der Westfeldzug Suvorovs in der
öffentlichen Meinung Englands. Wiesbaden 1976. Pp. 317.
Rev: *SEER.*, LVI, 1 (1977), 542-4.
Focus in fact on Anglo-Russian diplomatic relations, but
good study.

1335. SCHREYER-MÜHLPFORDT, B., 'Suvorov in der Darstellung Joh.
Peter Hebels', *JbfGSLE.*, I (1956), 129-134.

1336. AMBURGER, E., 'Michael Kutusow (1745-1813)', in: Grosse
Soldaten der europäischen Geschichte (Bonn 1961), pp. 195-
227.

1337. FRUMENKOV, G.G., 'Rossiia i semiletniaia voina', *Vop.
Ist.*, 9 (1971), 107-19.

1338. NOVICHEV, A., 'Turetskii istochnik o vnutrennem polozhenii
Osmanskoi imperii i prichinakh ee porazheniia v voine s
Rossiei v 1768-1774 gg.', *VLU(Ist.)*, 8 (1975), 80-89.

1339. SEMENOVA, I., Russko-moldavskoe boevoe sodruzhestvo
      (1787-1917). Kishinev 1968. Pp. 116.

9(d) - *Naval and Maritime*

There is no general history of the eighteenth-century Russian
navy and its operations; nos. 1340-42 are not adequate for
the period. Therefore, exceptionally, some important Russian
pre-revolutionary works have been included (1353-55). Recent
British interest has focussed principally on the British
contribution to the development of Russia's navy, particularly
in the later eighteenth century (1344-5, 1347-51). See also
2666.

1340. MITCHELL, M., The Maritime History of Russia, 848-1948.
      London 1949, N.Y. 1950, reprinted 1969. Pp. 543.
      Rev: *RR.*, 9 (1950), 334-6 (Sokol, A.E.).

1341. FAIRHALL, D., Russian Sea Power. Boston 1971. Pp. 287.
      Published in Britain under the title *Russia Looks To The
      Sea,* London 1971.

1342. MITCHELL, D., A History of Russian and Soviet Sea Power.
      N.Y. 1974. Pp. 657, plates.

1343. LONG, J.W., 'The Russian Naval Museum, Lakewood, New
      Jersey', *SR.*, XXX, 2 (1971), 350-55.

1344. ANDERSON, M.S., 'Great Britain and The Growth of the
      Russian Navy in the Eighteenth Century', *Mariner's
      Mirror*, 42, 1 (1956), 132-46.

1345. TURNER, E.H., 'The Russian Squadron with Admiral
      Duncan's North Sea Fleet, 1795-1800', *Mariner's Mirror*
      49, (1963), 212-40.

1346. MORISON, S., John Paul Jones. N.Y. 1959, reprinted 1964.
      Pp. 456.
      Jones in the Russian Navy, 1788-89.

1347. CHRISTIE, I., 'Samuel Bentham and the Western Colony at
      Krichev, 1784-1787', *SEER.*, XLVIII, 3 (1970), 232-247.
      Naval supply colony for Russian Black Sea fleet.

1348. CHRISTIE, I., 'Samuel Bentham and the Russian Dnieper
      Flotilla, 1787-1788', *SEER.*, L, 119 (1972), 173-197.

1349. CROSS, A.G., 'Samuel Greig, Catherine the Great's
      Scottish Admiral', *Mariner's Mirror*, 60, 3 (1974),
      251-265.

1350. CLENDENNING, P.H., 'Admiral Sir Charles Knowles and the Russian Navy, 1771-1774', *Mariner's Mirror*, 65, 1 (1975), 39-49.

1351. BARTLETT, R.P., 'Scottish Cannon-Founders and the Russian Navy, 1768-1785', *OSP.*, N.S., X (1977), 51-72.

1352. MORINEAU, M., 'Rations de marine (Angleterre, Hollande, Suède, Russie)', *Annales*, XX, 6 (1965), 1150-7.

1353. SOKOLOV, A.P., Russkaia Morskaia Biblioteka, 1701-1851. Ischislenie i opisanie knig, rukopisei i statei po morskomu delu za 150 let. St. P. 1883. Pp. 449.

1354. VESELAGO, F.F. (comp.), Opisanie del arkhiva Morskogo Ministerstva za vremia s poloviny XVII do nachala XIX stoletiia. St. P. 1880-1906. 11 vols.

1355. VESELAGO, F.F. (comp.), Materialy dlia istorii russkogo flota. 17 vols. St. P. 1865-1904.
Protocols of Admiralty College, copies of government decrees, etc., to Admiralty.

1356. SAL'MAN, G.IA., 'Morskoi ustav 1720 g. - pervyi svod zakonov russkogo flota', *I.Z.*, vol. 53 (1955), 310-22.

1357. TARLE, E.V., 'Chesmenskii boi i pervaia russkaia ekspeditsiia v Arkhipelag, 1769-1774', in: Sochineniia, ed. ERUSALIMSKII, A.S. et al., 12 vols (M. 1957-62), vol. X, 9-362.

1358. SHAPIRO, A., 'Ob usloviiakh pobed russkogo flota v kontse XVIII-nachale XIX vekov', *VLU(Ist.)*, 2 (1959), 61-73.

1359. ALEKSEEV, B.N. (ed.), Russkie i sovetskie moriaki na sredizemnom more. M. 1976. Pp. 264.
Provides nationalistic historic reasons for current Soviet activity.

SECTION 10 - GEOGRAPHY, DEMOGRAPHY, ETHNOGRAPHY

HARRIS (1361) is an exhaustive and highly professional guide to his field. KALESNIK (1375) provides a monumental geographical description of the Soviet Union, with some historical background (the Soviet counterpart to Semenov-T'ian-Shanskii's *Rossiia. Polnoe Opisanie Nashego Otechestva.*

As an historical geography PARKER (1364) is superior to, but less systematic than, DROBIZHEV (1382). Literature on explorers and travellers is extensive; only a sample is listed here (1370, 1384-89; see also Sections 14 and 15).

For historical atlases, besides 1362-63, 1368, see nos. 61-63, 1417. For demography, standard general works are KABUZAN (1398, 1400) and VODARSKII (1392). On the peasantry see also SHCHEPUKHOVA (702). For ethnography BROMLEY (1407) provides a clear over-view; TOKAREV (1411) is the standard Soviet account. See also no. 795.

10(a) - Geography and Exploration

1360. HARRIS, C.D., Bibliography of Geography. Part 1: Introduction to General Aids. Chicago 1976. Pp. 276. Includes serials and bibliographies in Russian.

1361. HARRIS, C.D., Guide to Geographical Bibliographies and Reference Works in Russian or on the Soviet Union. Chicago 1975. Pp. 477. 2660 annotated items.

1362. ADAMS, A.E. et al., An Atlas of Russian and East European History. London-N.Y. 1967. Pp. 204.

1363. GOL'DENBERG, L.A., Russian Maps and Atlases as Historical Sources. (Trans. by J.R. Gibson). Toronto 1971. Pp. 76.

1364. PARKER, W.H., An Historical Geography of Russia. Chicago-London 1969. Pp. 416.

1365. UHRYN, K., La notion de "Russie" dans la cartographie occidentale, XVIe-XVIIIe siècles. München 1975. Pp. 142.

1366. MOROZOVA, M., STEPANOVA, E. (comp.), Fizicheskaia geografiia. Annotirovannyi perechen' otechestvennykh bibliografii, izdannykh v 1810-1966 gg. M. 1968. Pp. 309. Useful for travel accounts, regional descriptions, etc.

1367. TIKHOMIROV, G.S., Bibliograficheskii ocherk istorii geografii v Rossii XVIII v. M. 1968. Pp. 135.

1368. LEMUS, N.V. (comp.), Russkie geograficheskie atlasy. XVIII vek. Svodnyi katalog. L. 1961. Pp. 243.

1369. MINTS, A., 'Istoriia geograficheskoi mysli (Obzor sov. lit za 1961-1970)', in: *Teoret. vopr. fiz. i ekon. geografii*, vol. I (M. 1972), pp. 26-43.

1370. ISAENKO, G., 'Obshchie raboty po istorii geograficheskikh
otkrytii v severo-vostochnoi chasti Tikhogo okeana i o
russko-iaponskikh otnosheniakh v XVIII–XIX vv.', in:
GOLOVIN, V., Zapiski flota kapitana Golovnina o
prikliucheniiakh ego v plenu u iapontsev v 1811, 1812 i
1813 godakh... (Khabarovsk 1972), pp. 516–522.

1371. KOLGUSHKIN, V.V. (comp.), Opisanie starinnykh atlasov, kart
i planov XVI, XVII, XVIII, i poloviny XIX vv. ... v arkhive
Tsentral'nogo Kartograficheskogo Proizvodstva VMF. L. 1958.
Pp. 270.

1372. NAVROT, M.I., 'Katalog rukopisnykh istoricheskikh kart
Rossii, XVIII–XIX vv. ... v fondakh Gos. Istoricheskogo
Muzeia ...', *Istoriia geograficheskikh znanii:
istoricheskaia geografiia*, 2 (1967), 17–19; 4 (1970),
39–43; 5 (1971), 34–8.

1373. A.N. SSSR, Geograficheskoe Obshchestvo SSSR, Opisanie
kollektsii rukopisei nauchnogo arkhiva geograficheskogo
obshchestva SSSR, vypusk 1. L. 1973. Pp. 88.

1374. GRIGOR'EV, A. (ed.), Kratkaia geograficheskaia
entsiklopediia. M. 1960–66. 5 vols.

1375. KALESNIK, S. et al. (eds), Sovetskii Soiuz. Geograficheskoe
opisanie v 22 tomakh. M. 1966–1972.

1376. IATSUNSKII, V.K., Istoricheskaia geografiia. Istoriia ee
vozniknoveniia i razvitie v XIV–XVIII vekakh. M. 1955.
Pp. 332.

1377. LEBEDEV, D.M., Ocherki po istorii geografii v Rossii XVIII
veka (1725–1800 gg.). M. 1957. Pp. 272.

1378. BELOV, M. (ed.), Voprosy geografii petrovskogo vremeni.
L. 1975. Pp. 79.

1379. GREKOV, V.I., Ocherki iz istorii russkikh geograficheskikh
issledovanii v 1725–1765 gg. M. 1960. Pp. 425.

1380. MARKOVA, K., SAUSHKINA, IU. (eds), Geografiia v Moskovskom
Universitete za 200 let, 1755–1955. M. 1955. Pp. 285.

1381. DIK, N.E., Lomonosovskii period v razvitii russkoi
geografii. M. 1976. Pp. 127.

1382. DROBIZHEV, V.Z., KOVAL'CHENKO, I.D., MURAV'EV, A.V.,
Istoricheskaia geografiia SSSR. M. 1973. Pp. 320.
Student textbook. Chaps 12–14 cover eighteenth- early
nineteenth centuries. Rev: *Vop. Ist.*, no. 8 (1973), 152–4.

1383. NAROCHNITSKII, A.L. (ed.), Istoricheskaia geografiia Rossii
XII-nachalo XX vv. Sb. statei k 70-letiiu prof. L.G.
Beskrovnogo. M. 1975. Pp. 347.
Some articles listed separately (nos 979, 1029, 1099, 1116).

1384. GEKHTMAN, G., Vydaiushchiesia geografy i puteshestvenniki.
Tbilisi 1962. Pp. 304.

1385. NOVLIANSKAIA, M.G., 'I.K. Kirilov i ego Atlas
Vserossiiskoi Imperii', accompanying Academy of Sciences
reprinting of Kirilov's Atlas Imperii Russici (1731),
L. 1959. Pp. 77.

1386. NOVLIANSKAIA, M.G., Ivan Kirilovich Kirilov, geograf XVIII
veka. L. 1964. Pp. 140.

1387. NOVLIANSKAIA, M.G., Daniil Gottlib Messerschmidt i ego
raboty po issledovaniiu Sibiri. L. 1970. Pp. 184.
D. Messerschmidt (1685-1735). See no. 2629.

1388. NOVLIANSKAIA, M.G., Filipp Iogann Stralenberg i ego
paboty po issledovaniiu Sibiri. L. 1966. Pp. 93.
Ph.J.T. von Strahlenberg (1676-1747).

1389. RASKIN, N., SHAFRANOVSKII, I., Erik Laksman.
Vydaiushchiisia puteshestvennik i naturalist XVIII v.
L. 1971. Pp. 273.

10(b) - Demography

1390. Annual current and retrospective demographic bibliography
in: Annales de démographie historique (Paris).

1391. BURNASHEV, E.IU., VALENTEI, E.D. (eds), Bibliografiia po
problemam narodonaseleniia, 1960-71. M. 1974. Pp. 343.
On-going. Later volumes cover succeeding years.

1392. VODARSKII, IA.E., Naselenie Rossii za 400 let (XVI nachalo
XX vv). M. 1973. Pp. 158.
Many tables. Introdn. by S.S. Dmitriev, pp. 3-21.

1393. PEREVEDENTSEV, V.I., Metody izucheniia migratsii
naseleniia. M. 1975. Pp. 231.
Much statistical material.

1394. VISHNEVSKII, A. (ed.), Brachnost', rozhdaemost', smertnost'
v Rossii i v SSSR. M. 1977. Pp. 247.

1395. VODARSKII, IA.E., Naselenie Rossii v kontse XVII-nachale
XVIII veka: chislennost', soslovno-klassovyi sostav,
razmeshchenie. M. 1977. Pp. 263.
Rev: *Kritika* XV, 1 (1979), 40-9 (Meehan-Waters, B.).

1396. IATSUNSKII, V.K., 'Izmeneniia v razmeshchenii naseleniia
Evropeiskoi Rossii v 1724-1916 gg.', *Ist. SSSR*, 1 (1957),
192-224.

1397. KABUZAN, V., SHEPUKOVA, N., 'Tabel' pervoi revizii
narodonaseleniia Rossii (1718-1727 gg.)', *Ist. Arkhiv.*,
3 (1959), 126-165.

1398. KABUZAN, V.M., Narodonaselenie Rossii v XVIII-pervoi
polovine XIX v. (po materialam revizii). M. 1963. Pp. 228,
tables.
Rev: *Vop. Ist.*, 4 (1964) (Ulashchik, N.N.).

1399. KABUZAN, V.M., 'Istochniki dlia sostavleniia kart
etnicheskogo sostava naseleniia Rossii XVIII v.-pervoi
poloviny XIX v.', *Vop. Geografii*, 83 (1970), 126-132.

1400. KABUZAN, V., Izmeneniia v razmeshchenii naseleniia Rossii
v XVIII-pervoi polovine XIX v. (Po materialam revisii).
M. 1971. Pp. 190, charts.

1401. KABUZAN, V.M., Kak zaselialsia Dal'nii Vostok. (Vtoraia
polovina XVII-nachalo XX v.) Khabarovsk 1973. Pp. 192.

1402. KABUZAN, V.M., Narodonaselenie Bessarabskoi oblasti i
levoberezhnykh raionov Pridnestrov'ia: konets XVIII-pervaia
polovina XIX v. Kishinev 1974. Pp. 157.

1403. KABUZAN, V.M., Zaselenie Novorossii (Ekaterinoslavskoi i
Khersonskoi gubernii) v XVIII-pervoi polovine XIX veka
(1719-1858 gg.). M. 1976. Pp. 307.

1404. PULLAT, R., Gorodskoe naselenie Estonii s kontsa XVIII
veka do 1940 goda. Istoriko-demograficheskoe issledovanie.
Tallin 1976. Pp. 224.
Rev: *Ist. SSSR.*, 2 (1978), 189-90.

1405. FEDOROVA, S.G., Russkoe naselenie Aliaski i Kalifornii.
Konets XVIII v.-1867 g. M. 1971. Pp. 269.

1405a. PALLI, KH., 'O nekotorykh metodicheskikh voprosakh obrabotki
istochnikov po istoricheskoi demografii ESSR na EBM(IBM)',
in Koval'chenko, I.,(ed.), Matematicheskie metody v istori-
ko-ekonomicheskikh i istoriko-kul'turnykh issledovaniakh.
(M. 1977), 82-98.
IBM computers and Estonian demographic analysis.

1406. HALPERN, J. et al. (comps), Bibliography of Anthropological
      and Sociological Publications on Eastern Europe and the
      USSR. With a Supplement of Siberian travel accounts com-
      piled by R.H. Fisher. Los Angeles 1961.Pp. 142.

1407. BROMLEY, IU.V., Soviet Ethnography: Main Trends. M.1977,
      Pp. 208.

1408. ERZIN, S., EBIN, F. (eds), Literatura i fol'klor narodov
      SSSR. Ukazatel' otechestvennykh bibliograficheskikh posobii
      i spravochnykh izdanii, 1926-1970. M. 1975. Pp. 235.
      Selective bibliography of bibliographies on literature and
      folklore of 42 Soviet nationalities.

1409. MEL'TS, M., 'Istoricheskoe razvitie russkogo fol'klora.
      Materialy k bibliografii. (Sistematicheskii ukazatel')',
      Russkii fol'klor 16 (1976), 279-91.

1410. TOKAREV, S.A. et al. (eds), Ocherki po etnografii narodov
      SSSR (evropeiskaia chast'). Uchebnoe posobie. M. 1962.
      Pp. 127.

1411. TOKAREV, S.A., Istoriia russkoi etnografii. M. 1966.
      Pp. 455.
      Rev: *SR.*, XXVII, 3 (1968), 486-488.

1412. SOKOLOVA, V., Russkie istoricheskie predaniia. M. 1970.
      Pp. 287.
      Rev: *Kritika*, VIII, 2 (1972), 72-9 (Okenfuss, M.).
      Fascinating account of historical folktales.

1413. LEVIN, M.G. (ed.), Istoriko-Etnograficheskii Atlas Sibiri.
      M.-L. 1961. Pp. 498.

1414. MINENKO, N.A., Russkaia krest'ianskaia sem'ia v Zapadnoi
      Sibiri (XVIII-pervoi poloviny XIX v.). Novos.1979. Pp. 350.
      See also no. 2533.

1415. IVANOV, V., Russkie uchenye o narodakh Severo-Vostoka
      Azii. XVII-nachalo XX vv. Iakutsk 1978. Pp. 320.

1416. IVANOV, S., Skul'ptura altaitsev, khakasov i sibirskikh
      tatar, XVIII-pervaia chetvert' XX vv. L. 1979. Pp. 194.

1417. TOLSTOV, S.P. et al. (eds), Russkie. Istoriko-
      etnograficheskii atlas. M. 1967. Plates, maps.

1418. ALEKSANDROV, V. (ed.), Etnograficheskoe kartografirovanie
      material'noi kul'tury narodov Pribaltiki. M. 1975.
      Pp. 239.
          Rural conditions and agricultural implements described.

Arrangement is alphabetical, with usual divisions within each
name entry. Writing on belles lettres (where relevant) has
been largely, but *not* wholly, excluded: guides to that area
may be found in Section 12. Monarchs are covered in Section 5.
See also no. 121.

Bogdanov.

1419. KOBLENTS, I.N., Andrei I. Bogdanov, 1692-1766. L. 1958.
Pp. 216.

Bolotov.

1420. RICE, J.L., 'The Memoirs of A.T. Bolotov and Russian
Literary History', in: CROSS (ed.), *Russian Literature*
(no. 1988), pp. 17-44.

1421. RICE, J.L., 'The Bolotov Papers and Andrei Timofeevich
Bolotov Himself', *RR.*, XXXV, 2 (1976), 125-54.

1422. BROWN, J.H., 'A Provincial Landowner: A.T. Bolotov (1738-
1833)', Princeton Ph.D., 1977.
Book announced, publication in 1981.

_____

1423. BOLOTOV, A.T., Zhizn' i prikliucheniia A.A. Bolotova.
M. 1931, 3 vols, reprinted 1973 in one volume, with new
introduction by M. Raeff.
The 1931 edition is an abridgement of Bolotov's diary
published in *Russkaia Starina,* 1870.

Boltin.

1424. LIPSKI, A., 'Boltin's Defense of Truth and Fatherland',
CalSlSt., II (1963), 39-52.

_____

1425. NIKITIN, A.L., 'Boltinskoe izdanie Pravdy Russkoi', *Vop.
Ist.*, 11 (1973), 53-65.

Dashkova.

1426. DASHKOVA, Princess E.R., The Memoirs of Princess Dashkov.
Trans. and ed. FITZLYON, K. London 1958. Pp. 322.
French edition, ed. PONTREMOLI, P. Paris 1966. Pp. 377.
Best Russian ed. St. P. 1907.

_____

1427. KRASNOBAEV, B.I., 'Glava dvukh akademii', *Vop. Ist.*, 12
(1971), 84-98.

1428. LOZINSKAIA, L.IA., Vo glave dvukh akademii. M. 1978.
Pp. 143.
Rev: *SGECRN.*, 6 (1978), 71-76 (Cross, A.G. - gives full
bibliography).

Derzhavin

1429. SMITH, G.S., 'G.R. Derzhavin: A Concise Bibliography of Works Published Outside the USSR', *SGECRN.*, 3 (1975), 52-6.

1430. CLARDY, J., G.R. Derzhavin: A Political Biography. The Hague 1967. Pp. 228.

1431. SPRINGEN, A.R., 'The Public Career and Political Views of G.R. Derzhavin', UCLA Ph.D., 1971.

1432. DERZHAVIN, G.R., Zapiski Derzhavina, St. P. 1861, reprinted with new introduction, Cambridge 1973. Pp. 508.
Reprints part of vol. 6 of Grot's *Sochineniia Derzhavina*.

Dmitriev

1433. DMITRIEV, I.I., Vzgliad ma moiu zhizn'. St. P. 1895, reprinted with introduction by A.G. Cross, Cambridge 1974. Pp. 128.

Eisen.

1434. DONNERT, E., Johann Georg Eisen (1717-1779). Ein Vorkämpfer der Bauernbefreiung in Russland. Leipzig 1978. Pp. 200.
Rev: *SR.*, XXXVIII, 3 (1979), 488-9 (Kirchner, W.).

Fonvizin.

1435. KANTOR, M. (trans. and intro.), The Dramatic Works of Denis Ivanovich Fonvizin. Bern-Frankfurt 1974. Pp. 150.

1435a. MOSER, C., Denis Fonvizin. Boston 1979. Pp. 151.

1436. MAKOGONENKO, G. (ed.), Denis Fonvizin: Sobranie sochinenii. M.-L. 1959. 2 vols.
The standard edition.

1437. MAKOCONENKO, G., Denis Fonvizin: tvorcheskii put'. M.-L. 1961. Pp. 442.

1438. KULAKOVA, L.I., Denis Ivanovich Fonvizin. L. 1966. Pp. 166.

Huyssen.

1439. PETSCHAUER, P., 'In Search of Competent Aides: Heinrich von Huyssen and Peter the Great', *JbfGO.*, XXVI, 4 (1978), 481-502.

Iakubovskii.

1440. IAKUBOVSKII, I.A., Karlik favorita; istoriia zhizni Ivana Andreevicha Iakubovskogo, karlika Sv. Kn. P.A. Zubova, pisannaia im samim. Intro. Ct. V.P. Zubov. München 1968. Pp. 424.

Kantemir, A.D.

1441. EVANS, R.J., 'Antiokh Kantemir: A Study of His Literary, Political and Social Life in England, 1732-38', London Ph.D., 1960.

1442. EHRHARD, M., 'Lettres sur la nature et l'homme du Prince A. Kantemir', *Revue des Etudes Slaves*, 34 (1957), 51-60.

1443. GRASSHOFF, H., A.D. Kantemir und Westeuropa. Ein russischer Schriftsteller des 18. Jahrhunderts und seine Beziehungen zur westeuropäischen Literatur und Kunst. Berlin 1966. Pp. 340.

1444. PRIIMA, F.IA., 'Antiokh Dmitrievich Kantemir' in: Antiokh Kantemir. Sobranie Stikhotvorenii (L., Biblioteka Poeta, 1956), pp. 5-48.

1445. RADOVSKII, M.I., Antiokh Kantemir i Peterburgskaia Akademiia Nauk. L. 1959. Pp. 112.

Kantemir, D.

1446. Ein bedeutender Gelehrter an der Schwelle zur Frühaufklärung: Dimitrie Cantemir (1673-1723). Berlin 1974. Pp. 96. (Sitzungsberichte der Akad. der Wissenschaften der DDR, Jg. 1973, no.13). Rev: *ZfG.*, XXIII (1975), 846 (Winter, E.).

1447. KANTEMIR, D., Opisanie Moldavii. Kishinev 1973. Pp. 222. Reprint of 1789 Russian translation of 1769 German original. Rev: *Vop. Ist.*, no. 8 (1975), 168-70 (Moiseeva, G.N.).

1448. ERMURATSKII, V., Dmitrii Kantemir - myslitel' i gosudarstvennyi deiatel'. Kishinev 1973. Pp. 154.

1449. LUCHINSKII, P.K., 'Dmitrii Kantemir - obshchestvenno-politicheskii deiatel', uchenyi, patriot', *Vop. Ist.*, 10 (1973), 34-46.

1450. KORBU, KH., CHOBANU, L., Nasledie Dmitriia Kantemira i sovremennost'. Kishinev 1976. Pp. 230.

Karamzin. See also no. 1876.

1451. PIPES, R., 'Karamzin's Conception of Monarchy', *Harvard SS.*, IV (1957), 35-58.

1452. PIPES, R. (ed. and intro.), Karamzin's Memoir on Ancient and Modern Russia. A Translation And Analysis. Cambridge, Mass. 1959, N.Y. 1966. Pp. 266.

1453. NEBEL, H.M., Jr., N.M. Karamzin, A Russian Sentimentalist. The Hague 1967. Pp. 190.

1454. CROSS, A.G., N.M. Karamzin: A Study of His Literary Career, 1783-1803. Carbondale 1971. Pp. 306.
Based on Cambridge Ph.D. thesis, 1966.

1455. COLE, E.A., 'The Enlightened Nationalism of N.M. Karamzin, 1766-1826', UC Berkeley Ph.D., 1972.

1456. KOCHETKOVA, N., Nikolay Karamzin. Boston 1975. Pp. 154.
Rev: *SEER.*, LIV, 2 (1976), 274-6.

1457. BLACK, J.L., Nicholas Karamzin and Russian Society in the Nineteenth Century. A Study in Russian Political and Historical Thought. Toronto 1975. Pp. 264.

1458. BLACK, J.L. (ed.), Essays on Karamzin: Russian Man-of-Letters, Political Thinker, Historian, 1766-1826. The Hague-Paris 1975. Pp. 232.
Includes K. as historian (Black); *Letters of a Russian Traveller* (Anderson); K. and the French Revolution (Kisliagina); K.'s spiritual crisis (Neuhäuser).

1459. BLACK, J.L., 'N.M. Karamzin and the Dilemma of Luxury in Eighteenth Century Russia', *Studies on Voltaire and the Eighteenth Century*, CLI-CLV (1976), 313-22.

1460. MITTER, W., 'Die Entwicklung der politischen Anschauungen Karamzins', *Forschungen zur osteuropäischen Geschichte*, II, (Berlin 1955), 165-285.

1461. BRYNER, F., N.M. Karamzin, Eine kirchen- und frömmig-keitsgeschichtliche Studie. Erlangen 1974. Pp. 289.

1462. KISLIAGINA, L.G., Formirovanie obshchestvenno-politicheskikh vzgliadov N.M. Karamzina, 1785-1803 gg.
M. 1976. Pp. 197.
Rev: *Ist. SSSR.*, 5 (1977), 197-200.

1463. TEPLOVA, B.A., '"Vestnik Evropy" Karamzina o velikoi frantsuzskoi revoliutsii i formakh pravlenii', *XVIII Vek.*, Sb. 8 (1969) |Derzhavin i Karamzin v literaturnom dvizhenii XVIII-nachala XIX v.|, pp. 269-280.

Karzhavin. See also no. 1245.

1464. RABINOVICH, V.I., Revoliutsionnyi prosvetitel' F.V. Karzhavin. M. 1966. Pp. 79.

1465. RABINOVICH, V.I., S gishpantsami v Noge, Novyi Iiurk i Gavanu (Zhizn' i puteshestvie F.V. Karzhavina). M. 1967. Pp. 87.

Kirilov. See nos. 367, 1385-6, 1577.

Kozel'skii.

1466. KOGAN, M.IA., Prosvetitel' XVIII veka IA. P. Kozel'skii.
    M. 1958. Pp. 188.

Krechetov.

1467. SIVKOV, K.V., PAPARIGOPULO, S.U., 'O vzgliadakh Fedora
    Krechetova', *Vop. Ist.*, 3 (1956), 121-128.

Kulibin.

1468. RASKIN, N.M., Ivan Petrovich Kulibin, 1735-1818. M.-L.
    1962. Pp. 207.
    Rev: *ZfG.*, XI (1963), 1012-3 (Grau, C.).

Lomonosov. See also nos. 627, 1381, 1732, 1985, 2080a,2196.

1469. MENSHUTKIN, B.N., Russia's Lomonosov; chemist, courtier,
    poet. Princeton 1952, reprinted Westport, Conn. 1970.
    Pp. 208.
    Translation of 1937 Russian original.

1470. HUNTINGTON, W.C., 'Michael Lomonosov and Benjamin Franklin:
    Two self-made Men of the Eighteenth Century', *RR.*, 18
    (1959), 294-306.

1471. JONES, D.N., 'M.V. Lomonosov: The Formative Years, 1711-
    1742', North Carolina Ph.D., 1969.

1472. KOGAN, IU.IU., 'M.V. Lomonosov and Religion', *Cahiers
    d'Histoire Mondiale – Journal of World History – Cuardernos
    de Historia Mundial*, X (1967), 519-50.

1473. LANGEVIN, L., 'Lomonosov and the Science of His Day',
    Impact of Science on Society, XIII (1963), 93-119.

1474. LEICESTER, H.M. (trans. and intro.), Michael Vasilievich
    Lomonosov on the Corpuscular Theory. Cambridge, Mass.
    1970. Pp. 289.

1475. LANGEVIN, L. (ed.), Lomonossov, 1711-1765. Sa vie, son
    oeuvre. Introduction, choix et traduction des textes,
    notes et commentaires ... L. Langevin. Paris 1967.
    Pp. 319.

1476. CHEVALIER, B., 'La Personnalité de Lomonosov (1711-1765)'.
    Thèse 1973, 3ème cycle. Lettres – Paris X. Pp. 290.

1477. LOMONOSOW, M.W., Ausgewählte Schriften in zwei Bänden.
    I: Naturwissenschaften, II: Geschichte, Sprachwissenschaft
    und Anderes, Briefe. Berlin 1961. Pp. 586, 317.
    Rev: *ZfG.*, IX (1961), 1404-7 (Hoffmann, P.).

1478. HOFFMANN, P., 'Lomonosovs Stellung in der russischen
      Geschichtsschreibung des 18. Jahrhunderts. Zum 250.
      Geburtstag M.V. Lomonosovs', ZfG., IX (1961), 1554-65.

1479. HOFFMANN, P., 'Lomonosov als Historiker', JfGSLE., V
      (1961), 361-73.

1480. LOTMAN, IU., 'Lomonosows Stellung in der Geschichte des
      russischen gesellschaftlichen Denkens. (Zum 200. Todestag
      M.V. Lomonosows)'. ZfSl., X (1965), 682-701.

1481. HOFFMANN, P., 'Lomonosov und Voltaire', StGrL., 3 (1968),
      417-425, 600-603.

1482. KUNTSEVICH, G.Z., Bibliografiia izdanii sochinenii M.V.
      Lomonosova na russkom iazyke. Petrograd 1918, reprinted
      Vaduz 1963. Pp. 231.
      Vol. 6 of 'Vystavka "Lomonosov i elizavetinskoe vremiia"'
      (1918).

1483. LOMONOSOV, M.V., Polnoe sobranie sochinenii, Moscow-
      Leningrad 1950-59, 10 vols.

1484. TORCHIEV, A.V., FIGUROVSKII, N.A., CHENAKAL, V.L.,
      Letopis' zhizni i tvorchestva M.V. Lomonosova. L. 1961.
      Pp. 435.

1485. CHENAKAL, V.L. (comp.), M.V. Lomonosov v portretakh,
      illiustratsiiakh, dokumentakh. M.-L. 1965. Pp. 316.
      Rev: ZfSl., XII (1967), 165-6 (Hoffman, P.).

1486. AKADEMIIA NAUK SSSR, Inst. Istorii Estestvoznaniia i
      Tekhniki. Muzei M.V. Lomonosova v Leningrade. L. 1974.
      Pp. 69.

1487. PAVLOVA, G.E., FEDOROV, A.S., Mikhail Vasil'evich
      Lomonosov. M. 1978.
      Popular illustrated biography.

1488. KON'KOV, N.L., 'Izvestiia kurostrovskikh aktov o
      sovremennikakh M.V. Lomonosova', Ist. SSSR., 6 (1978),
      164-70.

1489. KOROVIN, G.M., Biblioteka Lomonosova; materialy dlia
      kharakteristiki literatury, ispol'zovannoi Lomonosovym v
      ego trudakh, i katalog ego lichnoi biblioteki. L. 1961.
      Pp. 484.

1490. KULIABKO, E., BESHENKOVSKY, E., Sud'ba biblioteki i
      arkhiva M.V. Lomonosova. M. 1975. Pp. 226.

1491. AZARENKO, E.K., Mirovozzrenie M.V. Lomonosova. Minsk
      1959. Pp. 268.

1492. LYSTSOV, V., M.V. Lomonosov o sotsial'no-ekonomicheskom
      razvitii Rossii. Voronezh 1969. Pp. 262.
11-Individuals   131

1493. BELIAVSKII, M.T., M.V. Lomonosov i osnovaniie Moskovskogo
Universiteta. K 200-letiiu Moskovskogo universiteta.
Moscow 1955. Pp. 308.

1494. RADOVSKII, M., M.V. Lomonosov i Petersburgskaia
Akademiia Nauk. M.-L. 1961. Pp. 334.

1495. BOBROVNIKOVA, V.K., Pedagogicheskie idei i deiatel'nost'
M.V. Lomonosova. M. 1961. Pp. 181.

1496. KULIABKO, E.S., M.V. Lomonosov i uchebnaia deiatel'nost'
Peterburgskoi Akademii Nauk. M.-L. 1962. Pp. 216.

1497. PRIMA, F.IA., 'Lomonosov i "Istoriia Rossiskoi Imperii pri
Petre Velikom" Vol'tera', *XVIII Vek.*, Sb. 3 (1958), pp.
170-186.
Lomonosov's part in the preparation and revision of
Voltaire's work.

1498. BELIAVSKII, M.T., 'M.V. Lomonosov i russkaia istoriia',
Vop. Ist., 11 (1961), 90-106.
250th anniversary of birth.

1499. RASKIN, N.M., Khimicheskaia laboratoriia M.V. Lomonosova.
Khimiia v Peterburgskoi Akademii nauk vo vtoroi polovine
XVIII v. M.-L. 1962. Pp. 339.

1500. DANILEVSKII, V.V., Lomonosov i khudozhestvennoe steklo.
L. 1964. Pp. 441.

Lopukhin.

1501. TORKE, H.J., 'Introduction' in: I.V. Lopukhin, Zapiski
(London 1860; reprinted Newtonville, Mass., 1976),
pp. 1-7.

Mazepa. See nos. 2605-11

Menshikov.

1502. OVCHINNIKOV, R.V. (ed.), 'Krushenie poluderzhavnogo
vlastelina. Dokumenty sledstvennogo dela Kniazia A.D.
Menshikova', *Vop. Ist.*, 9 (1970), 87-104.

Merkel. See also no. 1786

1503. JENNISON, E.W., Jnr., 'Christian Garve and Garlieb Merkel:
two theorists of peasant emancipation during the ages of
enlightenment and revolution', *J. Baltic Studies* 4 (1973),
344-363.

1504. MILLER, V.O., MEL'KISIS, E.A., Politiko-pravovye
vzgliady Garliba Merkelia. M. 1977. Pp. 160.
Rev: *SGECRN.*, 6 (1978), 76-81 (Bartlett, R.P.).

Miranda. See also no. 2621

1505. BENEDIKT, H., 'Miranda in Russland', in: Studien zur
älteren Geschichte Osteuropas, II (Graz-Köln 1959).

1506. FEDOSEEV, P. et al. (eds), Presencia de Miranda, Bolivar i
Paez en los archivos de la URSS. M. 1976. Pp. 145.

1507. GRIGULEVICH, I., Frantsisko de Miranda i bor'ba za
nezavisimost' ispanskoi Ameriki. M. 1976. Pp. 274.
Good on Miranda in Russia.

Mordvinov.

1508. REPCZUK, H., 'Nicholas Mordvinov (1754-1845), Russia's
Would-Be-Reformer', Columbia Ph.D., 1962.

1509. DMYTRYSHIN, B., 'Admiral Nikolai S. Mordvinov: Russia's
Forgotten Liberal', *RR.,* 30, 1 (1971), 54-64.

Müller. See also no. 1752

1510. CHEREPNIN, L.V., 'G.F. Müllers Bedeutung für die
Quellenkunde der russischen Geschichte', in: *Ost und
West* (1737),   303-311.

Münnich. See also no. 387.

1511. LEY, FRANCIS, Le Maréchal de Münnich et la Russie au
XVIIIe siècle. Paris 1959. Pp. 319.

Novikov.

1512. McARTHUR, G.H., 'The Novikov Circle in Moscow, 1779-1792',
Rochester Ph.D., 1968.

1513. McARTHUR, G.H., 'Catherine II and the Masonic Circle of
N.I. Novikov', *CanAmSlSt.,* IV, 3 (1970), 529-546.

1514. JONES, W.G., 'The Closure of Novikov's "Truten"', *SEER.,*
L, 118 (1972), 107-111.

1515. JONES, W.G., 'Novikov's Naturalized "Spectator"', in:
GARRARD (ed.), (no.1595), pp. 149-165.
The 'Drone' as a 'Spectator-type' periodical.

1516. WEINBAUM, A.T., 'N.I. Novikov (1744-1818): An Interpretation of His Career and Ideas', Columbia Ph.D., 1975.

1517. HERZEN, M.A. von., 'Nikolai Ivanovich Novikov: The St.
Petersburg Years', Ph.D., Berkeley, Calif. 1975.

1518. OKENFUSS, M.J., 'The Novikov Problem: An English
Perspective', in: CROSS (ed.) *Proceedings* (no. 1794),
pp. 97-108.

1519. SHABAEVA, M.F. (ed.), TRUSHIN, N.A. (comp.),
N.I. Novikov: izbrannye pedagogicheskie sochineniia.
M. 1959. Pp. 254.

1520. ZAPADOV, A.V., Novikov. M. 1968. Pp. 192.

1521. LIKHOTKIN, G.A., Oklevetannyi Kolovion. L. 1972. Pp. 39.

1522. DERBOV, L.A., Obshchestvenno-politicheskie i
istoricheskie vzgliady N.I. Novikova. Saratov 1974.
Pp. 369.
Rev: *SGECRN.*, 3 (1975), 67-71 (Jones, W.G.).

1523. FILIMONOVA, N.I., 'Ekonomicheskii otdel "Pribavlenii k
Moskovskim vedomostiam" N.I. Novikova (1783-1784 gg)',
VMU(Ist.), 4 (1960), 40-52.

1524. BEREZINA, V., 'O formakh i metodakh satiry v
zhurnalakh N.I. Novikova, "Truten" (1769-1770) i
"Zhivopisets" (1772-1773)', *VLU(Ist.)*, 20 (1968), 74-84.

1525. OMEL'CHENKO, O.A., '"Drevniaia Rossiiskaia vivliofika"
N.I. Novikova i M.M. Shcherbatov', *A. Ezh.* (1975), 82-8.

1526. BUDIAK, L.M., Novikov v Moskve i Podmoskov'e. M. 1970.
Pp. 128.

1527. BELIAVSKII, M.T., 'Opis' novikovskogo sela Avdot'ina v
1792 g.', *Ezh. A.I.* (1973), 280-293.

1528. MAKOGONENKO, G.P. (ed.), 'N.I. Novikov i obshchestvenno-
literaturnoe dvizhenie ego vremeni', *XVIII vek.*, Sb. 11
(1976). Pp. 257.
Latest Soviet contributions on Novikov and related topics.
Rev: *SGECRN.*, 5 (1977), 78-82 (Jones, W.G.).

Ostermann.

1529. STÄHLIN, K., 'Graf Heinrich Ostermann', *Westfälische
Lebensbilder* IV (1959), 37-59.

1530. AMBURGER, E., Der russische Staatsmann Heinrich Ostermann.
Berlin-Dahlem 1961.

1531. KLUETING, H., Heinrich Graf Ostermann. Von Bochum nach
St. Petersburg: 1687 bis 1747. Bochum 1976. Pp. 114.
The third book on Ostermann by this author. An English
version has been announced for publication in 1981.
See also 1139.

Pnin.

1532. CROSS, A.G., 'Pnin and the Sankt - Peterburgskii
Zhurnal (1798)', *CanAmSlSt.*, VII, 1 (1973), 78-85.

1533. RAMER, S.C., 'The Traditional and the Modern in the
Writings of Ivan Pnin', *SR.*, XXXV, 3 (1975), 539-59.

Potemkin.

1534. SOLOVEYTCHIK, G., Potemkin, a picture of Catherine's
      Russia. Freeport, N.Y. 1938, reprinted N.Y. 1972. Pp. 349.

Prokopovich: see nos. 1592, 2307-14.

Protasov.
1535. LUKINA, T.A., A.P. Protasov - russkii akademik XVIII v.
      M. 1962. Pp. 187.

Radishchev.

1536. SMITH, G.S., 'Radishchev: A Concise Bibliography of Works
      Published Outside The Soviet Union', *SGECRN.*, 2 (1974),
      53-61.

1537. RADISHCHEV, A.N., A Journey from St. Petersburg to Moscow.
      (Trans. L. Wiener, ed. and intro. R.P. Thaler). Cambridge,
      Mass. 1958. Pp. 286.
      Rev: *ASEER.*, 19 (1960), 108-109 (McConnell, A.); *SEER.*,
      XXXVII (1958-9), 516-8 (Lang, D.M.).
      Standard English version, with useful introduction and
      notes.

1538. LANG, D.M., The First Russian Radical: Alexander
      Radishchev, 1749-1802. London 1959. Pp. 298.
      Developed from London Ph.D. thesis, 1950.

1539. CLARDY, J., The Philosophical Ideas of Alexander N.
      Radishchev. L. 1963. Pp. 155.
      Based on U. Michigan Ph.D. 1961.

1540. McCONNELL, A., A Russian Philosophe: Alexander
      Radishchev, 1749-1802. The Hague 1964. Pp. 228.

1541. PAGE, T., 'The Spiritual Conflict of A.N. Radiščev
      (1749-1802)', Columbia Ph.D., 1974.

1542. PAGE, T., 'Radishchev's Polemic against Sentimentalism
      in the Cause of Eighteenth-Century Utilitarianism', in:
      CROSS (ed.) (no. 1988), pp. 141-72.

1543. REGEMORTER, J.L. van, 'Deux images idéales de la
      paysannerie russe à la fin du XVIIIe siècle', *CMRS.*, IX,
      1 (1968), 5-19.
      Peasants in Radishchev and Karamzin. Cf. similar study
      by Piksanov in *XVIII vek,* Sb. 3 (1958).

1544. COLIN, M., 'Radiščev fut-il un écrivain révolutionnaire?'
      Revue des Etudes Slaves, 50, 1 (1977), 97-105.

1545. HOFFMANN, P., 'Stand und Aufgaben der Radiščev Forschung',
      JfGSLE., V (1961), 375-90.

1546. TATARINCEV, A., 'Radiščev und die Freimaurer', *JfGSLE.*,
      IX (1966), 171-191.

1547. HOFFMANN,P., 'Radiščevs Tod - Selbstmord oder Unglücksfall', *StGrL.*, 3 (1968), 526-539; 638-640.

1548. GRASSHOFF, H., 'Eine deutsche Quelle fur Radiščevs "Kurzen Bericht über die Entstehung der Zensur" aus der "Reise von Petersburg nach Moskau",' *StGrL.*, 4 (1970), 333-366.

1549. TATARINCEV, A., 'Zur Frage der deutschen Beziehungen A.N. Radiščevs', *ZfSl.*, XVI (1971), 896-900. German acquaintances in Leipzig and Russia.

1550. HEXELSCHNEIDER, E. (red.), Zum 175. Todestag A.N. Radiščevs. = *Wissenschaftliche Zeitschrift* der Karl-Marx-Universität, Leipzig, *Gesellschafts- und Sprachwissenschaftliche Reihe*, 26 Jg. (1977), 4, 1-377. Major Soviet-E.German symposium. Rev: *ZfSl.*, 6 (1978), 923-5 (Lehmann, U.).

1551. MAKOGONENKO, G.P., Radishchev i ego vremia. Moscow 1956. Pp. 774. Rev: *Ist. SSSR.*, 6 (1958), 174-183 (Beliavskii, M.).

1552. KARIAKIN, IU., PLIMAK, E., 'O nekotorykh spornykh problemakh mirovozzreniia A.N. Radishcheva', *I.Z.*, vol. 66 (1960), 137-205.

1553. KARIAKIN, IU.F., PLIMAK, E.G., Zapretnaia mysl' obretaet svobodu, 175 let bor'by vokrug ideinogo naslediia Radishcheva. M. 1966. Pp. 304. Valuable, if partisan, discussion of Soviet and Western views on Radishchev.

1554. BABKIN, D., A.N. Radishchev. Literaturno-obshchestvennaia deiatel'nost'. M.-L. 1966. Pp. 362. Rev: *Kritika*, III (1966), 23-39 (Ryu, In-Ho.).

1555. KULAKOVA, L.I., ZAPADOV, V.A., A.N. Radishchev, "Puteshestvie iz Peterburga v Moskvu". Kommentarii. Posobie dlia uchitelei. Leningrad 1974. Pp. 256. Recent Soviet commentary.

1556. SHTORM, G., Potaennyi Radishchev. Vtoraia zhizn' "Puteshestviia iz Peterburga v Moskvu". 3rd ed. M. 1974. Pp. 415. Intriguing pursuit of theory that Radishchev continued work on the 'Journey' after his return from exile. Many new facts, but thesis rejected by Radishchev scholars. Previous edition, 1965.

1557. MAKOGONENKO, G.P. (ed.), *XVIII Vek*, Sb. 12: A.N. Radishchev i literatura ego vremeni. L. 1977. Pp. 260. Whole issue devoted to Radishchev: latest Soviet contributions. Rev: *SGECRN.*, 5 (1977), 82-5 (Smith, G.).

1558. TATARINTSEV, A., Radishchev v Sibiri. M. 1977. Pp. 269.

Rychkov.

1559. KULIABKO, E.S., CHERNIKOV, A.M., 'Pervyi chlen-
korrespondent Akademii Nauk P.I. Rychkov', *Vestnik
A.N.SSSR.*, 2 (1962), 90-93.

1560. SIDORENKO, S.A., 'P.I. Rychkov kak istorik', *Vop. Ist.*, 7
(1975), 24-36.

Shcherbatov. See also nos. 1525, 1592.

1561. RAEFF, M., 'State and Nobility in the Ideology of M.M.
Shcherbatov', *ASEER.*, 19 (1960), 363-79.

1562. AFFERICA, J.M., 'The Political and Social Thought of
Prince M.M. Shcherbatov (1733-1790)', Harvard Ph.D., 1967.

1563. LENTIN, A. (trans., ed. and intro.), M.M. Shcherbatov,
'On the Corruption of Morals in Russia'. Cambridge,
England 1969. Pp. 339.
Notes and bibliography. Based on Ph.D. thesis,
Cambridge 1968.

1564. DONNERT, E., 'Mikhail Shcherbatov als politischer Ideologe
des russischen Adels in der zweiten Hälfte des 18. Jh.'
ZfSl., XVIII, 3 (1973), 411-21.

1565. FEDOSOV, I.A., Iz istorii russkoi obshchestvennoi mysli
XVIII stoletiia. M.M. Shcherbatov. M. 1967. Pp. 260.
Rev: *Vop. Ist.*, 4 (1968), 168-7 (Krasnobaev, B.I.);
Kritika VII, 3 (1971), 171-82 (Everett, L.).

Severgin.

1566. CARVER, J.S., 'Vasilii Mikhailovich Severgin, 1765-1826,
Russian Scientist, Technologist and Editor'. Temple
Ph.D. thesis, 1977.
Book announced 1980-81. See also no. 2671.

Skovoroda: see nos. 1621, 2269, 2694, 2695.

Soimonov. See also no. 2669.

1567. GOLDENBERG, L.A., Mikhail F. Soimonov, 1730-1804.
M. 1973. Pp. 120.
Distinguished technocrat, head of College of Mines.

Sumarokov.

1568. GLEASON, W., 'Sumarokov's Political Ideals: A
Reappraisal of His Role as a Critic of Catherine II's
Policies', *CSP.*, XVIII, 4 (1976), 415-27.

Tatishchev. See also nos. 204-6.

1569. LEVENTER, H.M., 'Tatishchev: Science and Service in 18th
Century Russia', Columbia Ph.D., 1972.

1570. DANIELS, R.L., V.N. Tatishchev: Guardian of the Petrine
      Revolution. Philadelphia 1973. Pp. 125.
      Based on Ph.D. thesis, Pennsylvania State U., 1971.

1571. BLANC, S., Un disciple de Pierre le Grand dans la Russie
      du XVIII siècle. V.N. Tatiščev (1686-1750). T. 1-2.
      (Thèse, Paris IVe, 1971). Lille 1972. Pp. 662, 60.

1572. BLANC, S., 'Tatishchev et la pratique du mercantilisme',
      in: *La Russie et l'Europe XVIe - XXe Siècles* (no. 579),
      pp. 169-184.
      Also appeared in *CMRS.*, X, 3-4 (1969), 353-70.

1573. GRAU, C., Der Wirtschaftsorganisator, Staatsmann und
      Wissenschaftler Vasilij N. Tatiščev (1686-1750). Berlin
      1963. Pp. 227.
      Rev: *Ist. SSSR.*, 5 (1966), 210-13 (Tomsinskii, S.).

1574. BAK, I.S., 'Ekonomicheskie vozzreniia V.N. Tatishcheva',
      I.Z., vol. 54 (1955), pp. 362-81.

1575. KOLOSOV, R.N., 'Novyye biograficheskie materialy o V.N.
      Tatishcheve', *A. Ezh.* (1963), 106-114.

1576. VALK, S.N., 'V.N. Tatishchev i nachalo novoi russkoi
      istoricheskoi literatury', *XVIII vek*, Sb. 7 (1966), 66-73.

1577. GOL'DENBERG, L., TROITSKII, S.M., 'O zaniatiiakh I.K.
      Kirilova russkoi istorii (Materialy k biografii I.K.
      Kirilova i V.N. Tatishcheva)', *A. Ezh.* (1970), 145-57.

1578. IUKHT, A.I., 'Poezdka Tatishcheva v Shvetsiiu (1724-1726
      gg.)', *I.Z.*, vol. 88 (1971), pp. 296-335.

1579. IUKHT, A.I., 'Proekty V.N. Tatishcheva 1721-1726 gg. o
      razvitii promyshlennosti i torgovli na Urale i v Sibiri',
      Ist. i ist. (1971), 293-331.

1580. KUZ'MIN, A.G., 'Stat'ia 1113 v "Istorii Rossiiskoi" V.N.
      Tatishcheva', *VMU(Ist.)*, 5 (1972), 79-90.

1581. IUKHT, A.I., 'Iz naslediia V.N. Tatishcheva (Materialy ob
      ekonomicheskom polozhenii Shvetsii v pervoi chetverti
      XVIII v.)', *Ist. i ist.* (1973), 298-322.

1582. SHAKINKO, I.M., 'V.N. Tatishchev kak gosudarstvennyi
      deiatel', *Vop. Ist.*, 4 (1975), 125-38.

1583. IUKHT, A.I., 'Sviazi V.N. Tatishcheva s Akademiei Nauk',
      in: CHEREPNIN, L. (ed.), Problemy istorii obshchestvennoi
      mysli i istoriografii (M. 1976), pp. 354-367.

1584. IUKHT, A.I., 'Deiatel'nost' V.N. Tatishcheva na Urale v
      1720-1722 gg.', *I.Z.*, vol. 97 (1976), pp. 124-199.

1585. IUKHT, A.I., 'Iz istorii izucheniia nauchnogo naslediia
V.N. Tatishcheva (S.N. Valk o trudakh Tatishcheva)', *I.Z.*,
vol. 99 (1977), pp. 297-311.

1585a. IUKHT, A.I., 'Pis'ma V.N. Tatishcheva 1742-1745 gg.',
I.Z., vol. 104 (1979), pp. 282-337.
Letters from Astrakhan.

Trediakovskii.

1586. LAKSHIN, V.IA., 'O deiatel'nosti V.K. Trediakovskogo -
prosvetitelia. (Perevod Knigi o Fr. Bekona)', *XVIII vek*,
Sb. 5 (1962), 223-248.
D. Mallet, The Life of Francis Bacon, Chancellor of
England, London 1740.

Vorontsov family. See also no. 1796

1587. HUMPHREYS, L.J., 'The Vorontsov Family: Russian Nobility in
a Century of Change, 1725-1875', Pennsylvania Ph.D., 1969.

1588. MARCUM, J.W., 'Semen R. Vorontsov: Minister to the Court of
St. James for Catherine II, 1785-1796', North Carolina
Ph.D., 1970.
Book announced for publication in 1980-81.

1589. ZIMMERMANN, J.S., 'Alexander Romanovich Vorontsov,
Eighteenth Century Enlightened Statesman, 1741-1805',
SUNY Ph.D., 1975.

1589a.KENNEY, J., 'The Vorontsov Party in Russian Politics,
1785-1803: An Examination of the Influence of an Aristo-
cratic Family at the Court of St. Petersburg in the Age
of Revolution'. Yale Ph.D. 1975.

Кн. Я. П. Шаховской.

12(a) - Intellectual History, Philosophy, The Enlightenment

A helpful reference work is the annual report on *Modern Language Studies* (1590). Recent Soviet historiography on the Enlightenment is discussed by GRIFFITHS (2683). On specific topics the collections edited by GARRARD (1595) and BERKOV (1621) are valuable. Intellectual trends are well discussed from a Marxist viewpoint by DONNERT (1617-19; also 453-58) and GRASSHOFF (1607, 1611); TSCHIZHEWSKIJ (1594, 1612) and KRASNOBAEV (1634) are both sound surveys of their subjects. SHTRANGE (1625) makes a stimulating but only partly successful attempt to prove the existence of a non-noble intelligentsia; LARAN (1602) and KURMACHEVA (1644) develop this theme.

1590. 'Russian Studies: The Eighteenth Century', *The Year's Work in Modern Language Studies*, vol. 26 (1974) onwards.

1591. ROGGER, H., National Consciousness in Eighteenth-Century Russia. Cambridge 1960. Pp. 319.
Based on Harvard Ph.D. thesis, 1956.

1592. RAEFF, M. (ed.), Russian Intellectual History: An Anthology. N.Y. 1966. Pp. 404.
Introduction by Isaiah Berlin. Includes Feofan Prokopovich, M.M. Shcherbatov. Rev: *Annales* Nov.-Dec. (1967), 1163-1205 (Confino, M.).

1593. BLAIR, L.B. (ed.), Essays on Russian Intellectual History. Austin 1971. Pp. 123.

1594. TSCHIZHEWSKIJ, D., Russian Intellectual History. Trans. from German by Osborne, J.C., ed. Rice, M.P. Ann Arbor 1978. Pp. 283.
Tenth to twentieth centuries. German edition: no. 1612.

1595. GARRARD, J.G. (ed.), The Eighteenth Century in Russia. Oxford 1973. Pp. 356.
Essays: The Emergence of Modern Russian literature and Thought (Garrard); The Enlightenment in Russia (Raeff); Classicism in Eighteenth-Century Russian literature (Segal); Feofan Prokopovich (Cracraft); Jesuit Origins of Petrine Education (Okenfuss); Russian Students Abroad Under Peter I (Okenfuss); Novikov's journals (W.G. Jones); Diderot in Russia (Wilson); Moscow Freemasons and Rosicrucians (Ryu); British in Catherine's Russia (Cross); influences in Russian Art and Architecture (Rice); Russian Music (Swan and Spiegelman); Urban Planning under Catherine (R.E. Jones).

1596. ROGGER, H., 'The Russian National Character: Some Eighteenth-Century Views', *Harvard Slavic Studies*, IV (1957), 17-34.
Studies of Fon-Vizin, Novikov, L'vov, Plavil'ščikov.

1597. AUTY, R., LEWITTER, L.R. (eds), Gorski Vijenac: A Garland of Essays Offered to Professor Elizabeth Mary Hill. Cambridge, Eng. 1970. Pp. 321. Essays include Repertory Theatre in 1750s (M. Burgess); Catherine II and England (A.G. Cross).

1598. VENTURI, F., 'The European Enlightenment', in: Italy and the Enlightenment. Studies in a Cosmopolitan century, trans., ed. and intro., CORSI, S. and WOOLF, S. (London 1972), pp. 1-33.

1599. RAEFF, M., 'The Enlightenment in Russia and Russian Thought in the Enlightenment', in: GARRARD (ed.) (no. 1595). pp. 25-47.

1600. BLANCHARD, R.R., Jr., 'A Proposal for Social Reform in the Reign of Catherine II: Aleksei Polenov's Response to the Free Economic Society Competition of 1766-68', SUNY, Binghamton Ph.D., 1973.

1601. GLEASON, W., 'Political Ideals and Loyalties of some Russian Writers in the early 1760's', SR., XXXIV, 3 (1975), 560-575.

1602. LARAN, M., 'La première génération de l'"intelligentsia" roturière en Russie, 1750-80', Revue d'Histoire Moderne et Contemporaine (1966), 137-56. Explicitly an extension of SHTRANGE (no. 1625).

1603. LABRIOLLE, F. de., 'Le Prosveščenie russe et les 'Lumières' en France (1760-1798)', Revue des Etudes Slaves, 45 (1966), 75-91.

1604. RAEFF, M., 'Les Slaves, les Allemands, et les "Lumières"' CanAmSlSt., I, 4 (1967), 521-51.

1605. JABLONOWSKI, H., 'Die geistige Bewegung in Russland in der zweiten Hälfte des 18. Jahrhunderts', in: Colloque slavistique: le movement des idées dans les pays slaves pendant la seconde môitié du XVIIIe siècle. Uppsala, 20-21 aôut, 1960. Commission Internationale des Etudes Slaves. Edizioni di Richerche Slavistique, pp. 7-25; 26-57. Much criticised in ensuing discussion (ibid.).

1606. LOTMAN, J., 'Die Frühaufklärung und die Entwicklung des gesellschaftlichen Denkens in Russland', StGrL., 3 (1968), 93-119; 557-637.

1607. GRASSHOFF, H., 'Der Fortschrittsgedanke in der russischen Literatur der Aufklärung', ZfSl., XIV (1969), 444-452. From Prokopovich to Radishchev and Karamzin.

1608. MÜLLER, O.W., Intelligencija. Untersuchungen zur Geschichte eines politischen Schlagworts. Frankfurt a/M. 1971. Pp. 419.

1609. LESKY, E., KOSTIC, St.K., MATL, J., RAUCH, G.V. (hrsg.),
ISCHREYT, H. (red.), Die Aufklärung in Ost- und
Südosteuropa. Aufsätze, Vorträge, Dokumentationen. Köln-
Wien 1972. Pp. 239.
8 articles, ranging across E. Europe. 1970 conference
proceedings of the Studienkreis für Kulturbeziehungen in
Mittel- und Osteuropa. Further proceedings published in
1973, 1976, 1977.

1610. TURCZYNSKI, E., 'Gestaltwandel und Trägerschichten der
Aufklärung in Ost- und Südosteuropa', in: LESKY (no. 1609)
pp. 23-49.

1611. GRASSHOFF, H., LAUCH, A., LEHMANN, U., Humanistische
Traditionen der russischen Aufklärung. Berlin 1973.
Pp. 249.

1612. TSCHIZHEWSKIJ, D., Russische Geistesgeschichte. München
1974, 2nd ed. Pp. 359.

1613. NIEDERHAUSER, R., 'Slawische Aufklärung - osteuropäische
Aufklärung', *ZfSl.*, XXI (1976), 449-55.

1614. HOESCH, E., Die Kultur der Ostslaven. Handbuch der Kultur-
geschichte. II. Abteilung - Kulturen der Völker.
Wiesbaden 1977. Pp. 363, plates.
Rev: *SEER.*, LVIII, 4 (1979), 632 (Fennell, J.).
Admirable, though slim on the eighteenth century.

1615. LEHMANN, U., 'Zum Anteil der russischen Literatur des 18.
Jahrhunderts an der Entwicklung des Nationalbewusstseins',
ZfSl., XIII (1968), 669-680.

1616. LEHMANN, U., 'Zur Rolle Peterburgs als
Ausstrahlungszentrum russischen Nationalbewusstseins im
18. und beginnenden 19. Jhdt.', *ZfSl.*, XV (1970), 857-80.

1617. DONNERT, E., 'Die Leibeigenschaft im Ostbaltikum und die
livländische Aufklärungs-geschichtsschreibung', *JfGSLE.*,
V (1961), 185-199.

1618. DONNERT, E., 'Aufklärung und antileibeigenschaftliches
Denken in Russland in der zweiten Hälfte des 18. Jhdt.',
ZfG., XX (1972), 974-996.

1619. DONNERT, E., 'Radiščev und die Pugačevbewegung', *ZfSl.*,
XXII (1977), 84-7.

1620. HARDER, H.-B. (ed.), Festschrift für Alfred Rammelmeyer.
München 1975. Pp. 450.
Includes essays (in German) on history of German theatre
in St. Petersburg; Schiller's *Räuber* in Russia; Kantemir's
satires; Lessing and Moscow University.

1621. BERKOV, P. (ed.), Problemy russkogo prosveshcheniia v literature XVIII veka. M. 1961. Pp. 271.

1622. BELIAVSKII, M.T., 'Prosvetiteli na konkurse o sobstvennosti krest'ian Rossii', *VMU(Ist.)*, 2 (1961).

1623. KLIBANOV, A.I., 'K kharakteristike novykh iavlenii v russkoi obshchestvennoi mysli vtoroi poloviny XVII-nachala XVIII vv.', *Ist. SSSR.*, 6 (1963), 85-103.

1624. KOVALENSKAIA, N., Russkii klassitsizm. M. 1964. Pp. 700, illustrations.

1625. SHTRANGE, M.M., Demokraticheskaia intelligentsiia v Rossii v XVIII veke. M. 1965. Pp. 306.
Rev: *Vop. Ist.*, 4 (1966), 136-9 (Beliavskii, M.); *JbfGO.*, N.F., XIV (1966), 441-3 (Kaplan, F.).

1626. SHTRANGE, M.M., 'Idei prosveshcheniia v russkoi istoriografii 50-70kh gg. XVIII v.', in: PASHUTO (no. 612), pp. 177-87.

1627. MATL', I., 'Epokha Prosveshcheniia v Rossii i ee otlichie ot Prosveshcheniia v drugikh slavianskikh stran', *XVIII Vek.*, Sb. 7 (1966), 199-206.

1628. SHCHIPANOV, I.IA. (ed.), Russkie prosvetiteli (ot Radishcheva go Dekabristov). Sobranie proizvedenii v dvukh tomakh. 2 vols. M. 1966. Pp. 440, 478.

1629. CHISTOV, K., Russkie narodnye sotsial'no-utopicheskie legendy. XVII-XIX vv. M. 1967. Pp. 339.
Rev: *Kritika*, VII (1968), 19-25 (Okenfuss, M.).

1630. TIKHOMIROV, M.N., Russkaia kul'tura X-XVIII vekov. M. 1968. Pp. 446.

1631. UTKINA, N.F., Estestvennonauchnyi materializm v Rossii XVIII veka. M. 1971. Pp. 196.

1632. SHCHIPANOV, I.IA., Filosofiia russkogo prosveshcheniia: vtoraia polovina XVIII veka. M. 1971. Pp. 284.

1633. KAMENSKII, A.A., Filosofskie idei russkogo prosveshcheniia (Deistichesko-materialisticheskaia shkola). M. 1972. Pp. 396.
Late eighteenth and early nineteenth centuries.

1634. KRASNOBAEV, B., Ocherki istorii russkoi kul'tury XVIII veka. M. 1972. Pp. 335, illustrations.
Rev: *Vop. Ist.*,4 (1974), 138-41 (Rogov, A.I.).

1635. KRASNOBAEV, B., 'Russkaia kul'tura XVIII veka', *Ist. SSSR.*, 6 (1976), 29-45.

1636. KRASNOBAEV, B.I., 'O nekotorykh poniatiakh istorii russkoi kul'tury vtoroi poloviny XVII-pervoi poloviny XIX veka', *Ist. SSSR.*, 1 (1978), 56-73.

1637. ZAPADOV, A. (ed.), Istoriia russkoi zhurnalistiki XVIII-XIX vekov. M. 1973. 3rd ed. Pp. 520.

1638. VOLGIN, V.P., Ocherki istorii sotsialisticheskih idei (s drevnosti do kontsa XVIII v.). M. 1975. Pp. 294.

1639. KIRAI, N., 'Russkaia kul'tura XVIII veka v rabotakh IU.M. Lotmana', *CanAmSlSt.*, IX, 1 (1975), 43-53.

1640. LEHMANN, U., 'O nekotorykh osobennostiakh russkogo prosveshcheniia', *XVIII Vek.* Sb. 10, [Russkaia literatura XVIII veka i ee mezhdunarodnye sviazi] (1975), 59-63.

1641. KLIBANOV, A.I., Narodnaia sotsial'naia utopiia v Rossii. Vyp. 1: Period feodalizma. M. 1977. Pp. 335. Vyp. 2: XIX vek. M. 1978. Pp. 342.

1642. BUSLOV, K.P. (ed.), Idei gumanizma v obshchestvenno-politicheskoi i filosofskoi mysli Belorussii (dooktiabr'-skii period). Minsk 1977. Pp. 279.

1643. KUZ'MIN, A.G., 'Russkoe prosvetitel'stvo XVIII veka', *Vop. Ist.*, no. 1 (1978), 106-25.

1644. KURMACHEVA, M.D., 'Krepostnaia intelligentsiia v Rossii XVIII v.', *Vop. Ist.*, 1 (1979), 82-94.

History of ideas, Philosophy

1645. KONSTANTINOV, A. (ed.), Filosofskaia entsiklopediia. M. 1960-70.

1646. EVGRAFOV, V. et al. (eds), Istoriia filosofii v SSSR. M. 1968-71. 4 vols.

1647. GALAKTIONOV, A., NIKANDROV, P., Russkaia filosofiia XI-XIX vekov. L. 1970. Pp. 691.
Rev: *Kritika*, IX, 1 (1972), 13-33 (Okenfuss, M.).

1648. BELEN'KII, I.L. et al. (comps), Istoriia russkoi filosofii. Ukazatel' literatury izdannoi v SSSR na russkom iazyke za 1917-1967 gg. M. 1975. 3 vols. 8245 entries; vols 2 and 3 deal with nineteenth century.

1649. SHCHIPANOV, I.IA. (ed.), Protiv sovremennykh fal'-sifikatorov istorii russkoi filosofii. M. 1960. Pp. 453.

1650. NIKITINA, P. (ed.), Ocherki po istorii logiki v Rossii. M. 1962. Pp. 256.

1651. KULAKOVA, L.I., Ocherki istorii russkoi esteticheskoi mysli
XVIII v. L. 1968. Pp. 343.
= *Uch. Zap. Leningradsk. gos. ped. in-ta im. A.I. Gertsena*,
t.358. Rev: *ZfSl.*, XV (1970), 944-7 (Hoffmann, P.).

1652. SHCHIPANOV, I.IA., Moskovskii universitet i razvitie
filosofskoi i obshchestvenno-politicheskoi mysli v Rossii.
M. 1957. Pp. 468.

1653. PETROV, L.A., Obshchestvenno-politicheskaia i filosofskaia
mysl' Rossii pervoi poloviny XVIII veka. Lektsii po
spetskursu 'Istoriia russkoi filosofii'. Irkutsk 1975.
Pp. 275.

1654. NICHIK, V.M., Iz istorii otechestvennoi filosofii kontsa
XVII-nachala XVIII vv. Kiev 1978. Pp. 297.

12(b) - RUSSIA AND THE WEST

(i) General

No one work adequately surveys the topic, but a great volume of
recent writing illuminates and contributes to the overall
mosaic. CROSS (1657) is a compendium of accounts written by
contemporaries and gives some insight into Western perceptions
of Russia. VENTURI (1664) presents a number of fascinating
vignettes that support the view that the Russian enlightenment
started in the 1750s. ALEKSEEV (1668-70) and ALPATOV (1671) complete the mosaic further with studies on important secondary
aspects of major figures.

1655. ROBERTS, H.L., RAEFF, M., SZEFTEL, M., discussion on
'Russia and The West: A Comparison and Contrast',
SR., XXIII, 1 (1964), 1-30.

1656. LEDNICKI, W., Russia, Poland and the West. Essays in
Literary and Cultural History. Port Washington 1955.
Pp. 419.

1657. CROSS, A.G., Russia Under Western Eyes, 1517-1825. London
1971. Pp. 400. 185 plates.
Rev: 'Russia Through European Eyes', *European Studies
Review*, VI, 2 (1976), 249-257 (Hollingsworth, B.).

1658. HANEY, B.M., 'Western Reflections of Russia, 1517-1812',
Washington, Seattle Ph.D., 1971.

1659. WREN, M.C., The Western Impact Upon Tsarist Russia.
Chicago 1971. Pp. 254.

1660. WITTRAM, R., Russia and Europe. N.Y. 1973. Pp. 180.

1661. TREADGOLD, D.W., The West in Russia and China: Religious
and Secular Thought in Modern Times. 2 vols. I: Russia,
1477-1917; 2: China, 1582-1949. N.Y. 1973. Pp. 324, 251.
Rev: *J. European Studies* 4 (1974), 103 (Bartlett, R.P.).

1662. ROWE, E., Hamlet - A Window on Russia. N.Y. 1976. Pp. 186.
"examines Russian life and culture through the perspective
provided by Russia's reaction to *Hamlet* from 1748 to the
present".

1663. RAUCH, G. von, 'Political Pre-Conditions for East-West
Cultural Relations in the Eighteenth Century', *CanAmSlSt.*,
XIII, 4 (1979), 391-411.
This number of *CanAmSlSt.* is a Special Issue on 'Russia
and the West'. An earlier German version of this article
appeared in LESKY (no. 1609), pp. 1-22.

1664. VENTURI, F., Europe des Lumières. Recherches sur le
dixhuitième siècle. Paris-The Hague 1971. Pp. 300.
Essays: Beccaria in Russia; Pietro Verri in Russia; the
Enlightenment in eighteenth-century Russia.

1665. LOCHER, T.J.G., Das abendländische Russlandbild seit dem
16ten Jahrhundert. Wiesbaden 1965. Pp. 35

1666. PAVLOVA-SIL'VANSKAIA, M.P., 'Problemy vneshnei politiki i
kul'turnykh sviazei Rossii pervoi chetverti XVIII veka v
nauchnoi literature sotsialisticheskikh stran', *Ist. SSSR.*,
4 (1972), 177-84.

1667. KONRAD, N., Zapad i vostok. M. 1966. Pp. 518.
Rev: *Kritika*, V, 3 (1969), 1-7 (Gleason, A.).

1668. ALEKSEEV, M.P. (ed.), Epokha prosveshcheniia. Iz istorii
mezhdunarodnykh sviazei russkoi literatury. M. 1967.
Pp. 363.
Essays: English journals in Russia; Rousseau, Voltaire,
Lessing and Goldoni in Russian translations and literature.

1669. ALEKSEEV, M.P. (ed.), Ot klassitsizma do romantizma. Iz
istorii mezhdunarodnykh sviazei russkoi literatury.
M. 1970. Pp. 391.
Essays: Dante and Russia; Voltaire in Russia; English
literature and Russian sentimentalism; English literature
and Russian translations 1745-1812; Wieland and Russia.

1670. ALEKSEEV, M.P. (ed.), Rossiia i zapad. M. 1973. Pp. 340.
Essays:Schiller and Siberia; Tasso in Russia, Viazemskii and
Voltaire.

1671. ALPATOV, M.A., Russkaia istoricheskaia mysl' i zapadnaia
Evropa, XVII-pervaia chetvert' XVIII vv. M. 1976. Pp. 455.
Essays: Petrine diplomats in the West; historical thought
in time of Peter the Great; Tatishchev and West European
history; St. P. *Vedomosti;* diaries of Patrick Gordon, J.
Korb, I. Yule, J. Perry, F. Weber.
Rev: *Vop. Ist.*, 3 (1978), 142-4 (Kurskov, IU.).

1672. KARATAEV, N. et al., Istoriia ekonomicheskikh uchenii
zapadnoi Evropy i Rossii. M. 1959. Pp. 549.

1673. LEVIN, IU., ROVDA, K. (eds), Vospriiatie russkoi literatury
na zapade. M. 1975. Pp. 279.
Essays: Russia and French tragedy; English journal
'Moskovit'(1714); Russian diaries of Poltava;
plus excellent bibliography of Pushkin House works
(1958-1975) on Russian-foreign literary relations.

*(ii) France and Russia: Cultural and Scientific
Relations and Influences*

There is no comprehensive recent treatment; HAUMANT (1679),
the older standard, is now dated. MOHRENSCHILDT (1674) and
LABRIOLLE (1603) examine the reciprocal impact of Russia upon
France. The role of the French *philosophes* is explored
especially in BERKOV's discussion of the select translations of
the *Encyclopédie* into Russian (1682); in 1686; and in 1696-
1702 and 1703-1713, which treat Diderot and Voltaire respectively. The impact of the French Revolution is covered elsewhere, in Section 8.

1674. MOHRENSCHILDT, D.S. von., Russia in the Intellectual Life
of Eighteenth Century France. N.Y. 1936, rep.1972.Pp.325.

1675. IGNATIEFF, L., 'French Emigrés in Russia, 1789-1825. The
Interaction of Cultures in Times of Stress', Michigan Ph.D.,
1963.

1676. HARCOURT, F., 'Madame Vigée le Brun in St. Petersburg,
1795-1801', *The Cornhill Magazine*, 1083-4 (1975), 143-162.

1677. MAGGS, B.W., 'Eighteenth-Century Russian Reflections on the
Lisbon Earthquake, Voltaire and Optimism', *Studies on
Voltaire and the Eighteenth Century*, CXXXXVII (1975), 7-29.

1678. SERMAN, I.Z., 'Fonvizin and Fénelon', *SGECRN.*, 5 (1977),
33-36.

1679. HAUMANT, E., La Culture Française en Russie, 1700-1900.
Paris, 2nd ed., 1913, reprinted ORP., Cambridge 1971.
Pp. 514.

1680. CALLEWAERT, J., 'Relations intellectuelles de la Russie et
de la France au XVIIIe siècle', *CSP.*, XII, 4 (1970), 431-41.

1681. GORDON, L.S., 'Gabriel-François Coyer et son oeuvre en
Russie', *Revue des Etudes Slaves*, 42 (1963), 67-82.

1682. BERKOV, P.N., 'Histoire de l'*Encyclopédie* dans la Russie du XVIII siècle', *Revue des Etudes Slaves*, XLIV, 1 (1965), 47-58.

1683. LANGEVIN, L., 'La pénétration des oeuvres de Lomonosov dans la France du XVIIIe siècle', *Dix-Huitième siècle*, 3 (1971), 237-252.

1684. NEVSKAJA, N.I., 'Joseph Nicolas Delisle (1688-1768)', *Revue d'Histoire des Sciences*, 3 (1973), 289-313. D's influence on Russian scientific personnel in the period 1720-1750.

1685. KNIAJETSKAJA, E., CHENAKAL, V.L., 'Pierre le Grand et les fabricants français d'instruments scientifiques', *Revue d'Histoire des Sciences*, 3 (1975), 243-58.

1686. KOGAN-BERNSHTEIN, F.A., 'Vliianie idei Montesk'e v Rossii v XVIII veke', *Vop. Ist.*, 5 (1955), 99-110.

1687. BELIAVSKII, M.T., 'Frantsuzskie prosvetiteli i konkurs o sobstvennosti krepostnykh krest'ian v Rossii (1766-1768 gg.)', *VMU(Ist.)*, 6 (1960), 26-52; 2 (1961), 58-77.

1688. LOTMAN, IU., 'Russo i russkaia kul'tura XVIII-nachala XIX veka', in: ALEKSEEV-POPOV, V.S. et al. (comp. and eds), Zhan-Zhak Russo, Traktaty. M. 1969. Pp. 703.

1689. KULIABKO, E., 'Nauchnye sviazi Zh.-L. Biuffona s Petersburgskoi Akademiei Nauk', *Frants. Ezh.*(1971), 282-7.

1690. KNIAZHETSKAIA, E.A., 'Petr I - chlen frantsuzskoi Akademii Nauk', *Vop. Ist.*, 12 (1972), 199-203.

1691. MORIAKOV, V.I., 'Russkii perevod "Istorii obeikh Indii" Reinalia', *VMU(Ist.)*, 1 (1972), 55-68.

1692. BUACHIDZE, G.S., Retif de la Bretonn v Rossii. Tbilisi 1972. Pp. 241. French résumé.

1693. EL'KINA, I.M., 'Frantsuzskie prosvetiteli i kniga Shappa d'Otrosha (Jean Chappe d'Auteroche) o Rossii', *VMU(Ist.)*, 6 (1973), 71-81.

1694. ZHANNE, D., 'Frantsuzskii iazyk v Rossii XVIII v. kak obshchestvennoe iavlenie', *VMU.* (Filosofiia), 1 (1978), 62-71.

1695. CHABAN, A., Progressivnaia sotsiologicheskaia mysl' Rossii i Ukrainy vtoroi poloviny XVIII-nachala XIX v. i frantsuzskoe Prosveshchenie. Kiev 1979.

1696. BARR, G., 'Natural Rights: the Soviet and the "bourgeois" Diderot', in: HEER, R., PARKER, R. (eds), Ideas in History. Essays presented to L. Gottschalk (Durham, N.C. 1965), pp. 330-48.

1697. SAUTER, U., 'Diderot, counsellor of Catherine II', *Revue Université d'Ottawa,* 42, 1 (1972), 108-72.

1698. WILSON, A., 'Diderot in Russia', in: GARRARD (no. 1595), pp. 166-197.

1699. DIDEROT, D., Oeuvres Politiques, ed.P. VERNIERE, Paris 1963. Pp. 523.
Section 'Diderot et Catherine II': pp. 214-458.

1700. DIDEROT, D., Mémoires pour Catherine II. Texte établi d'après l'autographe de Moscou ... Ed. P. VERNIERE, Paris 1966. Pp. 316.

1701. ALEKSEEV, M.P., 'D. Didro i russkie pisateli ego vremeni', *XVIII Vek.,* Sb. 3 (1958), 416-31.

1702. BIL'BASOV, V., Didro v Peterburge 1773-1774. St. P. 1884, reprinted Cambridge 1971. Pp. 320.
Reprint contains long introduction (in English), and bibliography, by A. Lentin.

- *Voltaire.* See also nos. 1481, 1497, 1668-9.

1703. REDDAWAY, W.F. (ed.), Documents of Catherine the Great; the correspondence of Voltaire and the Instruction of 1767 in the English text. Cambridge 1931, reprinted 1972. Pp. 349.

1704. LENTIN, A. (trans. and ed.), Voltaire and Catherine the Great: Selected Correspondence. Cambridge, Eng. 1974. Pp. 194.

1705. WILBERGER, C.H., Voltaire's Russia: window on the East. Oxford 1976. Pp. 287.
=*Studies on Voltaire and The Eighteenth Century,* CLXIV. Based on Ph.D. thesis, Cornell 1973.

1706. ZABOROV, P., 'Le théâtre de Voltaire en Russie au XVIIIe siècle', *CMRS.,* IX, 1 (1968), 145-76.

1707. HAINTZ, O., 'Peter der Grosse, Friedrich der Grosse und Voltaire. Zur Entstehungsgeschichte von Voltaires "Histoire de l'Empire de Russie sous Pierre le Grand"'. Akad. der Wissenschaften und der Literatur in Mainz, *Abhandlungen der geistes- und sozialwissenschaftlichen Klasse,* 5 (1961), 511-56.
Rev: *ZfSl.,* VIII (1963), 147-8 (Grau, C.).

1708. DONNERT, E., 'Voltaire und die Petersburger Freie
      Oekonomische Gesellschaft', *ZfSl.*, XIX, 1 (1974), 66-9.

1709. ALEKSEEV, M. (ed.), Biblioteka Vol'tera. Katalog knig.
      M.-L. 1961. Pp. 640.

1710. LIUBLINSKII, V.S., 'Novoe o russkikh sviaziakh Vol'tera',
      XVIII Vek., Sb. 3 (1958), 433-9.
      Critique of Bestermann's work on Voltaire's correspondence.

1711. IAM, K., 'Trudy Vol'tera v Rossii', *Frants. Ezh.* (1971),
      5-22.

1712. ZABOROV, P., '"Russkii Vol'ter" v rukopisnom otdele
      Pushkinskogo Doma', *Ezhegodnik ruk. otd. Push. Doma*
      (1974), 83-8.

1713. ZABOROV, P., Russkaia literatura i Vol'ter: XVIII-pervaia
      tret' XIX vv. M. 1978. Pp. 264.

*(iii) Germany and Russia: Cultural and Scientific
       Relations and Influences*

This field has attracted a large number of scholars in recent
years, particularly in E. and W. Germany, and produced much
new information on German-Russian relations and their impact
on Russian life. The doyen and inspirer of work in the D.D.R.
has been WINTER; appropriately, his Festschrift (1737) is of
special interest. In the B.R.D. AMBURGER (1731, 1741) and VON
RAUCH (1663, 1743) have been leading figures. The broad division here of German work into general and collective studies
(1729-47) and accounts of individuals (1748-78) reflects the
comprehensive coverage given. Leonhard Euler, who appears
under both, has been especially well covered - see also 1714,
1781. RAEFF (1604) is a valuable early exploration of the
German underpinnings of the Russian Enlightenment, based on
the new German research.

1714. TRUESDALL, C., 'Leonard Euler, Supreme Geometer (1707-
      1783)', in: PAGLIARO, H. (ed.), *Studies in Eighteenth
      Century Culture*, II (London 1972), pp. 51-95.

1715. HOME, R.W., 'Science as a Career: the Case of F.V.T.
      Aepinus', *SEER.*, LI, 122 (1973), 75-94.

1716. McGOLDRICK, J.J., 'Russia in the Writings of August von
      Kotzebue. A Study of his Satire and Irony', Ph.D., SUNY
      at Buffalo, 1975.

1717. BARTLETT, R.P., 'J.R. Forster's Stay in Russia, 1765-66:
      Diplomatic and Official Accounts', *JbfGO.*, XXIII, 1
      (1975), 489-95.

1718. HOARE, M., The Tactless Philosopher: Johann Reinhold Forster. Melbourne 1976. Pp. 419.

1719. BOND, M., 'A.L. von Schlözer: A German Political Journalist. Theory and Practice in the Light of the French Revolutions', *European Studies Review*, VI, 1 (1976), 61-72.

1720. CROSS, A.G., '"Nachricht von einigen russischen Schriftstellern" (1768): A New Document and a Bibliography', *SGECRN.*, 4 (1976), 32-43.

1721. HADLEY, M., 'The Sublime Housewife: An Eighteenth-Century German View of Catherine the Great', *Germano-Slavica*, II, 3 (1977), 181-8.

1722. PETSCHAUER, P., 'The Philosopher and The Reformer: Tsar Peter I, G.W. Leibniz and The College System', *CanAmSlSt.*, XIII, 4 (1979), 473-87.

1723. BERKOV, P., 'Deutsch-russische kulturelle Beziehungen im 18. Jahrhundert! (Translated from the Russian) . *Wissenschaftliche Annalen* VI (1957), 686-701. Also in no. 1727.

1724. BERKOV, P., 'Aus der Geschichte der deutsch-russischen Theaterbeziehungen im 18. Jhdt.', *ZfSl.*, I, 4 (1956), 9-13.

1725. WINTER, E., 'Zur Geschichte der deutsch-russischen Wissenschaftsbeziehungen im 18. Jhdt.', *ZfG.*, IX, 4 (1960), 844-55.

1726. GRAU, C., 'Russisch-sächsische Beziehungen auf dem Gebiet des Berg- und Hüttenwesens in der ersten Hälfte des 18. Jhdts', *Jahrbuch für Geschichte der UdSSR*, IV (1960), 302-330.

1727. WINTER, E. et al. (eds), Die deutsch-russische Begegnung und Leonhard Euler. Beiträge zu den Beziehungen zwischen der deutschen und der russischen Wissenschaft und Kultur im 18. Jhdt. Berlin 1958. Pp. 196.
Papers of 250th anniversary symposium. 16 articles cover Euler, Ludolf, Frisch, Prokopovich, Tatishchev, Gerstenberg.

1728. WINTER, E. et al. (eds), Die Berliner und die Petersburger Akademie der Wissenschaften im Briefwechsel Leonhard Eulers. I: Der Briefwechsel Eulers mit G. Müller (1737-67). Berlin 1959. Pp. 327. II: Briefwechsel Eulers mit Nartov, Razumovskij, Schumacher, Teplov und der Petersburger Akademie (1730-63). Berlin 1961. Pp. 464. III: Wissenschaftliche und wissenschaftsorganisatorische Korrespondenzen, 1726-74. Berlin 1976. Pp. 408. Rev: I: *ZfSl.*, VIII (1963), 146-7; II: *ZfG.*, X (1962), 990-1; III: *ZfG.*, XXV (1977), 1103-4.

1729. WINTER, E. (ed.), Leonhard Euler und Christian Goldbach. Briefwechsel,1729-1764. Berlin 1965. Pp. 420.

1730. MOHRMANN, H., Studien über russisch-deutsche Begegnungen in der Wirtschaftswissenschaft, 1750-1825. Berlin 1959. Pp. 146.

1731. AMBURGER, E., Beiträge zur Geschichte der deutsch-russischen kulturellen Beziehungen. Geissen 1961. Pp. 277. Studies on science, medicine and education.

1732. WINTER, E. (ed.), Lomonosov, Schlözer, Pallas: Deutsch-russische Wissenschaftsbeziehungen im 18. Jahrhundert. Berlin 1962. Pp. 358.

1733. MILLER, M., 'Deutsche-russische Wissenschaftsbeziehungen in der Mathematik im 18. Jh.', *JfGSLE.*, VII (1963), 361-66.

1734. JUSHKEVICH, A., 'Zu den russisch-deutschen Beziehungen auf mathematischen Gebiet in der Mitte des 18. Jahrhunderts', *JfGSLE.*, VIII (1964), 367-79.

1735. RÖSEL, H., Beiträge zur Geschichte der Slawistik an den Universitäten Halle und Leipzig im 18. und 19. Jahrhundert. Heidelberg 1964. Pp. 219.

1736. WINTER, E., Frühaufklärung. Der Kampf gegen den Konfessionalismus in Mittel- und Osteuropa und die deutsch-slawische Begegnung. Berlin 1966. Pp. 423. Includes Russia and Ukraine. Rev: *ZfG.*, XVII (1969), 641-3 (Wolfgramm, E.).

1737. STEINITZ, P.W., BERKOV, P., MOHR, H., GRAU, C. (eds), Ost und West in der Geschichte des Denkens und der kulturellen Beziehungen. Festschrift für Eduard Winter zum 70. Geburtstag. Berlin 1966. Pp. 816. Bibliography of Winter's works to 1966: pp. 5-27. Rev: *ZfG.*, XVI (1968), 371-3.

1738. GRAU, C., Petrinische kulturpolitische Bestrebungen und ihr Einfluss auf die Gestaltung der deutsch-russischen wissenschaftlichen Beziehungen im ersten Drittel des 18. Jhdts. Habilitationsschrift. Berlin 1967.

1739. SCHMIDT, H., 'Berührungen der deutschen und russischen Aufklärung in der Regierungszeit Katherinas II', *StGrL.*, 3 (1968), 443-464; 615-6.

1740. MUENTJES, M., Beiträge zum Bild des Deutschen in der russischen Literatur von Katharina bis auf Alexander II. Meisenheim am Glan 1971. Pp. 125.

1741. KRUEGER, H.-J. (ed.), Archivalische Fundstücke zu den russisch-deutschen Beziehungen: Erik Amburger zum 65. Geburtstag. Berlin 1973. Pp. 199.
Essays: French Mediation in Northern War (Schenk); R.-Latin American Studies, 1717-1915 (Lukin); Ludwig Gruno's diary (Krüger); Wilhelm Hetling's testimony on Paul's coronation (Elias); Peter the Great (Scheibert).

1742. GRASSHOFF, H., Russische Literatur in Deutschland im Zeitalter der Aufklärung; die Propagierung russischer Literatur im 18. Jahrhundert durch deutsche Schriftsteller und Publizisten. Berlin 1973. Pp. 476.

1743. LISZKOWSKI, U. (ed.), Russland und Deutschland. Stuttgart 1974. Pp. 334.
Festschrift for G. von Rauch. =*Kieler Historische Studien*, XXII. Essays: Königsberg Freemasons and Russia, 1760-63 (Ischreyt); German-Russian relations in Estonia (Weiss); H. von Fick and Peter I (Spieler); J.G. Eisen (Neuschäffer); Russian-German diplomatic relations and Poland (Zernack).

1744. HOEFERT, S., Russische Literatur in Deutschland. Tübingen 1974. Pp. 174.

1745. STRAUBE, F., 'Zur Deutschland-politik des zaristischen Russlands 1789 bis 1815', *JfGSLE.*, XIX, 1 (1975), 103-126.

1746. LEMKE, H., WIDERA, B. (eds), Russisch-deutsche Beziehungen von der Kiever Rus bis zur Oktoberrevolution. Berlin 1976. Pp. 329.

1747. MUEHLPFORDT, G., 'Die Petersburger Aufklärung und Halle', *CanAmClCt.*, XIII, 4 (1979), 488-500.

1748. WINTER, E., '"Einige Nachricht von Herrn Simeon Todorski", Ein Denkmal der deutsch-slawischen Freundschaft in 18. Jhdt.', *ZfSl.*, I (1956), 73-100.

1749. MUEHLPFORDT, G., 'Christian Wolff, ein Enzyklopädist der deutschen Aufklärung', *JfGSLE.*, I (1956), 66-102.

1750. MOROZOV, A., 'Christian Wolffs Leser in Russland', *JfGSLE.*, VII (1963), 411-23.

1751. WINTER, E., 'Ein Bericht von Johann Werner Paus aus dem Jahre 1732', *ZfSl.*, III (1958), 744-70.

1752. HOFFMAN, P., 'Gerhard Friedrich Müller', *ZfSl.*, III (1958), 771-86.

1753. FIGUROVSKIJ, N.A., Leben und Werk der Chemikers Tobias Lowitz (1757-1804). Ein Beitrag zur Geschichte der Begegnung deutscher und russischer Wissenschaft im 18 Jhdt. Mit einem Anhang von Dokumenten und Briefen hrsg. von E. Winter. Berlin 1959. Pp. 159.

1754. TETZNER, J., 'Die Leipziger Neue Zeitung von gelehrten Sachen über die Anfänge der Peterburger Akademie', *ZfSl.*, V (1960), 112-26.

1755. FEYL, D., 'Zwei Russlandbilder der Jenaer Aufklärung', *ZfSl.*, V, 1 (1960), 112-26.

1756. CHUCHMAREV, V., 'G.W. Leibniz und die russische Kultur zu Beginn des 18. Jahrhunderts', *Deutsche Zeitschrift für Philosophie*, 8 (1960), 94-107.

1757. WINTER, E., G.W. Leibniz und die Aufklärung. Berlin 1968. Pp. 14.

1758. HEXELSCHNEIDER, E., 'Zur frühen Fonvizin-Rezeption in Deutschland', *ZfSl.*, V (1960), 22-34.

1759. WINTER, E. et al. (eds), E.-W. von Tschirnhaus und die Frühaufklärung in Mittel- und Osteuropa. Berlin 1960. Pp. 346.
Rev: *ZfSl.*, VII (1962), 135-6 (Blaschke, W.).

1760. WINTER, E., 'E.-W. von Tschirnhaus (1651-1708) und die deutsch-slawische Wechselseitigkeit in der europäischen Aufklärung', *ZfSl.*, V (1960), 17-21.

1761. BUCHOLTZ, A., Die Göttinger Russlandsammlung Georgs von Asch. Giessen 1961. Pp. 189.

1762. SCHMIDT, H., 'Johann Heinrich Gottlob von Justi, ein vergessener Vertreter der deutschen Aufklärung des XVIII Jahrhunderts, und Russland', *Wissenschaftliche Zeitschrift der Universität Halle/Wittenberg, Gesellschafts- und Sprachwissenschaftliche Reihe*, X, 1 (1961), 272-79.

1763. WINTER, E. (ed.), August Ludwig Schlözer und Russland. Berlin 1961. Pp. 341.
Rev: *ZfSl.*, VIII (1963), 144-6 (Lehmann, U.).

1764. VOLK, O., 'Uber Keplers Manuskripte und ihren Ankauf durch Katharina II', *JfGSLE.*, VII (1963), 381-8.

1765. WINTER, E., 'Die russische und die deutsche Frühaufklärung und die Erforschung Sibiriens insbesondere durch Messerschmidt', *JfGSLE.*, VI (1962), 189-202.

1766. JAROSCH, G., 'Tabbert-Strahlenberg als Reisegefährte Messerschmidts', in: *Ost und West* (no. 1737), pp. 215-20.

1767. HOFFMAN, P., 'Anton Friedrich Büschings Wöchentliche
Nachrichten als Bibliographie der Russlandliteratur
siebziger und achtziger Jahre des 18. Jhdts., in: *Ost und
West* (no. 1737),pp. 321-331.

1768. LEHMANN, U., Der Gottsched-kreis und Russland. Deutsch-
russische Literaturbeziehungen im Zeitalter der Aufklärung.
Berlin 1966. Pp. 354.
Includes letters of J. Stählin from 1750s-1760s.

1769. GRASSHOFF, H., 'Gottsched als Popularisator und Übersetzer
russischer Literatur', *ZfSl.*, XV (1970), 189-207.

1770. GRAU, C., HOFFMAN, P., 'Zur Verbreitung der Petersburger
Akademiepublikation in Deutschland im 18. Jahrhundert',
StGrL., 2 (1968), 122-134; 398-400.

1771. STEINER, G., 'J.R. Forsters und Georg Forsters Beziehungen
zu Russland', *StGrL.*, 3 (1968), 245-311.

1772. SLAVISCHE SEMINAR, UNIVERSITÄT LEIPZIG, A.N. Radiščev und
Deutschland: Beiträge zur Literatur des ausgehenden 18.
Jahrhunderts. Berlin 1969. Pp. 132.

1773. LAUCH, A., Wissenschaft und kulturelle Beziehungen in der
russischen Aufklärung: zum Wirken H.L.Ch. Bacmeisters.
Berlin 1969. Pp. 444.
Includes a discussion of Bacmeister's bibliographically
important *Russische Bibliothek zur Kenntnis des
gegenwärtigen Zustandes der Literatur in Russland*. 11 vols.
St. P.-Riga-Leipzig; 1772-1789.   Rev: *CanAmSlSt.*, V, 3
(1971), 435-6 (Raeff, M.).

1774. HARDER, H., Schiller in Russland; Materialien zur einer
Wirkungsgeschichte 1789-1814. Bad Homburg 1969. Pp. 234.

1775. NEUMANN, F., 'Beiträge zur Aufnahme und Wirkung Kants in
Russland', *Jb. der Albertus-Universität zu Königsberg*, 21
(1971), 5-17.

1776. LOEW, R., 'Johann Heinrich von Busse und sein "Journal von
Russland" (1793-96)', *ZfSl.*, XVII (1972), 263-71

1777. WINTER, E., 'Friedrich Adelung: Ein Pionier der deutsch-
russisch-amerikanischer Sprachwissenschaftsbeziehungen',
East Central Europe, II, 2 (1975), 171-5.

1778. DONNERT, E., 'Antrittsrede Leonhard Eulers vor der Freien
Ökonomischen Gesellschaft zu St. Petersburg im Dezember
1766', *ZfSl.*, 2 (1979), 254-7.

1779. ZHITOMIRSKAIA, Z., I.V. Gete (Goethe), bibliograficheskii
ukazatel' ... na russkom iazyke, 1780-1971. M. 1972.
Pp. 616.

1780. POSPELOV, P., SHEELIA, G. (eds), Russko-germanskie
nauchnye sviazi mezhdu Akademiei Nauk SSSR i Akademiei
Nauk GDR, 1700-1974. M. 1975. Pp. 294.

1781. IUSHKEVICH, A.P., SMIRNOV, V.I. (eds), Leonard Eiler.
Perepiska. Annotirovannyi ukazatel'. L. 1967. Pp. 391.
Exhaustive index to Euler's correspondence.
Rev: *ZfG.*, XVI (1968), 1088 (Hoffmann, P.).

1782. 'KONFERENTSIIA o nemetsko-russkikh nauchnykh
otnosheniiakh vo vtoroi polovine XVIII v.', *Ist. SSSR.*, 5
(1960), 229-31.

1783. FEIGINA, S., 'Politicheskaia i kul'turnaia zhizn' Rossii v
nachale XVIII v. v osveshchenii zapadnogermanskogo istorika
Vittrama', in: KOROLIUK (ed.) (no. 1858), pp. 345-359.
Sympathetic discussion of *Peter I:Czar und Kaiser* (no.336).

1784. CHUCHMAREV, V., G.-V. Leibnits i russkaia kul'tura.
M. 1968. Pp. 48.
Based on his article (no. 1756). Rev: *Kritika*, VI, 1
(1969), 10-22 (Okenfuss, M.).

1785. NEDZEL'SKII, F.V., 'Eiler i Lomonosov. (Nekotorye aspekty
ikh otnosheniia k kartesianstvu i n'iutonianstvu)', in:
KOROLIUK, V.D. et al. (eds), Issledovaniia po slaviano-
germanskim otnosheniiam (M. 1971), pp. 322-45.

1786. IANKELOVICH, L., 'Iogann Gotfrid Gerder i Garlib Merkel'.
(O tvorcheskikh sviaziakh peredovykh myslitelei Germanii i
Latvii XVIII-XIX vv.)', *Uchenye Zapiski Latviiskogo Un-ta*
219 (1974), 86-106.

1787. MARTYNOV, I., 'Russkaia literatura i nauka v
Peterburgskikh nemetskikh zhurnalakh epokhi prosveshcheniia'
Die Welt der Slaven, XIX-XX (1974-75), 80-97.

1788. LUKIN, T., Karl Ber [Baer]: Peterburgskaia Akademiia Nauk:
Pis'ma deiateliam Peterburgskoi Akademii. L. 1975.
Pp. 245.
Letters in French & German with Russian translation.

1789. MAIER, L., 'K istorii russko-nemetskikh nauchnykh sviazei
v XVIII v.', *VMU(Ist.)*, 4 (1978), 29-36.
Lomonosov-Gmelin.

(iv) Great Britain and Russia: Cultural and
   Scientific Relations and Influences

ANDERSON (1790) has long remained the standard general survey, but the recent work of British and other scholars has revealed (as in the case with German-Russian relations) a veritable treasure trove of new material. The most recent major work is CROSS (1796); his *Proceedings* (1794) also provide essays on all aspects of the subject. General and collective treatments: 1790-1796; individuals and specific topics: 1797-1827. See also nos. 2675-76.

1790. ANDERSON, M.S., Britain's Discovery of Russia, 1553-1815. London 1958. Pp. 245

1791. MARTYNOV, I.F., 'English Literature and Eighteenth Century Russian Reviewers', *OSP.*, N.S., IV (1971), 30-42.

1792. CROSS, A.G., 'The British in Catherine's Russia: A Preliminary Survey', in: GARRARD (no.1595), pp. 233-67.

1793. CROSS, A.G. (comp.), Anglo-Russian Relations in the Eighteenth Century: A Catalogue of an Exhibition. Norwich 1977. Pp. 58.

1794. CROSS, A.G. (ed.), Great Britain and Russia in the Eighteenth Century: Contacts and Comparisons. Proceedings of An International Conference held at the University of East Anglia, Norwich, England 11-15 July 1977. Newtonville 1979. Pp. 323.

1795. CROSS, A.G., 'British Knowledge of Russian Culture (1698-1801)', *CanAmSlSt.*, XIII, 4 (1979), 412-35.

1796. CROSS, A.G., "By The Banks of The Thames". Russians in Eighteenth-Century Britain. Newtonville 1980. Pp. 350.

1797. McLEAN, H., "The Adventures of an English Comedy in Eighteenth-Century Russia: Dodsley's *Toy Shop* and Lukin's *Ščepetil'nik*," in: American Contributions to the Fifth International Congress of Slavists, Sofiia, September 1963, II: Literary Contributions (The Hague 1963), pp. 201-12.

1798. MAVOR, E., The Virgin Mistress. A Study In Survival. The Life of the Duchess of Kingston. London 1964. Pp. 208.

1799. CROSS, A.G., 'The Duchess of Kingston in Russia', *History Today*, XXVII (1977), 390-95.

1800. McLEISH, J., 'Illiteracy and Social Change: A Comparative Socio-Psychological Study of Certain Welsh, English, Russian and Polish Movements to Increase Popular Enlightenment in the Eighteenth, Nineteenth and Twentieth Centuries', Leeds Ph.D., 1964.

1801. PRESCOTT, J.A., 'The Russian Free Economic Society: Foundation Years', *Agricultural History* 51, 3 (1977) 503-12.
Develops articles published in *J. Royal Society of Arts*, 1965, 1967. Significance of Society of Arts and J. Sievers in the founding of the Free Economic Society. Jejune.

1802. URNESS, C. (ed.), A Naturalist in Russia: Letters from Peter Simon Pallas to Thomas Pennant. Minneapolis 1967. Pp. 189.

1803. PITCHER, H.J., 'A Scottish View of Catherine's Russia: William Richardson's "Anecdotes of the Russian Empire" (1784)', *Forum for Modern Language Studies*, III, 3 (1967), 236-71.

1804. SWANN,H., Home on the Neva. London 1968. Pp. 198. The Hynam family in Russia in the late eighteenth century.

1805. SPRIGGE, T., CHRISTIE, I., MILNE, A.T. (eds), Jeremy Bentham: Correspondence. London 1968-77. 6 vols to date. Letters from Jeremy's brother Samuel, in Russia in the 1780s and 1790s.

1806. PAPMEHL, K.A., 'Samuel Bentham and the *Sobesednik*, 1783', *SEER.*, XLVI (1968), 210-19. See also nos 1347-48.

1807. SWEET, J.M., 'Matthew Guthrie (1743-1807: An Eighteenth-Century Gemmologist', *Annals of Science*, XX, 4 (1964), 245-302.

1808. PAPMEHL, K.A., 'Matthew Guthrie - The Forgotten Student of Eighteenth Century Russia', *CSP.*, XI, 2 (1969), 167-182.

1809. CROSS, A.G., 'Arcticus and The Bee (1790-1794): An Episode in Anglo-Russian Cultural Relations', *OSP.*, N.S., II (1969), 62-76.
Matthew Guthrie

1810. CROSS, A.G., 'The Reverend William Tooke's Contribution to English Knowledge of Russia at the End of the Eighteenth Century', *CanSlSt.*, III, 1 (1969), 106-16.

1811. CROSS, A.G., 'John Rogerson: Physician to Catherine the Great', *CanAmSlSt.*, IV, 3 (1970), 594-601.

1812. CROSS, A.G., 'Chaplains to the British Factory in St. Petersburg, 1723-1813'., *Eur.St.Rev.*, II, 2 (1972), 125-42.

1813. CALINGER, R.S., 'The Introduction of the Newtonian Natural Philosophy into Russia and Prussia (1725-1772)', Chicago Ph.D., 1971.

1814. BOSS, V., Newton and Russia: the Early Influence, 1698-
1796. Cambridge, Mass. 1972. Pp. 309.
Based on Harvard Ph.D. thesis, 1962. Rev: *Ist. SSSR.*, 3
(1974), 212-4 (Kopelevich, IU.).

1815. CHENAKAL, V.L.,'Astronomical Instruments of John Rowley
in Eighteenth-Century Russia,' *Journal for the History of
Astronomy*, III (1972), 199-235.

1816. BARRATT, G., 'The Melancholy and the Wild: A Note on
Macpherson's Russian Success', *Studies in Eighteenth
Century Culture*, III (1973), 125-37.

1817. DUKES, P., 'Ossian and Russia', *Scottish Literary News*,
III, 3 (1973), 17-21.

1818. LEVIN, IU., 'Russian Responses to the Poetry of Ossian',
in: CROSS, *Proceedings* (no. 1794), pp. 48-65.

1819. CROSS, A.G., 'Yakov Smirnov: A Russian Priest of Many
Parts', *OSP.*, N.S., VIII (1975), 37-52.

1820. BUTLER, W.E., 'Yakov Smirnov and The Law of Nations',
O.S.P., N.S., XII (1979), 40-45.

1821. CROSS, A.G., 'Early Contacts of the Society of Arts with
Russia (i) Corresponding Members in Russia; (ii) Russian
Subscribing Members; (iii) The Visit of a Russian Serf',
Journal of the Royal Society of Arts, CXXIV, 5236 (March
1976), 204-7; 5237 (April 1976), 356-8; 5238 (May 1976),
334-6.

1822. CROSS, A.G., 'Mr. Fisher's Company of English Actors in
Eighteenth-Century Petersburg', *SGECRN.*, 4 (1976), 49-56.

1823. CROSS, A.G., 'Introduction' to: Sir George Macartney, An
Account of Russia, 1767. London 1768, reprinted F. Cass,
London 1977.

1824. MAKOGONENKO, G., 'Aleksandr Radishchev and Laurence
Sterne', in: CROSS, *Proceedings* (no.1794), pp. 84-97.

1825. HOME, R.W., 'Scientific links between Britain and Russia
in the Second Half of the Eighteenth Century', in: CROSS,
Proceedings (no. 1794), pp. 212-224.

1826. JOHNSON, C.A., 'Wedgwood and Bentley's "Frog" Service for
Catherine the Great', in CROSS, *Proceedings* (no. 1794),
pp. 123-134.

1827. DUKES, P., 'Some Aberdonian Influences on the Early
Russian Enlightenment', *CanAmSlSt.*, XIII, 4 (1979),
436-451.

1828. ALEKSEEV, M.P. (ed.), Shekspir i russkaia kul'tura. M.-L. 1965. Pp. 824.

1829. LEVIDOVA, I., Vil'iam Shekspir: Bibliograficheskii ukazatel' perevodov i kriticheskoi literatury na russkom iazyke, 1963-1975 gg. M. 1978. Pp. 187.

1830. DZHINCHARADZE, V.Z., 'Iz istorii russko-angliiskikh otnoshenii v XVIII v.', *Vestnik Mirovoi Kul'tury* V (1960), 63-76.

1831. RADOVSKII, M.I., Iz istorii anglo-russkikh nauchnykh sviazei. M. 1961. Pp. 216.

1832. CHENAKAL, V.L., 'Zerkal'nye teleskopy Vil'iama Gershelia v Rossii', *Istoriko-astronomicheskie issledovaniia*, IV (1958), 253-340.

1833. CHENAKAL, V.L., 'Dzhems Short i russkaia astronomiia XVIII v.', *Istoriko-astronomicheskie issledovaniia*, V (1959), 3-82.

1834. CHENAKAL, V.L., 'Astronomicheskie instrumenty Dzhona Berda v Rossii XVIII v.', *Istoriko-astronomicheskie issledovaniia*, VI (1960), 53-119.

1835. TIURINA, E., 'Dekart v russkikh izdaniakh - I. N'iuton v russkikh izdaniiakh', in: Fizika na rubezhe XVII-XVIII vv. (M. 1974), pp. 222-42.

1836. LEVIN, IU., 'Angliiskii zhurnal "Moskovit" (1714)', in: LEVIN, ROVDA (no. 1673), pp. 7-23.

1837. KROSS, A.G., 'Vasilii Petrov v Anglii (1772-74)', *XVIII Vek.*, Sb. 11 (1976), 229-47.

(v) U.S.A. and Russia: Cultural and Scientific Relations and Influences

ANSCHEL (1838) is the best survey of its subject to date. The Soviet authority on early relations is BOLKHOVITINOV (1839, 1843, 1847), well reviewed by SAUL (1840). See also BROWN (2634), who lists comprehensively the archival materials pertaining to Russia/USSR in the U.S.A.

1838. ANSCHEL, E. (ed.), The American Image of Russia, 1775-1917. N.Y. 1974. Pp. 259.
Rev: *RH.*, 1 (1976), 109-110 (Rose, J.).

1839. BOLKHOVITINOV, N.N., The beginnings of Russian-American relations, 1775-1815. Trans. E. Levin. Cambridge, Mass. 1975. Pp. 484.
Translation of no. 1161. Rev: no. 1840.

1840. SAUL, N., 'Russia and America, 1775-1815', *RR.*, 36, 3 (1977), 334-340.
Review essay on N. Bolkhovitinov's two books (nos. 1839, 1847).

1841. THALER, R.P., 'Radiščev, Russia and America', *Harvard Sl. St.*, IV (1957), 59-76.

1842. SHPRYGOVA, M.R., 'The American War of Independence as Treated by N.I. Novikov's Moscow Gazette', *Studies in Soviet History*, I (1962), 51-62.

1843. BOLKHOVITINOV, N., 'The American Revolution and the Russian Empire', in: Library of Congress (ed.), The Impact of the American Revolution abroad (Washington 1976), pp. 81-98.

1844. BODEN, D., Das Amerikabild im russischen Schrifttum bis zum Ende des 19. Jahrhunderts. Hamburg 1968. Pp. 209.

1845. FISCHER, A. et al. (eds), Russland-Deutschland-Amerika/ Russia-Germany-America. Wiesbaden 1978. Pp. 414. Mainly nineteenth and twentieth centuries.

1846. LIBMAN, V., Amerikanskaia literatura v russkikh perevodakh i kritike: Bibliografiia 1776-1975. M. 1977. Pp. 455.
7551 entries.

1847. BOLKHOVITINOV, N.N., Rossiia i voina SShA za nezavisimost' v 1775-1783. M. 1976. Pp. 272. Translated as no. 1155. Rev: *Ist. SSSR.*, 6 (1977), 189-191, and no. 1840.

1848. RADOVSKII, M., Veniamin Franklin i ego sviazi s Rossiei. L. 1958. Pp. 74.
See also Radovskii's biography of Franklin, L. 1965.

(vi) Russia and other non-Slavic European countries: Cultural Relations

1849. TURKEVICH, I., Spanish Literature in Russia and in the Soviet Union (1735-1964). Metuchen, N.J. 1967. Pp. 273. Rev: *CanSlSt.*, II, 1 (1968), 138-9 (Weiner, J.).

1850. BATALDEN, S.K., 'Eugenios Voulgaris in Russia, 1771-1806: A Chapter in Greco-Slavic Ties of the Eighteenth Century', Minnesota Ph.D., 1975.

1851. ALEKSEEV, M.P., Ocherki istorii ispano-russkikh
literaturnykh otnoshenii, XVI-XIXvv. L. 1964. Pp. 216.

1852. SKAZKIN, S. (ed.), Rossiia i Italiia. M. 1968. Pp. 462.
Essays include: Russian-Italian cultural relations
(Rutenberg, Venturi,); Archives of Venetian writer A.
Calogera in Leningrad (Vernadskaia); Beccaria's "On
Crimes and Punishments" in Russia (Berkov).
(vii) Russia and Other Slavic Peoples:
        Cultural Relations

1853. VAVRA, J., 'Böhmen und Russland im 18. Jahrhundert.
Zur Bedeutung der wirtschaftlichen, politischen und
kulturellen kontakte', *CanAmSlSt.*, XIII, 4 (1979),
510-543.

1854. FLOROVSKIJ, A., 'Peter I und die tschechische Kultur',
ZfSl., VII (1962), 537-55.

1854a. D'IAKOV, V. et al (eds), Slavianovedenie v dorevoliutsionnoi
Rossii: Biobibliograficheskii slovar'. M. 1979. Pp. 429.

1855. KALOEVA,I.(comp.), Sovetskoe slavianovedenie: Ukazatel'
literatury o zarubezhnykh slavianskikh stranakh, 1974-
1977. Moscow 1978. 7 vols. This continues previous coverage
for 1963-1968 (Moscow 1973-4. 7 vols.) and 1969-1973
(Moscow 1976. 7 vols.)

1856. KALOEVA,I.(comp.), Sovremennye slavianskie kul'tury,
razvitie, vzaimodeistvie, mezhdunarodnyi kontekst: Ukazatel' litertury 1970-78. M. 1979. 7 vols.

1857. BERKOV, P. (ed.), Russkaia literatura XVIII v. i
slavianskie literatury. M. 1963. Pp. 190.

1858. KOROLIUK, V. (ed.), Slaviano-germanskie kul'turnye sviazi
i otnosheniia. M. 1969. Pp. 367.
Essays. One of a series of vols edited by K. on this
theme: see nos. 1239, 1783, 1785.

1859. Vos'moi Mezhdunarodnyi S'ezd Slavistov - Zagreb, IX/1978
Doklady sovetskoi delegatsii v 3 tt. I: KOSTIUSHKO, I.
(ed.), Istoriia, kul'tura, etnografiia i fol'klor
slavianskikh narodov. M. 1978. Pp. 518. II: ALEKSEEV,
M. (ed.), Slavianskie literatury. M. 1978. Pp. 520.

1860. POPOVICH, K. (ed.), Ocherki moldavsko-russko-ukrainskikh
literaturnykh sviazei. Vyp. 1: S drevneishikh vremen-
1850g. Kishinev 1978. Pp. 236.

1860a. MARKOV, D. et al (eds), Slavianskie kul'tury v epokhu
formirovaniia i razvitiia slavianskikh natsii XVIII-XIXvv.
Materialy mezhdunarodnoi konferentsii(UNESKO) . M. 1978.
Pp. 399.

1860b. IAGICH, I., et al (eds), Slavianovedenie v dorevoliutsionnoi Rossii: bibliog. slovar'. M. 1979. Pp.429.

(viii) Russian Students Abroad
See also nos 575-6

1861. HANS, N.A., 'Russian Students at Leyden in the 18th Century', *SEER.*, XXXV (1956-7), 551-62.

1862. OKENFUSS, M.J., 'Russian Students in Europe in the Age of Peter the Great', in: GARRARD (no. 1595), pp. 131-48.

1863. CROSS, A.G., 'Russian Students in Eighteenth-Century Oxford (1766-75)', *JES.*, V (1975), 91-110.

1864. AMBURGER, E., 'Die russischen Studenten an deutschen Universitäten bis zum Ende des 18. Jahrhunderts', in: id. (no. 1731), pp. 214-32.

1865. KIRCHNER, P., 'Studenten aus der linksufrigen Ukraine an deutschen Universitäten in der zweiten Hälfte des 18. Jhdts', in: *Ost und West* (no. 1737), pp. 356-66.

1866. PENCHKO, N., 'Vydaiushchiesia vospitanniki Moskovskogo Universiteta v inostrannykh universitetakh (1758-1771gg.)' *Ist. Arkhiv.*, 2 (1956), 155-183.

12(c) - FREEMASONRY

Russian Freemasonry still awaits a modern historian; BASHILOV's tendentious account (1873) does not fill the gap. Apart from RYU (1867-68), the old works of PYPIN (1874) and VERNADSKII (1875) still provide the best foundation. See also nos. 1455-58, 1512-13, 1546.

1867. RYU, In-Ho L., 'Freemasonry under Catherine the Great: A Re-Interpretation', Harvard Ph.D., 1967.

1868. RYU, In-Ho L., 'Moscow Freemasons and The Rosicrucian Order', in: GARRARD (no. 1595), 198-232.

1869. CROSS, A.G., 'British Freemasons in Russia during the Reign of Catherine the Great', *OSP.*, N.S., IV (1971), 43-72.

1870. BAEHR, S.L., 'The Masonic Component in Eighteenth-Century Russian Literature', in CROSS (ed.) (no. 1988), pp. 121-40.

1871. GREEN, M., 'Masonry, Kheraskov and Mozart: A Footnote' *SGECRN.*, 7 (1979), 34-7.

1872. ISCHREYT, H., 'Die königsberger Freimaurerloge und die
Anfänge des modernen Verlagwesens in Russland (1760-
1763)', in: LISZKOWSKI (ed.) (no. 1743), pp. 108-119.

1873. BASHILOV, B., IVANOV, V., Istoriia russkogo masonstva.
Buenos Aires 1963. 8 vols.
Vols 1-3 cover the eighteenth- early nineteenth centuries.

1874. PYPIN, A.N., Russkoe masonstvo, XVIII i pervaia chetvert'
XIX v. (Issledovaniia i materialy po epokh Ekateriny II i
Aleksandra I.) Redaktsiia i primechaniia G.V. Vernadskogo.
Petrograd 1916, reprinted Düsseldorf 1970. Pp. 571.

1875. VERNADSKII, G.V., Russkoe masonstvo v tsarstvovanie
Ekateriny II. Petrograd 1917, reprinted Vaduz 1970.
Pp.560.

1876. KOCHETKOVA, N.D., 'Ideino - literaturnye positsii masonov
80-90 gg. XVIII v. i N.M. Karamzin', in *XVIII Vek.*, Sb.
6 (1967) [Russkaia literatura XVIII veka. Epokha
klassitsizma], pp. 176-196.

12(d) - EDUCATION

SHABAEVA (1900) offers the widest survey, though her critics
were severe; HANS (1877) is useful, if rather general.
OKENFUSS (1883) and EPP (1887) are thorough studies which
also offer extensive bibliographies; SYCHEV-MIKHAILOV (1901)
and PENCHKO (1904) provide valuable documentation. ·BLACK's
work (1886, 1895, 1897) is of considerable interest.
MADARIAGA (1888) gives the latest general account of the
system under Catherine II. See also nos. 2240, 2299.

1877. HANS, N.A., The Russian Tradition in Education. London
1963. Pp. 196.
Revised edition of his 1931 work. Rev: *SR.*, 23 (1964),
601 (Riasanovsky, N.).

1878. ROUCEK, J.S., 'Education within the Czarist Framework',
Paedagogica Historica, IV (1964), 392-443.

1879. ALSTON, P.L., Education and the State in Tsarist Russia.
Stanford 1969. Pp. 322.
Mainly nineteenth century.

1880. SINEL, A., 'Periodization in Russian Educational
History', *Slavic and European Education Review*, 2, (1977),
54-62.

1881. BECKER, C.B., 'The Church School in Tsarist Social and Educational Policy, from Peter to the Great Reforms', Harvard Ph.D., 1965.

1882. OKENFUSS, M.J., 'Education in Russia in the First Half of the 18th Century', Harvard Ph.D., 1971.

1883. OKENFUSS, M.J., Childhood and Education in Russia. The Evidence of the Slavic Primer. Newtonville 1980. Pp. 138.

1884. LIPSKI, A., 'The Beginnings of General Secondary Education in Russia', *History of Education Journal*, VI, 3 (1955), 201-10.

1885. BRYMER, C., 'Moscow University, 1755-1955', *RR.*, XIV, 2 (1955), 201-13.

1886. BLACK J.L., Citizens for the Fatherland: Education, Educators, and Pedagogical Ideals in Eighteenth Century Russia. With a translation of 'Book on the Duties of Man and Citizen' (St. P. 1783). Boulder-New York 1979. Pp. 273, illust.

1887. EPP, G., 'The Educational Policies of Catherine II of Russia, 1762-1796', Ph.D., Manitoba 1976.

1888. DE MADARIAGA, I., 'The Foundation of the Russian Educational System by Catherine II', *SEER.*, LVII, 3 (1979), 369-95.

1889. OKENFUSS, M.J., 'Education and Empire. School Reform in Enlightened Russia', *JbfGO.*, XXVII, 1 (1979), 41-69.

1890. WOLKOWSKI, L., 'Polish Commission for National Education, 1773-1794-Its Significance and Influence on Russian and American Education', Ph.D. Loyola(Chicago) 1979.

1891. HANS, N.A., 'H. Farquharson, Pioneer of Russian Education', *Aberdeen University Review*, XXXVIII, 120 (1959), 26-9.

1892. HANS, N.A., 'Dumaresq, Brown and Some Early Educational Projects of Catherine II', *SEER.*, XL (1961-2), 229-35.

1893. OKENFUSS, M.J., 'Technical Training in Russia under Peter the Great', *Hist. Ed. Q.*, XIII (1973), 325-45. See also no. 2299.

1894. BARAN, A., 'The Kievan Mohyla - Mazepa Academy and the Zaporozhian Cossacks', *Uk. Hist.* (1975), 70-6.

1895. BLACK, J.L., 'The Search for a "Correct" Textbook of National History in Eighteenth Century Russia', *The New Review of East-European History*, XVI, 1 (1976).

1896. JONES, W.G., 'The *Morning Light* Charity Schools, 1777-80', *SEER.*, LVI, 1 (1978), 47-68.

1897. BLACK, J.L., 'Educating Women in Eighteenth Century
   Russia: Myths and Realities', *CSP.*, XX, 1 (1978), 23-43.
1897a. NASH, C. S., ' The Education of Women in Russia, 1762-
   1796', Ph.D., New York, 1978.

1898. POLZ, P., 'Theodor Janković und die Schulreform in
   Russland', in: LESKY (no. 1609), pp. 119-74.
   A version of part of Polz's doctoral thesis on Janković
   (Graz 1970).
1899. SCHOLTZ, B., 'G.E. Lessing und die Gründung der Moskauer
   Lomonosov-Universität im Jahre 1755', in: Festschrift
   Alfred Rammelmeyer. Beiträge zur slavischen Philologie.
   München 1973.

1900. SHABAEVA, M. (ed.), Ocherki istorii shkoly i
   pedagogicheskoi mysli narodov SSSR, XVIII-pervaia polovina
   XIX v. M. 1973. Pp. 605.
   Rev: *Kritika*, XI, 1-2 (1975), 4-21 (Okenfuss, M.); *Vop.Ist.*
   5 (1974), 155-7 (Aizenberg, A.).

1901. SYCHEV-MIKHAILOV, M.V.,Iz istorii russkoi shkoly i
   pedagogiki XVIII veka. M. 1960. Pp. 255.

1902. BELIAVSKII, M.T., 'Shkola i sistema obrazovaniia v Rossii
   v kontse XVIII v.', *VMU(Ist.)*, 2 (1959), 105-121.

1903. TIKHOMIROV, M.N. (ed.), Istoriia Moskovskogo Universiteta,
   1755-1955, 2 vols; I: 1755-1917. M. 1955. Pp. 562.

1904. PENCHKO, N. (ed.), Dokumenty i materialy po istorii
   Moskovskogo universiteta vtoroi poloviny XVIII v. 3 vols.
   M. 1960-63. Pp. 414, 356, 365.
   Annotated selections from the University archives.

1905. SAKHAROV, A., Literatura po istorii Moskovskogo Universiteta, 1917-1967. Bibliog. ukazatel'. M. 1969. Pp. 116.

1906. POVAROVA, E.V., 'Nauchnaia pedagogicheskaia deiatel'nost'
   professorov i prepodavatelei peterburgskoi uchitel'skoi
   seminarii v XVIII v.', in: SHABAEVA, M.F. (ed.), Voprosy
   istorii pedagogiki. Sb. nauchnykh trudov (M. 1973),
   pp. 112-36.

1907. POVARENNYKH, A.S., 'Nachalo spetsial'nogo gornogo
   obrazovaniia v Rossii', *Ocherki po istorii geologicheskih
   znanii*, IV (1955), 150-66.

1908. ZOLOTAREV, B.V., 'K voprosu o nachale artilleriiskogo i
   voenno-inzhenerskogo obrazovaniia v Rossii', in: SHAPIRO
   (ed.) (no.220), pp. 195-206.

1909. ERMAKOVA-BITNER, G., 'Z.A. Goriushkin-vospitatel'
   rossiiskogo iunoshestva', *XVIII Vek.* Sb. 3 (1958),
   343-379.

12-Culture-Education   166

1910. FLOROVSKII, A.V., 'Latynskie shkoly v Rossii v epokhu
Petra I', *XVIII Vek.* Sb. 5 (1962), 316-335.

1911. LEPSKAIA, L.A., 'Sostav uchashchikhsia narodnykh uchilishch
Moskvy v kontse XVIII v.', *VMU(Ist.)*, 5 (1973), 88-96.

1912. MATL, I., 'F.IA. Iankovich i avstro-serbsko-russkie sviazi
v istorii narodnogo obrazovaniia v Rossii', *XVIII Vek.* Sb.
10 (1975), 76-81.

1912a. MOLEVA, N., BELIUTIN, F., Pedagogicheskaia sistema
Akademii Khudozhestv XVIII v. M. 1956. Pp. 518.

1912b. TORNAU, J. (ed.), Vilniaus universitetas: bibliografija,
1940-1977. Vilnius 1979.Pp. 341.
Contains 3,228 entries for history of university (1579-1977)

12(e) - PRINTING, BOOKS, LIBRARIES, THE PRESS, JOURNALISM

Annual bibliographies appear in KNIGA (1929). SIDOROV (1930)
provides a good historical survey, with illustrations; his
latest work (1937) contains a number of useful essays.
SLUKHOVSKII (1940) and LUPPOV (1935, 1936) describe in loving
detail the major book collectors and their collections;
institutional libraries are covered in 1927, 1941-1945. On
censorship, PAPMEHL (1917) is the best in English; further,
1916, 1928, 1949-1952. Individual presses, publishers,
book-sellers: 1918, 1924-1926, 1947, 1948. See also 1872,2349.

1913. SWINDLER, W.F., 'Recent Research Material on Russian
Journalism: A Survey of Important Studies of the Russian
Press from its 17th Century Beginnings to the Present',
Journalism Quarterly, 32 (1955), 70-5.

1914. AUTY, R., SIMMONS, J.S.G., 'Russian Writing and Printing',
in: AUTY, OBOLENSKY (no.283), II, pp. 41-55.

1915. SIMMONS, J.S.G., A History of Russian Hand Paper mills and
their Watermarks. Hilversum 1962. Pp. 381.
English translation and adaptation of Russian work by
Z. UCHASTKINA.

1916. BAYLEY, R.B.. 'Freedom and Regulation of the Russian
Periodical Press', Illinois Ph.D., 1968.

1917. PAPMEHL, K.A., Freedom of Expression in Eighteenth
Century Russia. The Hague 1971. Pp. 166.
Based on London Ph.D. thesis, 1965.

1918. CROSS, A.G., 'Printing at Nikolaev, 1798-1803', *Trans.
Cambridge Bibl. Soc.*, VI (1974), 149-57.

1919. TRYPUCKO, J., 'Moskovskija Vedomosti (1756-1917)',
in: Russian Newspapers on Microfilm (Zug 1975), pp. 13-18.
Discussion of microfiche project reprinting *Vedomosti*.

1920. MARKER, G., 'Publishing and the Formation of a Reading Public in Eighteenth Century Russia'. U. Cal. Berkeley Ph.D. 1977.

1921. ZAVIALOFF, N., 'Fonction de la presse et du livre en Russie au XVIIIe siècle', *Revue Française d'Histoire du Livre*, IV, 7 (1974), 111-27.

1922. ŠAFRANOVSKIJ, K., 'Les Salles de l'Académie des Sciences de Saint-Pétersbourg en 1741. Histoire d'un livre condamné', *CMRS.*, VIII, 4 (1967), 605-615.

1923. ISCHREYT, H., 'Buchgeschichte in der Sowjetunion. Zu einigen Neuerscheinungen', *Börsenblatt für den Deutschen Buchhandel*, 46 (June 1979), 368-372.

1924. AMBURGER, E., 'Buchdruck, Buchhandel und Verlage in St. Petersburg im 18. Jahrhundert', in: GOEPFERT, H., KOZIELEK, G., WITTMANN, R. (eds), Buch- und Verlagswesen im 18. und 19. Jahrhundert (Berlin 1977),pp. 201-216.

1925. LEHMANN, U., 'Der Verlag Breitkopf in Leipzig und die Petersburger Akademie in den 60-er und 70-er Jahren des 18. Jhdts.', *ZfSl.*, VIII (1963), 25-33.

1926. LEHMANN, U., 'Johann Friedrich Hartknochs Beitrag zur deutschen Russlandkenntnis im 18. Jhdt.', *ZfSl.*, XV (1970), 323-30.

1927. NIKITINA, N., Zur Geschichte des Bibliothekswesens an den russischen Hochschulen. Von den Anfängen bis 1917. Berlin 1970. Pp. 71. Translated from Russian.

1928. DONNERT, E., 'Öffentliche Meinung und Pressepolitik unter Katharina II', *ZfSl.*, XVIII (1973), 886-91.

1929. KNIGA, Issledovaniia i materialy. M. 1958- Year's work in "book science".

1930. SIDOROV, A.A. (ed.), 400 let russkogo knigopechataniia, 1564-1964: russkaia kniga do 1917 goda, 1564-1917. M. 1964. Pp. 662.

1931. EIKHENGOL'TS, A. (ed.), Khrestomatiia po istorii russkoi knigi 1564-1917. M. 1965. Pp. 377.

1932. NIZHEVA, D.N. et al., Russkie dorevoliutsionnye gazety v fondakh Gos. Biblioteki SSSR im. V.I. Lenina: 1702-1916 gg., alfavitnyi katalog. M. 1977, 2 parts.

1933. ZAPADOV, A.V., Istorii russkoi zhurnalistiki XVIII-XIX vekov. 3rd ed. M. 1973. Pp. 520.

1934. STAN'KO, A., Russkaia periodicheskaia pechat' XVIII veka.
Rostov n/D. 1979. Pp. 127.

1935. LUPPOV, S.P., Kniga v Rossii v pervoi chetverti XVIII v.
L. 1973. Pp. 373.

1936. LUPPOV, S.P., Kniga v Rossii v poslepetrovskoe vremiia,
1725-1740. L. 1976. Pp. 379.
Rev: *Kritika* XV, 2 (1979), 94-104 (Rosenburg, K.).

1937. SIDOROV, A., LUPPOV, S. (eds), Kniga v Rossii do serediny
XIX veka. L. 1978. Pp. 320.
Essays include: recent works dealing with Russian book
history (Luppov); books in the 'period of feudalism'
(Sidorov); Musin-Pushkin as editor (Moiseeva); Russian
translations of French works (Barenbaum); Lomonosov and
Enlightenment (Tiulichev); book trade in Lithuania
(Apinis).

1938. AGZAMOV, F. (ed.), Iz istorii Kazanskoi pressy. Kazan'
1977. Pp. 119.

1939. KLEPIKOV, S., Filigrani na bumage russkogo proizvodstva
XVIII-nachala XIX veka. M. 1978. Pp. 239.

1940. SLUKHOVSKII, M., Bibliotechnoe delo v Rossii do XVIII
veka. M. 1968. Pp. 231.

1941. BARASHENKOV, V.M. (ed.), Istoriia gosudarstvennoi
publichnoi biblioteki imeni M.E. Saltykova-Shchedrina.
L. 1963. Pp. 436.

1942. ATKINSON, D., 'The Library of the Free Economic Society',
SR., XXXIX, 1(1980), 97-104.

1943. LIKHACHEV, D.(ed.), BOBROVA, E.(comp.), Biblioteka Petra I.
Ukazatel'-spravochnik. L. 1978. Pp. 213.

1944. PENCHKO, N. et al., Istoriia Biblioteki Moskovskogo
Universiteta 1755-1967.Vol.1: Do 1812. M. 1969. Pp.162.

1945. KARPOVA, E. (ed.), Iz istorii fondov nauchnoi biblioteki
Moskovskogo Universiteta. M. 1978. Pp. 167, 26 illust.
Essays: first printed newspaper, various private
libraries.

1946. MAKEEVA, V., 'Iz istorii izdaniia "Slovaria Akademii
Rossiiskoi" (1789-1794)', *Kniga,* 13 (1966), 219-226.

1947. MARTYNOV, I.F., 'Knigoizdatel', literator i bibliograf
XVIII veka Petr Ivanovich Bogdanovich', *Kniga,* 21 (1970),
89-105.

1948. MARTYNOV, I.F., 'Knigotorgovets i knigoizdatel' XVIII v.
M.K. Ovchinnikov', *Kniga*, 24 (1972), 99–115.

1949. SHAMRAI, D.D., 'K istorii tsenzurnogo rezhima Ekateriny
II', *XVIII Vek.*, Sb. 3 (1958), 187–206.

1950. SHAMRAI, D.D., BERKOV, P.N., 'K tsenzurnoi istorii
"Trudoliubivoi pchely" A.P. Sumarokova', *XVIII Vek.*, Sb.
5 (1962), 399–406.

1951. ZAPADOV, V.A., 'Kratkii ocherk istorii russkoi tsenzury
60kh–90kh gg. XVIII v.' in: Russkaia literatura i
obshchestvenno-politicheskaia bor'ba XVIII–XIX vv.
(Uchenye Zapiski Leningradsk. Gos. Ped. In-ta im.
A.I. Gertsena, 414, 1971), pp. 94–136.

1952. SHITSGAL,A. Russkii tipografskii shrift. M. 1974. Pp.208.
Contains valuable bibliography.

12(f) – LITERATURE AND LANGUAGE

The section is divided into bibliographical works (1953–1973);
literature (1974–2038); language (2038–2051). It does not
seek to cover in detail the wide array of material on its
subjects, merely to indicate useful guides into the field, and
to suggest some major works and themes. Besides bibliographies listed here, BERKOV (119) and TERRY (165) are particularly valuable. DRAGE (1976) and BROWN (1977) are the latest
Western surveys, with bibliographies. In the English language
section attention has been paid to recent doctoral work in
the field, and to studies of individual figures. For the
latter see also Section 11.

Bibliographies on Literature and Language
Literature: 1953–1963; Language: 1964–1973, 2044.
See also no. 1590, and in general Section 1(c).

1953. ZENKOVSKY, S., ARMBRUSTER, D., A Guide to the Bibliographies of Russian Literature. Nashville 1970. Pp. 62.

1954. CROSS, A.G., SMITH, G.S., 'Bibliography of English-
Language Scholarship on Russian 18th Century Literature,
Thought and Culture, 1900–1974', in: CROSS, A.G. (ed.)
Russian Literature in the Age of Catherine the Great
(no. 1988), pp. 197–217.

1955. CROSS, A.G., SMITH, G.S., 'A Bibliography of English Language Scholarship on Eighteenth-Century Russian Literature, Thought and Culture since 1974', *SGECRN.*, 5 (1977), 55-65.
Continuation of no. 1954. On-going.

1956. JACKSON, W., The Kilgour Collection of Russian Literature, 1750-1920. Cambridge 1959.
First editions of Russian literature in Harvard's Houghton Library.

1957. WYTRZENS, G., Bibliografische Einführung in das Studium der slavischen Literaturen. Frankfurt/M. 1972. Pp. 348.

1958. WYTRZENS, G., Bibliographie der russischen Autoren und anonymen Werke. Frankfurt/M. 1975. Pp. 268.

1959. KANDEL', B. et al. (comps), Russkaia khudozhestvennaia literatura i literaturovedenie. Ukazatel' spravochno-bibliograficheskikh posobii s kontsa XVIII veka do 1974 god. M. 1976. Pp. 492.
2522 entries.

1960. LEBEDEVA, E.D., Tekstologiia russkoi literatury XVIII-XX vv. Ukazatel sovetskikh rabot na russkom iazyke, 1917-1975. M. 1978. Pp. 207.
2284 entries.

1961. 'Ukazatel' statei v izdaniiakh gruppy po izucheniiu russkoi literatury XVIII v 1935-1974 gg.', *XVIII vek.*, Sb. 10 (L. 1975), 303-314.

1962. SMIRNOV-SOKOL'SKII, N., Moia biblioteka. Bibliograficheskoe opisanie. 2 vols. M. 1969. Pp. 532, 573.

1963. GOL'DBERG, A. (comp.), et al., Biblioteka russkoi poezii I.N. Rozanova: Bibliograficheskoe opisanie. M. 1975. Pp. 479.
7943 entries concerning Russian poetry, works published in Russia and abroad.

1964. BIRKENMAYER, S., A Selective Bibliography of Works Related to the Teaching of Slavic languages and Literatures in the United States and Canada, 1942-1967. N.Y. 1967. Pp. 40.
Rev: *CSS.*, IV, 2 (1970), 337-8.

1965. UNBEGAUN, B.O., A Bibliographical Guide to the Russian Language. Oxford 1953. Pp. 174.

1966. MATEJKA, L., Introductory Bibliography of Slavic Philology. Ann Arbor 1965. Pp. 97.

1967. STANKIEWICZ, E., WORTH, D., A Selected Bibliography of
Slavonic Linguistics. 2 vols. The Hague-Paris 1966, 1970.
Pp. 315, 530.

1968. WORTH, D.S., A Bibliography of Russian Word-Formation,
Columbus, Ohio 1977. Pp. 317.

1969. LEWANSKI, R.C. (comp.), A Bibliography of Slavic
Dictionaries. Bologna 1972-73, 2nd ed. 4 vols.
Russian dictionaries: vol. III, and vol. IV (Supplement),
91-294. Academy dictionaries of 1789-94, 1806-22: III
nos 116, 117.

1970. ZALEWSKI, W., Russian-English Dictionaries with Aids for
Translators: A Selected Bibliography. Stanford 1976.
   400 entries.

1971. AAV, Y., Russian Dictionaries. Dictionaries and Glossaries
Printed in Russia 1627-1917. Zug 1977. Pp. 196.
Russian language dictionaries.

1972. KAUFMAN, I.M., Terminologicheskie slovari.
Bibliografiia. M. 1961. Pp. 420.

1973. BULAKHOV, M.G., Vostochnoslavianskie iazykovedy.
Bibliograficheskii slovar'. 3 vols. Minsk 1976-78.
Extensive bibliographies. Sixteenth century onwards.

   Literature   See also nos 554, 1429, 1454, 1536, 1624,
               1637.

1974. WEBER, H. (ed.), Modern Encyclopedia of Russian and
Soviet Literature. Gulf Breeze 1976-
Projected 50 volumes. Vols. 1-3 in print, 4-6 by end
1980.

1975. ČIŽEVSKIJ, D., History of Russian Literature from the XI
Century to the End of the Baroque. The Hague 1960. Pp. 451.

1976. DRAGE, C., Russian Literature in the Eighteenth Century:
the Solemn Ode, The Epic, other Poetic Genres, the Story,
the Novel, Drama. London 1978. Pp. 281.

1977. BROWN, W.E., A History of Eighteenth-Century Russian
Literature. Ann Arbor 1978. Pp. 650.

1978. SEGEL, H. (ed.), The Literature of Eighteenth Century
Russia. A History and Anthology. N.Y. 1967. 2 vols.
Selections in translation, with introduction.

1979. DRAGE, C., VICKERY, W. (comp. and eds), An XVIIIth Century
Russian Reader. Oxford 1969. Pp. 346.

1980. BUCSELA, J., 'The Problems of Baroque in Russian Literature', *RR.*, 31, 3 (1972), 260-272.

1981. SEGEL, H., 'Baroque and Roccoco in Eighteenth Century Russian Literature', *CSP.*, XV, 4 (1973), 556-566.

1982. BURGESS, M., 'The Age of Classicism", in: AUTY, OBOLENSKY (no. 283), II , 111-32.

1983. ARIAN-BAYKOV, I., 'The Beginnings of Russian Fiction', in: DAICHES, D., THORLBY, A. (eds), The Modern World: I. Hopes (London 1975), pp. 473-511.

1984. BUDGEN, D., 'The Concept of Fiction in Eighteenth-Century Russian Letters', in: CROSS, *Proceedings* (no. 1794) pp. 65-75.

1985. SILBAJORIS, R., Russian Versification. The Theories of Trediakovsky, Lomonosov and Kantemir. N.Y.-London 1968. Pp. 213.

1986. COOPER, B.F., 'The History and Development of the Ode in Russia', Cambridge Ph.D., 1972.

1987. WELSH, D., Russian Comedy, 1765-1823. The Hague-Paris 1966. Pp. 133.

1988. CROSS, A.G. (ed.), Russian Literature in the Age of Catherine the Great. Oxford 1976. Pp. 229. Essays: Bolotov's Memoirs (Rice); The Russian ode (Hart); Emin and the novel (Budgen); Russian classicism (Jones); sentimentalism (Smith); Radishchev and sentimentalism (Page); overview and bibliography (Cross).

1989. NEUHAUSER, R., Towards the Romantic Age: Essays on Sentimental and Preromantic Literature in Russia. The Hague 1974. Pp. 250.

1990. CROSS, A.G., 'The Russian Literary Scene in the Reign of Paul I', *CanAmSlSt.*, VII, 1 (1973), 39-52.

1991. GARRARD, J.G., Mixail Čulkov. An Introduction to his Prose and Verse. The Hague-Paris 1970. Pp. 162.

1992. GREEN, M.A., 'Mixail Xeraskov and His Contribution to the Eighteenth Century Russian Theatre', UCLA Ph.D., 1973.

1993. McCORMICK, P.A., 'The Critical Ideas of Vladimir Lukin', Georgetown Ph.D., 1973.

1994. CROSS, A.G., '"The Notorious Barkov": An Annotated Bibliography', *SGECRN.*, 2 (1974), 41-52.

1995. BUDGEN, D.E., 'The work of E.A. Emin (1735-70): Literary and Intellectual Transition in Eighteenth-Century Russia', Oxford D.Phil., 1976.

1996. STANCHFIELD, G.V., 'Russian Baroque: A.D. Kantemir',
Florida State U. Ph.D., 1977.

1997. YANCEY, J.V., 'Baroque elements in the poetry of M.V.
Lomonosov', British Columbia Ph.D., 1977.

1998. McKENNA, K.J., 'Catherine the Great's *Vsiakaia Vsiachina*
and the *Spectator* Tradition of the Satirical Journal of
Morals and Manners', Colorado Ph.D., 1977.

1999. HART, P., G.R. Derzhavin: A Poet's Progress.   Columbus
1978. Pp. 164.

2000. WORTH, G.H., 'Thoughts on The Turning Point in the
History of Literary Russian: The Eighteenth Century',
International Journal of Slavic Linguistics and Poetics
XIII (1970), 125-35.

2001. PLETNEV, R., Entretiens sur la littérature russe des
XVIIIe et XIXe siècles. Montréal 1964. Pp. 968.

2002. GATTO, ETTORE LO, Histoire de la littérature russe (des
origines à nos jours). Paris 1965. Pp. 923.
Translated from the Italian.

2003. LABRIOLLE, F. de, Ivan A. Krylov: ses oeuvres de jeunesse
et les courants littéraires de son temps, 1768 – 1808 – 1844.
Paris 1975. 2 vols. Pp. 806, 48.

2004. TRUBETSKOJ, N., Die russischen Dichter des 18. und 19.
Jahrhunderts. Abriss einer Entwicklungsgeschichte.
Nach einem nachgelassenen russischen Mt. hrsg. von R.
JAGODITSCH. Graz-Köln 1956. Pp. 148.

2005. LETTENBAUER, W., Russische Literaturgeschichte.   2nd ed.
Wiesbaden 1958. Pp. 336.

2006. DIECKMANN, E. et al., Geschichte der klassischen russischen
Literatur. Berlin-Weimar 1965. Pp. 1012.

2007. GRASSHOFF, H., Russische Literatur im Ueberblick.
Frankfurt/M. 1974. Pp. 500.

2008. HARDER, H., Studien zur Geschichte der russischen
klassizistichen Tragödie, 1747-1769. Wiesbaden 1962.
Pp. 162.

2009. KRONEBERG, B., Studien zur Geschichte der russischen
klassizistischen Elegie. Wiesbaden 1972. Pp. 243.

2010. LEO, M., Patriotische Färbung und Wirklichkeit in der
russischen Literatur im ersten Drittel des 18. Jahrhunderts
Münster 1969. Pp. 294.

2011. SURKOV, A.A. et al. (eds), Kratkaia literaturnaia entsiklopediia. 9 vols. M. 1962-78. (New ed. announced) See review by B. LEWIS and M. ULMAN in *SR.*,XXXIX,1(1980), 104-111.

2012. ORLOV, A.S. et al. (eds), Istoriia russkoi literatury. 10 vols. M. 1941-56. Eighteenth century: vols III, IV.

2013. BLAGOI, D.D., Istoriia russkoi literatury XVIII v. 3rd rev. ed. M. 1955. Pp. 568.

2014. KOKOREV, A. (comp.), Khrestomatiia po russkoi literature XVIII veka. 4th ed. M. 1965. Pp. 848.

2015. MAKOGONENKO, G.P. (comp.), Russkaia literatura XVIII veka. L. 1970. Pp. 832. Anthology.

2016. MAKOGONENKO, G.P. (comp.), Russkaia proza XVIII v. M. 1971. Pp. 719. Anthology.

2017. BERKOV, P., Vvedenie v izuchenie istorii russkoi literatury XVIII veka. Chast' I. Ocherki literaturnoi istoriografii XVIII veka. L. 1964. Pp. 261. Rev: *Kritika*, II, 1 (1965), 7-14 (Rice, J.).

2018. LIKHACHEV, D.S. et al. (eds), Rol' i znachenie literatury XVIII veka v istorii russkoi kul'tury. K 70-letiiu P.N.Berkova. M. 1966. Pp. 458.

2019. BLAGOI, D., Ot Kantemira do nashikh dnei. M. 1972. 2 vols. Pp. 559, 463.

2020. TATARINOVA, L., Istoriia russkoi literatury i zhurnalistiki XVIII v. M. 1975. Pp. 334.

2021. KRESTOVA, L.V., 'Otrazhenie formirovaniia russkoi natsii v russkoi literature i publitsistike pervoi poloviny XVIII v.'. in: DRUZHININ, N.M., CHEREPNIN, L.V. (eds), Voprosy formirovaniia russkoi narodnosti i natsii. Sb. statei (M.-L. 1958), pp. 253-96.

2022. ROBINSON, A., DERZHAVINA, O., LOMUNOV, K. (eds), Ranniaia russkaia dramaturgiia. XVII-pervaia polovina XVIII v. 5 vols. M. 1972-6.

2023. MAKOGONENKO, G. (ed.), Problemy literaturnogo razvitiia Rossii pervoi treti XVIII v. L. 1974. Pp. 354. *(XVIII Vek:* Sbornik 9).

2024. ROBINSON, A.N. (ed.), Novye cherty v russkoi literature i iskusstve XVII-nachalo XVIII v. M. 1976. Pp. 285. Includes early eighteenth-century drama and theatre.

2025. EGUNOV, A., Gomer (Homer) v russkikh perevodakh XVIII-XIX vekov. M. 1964. Pp. 439.

2026. MAKOGONENKO, G., Ot Fonvizina do Pushkina. M. 1969.
Pp. 508.

2027. SERMAN, I.Z., Russkii klassitsizm. Poeziia. Drama.
Satira. L. 1973. Pp. 284.

2028. GRUZDEV, A. (ed.), Zhanrovoe novatorstvo russkoi
literatury kontsa XVIII-XIX vv. L. 1974. Pp. 188.

2029. PAVLOVICH, S., Puti razvitiia russkoi sentimental'noi
prozy XVIII v. Saratov 1974. Pp. 223.

2030. ORLOV, P., Russkii sentimentalism. M. 1977. Pp. 269.

2031. STEPANOV, N., Russkaia basnia XVIII-XIX vekov. L. 1977.
Pp. 653.

2032. KURILOV, A. (ed.), Istoriia romantizma v russkoi
literature. Vozniknovenie i utverzhdenie romantizma v
russkoi literature, 1790-1825. M. 1979. Pp. 312.

2033. KASTORSKII, S. (ed.), Iz istorii russkikh literaturnykh
otnoshenii XVIII-XX v. M. 1959. Pp. 442.

2034. SMIRNOV-SOKOL'SKII, N., Russkie literaturnye al'manakhi i
sborniki XVIII-XIX vv. M. 1965. Pp. 591.

2035. BAZANOV, V.G. (ed.), Russkaia literatura i fol'klor.
Vyp. 1: XI-XVIII vv. L. 1970. Pp. 432.

2036. LIKHACHEV, D. (ed.), Drevnerusskaia literatura i
russkaia kul'tura XVIII-XX vv. L. 1971. Pp. 383.

2037. VASIL'IEV, V., Russkaia epigramma vtoroi poloviny XVII-
nachala XX v. L. 1975. Pp. 966.

2038. BERKOV, P., Istoriia russkoi komedii XVIII v. L. 1977.
Pp. 390.

Language See also nos 2204, 2672.

2039. VINOGRADOV, V.V., The History of the Russian Literary
Language from the Seventeenth Century to the Nineteenth.
Madison 1969. Pp. 275.

2040. VINOKUR, G., The Russian Language: A Brief History.
N.Y. 1971. Pp. 147.

2041. AUTY, R., 'History of the Language', in: AUTY, OBOLENSKY
(no. 283), II, 1-40.

2042. WORTH, G., Foreign Words in Russian. A Historical Sketch,
1550-1800. Los Angeles 1963. Pp. 132.

2043. BOND, A., German Loanwords in the Russian Language of the Petrine Period. Frankfurt 1974. Pp. 179.

2044. AVILOVA, N. (comp.), Bibliograficheskii ukazatel' literatury po russkomu iazykoznaniiu s 1825 po 1880g. M. 1954-56. 8 vols. (Index in vol. 8).

2045. BUKATEVICH, N., Istoricheskaia grammatika russkogo iazyka. Kiev 1974. Pp. 307.

2046. BORKOVSKII, V. (ed.), Istoricheskaia grammatika russkogo iazyka. M. 1979. Pp. 461.

2047. CHERNYSHEV, V.I. et al. (eds), Slovar' sovremennogo russkogo literaturnogo iazyka. M. 1950-65. 17 vols. The closest Russian equivalent to the Oxford English Dictionary.

2048. DAL', V.I., Tolkovyi slovar' zhivogo velikorusskogo iazyka. M. 1955. 6th ed., 4 vols. Based on edition of 1880-82.

2049. FASMER, M., Etimologicheskii Slovar' Russkogo Iazyka. Perevod s nemetskogo i dopolneniia O.N. Trubacheva. 4 vols, M. 1964-73. Translation, with additions, of Vasmer's *Russisches Etymologisches Wörterbuch*, Heidelberg 1950-58.

2050. GRIBBLE, C.E. (comp.), Slovarik russkogo jazyka 18-go veka / A Short Dictionary of 18th-Century Russian. Columbus, Ohio 1976. Pp. 103.

2051. SOROKIN, IU. S. (ed.), Slovar' russkogo iazyka XVIII veka: proekt. L. 1977. Pp. 163. Rev: *SGECRN.*, 6 (1978), 60-63 (Pennington, A.).

2051a. ARISTOVA, B., Anglo-russkie iazykovye kontakty (anglizmy v russkom iazyke) L. 1978. Pp. 151.

12(g) - THE ARTS

In English, ALPATOV (2055) is a useful recent study, as is the German-language BEHRENS (2059). The Russian series edited by ALEKSEEVA (2066, 2068-9, 2099) is outstanding. OSTROI (2060) lists art galleries and holdings by city. GRABAR' (2062) and VEIMARN (2063) are fundamental large scale surveys. GORINA (2077), when completed, will be the standard bibliographic source for individuals. See also HOESCH (1614).

2052. BOWLT, J., 'New Soviet Publications on Art', *RR.*,
XXXVIII, 3 (1979), 348-59.
Mainly on modern period, but a useful survey of the
current scene.

2053. HARE, R., The Art and Artists of Russia. London 1965.
Pp. 294, 209 plates.

2054. FRONCEK, TH. (ed.), The Horizon Book of the Arts of
Russia. N.Y. 1970. Pp. 384, illustrated.

2055. ALPATOV, M., Russian Impact on Art. Translated by I.
Litvinov. M. 1977. Pp. 352.

2056. KAGANOVICH, A.L., Arts of Russia: 17th and 18th Centuries.
Translated by J. Hogarth. N.Y. 1968. Pp. 173.

2056a. MASSIE, S., Land of the Firebird. The Beauty of
Old Russia. NY 1980. Pp. 495.

2057. TALBOT, RICE, T., 'The Conflux of Influences in
Eighteenth-Century Russian Art and Architecture: A
Journey from the Spiritual to the Realistic', in: GARRARD
(no. 1595), pp. 268-299.

2058. NETTING, A., 'Images and Ideas in Russian Peasant Art',
SR., XXXV, 1 (1976), 48-68.

2059. BEHRENS, E., Kunst in Russland: Ein Reiseführer zu
russischen Kunststätten. Köln 1969. Pp. 318.

2060. OSTROI, O.S., Russkie spravochnye izdaniia po izobraziteĽ-
nomu i prikladnomu iskusstvu. M. 1972. Pp. 280.

2061. ZUBOV, IU.S. et al., Bibliografiia iskusstva. M. 1973.
Pp. 303.

2062. GRABAR', I.E. et al. (eds), Istoriia russkogo iskusstva.
16 vols in 18. M.-L. 1955-64.
Vols 2-6 cover the eighteenth century.

2063. VEIMARN, B.V. et al. (eds), Istoriia Iskusstva Narodov
SSSR v 9 tomakh. M. 1971-
In progress. Vol. 4 (1974), ed. NUROK, A.IU., ORLOVA,
M.A.: Iskusstvo kontsa XVII-XVIII vekov.

2064. OSTROI, O., Izobrazitel'noe i prikladnoe iskusstvo.
Trudy. M. 1969. Pp. 216.

2065. KOVALENSKAIA, N., Istoriia russkogo iskusstva XVIII v.
M. 1962. Pp. 286, illustrations.

2066. ALEKSEEVA, T.V. (ed.), Russkoe iskusstvo XVIII v.
Materialy i issledovaniia. M. 1968. Pp. 311.

2067. KUZNETSOVA, E., Besedy o russkom iskusstve XVIII-nachala
XX veka. M. 1972. Pp. 182, illustrations.

2068. ALEKSEEVA, T.V. (ed.), Russkoe iskusstvo XVIII veka.
Materialy i issledovaniia. M. 1973. Pp. 196,
illustrations.

2069. ALEKSEEVA, T.V. (ed.), Russkoe iskusstvo pervoi chetverti
XVIII v. Materialy i issledovaniia. M. 1974. Pp. 234.

2070. KOMELEVA, G. (ed.), Kul'tura i iskusstvo Petrovskogo
vremeni. L. 1977. Pp. 200.
Rev: SGECRN, 6 (1978), 67-71 (Cross, A.G.).

2071. PIGAREV, K.V., Russkaia literatura i izobrazitel'noe
iskusstvo XVIII-pervaia chetvert' XIX veka. Ocherki.
M. 1966. Pp. 291, 52 illustrations.

2072. TRUCHIN, V.S., 'Slozhenie traditsii russkogo portretnogo
iskusstva', VMU(Ist.), 4 (1970), 86-96.

2073. MANIN, V., 'Akademiia khudozhestv i rasprostranenie
proizvedenii iskusstv v XVIII v.', Ist. SSSR, 1 (1965),
146-50.

2074. MOLEVA, N.M., 'Tsekhovaia organizatsiia khudozhnikov v
Moskve XVII-XVIII vv.', Vop. Ist., 11 (1969), 43-54.

Individuals

2075. BISCHOFF, I., 'Etienne Maurice Falconet: Sculptor of the
Statue of Peter the Great', RR., 24 (1965), 369-86.
See also no. 2133, and Appendix.

2076. RAE, I., Charles Cameron, Architect to the Court of
Russia. London 1971. Pp. 111.

2077. GORINA, T. (ed.), VOL'TSENBURG, O. (comp.), Khudozhniki
narodov SSSR v 6 tomakh. Bibliograficheskii slovar'.
M. 1970-
3 vols to date.

2078. SELINOVA, T.A., Ivan P. Argunov, 1729-1802. M. 1973.
Pp. 207, 70 illustrations.

2079. SAKHAROVA, I., Aleksei Petrovich Antropov, 1716-1795.
M. 1974. Pp. 237.
Portraitist.

2080. KRASHENINNIKOVA, N., TEL'TEVSKII, P., Arkhitektor V.I.
Bazhenov. (Dom Paskova). M. 1957. Pp. 30.

2081. ALEKSEEVA, T.V., Vladimir Lukich Borovikovskii i
russkaia kul'tura na rubezhe XVIII–XIX vekov. M. 1975.
Pp. 421. Résumé in English.

2082. DANILOVA I.(ed.), Narodnaia graviura i fol'klor v Rossii
XVII–XIX vv. (K 150-letiiu so dnia rozhdeniia D.A. Rovin-
skogo): Materialy nauch. konf. (1975). M. 1976. Pp. 369.

2083. NIKULINA, N., Nikolai L'vov. M. 1971. Pp. 132.

2084. MOLEVA, N., Ivan Nikitin. M. 1972. Pp. 248.
Life of Russia's first portrait painter. Rev: *Kritika,*
XII, 1 (1976), 16-25 (Okenfuss, M.).

2085. LEBEDEVA, T.A., Ivan Nikitin. M. 1975. Pp. 164.

2086. PETINOVA, E., B.K. Rastrelli, 1675-1744. L. 1979. Pp. 71.

2087. KOMELOVA, G.N., 'Russkii graver Gavriil Ivanovich
Skorodumov, 1755-1792', *Trudy Gos. Ermitazha,* XV (1974),
40-55.

2088. VZDORNOV, G.I., 'Arkhitektor P'etro Antonio Trezini i ego
postroiki' in: ALEKSEEVA (ed.) (no. 2066), pp. 139-56.

2089. LISOVSKII, V., Andrei Voronikhin. L. 1971. Pp. 140.

2090. LEBEDIANSKII, M.S., Graver petrovskoi epokhi Aleksei
Zubov. M. 1973. Pp. 48, plates.

ARCHITECTURE

PILIAVSKII (2097) is an important bibliography. Architectural
theory is well discussed by EVSINA (2098) and VIPPER (2100);
LUCAS (2094-5) and HUGHES (2096) give a stimulating account of
Russian architecture's debt to the West. Architectural theory
is also one of the subjects covered in ALEKSEEVA (2099),
together with palace interiors, baroque facades and the
Kremlin arsenal. KENNETT (2092) and FEDOROV (2093) are
excellently illustrated. See also 803-4, 808-9, 894.

2091. EGOROV, I., The Architectural Planning of St. Petersburg.
Athens, Ohio 1969. Pp. 237.
Translation of Soviet work.

2092. KENNETT, V. and A., The Palaces of Leningrad. L. 1973.
Pp. 287, illustrations.

2093. FEDOROV, B., Architecture of the Russian North: Twelfth to
Nineteenth Centuries. L. 1976. Pp. 298, 212 colour plates.

2094. LUCAS, R., 'Innovation in Russian Architecture in Early
Modern History: A Stylistic Survey', *SGECRN.*, 4 (1976),
17-24.

2095. MILNER-GULLAND, R., 'Reflections on R. Lucas' "Innovation
..."', *SGECRN.*, 5 (1977), 45-48. 'Reply' by R. Lucas,
48-54.

2096. HUGHES, L., 'Western European Graphic Material as a Source
for Moscow Baroque Architecture', *SEER.*, LV, 4 (1977),
433-443.

2097. PILIAVSKII, U.K., GORSHKOVA, N., Russkaia arkhitektura
XI-nachalo XX v. (Ukazatel' izbr. lit. na russk. iazyke za
1811-1975 gg.). L. 1978. Pp. 160.

2098. EVSINA, N.A., Arkhitekturnaia teoriia v Rossii XVIII veka
(1700-1760). M. 1975. Pp. 261.

2099. ALEKSEEVA, T.V. (ed.), Russkoe iskusstvo barokko.
Materialy i issledovaniia. M. 1977. Pp. 236, 168
illustrations.
Rev: *SGECRN.*, 6 (1978), 63-7 (Hughes, L.).

2100. VIPPER, B., Arkhitektura russkogo barokko. M. 1978.
Pp. 230.

2101. RIAZANTSEV, I., 'Kharakternye cherty arkhitektury rannego
klassitsizma v Rossii', *VMU(Ist.)*, 2 (1964), 62-70.

2102. EVANGULOVA, O.S., 'O nekotorykh osobennostiakh moskovskoi
arkhitekturnoi shkoly serediny XVIII v.' in: IANIN (no.
792), pp. 259-69.

2103. MAKSIMOV, A.A., 'Arkhitektura russkikh torgovykh riadov
(XVIII-pervaia polovina XIX v.)' *Ist. SSSR.*, 1 (1972),
220-7.

2104. BOROVKOV, A.A. et al., Arkhitekturnyi putevoditel' po
Leningradu. L. 1971. Pp. 293, map, illustrations.

2105. RASKIN, A., Petrodvorets: dvortsovo-parkovyi ansambl'
XVIII v. L. 1975. Pp. 148.

2106. POD'IAPOLSKAIA, E. (ed.), Pamiatniki arkhitektury
moskovskoi oblasti. Katalog. M. 1975. 2 vols.
Pp. 384, 316.

2107. IL'IN, M., MOISEEVA, T., Pamiatniki arkhitektury Moskvy i
Podmoskov'ia. M.-Leipzig 1978. Pp.376.
illustrations. Updates various editions appearing in 1960's.

2108. SHIL'NIKOVSKAIA, V., Velikii Ustiug. Razvitie
arkhitekhtury goroda do serediny XIX v. M. 1973.
Pp. 226.

12-The Arts-Architecture   181

2109. TEL'TEVSKII, P., Velikii Ustiug : arkhitektura i iskusstvo
XVII-XIX veka. M. 1977. Pp. 177.

2109a. BUNIN, A., SAVARENSKAIA, T., Istoriia gradostroitel'-
nogo iskusstva. 2nd ed. 2 vols. M. 1979. Pp.494,410.
Vol I mainly 16th-18th Centuries: Russian references.

PAINTING, ENGRAVING, PRINTS, PHOTOGRAPHS

The multi-volume British Museum Catalogue (2110) is often
over-looked but contains many illustrations concerning Russia
at the end of the century, especially of Catherine II.
OVSIANNIKOV (2112) and BAKHTIN (2119) cover the Russian broad-
side (*lubok*); SADOVEN' (2118) is an interesting look at war
art with a number of eighteenth century references.
IAMSHCHIKOV (2115) is a very useful survey of portrait art - a
topic that is now becoming very fashionable among Soviet art
historians.

2110. STEPHENS, F.G., GEORGE, M.D. (comp.), Catalogue of Prints
and Drawings in the British Museum. Division 1:
Political and Personal Satires. 11 vols, London 1870-1954.
II-IV: 1689-1720; V-VII: 1771-1800.

2111. VANDERBIET, P., Guide to the Special Collections of Prints
and Photographs in the Library of Congress, Washington
1968.
No. 599: Prokhudin-Gorskii Collection of photographs,
taken before 1917, of Russian monuments.

2112. OVSIANNIKOV, IU.M., The Lubok. 17-18th Century Russian
Broadsides. M. 1968. 83 illustrations.
Russian-English. English text by A. Shkarovsky-Raffe.

2113. HORDYNSKY, S., The Ukrainian Icon of the XIIth to
XVIIIth Centuries. (Trans. by W. Dushnyck). Philadelphia
1973. Pp. 212, 24 colour, 193 b/w illustrations.
Rev: *Uk. Q.*, XXX, 3 (1974), 289-90.

2114. BARABANOVA, N., The Female Portrait in Russian Art
(Twelfth to Twentieth Centuries). M. 1974. Pp. 232.
Russian and English text and captions.

2115. IAMSHCHIKOV, S., Russian Portraits of the 18th and 19th
Centuries in the Museums of the RSFSR. M. 1976. Pp. 248,
109 colour plates. English/Russian text.

2116. BELECKIJ, P., 'Le Portrait dans la Peinture Ukrainienne
("Parsuna") des XVIIe et XVIIIe siècles', *CMRS.*, I, 4
(1960), 630-7.

2117. MAKAROVA, V., Russkaia svetskaia graviura pervoi chetverti
XVIII veka. Annotirovannyi svodnyi katalog. L. 1973.
Pp. 367.

2118. SADOVEN', V.V., Russkie Khudozhniki Batalisty. M. 1955.
Pp. 370, illustrations.

2119. BAKHTIN, V., MOLDAVSKII, D. (comp.), ADRIANOVA-PERETS, V.P.
(ed.), Russkii Lubok, XVII-XIX vv. M.-L. 1962.
87 illustrations.

APPLIED ARTS, SCULPTURE

This field is well illustrated, though sculpture is poorly
represented (2132). KORSHUNOVA (2122) is a particularly fine
volume on St. Petersburg's attempt to reproduce Gobelin.

2120. OVSIANNIKOV, IU.M., Russian Folk Arts and Crafts.
Translated from the Russian by A. Shkarovsky. M. 1966.
Pp. 238.

2121. ONASSIS, J., (ed.), In the Russian Style. NY 1976. Pp. 184.
Includes pictures of Catherine the Great's coronation dress
etc. as featured in a Met. Museum of Art exhibition.

2122. KORSHUNOVA, T., Russian Tapestry. L. 1975. Pp. 270, 183
plates.
Imperial Tapestry Manufacture 1716-1859. Russian text
with English, French, German summaries.

2123. IVANOVA, E., Russian Applied Art: 18th to Early 20th
Century. L. 1976. Pp. 200, 171 illustrations.

2124. TURNAU, I., 'Un aspect de l'artisanat russe: la
bonneterie aux XVIIe et XVIIIe siècles', *CMRS.*, IX, 1
(1968), 209-226.

2125. BERMAN, E.M., RYNDIN, V., Russkii Kostium 1750-1917.
M. 1960-1972. 5 vols, illustrations.
Vol. I: eighteenth century.

2126. SHCHUKINA, E.S., Medal'ernoe iskusstvo v Rossii XVIII
veka. L. 1962. Pp. 128.

2127. VASIL'EVA, V., GLINKA, V., Pamiatniki russkoi kul'tury
pervoi chetverti XVIII veka. Katalog. L. 1966. Pp. 352,
illustrations.
Valuable catalogue and illustrations of Hermitage holdings,
items relating to 1700-1725.

2128. SOKOLOVA, T., ORLOVA, K., Russkaia mebel' v gosudarstvennom
      Ermitazhe. L. 1973. Pp. 254, 195 illustrations.
      Russian/English text, captions.

2129. POSTNIKOVA-LOSEVA, M.M., Russkoe iuvelirnoe iskusstvo. Ego
      tsentry i mastera XVI-XIX vv. M. 1974. Pp. 371,
      illustrations.

2130. BARTENEV, I.A., Russkii inter'er XVIII-XIX vv. L. 1977.
      Pp. 128, illustrations.

2131. SHCHUKINA, E., '"Natural'nyi sad" russkoi usad'by v kontse
      XVIII v.', in: ALEKSEEVA (ed.) (no. 2068), pp. 109-117.

2132. MOLEVA, N., 'I snova mednyi vsadnik ...' *Novyi Mir,* 3
      (1974), 195-208.
      Creation of Falconet's monument, role in it and in his
      life of Marie-Anne Collot.

MUSIC

The principal writer in English is SEAMAN (2134, 2138-41).
Russian reference and bibliographic works: 2144-48. Useful
recent general studies are KELDYSH (2149) and RABINOVICH
(2151). See also TERRY (165).

2133. MOLDON, D., A Bibliography of Russian Composers. London
      1976. Pp. 364.
      Small section on the eighteenth century.

2134. SEAMAN, G.R., A History of Russian Music. Oxford-N.Y.
      1967. Pp.303. Amplification of author's 1961 thesis.

2135. BELIAEV, V.M., Central Asian Music: Essays in the History
      of Music of the Peoples of the USSR (ed. and trans. SLOBIN,
      M.). Middletown, Conn. 1975. Pp. 340.

2136. SWAN, A. and J., 'The Survival of Russian Music in the
      Eighteenth Century', in: GARRARD (no. 1595), pp. 300-310.
      The continuation of native traditions in church and folk
      music.

2137. WHAPLES, M.K., 'Eighteenth Century Russian Opera in the
      Light of Soviet Scholarship', *Indiana Sl. St.,* 2 (1958),
      113-34.

2138. SEAMAN, G.R., 'Russian Folk-Songs in the Eighteenth
      Century', *Music and Letters,* 40 (1959), 253-60.

2139. SEAMAN, G.R., 'Folk-Song in Russian Opera of the 18th Century', *SEER.*, 41 (1962-3), 144-57.

2140. SEAMAN, G.R., 'Russian Opera Before Glinka', in: LEGHTERS, L.H. (ed.), Russia. Essays in History and Literature (Leiden 1972), pp. 56-78.

2141. SEAMAN, G.R., 'The Influence of Folk-Song on Russian Opera up to the Time of Glinka', Oxford D.Phil., 1972.

2142. SPIEGELMANN, J., 'Style Formation in Early Russian Keyboard Music', in: GARRARD (no. 1595), pp. 311-320.

2143. LABRIOLLE, F. de., 'L'opéra-comique russe et le drame en France, 1765-1795', *CMRS.*, VI, 3 (1965), 399-412.

2144. KOLTYPINA, G.B. (comp.), Spravochnaia literatura po muzyke. Slovari, sborniki, biografii, kalendari, ... ukazatel' izdanii ... 1773-1962. M. 1964. Pp. 249.

2145. BERNANDT, G., IAMPOL'SKII, I., Kto pisal o myzyke. Biobibliograficheskii slovar' muzykal'nykh kritikov i lits, pisavshikh o muzyke v dorevoliutsionnoi Rossii i SSSR. M. 1971-78.
3 vols.

2146. BIBLIOTEKA SSSR im. V. LENINA, Muzykal'nye biblioteki i myzykal'nye fondy v bibliotekakh SSSR. Spravochnik. M. 1972. Pp. 176. Rotaprint.

2147. BERNANDT, G., Slovar' oper, vpervye postavlennykh ... v Rossii, 1736-1959. M. 1962. Pp. 554.

2148. SIDEL'NIKOV, V.M. (comp.), Russkaia narodnaia pesnia, bibliograficheskii ukazatel', 1735-1945 gg. M. 1962. Pp. 121.

2149. KELDYSH, IU., Muzyka XVIII v. M. 1965. Pp. 463.

2150. LIVANOVA, T.N., 'Russkaia muzyka v period obrazovaniia russkoi natsii', in: DRUZHININ, N.M., CHEREPNIN, L.V. (eds), Voprosy formirovaniia russkoi narodnosti i natsii. Sb. statei (M.-L. 1958), pp. 347-87.
Seventeenth to nineteenth centuries.

2151. RABINOVICH, V.I. (ed.), KIKNADZE, L.V. (comp.), Traditsii russkoi muzykal'noi kul'tury XVIII v. M. 1975. Pp. 205.

2152. BRAZHNIKOV, M., Drevnerusskaia teoriia muzyki, po rukopisnym materialam XV-XVIII vekov. L. 1972. Pp. 424.

2153. BRAZHNIKOV, M., Stat'i o drevnerusskoi muzyke. L. 1975. Pp. 119.

2154. RAPHAEL, J.E., 'An Annotated And Critical Bibliography of the Works Written in English since 1900 on the Pre- and Post- Revolutionary Russian Theatre ', Michigan State Ph.D., 1971.

2155. SLONIM, M., Russian Theater from the Empire to the Soviets. N.Y. 1961, London 1963. Pp. 354. Rev: *RR.*, 21 (1962), 387-8 (Gibian, G.).

2156. BURGESS, M.A.S., 'The Early Theatre', in: AUTY, OBOLENSKY (no. 283), II, pp. 111-32.

2157. BURGESS, M.A.S., 'Russian Public Theatre Audiences of the 18th and Early 19th Centuries', *SEER.*, XXXVII (1958-9), 160-83.

2158. BURGESS, M.A.S., 'Fairs and Entertainers in 18th-Century Russia', *SEER.*, XXXVIII (1959-60), 95-113.

2159. MAGGS, B.W., 'Firework Art and Literature: Eighteenth Century Pyrotechnical Tradition in Russia and Western Europe', *SEER.*, LIV, 1 (1976), 24-40.

2160. BAEHR, S.L., '"Fortuna Redux": The Courtly Spectacle in Eighteenth-Century Russia', in: CROSS, *Proceedings* (no. 1794), pp. 109-123.

2161. PARGMENT, L., 'Serf Theatres and Serf Actors', *AATSEEL*, 14, 3 (1956), 71-8.

2162. COOKS, J.B., 'The Serf Theatre of Imperial Russia', Kansas Ph.D., 1970.
_____

2163. KHOLODOV, E. (ed.), Istoriia russkogo dramaticheskogo teatra v 7 tomakh. M. 1977- Vol. I: Do 1800 g. In progress.

2164. AL'TSHULLER, A. (ed.), Ocherki istorii russkoi teatral'- noi kritiki. Konets XVIII-pervaia polovina XIX veka. Vol. I: 1770-1850. L. 1975. Pp. 385.

2165. LEVINA, L. et al., Russkii sovetskii dramaticheskii teatr: Ann. ukaz. bibliografii i spravochnykh materialov, 1917-1973. M. 1977-8. 3 vols.

2165a. KROSS, A.G.,' Russkaia zriteli v angliiskom teatr XVIII veka', in: Russkie kul'tura XVIII veka i zapadnoevropeiskie literatury (L. 1980), 162-73.

The only recent work in English is KOPELEVICH (2166), which is
a good précis of her longer Russian work (2179). KASACK
(2167) includes much useful reference material, in German and
Russian. OSTROVITIANOV (2172) is the old standard Soviet
account, now in process of renewal. LUPPOV (2174) provides an
interesting account of the growth of the Academy's library.
See also nos. 34-8, 97, 1445, 1494, 1499, 1583, 1689-90, 1754,
1780, 1788, 1922, 1925, 2692.

2166. KOPELEVICH, IU., 'The Creation of the Petersburg
      Academy of Sciences as a New Type of Scientific and State
      Institution', in CROSS (ed.), *Proceedings* (no. 1794),
      pp. 204-11.

2167. KASACK, W., Die Akademie der Wissenschaften der UdSSR.
      Ueberblick über Geschichte und Struktur. Verzeichnis der
      Institute. 3rd ed. Boppard 1978. Pp. 157.

2168. WINTER, E. (ed.), 'L. Blumentrost der Jüngere und die
      Anfänge der Petersburger Akademie der Wissenschaften',
      JfGSLE., 8 (1964), 247-69.

2169. VÁVRA, J., 'Die Olmützer Societas Incognitorum und die
      Petersburger Akademie der Wissenschaften', in: *Ost und
      West* (no. 1737), pp. 278-289.

2170. BYKOVA, T., 'Zur Geschichte der ersten deutschsprachigen
      Zeitung der Petersburger Akademie', *StGrL.*, 4 (1970),
      273-284.
      Translated from the Russian.

2171. GRAU, C., 'Robert Areskin und die Vorgeschichte der
      Petersburger Akademie der Wissenschaften:
      Wissenschaftsorganization und Forschungsreisen in Russland
      im zweiten Jahrzehnt des 18. Jhdts', *JbfGSLE.*, 16 (1977),
      7-31.

2172. OSTROVITIANOV, K. (ed.), Istoriia Akademii Nauk SSSR.
      3 vols. I: 1724-1803. M. 1958. Pp. 483.
      The standard history. A new edition in 2 vols, ed.
      Komkov, Levshin, Semenov, is in progress (vol. 2 (1917-76):
      M. 1977, vol. 1 forthcoming).

2173. KOLDOBSKAIA, R., ELAGINA, L. (comps), Akademii Nauk
      SSSR - 250 let. Rekomendatel'nyi ukazatel' literatury.
      Alma Ata 1974. Pp. 103.

2174. LUPPOV, S. (ed.), Istoriia biblioteki Akademii Nauk SSSR,
      1714-1964. M.-L. 1964. Pp. 600.

2175. AVTOKRATOVA, M., 'Dokumenty TsGADA po istorii Akademii
      Nauk pervoi poloviny XVIII v.', *A. Ezh.* (1974), 245-54.

2176. LEVSHIN, B., 'Nachalo Akademii nauk v Rossii', *Ist. SSSR*,
2 (1974), 94-108.

2177. BELIAVSKII, M.T., 'Osnovanie Akademii nauk v Rossii', *Vop.
Ist.*, 5 (1974), 16-27.

2178. PUSHKAREV, L.N., 'Akademiia nauk i russkaia kul'tura
XVIII v.', *Vop. Ist.*, 5 (1974), 28-38.

2179. KOPELEVICH, IU., Osnovanie Peterburgskoi Akademii Nauk.
L. 1977. Pp. 211.

2180. SKRIABIN, G. (ed.), 250 let Akademii Nauk SSSR. Sbornik
dokumentov i materialy iubeleinykh torzhestv. M. 1978.
Pp. 585.

2180a. KULIABKO, E., Zamechatel'nye pitomtsy Akademicheskogo
Universiteta. L. 1977. Pp. 228.
Biographical sketches of Lomonosov's pupils.

12(i) - SCIENCE

Writing in this area has tended to fall into opposing trends.
Western authors have stressed the dependence of Russian
writers upon the West, while Soviet writing has emphasised the
role of figures such as Lomonosov and Russia's own development.
The most useful English language survey, though now dated, is
VUCINICH (2182). Essential bibliographical coverage of Soviet
writing is provided in 2184-91. The latest general study is
MIKULINSKII (2193); attention should also be drawn to the out-
standing older work, very wide-ranging, of LUKIANOV (2201).
For individuals (including Lomonosov) see Section 11; interactions with the West, 12(b); Academy of Sciences, 12(h);
Medicine 12(j).

General

2181. WHITROW, M. (ed.), ISIS Cumulative Bibliography. A
Bibliography of the History of Science formed from ISIS
Critical Bibliographies 1-90 (1913-1965). London 1976. 3
vols.: I-II Personalities/Institutions, III: Subjects.

2182. VUCINICH, A., Science in Russian Culture: A History to
1860. Stanford 1963. Pp. 463.
Rev: *SR.*, 25 (1966), 367-9 (Joravsky, D.); *History of
Science*, 5 (1966), 52-61 (Ryan, W.).

2183. VERNADSKY, G., 'Rise of Science in Russia, 1700-1917',
RR., 28, 1 (1969), 37-53.

2184. AKADEMIIA NAUK SSSR, INSTITUT ISTORII ESTESTVOZNANIIA
I TEKHNIKI, Istoriia estestvoznaniia. Literatura, o-
publikovannaia v SSSR. M. 1949-
On-going bibliography. 6 vols to date (1949-1977),
covering publications 1917-66.

2185. BALDAEV, R. (comp.), Ukazatel' osnovnykh otechestvennykh
bibliografii i spravochnykh izdanii po estestvennym i
fiziko-matematicheskim naukam. L. 1966. Pp. 385.

2186. Bibliografiia Tekhniki. I, BRONSHTEIN, M.P., FIRSOV, G.G.
(eds), Bibliografiia tekhniki. M. 1975. Pp. 272. II,
GASTFER, M.P., GEDRIMOVICH, G.B. (eds), Bibliografiia
tekhnicheskoi literatury. M. 1978. Pp. 218.

2187. AKADEMIIA NAUK SSSR. BIBLIOTEKA. Bibliografiia
otechestvennykh bibliografii po geologii XVIII v.-1973 g.
M.1976-8. 2 vols. Pp. 326, 408.

2188. SHMELA, A. et al., Periodicheskaia pechat' Rossii.
Estestvennye nauki, tekhnika, promshlennost', transport,
gos. khoziaistvo, kustarnye promysly. 1703-1917. (Katalog-
spravochnik). M. 1975-
Vol. I: A-N, vol. II: K-O (with bibliographies for each
section).

2189. PAVLOVA, L., PIL'SHCHIKOVA, P., 'Sovetskie periodicheskie
izdaniia po istorii estestvoznaniia i tekhniki (s 20kh
godov po nastoiashchee vremiia): bibliograficheskii
ukazatel'', *Voprosy istorii estestvoznaniia i tekhniki*, 1
(1975), 84-88.

2190. AVTUKHOVA, I. et al. (comp.), 'Soderzhanie vypuskov 21-40
sbornika *Voprosy istorii estestvoznaniia i tekhniki* (1967-
1972), *Voprosy istorii estestvoznaniia i tekhniki* 3
(40) (1972), 102-19.

2191. ZUBOV, V.P., Istoriografiia estestvennykh nauk v Rossii
(XVIII v.-pervaia polovina XIX v.). M. 1956. Pp. 575.

2192. FIGUROVSKII, N., ZUBOV, V.P. et al., Istoriia
estestvoznaniia v Rossii. M. 1957-62. T. 1, chast' 1
(M. 1957): do kontsa XVIII v. Pp. 495.

2193. MIKULINSKII, S.R., IUSHKEVICH, A.P., Razvitie
estestvoznaniia v Rossii, XVIII-nachalo XX v. M. 1977.
Pp. 507.
Extensive bibliography, pp. 494-507.

2194. AKADEMIIA NAUK SSSR, INSTITUT ISTORII ESTESTOVOZNANIIA I
TEKHNIKI, Razvitie fiziko-geograficheskikh nauk XVII-XX vv.
M. 1975. Pp. 434.
Bibliography: pp. 418-32.

2195. CHENAKAL, V.L., Watchmakers and Clockmakers in Russia, 1400–1850 (Trans. from the Russian by W.F. Ryan) London 1972. Pp. 64.
(Antiquarian Horological Society Monograph, no. 6).

2196. LEICESTER, H.M., 'The Electrical Theories of M.V. Lomonosov', *Annals of Science*, 30 (1973), 299–310.

2197. TURNER, G.L'E., 'Forms of Patronage and Institutionalisation of Science in the Eighteenth Century', in Cross, *Proceedings* (no. 1794), pp. 193–203.

2198. FEDOSEEV, I., Razvitie gidrologii sushi v Rossii. M. 1960. Pp. 301.
Contains useful bibliography.

2199. IUSHKEVICH, A.P. (ed.), Istoriia matematiki s drevneishikh vremen do nachala XIX stoletiia. M. 1970–72. 3 vols. Pp. 352., 300, 496.

2200. SHTOKALS, I., Istoriia otechestvennoi matematiki. 5 vols. Kiev 1966–70.
Vol. I: to 1800.

2201. LUKIANOV, P., Istoriia khimicheskikh promyslov i khimicheskoi promyshlennosti Rossii do kontsa XIX v. M.-L. 1948–65. 6 vols.
Bibliographies in each volume.

2202. FIGUROVSKII, N.et al., Khimiia v Moskovskom Universitete za 200 let. M. 1955. Pp. 141.

2203. GORDEEV, D., Istoriia geologicheskikh nauk v Moskovskom Universitete. M. 1962. Pp. 351.

2204. KUTINA, L., Formirovanie terminologii fiziki v Rossii (1700–1730). M.-L. 1966. Pp. 289.

2205. BOGOLIUBOV, A.N. (ed.), Fizika na rubezhe XVII–XVIII vv. Sbornik statei. Moscow 1974. Pp. 246.

2206. NOVITSKII, G., 'Razvitie nauki v Moskovskom Universitete vo vtoroi polovine XVIII veka', *(VMU(Ist.),* 6 (1961),16–27.

2207. KAMENTSEVA, E.I., USTIUGOV, N.V., Russkaia metrologiia. M. 1965. Pp. 255.
Russian systems of measurement, eleventh- twentieth centuries. Rev: *ZfSl.*, XIII (1965), 1472, Hoffmann, P.

2208. KAMENTSEVA, E.I., 'Mery zhidkostei v pervoi polovine XVIII v.', *A. Ezh.* (1960), 57–66.

2208a. TIKHOMIROV, V., Geologiia v Akademii Nauk (Ot Lomonosov do Karpinskogo). M. 1979. Pp. 295.

2209. SHUKHARDIN S. (ed.), Tekhnika v ee istoricheskom razvitii ot noiavleniia ruchnykh orudii truda do stanov-
leniia tekhniki mashinno-fabrichnogo proizvodstva.
M. 1979. Pp. 412. Bibliography, pp. 380-392.

2210. ZAGORSKII, F.N., L.F. Sabakin, mekhanik XVIII veka.
M.-L. 1963. Pp. 86.

2211. ASHURKOV, V., Oruzheinogo dela nadziratel'. Zhizn' i
deiatel'nost' tul'skogo mekhanika Alekseia Surnina (1767-
1811 gg.). Tula 1969.

2212. ZAGORSKII, F., Andrei Konstantinovich Nartov, 1693-1756.
L. 1969. Pp. 164.

2213. NEVSKAIA, N.I. (comp.), Nikita Ivanovich Popov, 1720-
1782. L. 1977.
First Russian professor of astronomy at Academy of
Sciences. Bibliography: pp. 95-100.

2214. RASKIN, P.M., Iakov Dmitrievich Zakharov (1765-1836):
fizik i khimik kontsa XVIII i nachala XIX v. L. 1979.
Pp. 106.

2214a. RASKIN, P.M., Fedor P. Moiseenko, mineralog XVIII
veka, 1754-1781. L. 1974. Pp.177.

2214b. RASKIN, P.M., A.M. Karamyshev, 1744-1791. L. 1975. Pp.131.

12(j) - MEDICINE

Russian medical history has become a popular topic with some
excellent results. ALEXANDER (2217) offers the best comment
as well as a good bibliography. KAISER (2225) outlines the
German influence. MÜLLER-DIETZ (2226) is inadequate and must
be supplemented by PALKIN (2240) and older studies cited in
ROSSIISSKII (2229). There are several outstanding reference
works: ROSSISSKII (2229) is a classic, though unfortunately
not found in most libraries; GROMBAKH (2230) is well annotated; SHIBKOV (2231) indicates the extent to which Western
preventive military medicine penetrated into Russia.

2215. ALEXANDER, J.T., 'Medical Developments in Petrine Russia',
CanAmSlSt., VIII, 2 (1974), 198-222.

2216. HAIGH, B., 'Design for a Medical Service: Peter the
Great's Administrative Regulations (1722)', *Medical
History*, XIX (1975), 129-46.

2217. ALEXANDER, J. T., Bubonic Plague in Early Modern Russia.
Public Health and Urban Disaster. Baltimore 1980. Pp.
385. The 1771-72 plague.

2217a. WELLCOME INSTITUTE, Current Work in the History of Medicine: An International Bibliography. London 1954-.qrly.

2218. GRMEK, M., 'The History of Medical Education in Russia', in: O'MALLEY, C.D. (ed.), The History of Medical Education (Berkeley 1970), pp. 303-27.

2219. BOXER, C., 'An Enlightened Portuguese: Dr. Ribeiro Sanches', *History Today*, XX, 4 (1970), 270-77.

2220. CLENDENNING, P.H., 'Dr. Thomas Dimsdale and Smallpox Inoculation in Russia', *Journal of the History of Medicine*, XXVIII, 2 (1973), 109-125.

2221. WILSON, J.B., 'Three Scots in the Service of the Czar', *The Practitioner*, vol. 210 (April 1973), 569-74; (May 1973), 704-708.

2222. DE MERTENS, C., An Account of the Plague which Raged at Moscow, 1771. London 1798, reprinted Newtonville 1977. Pp. 128.
Reprint provides a long introduction and bibliography by J.T. Alexander.

2223. ROWELL, M., 'Medicinal Plants in Russia in the 18th and early 19th Centuries', Kansas Ph.D., 1977.

2224. WILLEMSE, D., Antonis Nũnes Ribeiro, élève de Boerhaave, et son importance pour la Russie. Leyden 1966. Pp.188,93.

2225. KAISER, W., KROSCH, K.-H., Wissenschaftsbeziehungen Halle-Russland aus medizinischer Sicht (18. Jahrhundert). Halle 1967. Pp. 72.

2226. MÜLLER-DIETZ, H., Der russische Militärarzt im 18. Jahrhundert. Berlin 1970. Pp.188.

2227. MÜLLER-DIETZ, H., Aerzte im Russland des achtzehnten Jahrhunderts. Esslingen/Neckar 1973. Pp.111.

2228. MÜLLER-DIETZ, H., 'Die Anfänge der Stadtphysikats in Moskau und St. Petersburg', *Sudhoffs Archiv*, 60, 2 (1976), 194-206.

2229. ROSSIISKII, D., Istoriia vseobshchei i otechestvennoi meditsiny i zdravookhraneniia. Bibliografiia (996-1954 gg.). M. 1956. Pp. 935.

2230. GROMBAKH, S.M., Russkaia meditsinskaia literatura XVIII veka. M. 1953. Pp. 282.

2231. SHIBKOV, A.A., Kratkii bibliograficheskii spravochnik russkoi voenno-meditsinskoi literatury (1700-1968 gg.). L. 1970. Pp. 192.

2232. CHERNOV, E., (comp.), Sistematicheskii katalog otechest-vennykh periodicheskikh i prodolzhaiushchikhsiia izdanii po meditsine 1792-1960. L. 1965. Pp. 495.

2233. BLIAKHER, L., Istoriia embriologii Rossii, 1750-1850.
M. 1955. Pp. 375.

2234. FEDOTOV, D., Ocherki po istorii otechestvennoi
psikhiatrii. M. 1957. 2 vols.
Vol. 1: 1750-1825. Pp. 318.

2235. IAROSHEVSKII, M.G., Istoriia psikhologii. 2nd rev. ed.
M. 1976. Pp. 462.

2236. VASIL'EV, K., SEGAL, A., Istoriia epidemii v Rossii.
Materialy i ocherki. M. 1960. Pp.396.

2237. SHERSHAVIN, S., Istoriia otechestvennoi sudebno-
meditsinskoi sluzhby. M. 1968. Pp. 181.

2238. ROSSIISKII, D., 200 let meditsinskogo fakul'teta
Moskovskogo gosudarstvennogo universiteta. M. 1955.
Pp. 241.

2239. MIKHAILOV, S., Meditsinskaia sluzhba russkogo flota v
XVIII veke. Materialy k istorii otechestvennoi meditsiny.
L. 1957. Pp. 231.

2240. PALKIN, B., Russkie gospital'nye shkoly XVIII veka i ikh
vospitanniki. M. 1959.

2241. SEMEKA, S., Meditsinskoe obespechenie russkoi armii vo
vremia semiletnei voiny 1756-1763 gg. M. 1961.

2242. VOSTRIKOV, L.A., Svetia drugim. Ocherki o vrachakh Sibiri
i Dal'nego Vostoka XVIII-nachala XX veka. Khabarovsk
1974. Pp. 212.

2242a. VASIL'EV, K., Materialy po istorii meditsyny i zdravookhraneniia Latvii. Riga 1959. Pp. 359.

2242b. PALKIN, B., Ocherki istorii meditsiny i zdravookhraneniia Zapadnoi Sibiri i Kazakhstana v period prisoedine-
niia k Rossii, 1716-1868. Novos. 1967. Pp. 578.

KASINEC (2243) provides the most recent bibliographical survey: for another full bibliography on the Russian Orthodox Church and Old Believers see VERNADSKY (183). SMOLITSCH (2248) is very thorough; BLANC (2247) a solid and perceptive article. Among particular topics, the Petrine reforms have, not surprisingly, claimed much attention (2257-62); FREEZE (2265) is another and excellent contribution. For the Old Believers, DRUZHININ (2285) is essential. Catholic and Jesuit history is well covered (2295-8, 2301-3); the Uniates have been neglected (2302). Soviet historians have been in general reticent about eighteenth-century religion, but SAKHAROV (2256) is useful. Prokopovich has been well served by Western and Eastern scholars (2306-13). For Judaism and the Jews, see Section 14(b).

For reference books, see 2702-4.

(i) General

2243. KASINEC, E., 'A Bibliographical Essay on the Documentation of Russian Orthodoxy During The Imperial Era', and 'Guide to Further Reading In Western Languages', in: NICHOLS, STAVROU (no. 2246), pp. 205-28, 229-37.

2244. BLANE, A. (ed.), Russia and Orthodoxy: Essays in Honour of Georges Florovsky. 3 vols. The Hague 1973-74.

2245. TREADGOLD, D., A History of Christianity. Belmont, Mass. 1978. Pp. 151.

2246. NICHOLS, R.L., STAVROU, T.G. (eds), Russian Orthodoxy Under The Old Regime. Minneapolis 1978. Pp. 261. Includes essays on Prokopovich (Cracraft); Orthodoxy and Enlightenment (Nichols); Peter the Great as inquisitor (Müller); Church and State (Szeftel).

2247. BLANC, S., 'L'Eglise russe à l'aube du "Siècle des lumières"', *Annales*, XX, 3 (1965), 442-464.

2248. SMOLITSCH, I., Geschichte der russischen Kirche 1700-1917. Band I. Leipzig 1964. Pp. 734. Rev: *JbfGO.*, N.F., 13, 2 (1965), 254-5 (Amburger, E); *Kyrios*, N.F. 5 (1965), 179-85 (Müller, L.).

2249. ONASCH, K., Grundzüge der russischen Kirchengeschichte. Göttingen 1967. Pp. 133.

2250. IVANKA, E. von. (ed.), Handbuch der Ostkirchenkunde. Düsseldorf 1971. Pp. 839. Some eighteenth-century general history

2251. STUPPERICH, R., Kirche im Osten. Studien zur osteuropaischen Kirchengeschichte und Kirchenkunde. Göttingen 1977. Pp. 195.

2252. Polnyi pravoslavnyi bogoslovskii entsiklopedicheskii
slovar'. St. P. 1913, reprinted 1971. 2 vols. Pp. 2,463.

2253. KARTASHOV, A.V., Ocherki po istorii russkoi tserkvi. 2
vols. Paris 1959.

2254. KOCAN, IU., Ocherki po istorii russkoi ateisticheskoi
mysli XVIII v. M. 1962. Pp. 344.
Rev: *Vop. Ist.*, 11 (1963), 122-4 (Dunaevskii, L.R.);
Kritika I, 2 (1964-65), 11-18 (Ryu, In-Ho.).

2255. SMIRNOV, N.A. et al. (eds), Tserkov' v istorii Rossii.
IX v.-1917 g. Kriticheskie ocherki. M. 1967. Pp. 335.

2256. SAKHAROV, A. (ed.), Religiia i tserkov'v istorii Rossii
Sovetskie istoriki o pravoslavnoi tserkvi v Rossii.
M. 1975. Pp. 255.

(ii) Specific topics   See also no. 2485

2257. BISSONNETTE, G., 'The Church Reforms of Peter the Great as
a Problem in Soviet Historiography', *Et. Slav. Est.-Eur.*,
I (1956-57), 146-157; 195-207.

2258. BISSONNETTE, G., 'Pufendorf and the Church Reform of Peter
the Great', Columbia Ph.D., 1962.

2259. BISSONNETTE, G., 'Peter the Great and the Church as an
Educational Institution', in: CURTISS, J.S. (ed.),
Essays in Russian and Soviet History in Honor of G.T.
Robinson (Leiden 1963), pp. 3-19.

2260. CRACRAFT, J., The Church Reform of Peter the Great.
Stanford 1971. Pp. 336.
Based on D.Phil. thesis, Oxford 1969. Rev: *RR.*, 31, 1
(1972), 77-79.

2261. MULLER, A.V. (trans. and ed.), The Spiritual Regulation
of Peter the Great. Seattle 1972. Pp. 150.

2262. MULLER, A.V., 'Historical Antecedents of the Petrine
Ecclesiastical Reforms', Washington, Seattle Ph.D., 1973.

2263. FREEZE, G., 'Social Mobility and the Russian Parish
Clergy in the Eighteenth Century', *SR.*, XXXIII, 4 (1974),
641-662.

2264. FREEZE, G., 'The Disintegration of Traditional
Communities: The Parish in Eighteenth-Century Russia',
JMH., 48, 1 (1976), 32-51.

2264a. BOLSHAKOFF, S., Russian Mystics: Introduction by T. Merton.
Kalamazoo/London 1977. Pp. 303. (Trans. from the Italian
edition , Torino 1962).
Essays on Russian monasticism in 18th C.

2265. FREEZE, G., The Russian Levites. Parish Clergy in the Eighteenth Century. Cambridge, Mass. 1977. Pp. 325. Based on Ph.D. thesis, Columbia 1972. Rev: *AHR.*, 83, 3 (June 1978), 769 (Orlovsky, D.).

2266. MALONEY, G., A History of Orthodox Theology Since 1453. Belmont, Mass. 1976. Pp. 388.

2267. SYDORENKO, A., 'Scholastic, Humanist and Baroque Strains in Orthodox Spirituality', Illinois Ph.D., 1974.

2268. WIDNER, E., The Russian Ecclesiastical Mission in Peking. Cambridge 1976. Pp. 250. Based on Ph.D. thesis, Harvard 1970.

2269. SCHERER, S.P., 'The Life and Thought of Russia's First Lay Theologian, Grigorij Savvic Skovoroda (1772-1794)', Ohio State Ph.D., 1969.

2270. SOLDATOV, G.M., Arsenii Matseevich Mitropolit Rostovskii, 1696-1772. St. Paul 1971 Pp. 130. Chief clerical opponent of secularization in Russia.

2271. PAPMEHL, K., Metropolitan Platon of Moscow (1737-1812). The Enlightened Churchman, Scholar and Educator. Newtonville 1981. Pp. 125.

2272. ARMINJON, V., La Russie monastique. Présence 1975. Pp. 236.

2273. MAZON, A., 'Ivan Bykovskii, Ioil L'Archimandrite et l'auteur de *La Vérité ou Extraits de Notes sur la vérité*, *Revue des Etudes Slaves*, 44 (1965), 59-88. Book published in Iaroslavl, 1787. Extract from many writers in tolerant, eighteenth-century vein - including *Encyclopédie*.

2274. SMOLITSCH, I., Leben und Lehre der Starzen. Köln 1952. Pp. 230. Translated into French as: Moines de la Sainte-Russie. Paris 1967.

2275. FINK, H., Die Auswirkungen der Reformen Peters des Grossen auf das Kirchenrecht der russischen orthodoxen Kirche. Erlangen-Nürnberg 1963. Pp. 169.

2276. NOLTE, H.-H., Religiöse Toleranz in Russland, 1600-1725. Göttingen 1969. Pp. 216.

2277. NOLTE, H.-H., 'Verständnis und Bedeutung der religiösen Toleranz in Russland, 1600-1725', *JbfGO.*, N.F. 17, 3 (1969), 494-530.

2278. HOESCH, E., Orthodoxie und Häresie im alten Russland. Wiesbaden 1975. Pp. 321.

2279. ZANDER, V., Seraphim von Sarov. Ein Heiliger der orthodoxen Christenheit (1759-1833). Düsseldorf 1965. Pp. 176.
Rev: *Kyrios*, N.F., 6 (1966), 191-2

2280. OLTOW, M., LENZ, W. (eds), Die Evangelischen Prediger Livlands bis 1918. Köln/Wien 1977. Pp. 529.
Biographical dictionary of Lutheran pastors, 1512-1918.

2281. MAIKOVA, T., 'Petr I i pravoslavnaia tserkov'', *Nauka i religiia* 7 (1972), 38-46.

2282. BULYGIN, I.A., 'Tserkovnaia reforma Petra I', *Vop. Ist.*, 5 (1974), 79-93.

(iii) Old Believers

2283. CHERNIAVSKY, M., 'The Old Believers and the New Religion', *SR.*, XXV (1960).

2284. CRUMMEY, R.O., The Old Believers and the World of Antichrist: the Vyg Community and the Russian State, 1694-1855. Madison 1970. Pp. 258.
Based on Ph.D. thesis, Chicago 1964.

2285. DRUZHININ, V.G., Pisaniia russkikh staroobriadtsev, perechen' spiskov, sostavlennykh po pechatnym opisaniiam rukopisnykh sobranii. St. P. 1912, reprint scheduled Newtonville 1981. Pp. 534.
Reprint includes 50-page bibliography of recent works by V. Teteriatnikov.

2286. POKROVSKII, N.N., Antifeodal'nyi protest uralo-sibirskikh krest'ian-staroobriadsev v XVIII v. Novosibirsk 1974. Pp. 391.

2287. POKROVSKII, N.N., 'Predstavleniia krest'ian-staroobriadtsev Urala i Sibiri XVIII v. o svetskikh vlastiakh', *Ezh. A.I.* (1971), 167-76.

2288. SOKOLOVSKAIA, M., 'Severnoe raskol'nich'e obshchezhitel'-stvo pervoi poloviny XVIII veka i struktura ego zemel', *Ist. SSSR.*, I (1978), 157-68.

(iv) Doukhobors

2289. HORVATH, M., A Doukhobor Bibliography. Vancouver 1968-70. 3 parts.

2290. HORVATH, M., A Doukhobor Bibliography based on material in the University of British Columbia Library. Vancouver 1972.
651 items.

2291. WOODCOCK, G., AVAKUMOVIC, I., The Doukhobors. Toronto
1968. Pp. 382.

2292. POPOFF, E.A., Historical Exposition on the origin and
evolvement of the basic tenets of the Doukhobor life-
conception. Grand Forks, B.C. 1966. Pp. 58.

(v) Islam See also no. 2444

2293. Encyclopaedia of Islam. 1st ed. 4 vols. Leiden/London
1913-38. 2nd ed. London/Leiden 1960. 4 vols to date.
Good bibliographies.

2294. FISHER, A.W., 'Enlightened Despotism and Islam under
Catherine II', *SR.*, XXVII, 4 (1968), 542-54.

2295. LEMERCIER-QUELQUEJAY, C., 'Les missions orthodoxes en
pays musulmans de Moyenne et Basse-Volga, 1552-1865',
CMRS., VIII, 3 (1967), 369-403.

(vi) Catholic, Jesuits, Uniats and Protestant confessions

2296. ZATKO, J.J., 'The Organisation of the Catholic Church in
Russia, 1772-84', *SEER.*, 43 (1964-5), 303-13.

2297. SMAL-STOCHI, R., 'Catherine II of Russia and the Jesuits',
Uk. Q., XXVI, 1 (1970), 73-78.

2298. JAMES, W.A., 'Paul I and the Jesuits in Russia',
Washington, Seattle Ph.D., 1977.

2299. OKENFUSS, M., 'The Jesuit Origins of Petrine Education',
in: GARRARD (no. 1595), pp. 106-30.

2300. SCOTT, R., Quakers in Russia. London 1964. Pp. 302.
W. European and American Quaker contacts and activities.
Chap. 2 covers the eighteenth century.

2301. REMPEL, D.G., 'The Mennonite Commonwealth in Russia. A
Sketch of its Founding and Endurance, 1789-1919',
Mennonite Quarterly Review, XLVII (Oct. 1973), XLVIII
(Jan. 1974).

2302. BEAUVOIS, D., 'Les jésuites dans l'Empire russe (1772-
1820)', *Dix-Huitième siècle*, 8 (1976), 257-272.

2303. BEAUVOIS, D., 'Les Lumières au Carrefour de l'Othodoxie
et du Catholicisme. Le cas des Uniates de l'Empire russe
au début du XIXe siècle', *CMRS.*, XIX, 4 (1978), 423-441.

2304. WINTER, E., 'Die Jesuiten in Russland (1772-1820). Ein
Beitrag zur Auseinandersetzung zwischen Aufklärung und
Restauration', in: Forschen und Wirken. Festschrift zur
150-Jahr-Feier der Humboldt-Universität zu Berlin, 1810-
1960. Bd. 3 (Berlin 1960), pp. 167-91.

2305. AMBURGER, E., Geschichte des Protestantismus in Russland. Stuttgart 1961. Pp. 210.

2306. KAHLE, W., Aufsätze zur Entwicklung der Evangelischen Gemeinden in Russland. Leiden-Köln 1962. Pp. 267.

(vii) Feofan Prokopovich See also nos. 358, 1592, 1727.

2307. CRACRAFT, J., 'Feofan Prokopovich', in GARRARD (no. 1595), pp. 75-105.

2308. CRACRAFT, J., 'Feofan Prokopovich: A Bibliography of His Works', *OSP.*, N.S., VIII (1975), 1-36.

2309. CRACRAFT, J., 'Feofan Prokopovich and the Kiev Academy', in: STAVROU, NICHOLS (2246), pp. 44-64

2310. CRACRAFT, J., 'Prokopovyc's Kiev Period Reconsidered', *Harvard Ukrainian Studies*, II, 2 (1978), 138-158.

2311. HARTEL, H.-J., Byzantinisches Erbe und Orthodoxie bei Feofan Prokopovich. Würzburg 1970.

2312. PROSINA, A., 'Teoreticheskoe obosnovanie F. Prokopovichem reform Petra I', *VMU.* (Pravo), 6 (1969), 63-71.

2313. WINTER, E., 'Feofan Prokopovich i nachalo russkogo Prosveshcheniia', in: XVIII Vek. Sb. 7 [Rol' i znachenie literatury XVIII v. v istorii russkoi kul'tury] (M.-L. 1966), pp. 43-46.

2314. NICHIK, V.M., Feofan Prokopovich. M. 1977. Pp.192.

Sub-section (a) deals with colonization processes and expansion generally. These processes in particular areas are
covered in the succeeding regional sub-sections. Similarly
sub-section (b) on minorities lists general works and covers
groups who had no single or specific territorial affiliation
(the Jews, German-Russians).

14(a) - COLONIZATION AND EXPANSION

HUNCZAK (2317) includes a valuable bibliographical essay by
R. Hatton. WIECZYNSKI (2318) examines an important subject,
ranging over a wide time scale, but with limited success.
NOLDE (2320) remains fundamental.

2315. FOOTE, J., Russian and Soviet Imperialism. Richmond 1972.
        Pp. 272.

2316. LANTZEFF, G.V., PIERCE, R., Eastward to Empire:
        Exploration and Conquest on the Russian Open Frontier to
        1750. Montreal 1973. Pp. 276.

2317. HUNCZAK, T. (ed.), Russian Imperialism from Ivan the Great
        to the Revolutions. New Brunswick, N.J., 1974. Pp. 396.
        Rev: *RH.*, III, 3 (1976), 247 (Fisher, R.).

2318. WIECZYNSKI, J., The Russian Frontier. The Impact of
        Borderlands on Early Russian History. Charlottesville
        1976. Pp. 108.
        Rev: *SEER.*, 56, 3 (1978), 455-6 (French, R.A.).

2319. BARTLETT, R.P., Human Capital. The Settlement of
        Foreigners in Russia, 1762-1804. Cambridge 1979. Pp. 358.
        Based on D.Phil. thesis, Oxford 1972.

2320. NOLDE, B., La Formation de l'Empire Russe. Etudes, Notes,
        Documents. Paris 1952-3. 2 vols.

2321. SZEFTEL, MARC, 'La formation et l'évolution de l'Empire
        russe jusqu'en 1918', *Recueils de la Société Jean Bodin*,
        31 (1973), 422-32.

2322. MAMONTOV, A.V., Kraevedcheskaia bibliografiia v Rossii v
        dorevoliutsionnyi period. L. 1974. Pp. 24.

2323. EFIMOV, A.V., '"Svobodnye zemli" Ameriki i istoricheskaia
        kontseptsiia F.D. Ternera', in: PANKRATOVA, A.M. et al.
        (eds), Iz istorii obshchestvennykh dvizhenii i
        mezhdunarodnykh otnoshenii. Sb. statei v pamiat' akad.
        E.V. Tarle (M. 1957), pp. 548-60.
        A Soviet comment on F.J. Turner, whose theory inspired
        no. 2318.

2324. IATSUNSKII, V.K., 'Rol' migratsii i estestvennogo prirosta
naseleniia v zaselenii kolonizovavshchikhsia raionov
Rossii', *Voprosy Geografii*, 83 (1970), 34-44.

14(b) - NATIONALITIES AND ETHNIC MINORITIES

General works in English tend to concentrate on the Soviet
period (2325-6), but provide historical background. See also
no. 178. On the Jews, LANDAU (2340) is somewhat dated, but
still a valuable guide to nineteenth-century literature;
BARON (2330) remains the most comprehensive recent survey;
GILBERT (2331) is weak, KLIER (2333-4) good.

- general

2325. GOLDHAGEN, E. (ed.), Ethnic Minorities in the Soviet
Union. N.Y. 1968. Pp. 351.

2326. KATZ, Z. et al. (ed.), Handbook of Major Soviet
Nationalities. N.Y. 1975. Pp. 481.

2327. LEMBERG, H. et al. (eds), Osteuropa in Geschichte und
Gegenwart. Festschrift für Günther Stökl zum 60.
Geburtstag. Köln 1977. Pp. 461.
Essays include: Soviet views on national minorities in the
Pugachev movement (Nitsche); problems of national minori-
ties in Russian history (Raeff); the autocracy in Russia
(Ruffman).

- Jews

2328. DUBNOW, S.M., History of the Jews in Russia and Poland:
From the Earliest Times Until the Present Day.
Philadelphia 1916-20, reprinted N.Y. 1975. 3 vols.

2329. ABRAMOWITZ, R., 'The Jews under the Tsars and Commissars:
The History and Culture of Russian Jewry', Miami Ph.D.,
1975.

2330. BARON, S.W., The Russian Jew under Tsars and Soviets.
N.Y. 1964. Pp. 427. 2nd rev. ed. N.Y. -London 1976.
Pp. 467.
Rev: *RR.*, 24 (1965), 190-3 (Kucherov, S.).

2331. GILBERT, M., The Jews of Russia. London 1977. Pp. 80,
maps.

2332. PIPES, R., 'Catherine II and the Jews: The Origin of the
Pale of Settlement', *Soviet Jewish Affairs*, 2 (1975),
3-20.

2333. KLIER, J.D., 'The Origins of the Jewish Minority Problem in Russia, 1772-1812', Illinois Ph.D., 1975.

2334. KLIER, J.D., 'The Ambiguous Legal Status of Russian Jewry in the Reign of Catherine II', *SR.*, XXXV, 3 (1976), 504-17.

2335. SPRINGER, A., 'Gavriil Derzhavin's Jewish Reform Project of 1800', *CanAmSlSt.*, X, 1 (1976), 1-23.

2336. ELIACH, Y., 'Jewish Hasidim, Russian Sectarians, Non-Conformists in the Ukraine, 1700-1760', C.U.N.Y. Ph.D., 1973.

2337. LEVINE, H., 'Menahem Mendel Letin (1749-1826): A Case Study of Judaism and Modernization', Harvard Ph.D., 1974.

2338. REST, M., Die russische Judengesetzgebung von der ersten polnischen Teilung bis zum 'Polozhenie dlja Evreev', 1804. Wiesbaden 1975. Pp. 296.

2339. WEINRYB, B., Das Wirtschaftsleben der Juden in Russland und Polen von der I. polnischen Teilung bis zum Tode Alexanders II (1772-1881). Hildesheim 1972, 2nd ed. Pp. 282.

2340. LANDAU, A.E. (comp.), Sistematicheskii ukazatel' literatury ob evreiakh na russkom iazyke so vremeni vvedenii grazhdanskago shrifta, 1708 po dekabr' 1889 gg. St. P. 1892, reprinted ORP.,1973. Pp. 579.

    – *German Russians*. See also nos. 2319, 2497

2341. LONG, J., The German-Russians. A Bibliography of Russian-language Materials. Santa Barbara-Oxford 1979. Pp. 137.
438 entries.

2342. STUMPP, K., Das Schrifttum über das Deutschtum in Russland. Eine Bibliographie. 3rd ed. Stuttgart 1971 Pp. 77.

2343. GIESINGER, A., From Catherine to Khrushchev: the Story of Russia's Germans. Battleford, Saskatchewan 1974. Pp. 443.

Baltic bibliographies are published regularly in *J. Baltic Studies* and *ZfO*. 2351-3 are useful sources for Soviet writing. WESTINGHAUSEN (2363), NEUSCHAEFFER (2381) and ELIAS (2382) are significant new Western contributions. PLAKANS (2357-8) breaks new ground; GRIMSTED (2377) is a major new publication on source material. LENZ (2350) is of considerable value. See also no. 1404,1912b (inc. English language items).
- *general*

2344. INSTITUTE OF HISTORY, COPENHAGEN, History of the Baltic and the North Sea: A Select Bibliography of Works published in 19-- (annual)

2345 KANTAUTAS, A. and F., A Lithuanian Bibliography. Edmonton 1975. Pp. 725.

2346. SUŽIEDELIS, S. (ed.), Encyclopedia Lituanica. Boston 1970-77. 6 vols.

2347. RUTKIS, J. (ed.), Latvia: Country and People. Stockholm 1967. Pp. 681.

2348. BERKIS, A.V., The History of the Duchy of Courland (1561-1795). Towson, Maryland 1969. Pp. 336.

2349. ZIEDONIS, A., WINTER, W.L., VALGEMAE, M., Baltic History. Columbus 1974. Pp. 341.
Essays on "the Baltic Question" after Nystad (Misiunas); Courland and Mirabeau (Jennison); Französische Revolution und die baltischen Provinzen (Rauch); Studien zum Kurländischen Verlagswesen (Ischreyt).

2350. LENZ, W. (ed.), Deutschbaltisches Biographisches Lexikon, 1710-1960. Wien 1970. Pp. 930.

2351. AKADEMIIA NAUK LITOVSKOI SSR, TSENTRAL'NAIA BIBLIOTEKA (Vilnius), Bibliografiia istorii Litovskoi SSR. Vilnius 1969. Pp. 711.
Covers writing in years 1940-1963.

2352. ARJAS, E. et al., Latyshskaia periodika 1768-1940: Bibliograficheskii ukazatel' v 3-kh tomakh. T. 1: 1768-1916. Riga 1977. Pp. 556.

2353. BIRON, A., DOROSHENKO, V.V., Sovetskaia istoriografiia Latvii. Riga 1970. Pp. 498.

2354. KRASTYN, IU. (ed), Istochnikovedcheskie problemy istorii narodov Pribaltiki. Riga 1970. Pp. 486.

2355. STRODS, KH., 'Istoriia pribaltiiskikh narodov i poslevoennyi ostforshung', *Ist. SSSR.*, 2 (1972), 154-65.

2356. KANALE, V.IA., STEPERMANIS, M., Istoriia Latviiskoi SSR
Riga 1974. 3rd ed. Pp. 311.

- *social and economic history*

2357. PLAKANS, A., 'Seigneurial Authority and Peasant Family
Life: The Baltic Area in the Eighteenth Century', *Journal
of Interdisciplinary History*, V, 4 (1975), 629-655.

2358. PLAKANS, A., 'Peasant farmsteads and households in the
Baltic littoral, 1797', *Comparative Studies in Society and
History*, 17 (1975), 2-35.
See also this author's contribution in no. 550.

2359. KAHK, J. et al., 'Sur l'histoire démographique de
l'Estonie', *Annales de démographie historique* (1972),
425-46.

2360. ELIAS, O.H., 'Zur Lage der undeutschen Bevölkerung in
Riga des 18. Jhdt.', *JbfGO.*, N.F., XIV, 4 (1966), 481-4.

2361. ELIAS, O.H., 'Revaler Handelsschiffahrt im 18.
Jahrhundert', *JbfGO.*, N.F., XV, 1 (1967), 16-28.

2362. PÖNICKE, H., 'Ländliche Industrieunternehmungen in den
baltischen Provinzen Russlands im 18. und 19. Jhdt.',
Vierteljahrschrift für Sozial- und Wirtschaftsgeschichte,
60, 3 (1973), 459-89.

2363. WISTINGHAUSEN, H. von, Quellen zur Geschichte der
Rittergüter Estlands im 18. und 19. Jahrhundert (1772-
1889). Hanover 1975. Pp. 365.
Rev: *JbfGO.*, XXV, 1 (1977), 116-8.

2364. SEEBERG-ELVERFELDT,R. Revaler Regesten. Göttingen 1966-75.
3 vols.
Bd. 1. Beziehungen zwischen den deutschen Staaten und Reval
1500-1807.
Bd. 2. Niederländische und scandinavische Beziehungen mit
Reval, 1500-1795.
Bd. 3. Testamente Revaler Bürger und Einwohner aus den
Jahren 1369-1851.

2365. GERMANIS, I., 'Die Agrargesetzgebung auf den herzoglichen
Domänen Kurlands zur Zeit Birons', *Acta Baltica*, XVI
(1976), 198-254.

2366. DONNERT, E., 'Gesellschaftspolitisches Denken und soziale
Bewegungen in Kurland im Wirkungsbereich der
amerikanischen und französischen Revolution', *ZfSl.*,
XXIII (1978), 196-204.

2367. PALLI, KH. (comp.), Bibliografiia po istoricheskoi
demografii Estonii. Tallin 1969. Pp. 132.

2368. STRODS, KH., 'Agrarnaia istoriia Pribaltiki XVIII-XIX vv.
v burzhuaznoi istorii FRG', *Vop. Ist.*, 3 (1967), 30-41.

2369. STEPERMANIS, M.K., 'Vliianie frantsuzskoi revoliutsii 1789–
94 gg. na agrarnyi vopros v Latvii', *Ezh. A.I.* (1964),
320–331.
S.'s last (posthumous) book (Riga 1971), in Latvian with
Russian résumé, treats the Fr. Revn. in Latvia at length.

2370. STRODS, KH., 'Zheleznyi inventar' i ego rol' v sotsial'-
no-ekonomicheskom razvitii Latvii vo vtoroi polovine
XVIII i v. pervoi polovine XIX v.', *Ezh. A.I.* (1966),
337–348.

2371. IUCHAS, M., 'Naemnyi trud v krest'ianskom khoziastve
pomeshchich'ei derevni Litvy vtoroi poloviny XVIII v.',
Ist. SSSR., 1 (1967), 93–103.

2372. DOROSHENKO, V.V., 'Myza, korchma, i krest'ianin v
Lifliandii XVI–XVIII vv.', *Ezh. A.I.* (1968), 62–75.

2373. DOROSHENKO, V.V., 'K probleme tovarnosti myzno-
barshchinnogo khoziaistva v Lifliandii XVIII v.', *Ist.
SSSR.*, 5 (1971), 123–35.

2374. VIIRES, A., 'Upriazhnye voly i loshadi v Pribaltike
(XIII–XIX vv.)', in: ALEKSANDROV, V. (ed.),
Etnograficheskoe kartografirovanie material'noi kul'tury
narodov Pribaltiki. (no. 1418), pp. 1–34.

2375. RIKHTER, E.V., Russkoe naselenie zapadnogo Prichud'ia.
Tallin 1977. Pp. 292.

2376. DUKHANOV, M. Ostzeitsy: politika ostzeiskogo dvorianstva
v 50–70-kh gg. XIX v. i kritika ee apologeticheskoi istoriografii. Riga 1978. 2nd ed. Pp. 472.
Extensive historical material provided.

- *political and international relations*

2377. GRIMSTED, P., SUŁKOWSKA-KURASIOWA, I. (eds), The
'Lithuanian Metrica' in Moscow and Warsaw. A Re-edition
of the Ptasycki 1887 Inventory, with an Introduction,
Indication of Current Locations, and Supplemental
Correlation Tables. Newtonville 1981. Pp. 60, 276.
Reprint of the original Moscow inventory of the royal
Chancellery registers of the Grand Duchy of Lithuania,
from the fifteenth to eighteenth centuries.

2378. BARTON, H.A., 'Gustav III of Sweden and the East Baltic,
1771–1792', *J. Baltic Studies*, VII, 1 (1976), 13–30.

2379. MEDIGER, W., 'Russland und die Ostsee im 18ten Jahrhundert'
JbfGO., N.F., 16, 1 (1968), 85–103.

2380. RUFFMANN, K.-H., 'Der Ostseeraum im Siebenjährigen Krieg',
ZfO., V, 3 (1956), 500-511.

2381. NEUSCHAEFFER, H., Katharina II und die baltischen
Provinzen. Hannover-Döhren 1975. Pp. 509.

2382. ELIAS, O.-H., Reval in der Reformpolitik Katherinas II
(1783-1796). Bonn-Godesberg 1978. Pp. 230.
Rev: *ZfO.*, XXVII, 4 (1978), 686-8 (Kenez, C.).

2383. PALLI, KH., Mezhdu dvumia boiami za Narvu. Estoniia v
pervye gody Severnoi voiny 1701-1704. Tallin 1966.
Pp. 343.

    - *culture.*
      See also nos 1434, 1505-6, 1743, 1786, 2280

2384. NEANDER, I., 'Die Aufklärung in den Ostseeprovinzen',
in: WITTRAM, R. (hrsg.), Baltische Kirchengeschichte
(Göttingen 1956), pp. 130-149.

2385. DONNERT, E., 'Die Leibeigenschaft im Ostbaltikum und die
livländische Aufklärungsgeschichtsschreibung',
Wissenschaftliche Zeitschrift der Fr.-Schiller-Universität,
Jena, Gesellschafts- und Sprachwissenschaftliche Reihe
2 (1960/61), 239-47.

2386. RAUCH, G. von, Die Universität Dorpat und das Eindringen
der frühen Aufklärung in Livland 1690-1710. Essen 1943;rep.
1969 with a new introduction by M. Hellmann. Pp. 471.

2387. JOHANSONS, A., Latvijas kultūras vēsture, 1710-1800.
Stockholm 1975. Pp. 647.
History of Latvian culture. German résumé, pp. 629-647.

2388. VALESKALN, P.I., Ocherk razvitiia progressvnoi filosofskoi
i obshchestvenno-politicheskoi mysli v Latvii. Riga 1967.
Pp. 247.

2389. VALESKALN, P.I. (ed.), Nauchnye sviazi Pribaltiki XVIII-
XIX vv. Materialy VII Pribaltiiskoi konferentsii po
istorii nauki. Riga 1968. Pp. 265.

2390. AKADEMIIA NAUK LATVIISKOI SSR, FUNDAMENTAL'NAIA
BIBLIOTEKA, Biblioteke 450: K iubileiu fundamental'noi
biblioteki Akademii Nauk Latviiskoi SSR, 1524-1974. Riga
1974. Pp. 199.

2391. KALNYN', IA. et al. (eds), Istoriia Latyshskoi Literatury.
2 vols. Riga 1971.

2392. LANKUTIS, I. (ed.), Istoriia Litovskoi literatury.
Vilnius 1977. Pp. 957.

Some materials on Belorussia will be found in other sections.
VAKAR (2393) is now very outdated.

- *general*

2393. VAKAR, N.P., A Bibliographical Guide to Belorussia.
Cambridge 1956. Pp. 63.

2394. SAKOL'CHIK, A. (comp.), Dooktiabr'skaia kniga na russkom
iazyke o Belorussii (1768-1917 gg.). Bibliograficheskii
ukazatel'. Minsk 1976. Pp. 425. 3821 titles.

2395. ABETSEDARSKII, L.S. et al. (eds), Istoriia Belorusskoi
SSR. Minsk 1961. 2 vols. Pp. 655, 703.

2396. CHEPKO, V.V. (ed.), Belorussiia v epokhu feodalizma.
Minsk 1959-79. 4 vols.
Vol. 3 (M.1961. Pp. 624), 1772-1800.

2397. SHTYKHOV, G. et al., Istoriia Belorusskoi SSR. Minsk
1977. Pp. 630.

2398. KRAVCHENKO, I. (ed.), Istoriia Minska. Minsk 1957.
Pp. 540.

2399. ULASHCHIK, N.N., Ocherki po arkheografii i
istochnikovedeniiu istorii Belorussii feodal'nogo perioda.
M. 1973. Pp. 303.

2400. MUSAVEVA, A.V., Puteshestvie v istoriiu Belorussii.
Minsk 1974. Pp. 87.

- *social and economic*

2401. SAVOCHKIN, P. (ed.), Sovetskoe slavianovedenie. Materialy
IV konferentsii istorikov-slavistov (Minsk 31 ianvaria-
3 fevralia 1968 g.). Minsk 1969. Pp. 668.
Essays: Belorussian-Polish economic relations in eight-
eenth century (Meleshko); Ukrainian-Belorussian economic
relations in eighteenth century (Shul'ga); Cities in
Belorussia in eighteenth century (Karpachev); Vitebsk-
Riga trading links (Adamshchik).

2402. MELESHKO, V.I., Ocherki agrarnoi istorii vostochnoi
Belorussii (vtoraia polovina XVII-XVIII vv.). Minsk 1975.
Pp. 247.

2403 KOPYSSKY, Z.IU., Ekonomicheskoe razvitie gorodov
Belorussii v XVI-pervoi polovine XVIII v. Minsk 1966.
Pp. 228.
Rev: *SR.*, XXIX, 2 (1970), 304-6.

2404. POKHILEVICH, D.L., Krest'iane Belorussii i Litvy v XVI-
XVIII vv. L'vov 1957. Pp. 175.
Rev: *Vop. Ist.*, 3 (1960), 175-80 (Ulashchik, N.). See
also no. 689.

2405. KOZLOVSKII, P., 'Polozhenie krest'ian v magnatskikh
votchinakh Belorussii vo vtoroi polovine XVIII v.', *Ezh.
A.I.* (1965), 205-219. See also no. 690.

2406. KOZLOVSKII, P., 'Razvitie proizvoditel'nykh sil v
magnatskom pomest'e zapadnoi i tsentral'noi Belorussii vo
vtoroi polovine XVIII v.', *Ist. SSSR.*, 2 (1972), 52-70.

2407. KOZLOVSKII, P., Magnatskoe khoziastvo Belorussii vo
vtoroi polovine XVIII v. Minsk 1974. Pp. 162.

2408. KOZLOVSKII, P., 'Tarify podymnogo naloga belorusskikh
povetov 1775 i 1790 gg.', *A. Ezh.* (1972), 135-141.

- *culture*

2409. McMILLIN, A.R., A History of Byelorussian Literature.
Giessen 1977. Pp. 448.

2410. NAUKA i nauchno-issledovatel'skaia rabota v Belorussii
1918-1973 gg.: bibliograficheskii ukazatel' v 5-ti tomakh.
Minsk 1975-
Vol. 1: Razvitie nauki; istoriia ... Pp. 323.

2411. NEMIROVSKII, E.L., Nachalo knigopechataniia v Belorussii i
Litve, zhizn' i deiatel'nost Frantsiska Skoriny:
Opisanie izdanii i ukazatel' literatury 1517-1977.
M. 1978. Pp. 160.

2412. AN BSSR, FUNDAMENTAL'NAIA BIBLIOTEKA IM. IAKUBA KOLASA.
Iz istorii knigi, bibliotechnogo dela i bibliografii v
Belorussii. Minsk 1970. Pp. 195.

2413. CHEMERITSKII, V., BORISENKO, V. et al. (eds), Istoriia
belorusskoi dooktiabrskoi literatury. Minsk 1977.
Pp. 639.

14(e) - BESSARABIA, MOLDAVIA   See also no. 955

2414. JEWSBURY, G.F., The Russian Annexation of Bessarabia:
1774-1828. Boulder 1976. Pp. 199.

2415. HAUPT, G., 'La Russie et les principautés danubiennes en 1790. Le prince Potemkin-Tavriceskij et le *Courrier de Moldavie'*, *CMRS.*, VII, 1 (1966), 58-62.

2416. KOZHUKAR, P.M., SHPAK, I. (comps.), Istoriia, arkheologiia, etnografiia Moldavii. Ukazatel' sovetskoi literatury, 1918-1968. Kishinev 1973. Pp. 563. 5330 entries; index.

2417. GROSUL, IA.(ed.), Istoriia narodnogo khoziaistva Moldavskoi SSR. 3 vols. Kishinev 1974-7. Pp.433,347,375. Vol I: to 1812.

14(f) - CAUCASUS, TRANSCAUCASIA, CASPIAN AND CRIMEA

See also Section 8, and for the Crimea 14(1). FISHER (2418) and BENNIGSEN (2419) are major new contributions on the Crimean Tatars. Armenia and Georgia, outside the Empire, have been covered briefly. See also 2510.
   - *general*

2418. FISHER, A., The Crimean Tatars. Stanford 1978. Pp. 264. First in series 'Nationalities of the USSR';includes an historical overview.

2419. BENNIGSEN, A., Le Khanat de Crimée dans les archives de musée du Palais de Topkapi. Paris 1978. Pp. 458.

2420. MIANSAROV, M., Bibliographia Caucasica et Transcaucasica. St. P. 1874-76, reprinted Amsterdam 1975. Pp. 804.

2421. FADEEV, A.V., 'Vopros o sotsial'nom stroe kavkazskikh gortsev XVIII-XIX vv. v novykh rabotakh sovetskikh istorikov', *Vop. Ist.*, 5 (1958), 130-38.

2422. VINOGRADOV, V.B., 'Rossiia i Severnyi Kavkaz (obzor literatury za 1971-75 gg.)', *Ist. SSSR.*, 3 (1977), 158-167.

2423. FADEEV, A.V., Ocherki ekonomicheskogo razvitiia stepnogo Predkavkaz'ia v doreformennyi period. M. 1957. Pp. 256. Rev: *Vop. Ist.*, 9 (1958) (Golobutskii, V.).

2424. KOSVEN, M. (ed.), Istoriia, geografiia i etnografiia Dagestana XVIII-XIX vv., arkhivnye materialy. M. 1958. Pp. 371.

2425. SMIRNOV, N.A., Politika Rossii na Kavkaze v XVI-XIX
vekakh. M. 1958. Pp. 224.
Rev: *Vop. Ist.*, 5 (1961), 134-6 (Abdullaev,G., Efendiev,
M.).

2426. ABDULLAEV, G., Azerbaidzhan v XVIII veke i
vzaimootnosheniia ego s Rossiei. Baku 1965. Pp. 620.

2427. BLIEV, M.M., Russko-osetinskie otnosheniia. 40-e gody
XVIII v.- 30-e gody XIX v. Ordzhonikidze 1970. Pp. 380.

2428. NOVOSEL'TSEV, A.P., 'Osvoboditel'naia bor'ba narodov
Zakavkaz'ia v XVIII v.', *Vop. Ist.*, 5 (1972), 110-122.

2429. VOLKOVA, N., Etnicheskii sostav naseleniia severnogo
Kavkaza v XVIII-nachale XX veka. M. 1974. Pp. 275.

2430. GOL'DENBERG, L.A., 'Rukopisnye karty i plany XVIII veka
kak istochnik po istorii goroda Derbenta', *A. Ezh.* (1963),
115-141.

2431. IUKHT, A.I., 'Russko-vostochnaia torgovlia v XVII-XVIII
vekakh i uchastie v nei indiiskogo kupechestva', *Ist.
SSSR.* 6 (1978), 42-59.

  - *Armenia*   See also 2710.

2432. SARKISYANZ, E., A Modern History of Transcaucasian
Armenia. Leiden 1975. Pp. 413.

2433. LANG, D., Armenia: Cradle of Civilization. London. 2nd
ed., 1978. Pp. 320.

2434. SALMASLIAN, A., Bibliographie de l'Arménie. Erevan 1969.
Pp. 470.
Covers works in languages other than Russian and Armenian.

2435. BABADZHANIAN, R.A., Armeniia i armianskaia kul'tura v
dorevoliutsionnykh izdaniiakh Akademii Nauk SSSR.
Bibliografiia. Erevan 1974. Pp. 87.

2436. AKOPIAN, T., Ocherk istorii Erevana. Erevan 1977.
Pp. 490.

2437. GRIGOR'IAN, K., Iz istorii russko-armianskikh literaturnykh i kulturnykh otnoshenii (X-nachalo XX vv.).Erevan
1974. Pp.366.
Essays include first Armenian press in Russia; Russia and
Armenian colony at New Djulfa (Persia); bibliography.

  - *Georgia*

2438. DUMBADZE, N. et al., Bibliografiia literatury o Gruzii
izdannoi na nemetskom, angliiskom i frantsuzskom
iazykakh. Tbilisi 1974. Pp. 112.

2439. AKADEMIIA NAUK GrSSR, Bibliografiia literatury i trudov v
oblasti istoricheskikh nauk. Tbilisi 1977 –
Annual publication.

2440. TATISHVILI, V., Gruziny v Moskve, 1653–1772. Tbilisi
1959. Pp. 232.

2441. GORGIDZE, M., Gruziny v Peterburge. Stranitsy letopisi
kul'turnykh sviazei. Tbilisi 1976. Pp. 407.

14(g) – CENTRAL ASIA

While this area lay largely outside the Empire in the 18th century, its relations with Russia and the history and development of its peoples have both been studied by Soviet and
other historians. ALLWORTH (2442) is a scholarly and helpful
compilation. SARKISYANZ (2446) has a good but brief bibliography. VITKIND (2447), an important listing, is updated in
part by AGEEVA (2449). See also no. 895.

2442. ALLWORTH, E., Soviet Asia: Bibliographies. A Compilation
of Social Science and Humanities Sources on the Iranian,
Mongolian and Turkic Nationalities with an Essay on the
Soviet-Asian Controversy. N.Y. 1975. Pp. 686.

2443. VUCINICH, W.S. (ed.), Russia and Asia: Essays on the
Influence of Russia on the Asian Peoples. Stanford 1972.
Pp. 521.

2444. ZENKOVSKY, S.A., Pan-Turkism and Islam in Russia.
Cambridge, Mass. 1960. Pp. 345.

2445. DONNELLY, A., 'Peter the Great and Central Asia', *CSP.*,
XVII, 2-3 (1975), 202-218.

2446. SARKISYANZ, E., Geschichte der orientalischen Völker
Russlands bis 1917. Eine Ergänzung zur ostslawischen
Geschichte Russlands. Munich 1961. Pp. 422.

2447. VITKIND, N.IA., Bibliografiia po Srednei Azii. Ukazatel'
literatury po kolonial'noi politike tsarisma v Srednei
Azii. M. 1929, reprinted Cambridge, Eng. 1971. Pp. 165.

2448. AMITIN-SHAPIRO, Z., Annotirovannyi ukazatel' literatury
po istorii, arkheologii i etnografii Kirgizii (1750-1917).
M. 1957. Pp. 349.
Rev: *Ist. SSSR.*, 5 (1958), 194-6 (Musin, KH.).

2449. AGEEVA, E.E. et al. (comp.), BEKMANOV, E.B. (ed.),
Bibliografiia po istorii Kazakhstana. Annotirovannyi
ukazatel'. Vypusk I: Dorevoliutsionnyi period. Alma
Ata 1964. Pp. 410, 2483 entries.
Rev: *Vop. Ist.*, 10 (1965), 153-4 (Galuzo, P.G.,
Kalistratos, N.P.). Gives addenda.

2450. SHEVCHENKO, Z., Bibliografiia bibliografii Tadzhikistana.
Dushanbe 1966. Pp. 168.

2451. NOVICHENKO, E., Bibliografiia bibliografii Kirgizii,
1852-1967, annotirovannyi ukazatel' literatury. Frunze
1969. Pp. 192.

2452. BAZIIANTS, A. et al. (eds), Aziatskii muzei - Leningrads-
koe otdelenie instituta vostokovedeniia A.N. S.S.S.R.
M. 1972. Pp. 595.
Exhaustive description of holdings; much on the
eighteenth century.

2453. APOLLOVA, N., Ekonomicheskie i politicheskie sviazi
Kazakhstana s Rossiei vo vtoroi polovine XVIII-nachalo
XIX veka. M. 1960. Pp. 456.
Rev: *Vop. Ist.*, 10 (1962), 136-8 (Zimanov, S.Z.).
Continuation of previous work, Prisoedinenie Kazakhstana k
Rossii (Alma-Ata 1948).

2454. AKADEMIIA NAUK KAZAKHSKOI SSR, Kazakhsko-russkie
otnosheniia v XVI-XVIII vekakh. Sbornik dokumentov i
materialov. Alma-Ata 1961. Pp. 744.
See also later edition for eighteenth and nineteenth
centuries (1771-1867), Alma-Ata 1964. Pp. 576.

2455. IBRAGIMOV, S. (ed.), Materialy po istorii kazakhskikh
khanstv XV-XVIII vekov. Alma Ata 1969. Pp. 648.
Includes Persian and Turkish sources.

2456. AZAT'IAN, A. et al., Istoriia otkrytiia i issledovaniia
Sovetskoi Azii. M. 1969. Pp.535.

2457. BASIN, V.IA., Rossiia i kazakhskie khanstva v XVI-XVIII vv.
Kazakhstan v sisteme vneshnei politiki Rossiiskoi
Imperii. Alma-Ata 1971. Pp. 274.
Rev: *Vop. Ist.*, 2 (1972), 151-5 (Apollova, N.).

2458. ANNANEPESOV, M., Khoziaistvo Turkmen v XVIII-XIX vv.
Ashkhabad 1972. Pp. 284.

2459. APOLLOVA, N., Khoziaistvennoe osvoenie Poirtysh'ia v
kontse XVI-pervoi polovine XIX v. M. 1976. Pp. 370.
Mainly Kazakhstan.

This area has recently been the focus of great interest among American and Canadian scholars: the latest results are the Kennan Centre Occasional Papers (2462, 2480-83, 2485-6). KERNER (2460) and LADA-MOCARSKI (2461) are important for earlier writing, as is MAKAROVA (2488) for recent Soviet scholarship. Major recent productions are the translations of FEDOROVA (2473) and TIKHMENEV (2469).

2460. KERNER, R.J., Northeastern Asia, a selected bibliography. Berkeley 1939, reprinted N.Y. 1968. 2 vols. Vol. 2: The Russian Empire and the Soviet Union in Asia and on the Pacific.

2461. LADA-MOCARSKI, V. (comp.), Bibliography of Books on Alaska published before 1868. New Haven 1969. Pp. 567. Russian titles translated.

2462. PIERCE, R.A., FEDOROVA, S., 'Little Known Bibliographic and Archival Materials on Russian America', Kennan Institute for Advanced Russian Studies (Wilson Center, Washington D.C.), Occasional Paper no. 66 (1979).

2463. EFIMOV, A.V., Atlas of Geographical Discoveries in Siberia and North-Western America XVII-XVIII Centuries. M. 1964. Pp. 134, 189 maps.

2464. NEATBY, L.H., Discovery in Russian and Siberian Waters. Athens, Ohio 1973. Pp. 226.

2465. MURPHY, R., The Haunted Journey: An Account of Vitus Bering's Voyages of Discovery. London 1962. Pp. 212.

2466. FISHER, R., Bering's Voyages. Whither and Why. Seattle 1977. Pp. 217. Rev: *SR.*, XXVIII, 2 (1979), 297-99.

2467. WHEELER, M.E., 'The Origins and Formation of the Russian-American Company', North Carolina Ph.D., 1965.

2468. KHLEBNIKOV, K., Baranov: Chief manager of the Russian colonies in America. (Trans. Bearne, C.). Kingston, Ont. 1973. Pp. 140.

2469. TIKHMENEV, P., A History of the Russian-American Company Translated and edited by R.A. Pierce and A.S. Donnelly. Seattle-London 1978. Pp. 522. Rev: *SR.*, XXXVIII, 2 (1979), 299 (Mackay, J.P.).

2470. WHEELER, M.E., MARTINOV, A., 'The Russian-American Company and the Imperial Company', Kennan Institute for Advanced Russian Studies, Occasional Paper no. 67 (1979).

2471. COPPOCK, H.A., 'Interactions between Russians and Native Americans in Alaska, 1741-1840', Michigan State Ph.D., 1970.

2472. HARRISON, J.A., The Founding of the Russian Empire in Asia and America. Coral Gables. 1971. Pp. 156.

2473. FEDOROVA, S.G., The Russian Population in Alaska and California, late Eighteenth Century - 1867. Translated from the Russian, M. 1971 / and edited by Pierce, R.A., Donnelly, A.S. Kingston, Ont. 1973. Pp. 376.
Rev: *Vop. Ist.*, 8 (1972), 150-2 (Makarova, R.V.).

2474. MAKAROVA, R.V., Russians on the Pacific in the Second Half of the Eighteenth Century. Kingston, Ont. 1973. Translated from Russian (M. 1968).

2475. KUSHNER, H.I., Conflict on the Northwest Coast: American-Russian Rivalry in the Pacific Northwest, 1790-1867. Westport, Conn. 1975. Pp. 228.
Based on Ph.D. thesis, Cornell 1970.

2476. GIBSON, J.R., Feeding the Russian Fur Trade - Provisionment of the Okhotsk Seaboard and the Kamchatka Peninsula, 1639-1856. Madison 1969. Pp. 337.
Based on Ph.D. thesis, Wisconsin 1967.

2477. GIBSON, J.R., 'Russian Occupance of the Far East, 1639-1750', *CSP.*, XII, 1 (1970), 60-78.

2478. GIBSON, J.R., Imperial Russia in Frontier America: The Changing Geography of Supply of Russian America, 1784-1867. N.Y. 1976. Pp. 256.

2479. STARR, J.L., 'The Cultural and Educational Development of Aborigines and Settlers in Russian America, 1784-1867', New York Ph.D., 1967.

2480. SARAFIAN, W., MAKAROVA, R., 'Economic Foundations of Russian America', Kennan Institute for Advanced Russian Studies, Occasional Paper no. 68 (1979).

2481. GIBSON, J., LIAPUNOVA, R., 'Russian Dependence upon the Natives of Russian America', Kennan Institute for Advanced Russian Studies, Occasional Paper no. 70 (1979).

2482. KUSHNER, H.I., BOLKHOVITINOV, N.N., 'The United States, Russia, and Russian-America', Kennan Institute for Advanced Russian Studies, Occasional Paper no. 71 (1979).

2483. GIBSON, J., 'Russian Expansion in Siberia and America: Critical Contrasts', Kennan Institute for Advanced Russian Studies, Occasional Paper no. 72 (1979).

2484. SHIMKIN, D.B., 'S.P. Krasheninnikov's *Opisanie zemli Kamchatki* (Description of Kamchatka Land): An Eighteenth-Century Scientific Masterpiece. A Review Article', *CanAmSlSt.*, IX, 3 (1975), 374-80.

2485. PIERCE, R. (ed.), The Russian Orthodox Religious Mission in America, 1794-1837,, with Materials concerning the Life and Works of the Monk German and Ethnographic Notes by the Hieromonk Gideon. Kingston, Ontario 1978. Pp. 186.

2486. SENKEVITCH, A., DEREVIANKO, A., 'Architecture and Everyday Life in Russian America', Kennan Institute for Advanced Russian Studies, Occasional Paper no. 69 (1979).

2486a. BARRATT, G., Russia in Pacific Waters, 1715-1825: A Survey. Origins of Russia's Naval Presence in the North and South Pacific. Vancouver 1980. Pp. 359.

2487. PONIATOWSKI, M., Histoire de la Russie d'Amérique et de l'Alaska. 2nd ed. Paris 1978. Pp. 481, maps.

2488. MAKAROVA, R.V., 'Russkaia Amerika v trudakh sovetskikh istorikov (60-70kh godov)', *Trudy Mosk. ist-arkhiv. instituta*, 30, 1 (1974), 51-60.

14(i) - THE RUSSIAN NORTH   See also Section 7(c)

2489. BÖSS, O., 'Geschichte des russischen Nordens (1725-1917). Ein Bericht über das sowjetrussische Schrifttum seit 1945'. *JbfGO.*, N.S., XIII, 4 (1965), 539-84.

2490. GORBACHEVA, N. (comp.), BALAGUROV, IA. (ed.), Istoriia, arkheologiia, etnografiia Karelii; bibliograficheskii ukazatel' sovetskoi literatury za 1917-1965 gg. Petrozavodsk 1967. Pp. 267.

2491. IVANKINA, L.P., Arkhangel'skaiia oblast': rekomendatel'nyi ukazatel' sovetskoi literatury. Archangel'sk 1973. Pp. 239.

2492. KOLESNIKOV, P., 'K istorii naselennykh punktov i dvizheniia sel'skogo naseleniia Evropeiskogo severa v XVII-XIX vv.', *Ezh. A.I.* (1966), 179-193.

2493. KOLESNIKOV, P., Severnaia derevnia v XV-pervoi polovine XIX veka. K voprosu ob evoliutsii agrarnykh otnoshenii v russkom gosudarstve. Vologda 1976. Pp. 416.

2494. BOCHAROV, G., VYGOLOV, V., Vologda. Kirilov. Ferapontovo. Belozersk. M. 1969. Pp. 295, 123 illustrations. French and Russian captions.

2495. DONNELLY, A., The Russian Conquest of Bashkiria, 1552–1740: A Case Study in Imperialism. New Haven-London 1968. Pp. 214.
Based on Ph.D. thesis, U.C. Berkeley 1960.

2496. SHAW, D.J.B., 'Settlement, Urbanism and Economic Change in a Frontier Context: The Voronezh Province of Russia, 1615–1800', London Ph.D., 1973.

2497. KOCH, F.C., The Volga Germans in Russia and the Americas, from 1763 to the Present. Univ. Park, Pennsylvania-London 1977. Pp. 365.
Rev: *RH.*, IV, 2 (1977), 197–9 (Bartlett, R.P.).

2498. KOHLS, W.A., 'German Settlement on the Lower Volga. A Case Study: the Moravian Community at Sarepta, 1763–1892', *Trans. Moravian Hist. Society*, XXII, 2 (1971), 47–99.

2499. LEMERCIER-QUELQUEJAY, C., 'Les Kalmuks de la Volga entre l'Empire russe et l'Empire Ottoman sous le règne de Pierre le Grand', *CMRS.*, VII, 1 (1966), 63–76.

2500. KAPPLER, A., 'Die Geschichte der Völker der Mittleren Wolga (vom 10. Jh. bis in die zweite Hälfte des 19. Jh.) in der sowjetischen Forschung', *JbfGO.*, N.F., XXVI (1978), 222–57.

2501. USTIUGOV, N. (ed.), Materialy po istorii Bashkirskoi ASSR. 6 vols. M.-L. 1949–56.

2502. DEMIDOVA, N., 'Upravlenie Baskhirii i povinnosti naseleniia Ufimskoi provintsii v pervoi treti XVIII v.', *I.Z.*, 68 (1961), 211–237.

2503. KUL'SHARIPOV, M.M., 'Zemel'naia politika tsarizma v Bashkirii v kontse XVIII – nachale XIX v.', *VMU(Ist.)*, 4 (1972), 49–62.

2504. PREOBRAZHENSKII, A.A., Ocherki kolonizatsii zapadnogo Urala v XVII-nachale XVIII v. M. 1956. Pp. 302.

2505. DMITRIEV, V.D., Istoriia Chuvashii XVIII v. Cheboksary 1959.

2506. KUSHEVA, E., 'Saratov v pervoi polovine XVIII v.', in: IVANOV, L. et al. (eds), Problemy sotsial'no-ekonomicheskoi istorii Rossii (no. 214), pp. 26–52.

2507. VAS'KIN, N.M., 'Pomeshchich'e zemlevladenie v Astrakhanskom krae vo vtoroi polovine XVIII v.', *Problemy Istorii SSSR*, V (1976), 181–93.

2508. IUKHT, I.A., 'Indiiskaia koloniia Astrakhani', *Vop. Ist.*, 3 (1957), 135-43.

2509. KHACHATURIAN, V.A., 'Naselenie armianskoi kolonii v Astrakhani vo vtoroi polovine XVIII v.', *Izv. A.N. Armianskoi SSR (obshchestv. nauki)*, 7 (1965), 77-87.

2510. PRONSHTEIN, A.P. et al. (eds), Don i stepnoe Predkavkaz'e, XVIII - pervaia polovina XIX v.: sotsial'nye otnosheniia, upravlenie, klassovaia bor'ba. Rostov n/D 1977. Pp. 207.

14(k) - SIBERIA (including IAKUTIIA, FAR EAST)

Since MEZHOV's monumental work (2515), bibliographical aids to the huge literature on Siberia have become much more plentiful (2516-21, 2555). OKLADNIKOV (2529) is polemical, but valuable both as a survey and for references; his summary of scholarship (2524) is also useful. GLINKA (2527), a classic, has a good historical survey, and the reprint includes a short bibliography; the work's unique value is in its 800 photographs of old Siberia, many of which mirror eighteenth century conditions. Individual Siberian towns are dealt with here in nos. 2550-5 : see generally nos. 800-801. On Siberia's peasantry see, besides 2546, nos 723, 728.

- *general*

2511. GIBSON, J.R., 'The Significance of Siberia to Tsarist Russia', *CSP.*, XIV, 3 (1972), 442 454.

2512. ARMSTRONG, T., Russian Settlement in the North. Cambridge 1965. Pp. 224.

2513. POTAPOV, L.P., The Peoples of Siberia. Translation from the Russian. Chicago 1964. Pp. 948.

2514. COQUIN, F.-X., La Sibérie: peuplement et immigration paysanne au XIXe siècle. Paris 1969. Pp. 789. Includes eighteenth-century background.

2515. MEZHOV, V.I., Sibirskaia bibliografiia. St. P. 1892-1903, reprinted 1969. 3 vols.

2516. LEBEDEVA, A. et al. (comp.), Ukazatel' bibliograficheskikh posobii po Sibiri i Dal'nemu Vostoku (XIX v.-1968 g.). Novosibirsk 1975. Pp. 630. Issued by Gos. Publ. nauchno-tekhnich. biblioteka, Sibirsk. otd. Akad. Nauk SSSR.

2517. AKADEMIIA NAUK, NAUCHNAIA BIBLIOTEKA VOSTOCHNO-SIBIRSKOGO
FILIALA (Irkutsk), Geografiia naseleniia Sibiri i
Dal'nego Vostoka, bibliograficheskii ukazatel'. Irkutsk
1968. Pp. 224.

2518. NIKOLAEV, V.A. (comp.), Bibliografy Sibiri i Dal'nego
Vostoka: Biobibliograficheskii Slovar'. Novosibirsk
1973. Pp. 174.

2519. KRIAZHINSKAIA, N. (ed.), TARMAKHANOVA, V.A. et al. (comp.),
Pisateli Vostochnoi Sibiri: Bio-bibliograficheskii
ukazatel'. Irkutsk 1973. Pp. 330.

2520. ISTORIIA SIBIRI. Tekushchii ukazatel' literatury. Izd. s
1966 g. Novosibirsk.
Quarterly.

2521. BURTSEVA, V.P., GULIAEVA, E.P., Krai rodnoi-Iakutiia:
Rekommendatel'nyi ukazatel' literatury. Iakutsk 1978.
Pp. 99.

2522. MIRZOEV, V.G., Istoriografiia Sibiri (XVIII v.).
Kemerovo 1963. Pp. 262.
Rev: *Vop. Ist.*, 7 (1964), 143-5 (Kabanov, P.I.).

2523. MIRZOEV, V.G., Istoriografiia Sibiri. M. 1970. Pp. 392.

2524. OKLADNIKOV, A. (ed.), Itogi i zadachi izucheniia istorii
Sibiri dosovetskogo perioda. Novosibirsk 1971. Pp. 215.

2525. BASHARIN, G.P., Nekotorye voprosy istoriografii
vkhozhdeniia Sibiri v sostav Rossii. Iakutsk 1971.
Pp. 136.

2526. POKROVSKII, N., DERGACHEVA-SKOP, E., Arkheografiia i
istochnikovedenie Sibiri. Novos. 1975-77. Pp. 213, 256.

2527. GLINKA, G.L., Aziatskaia Rossiia. 3 vols. St. P. 1914,
reprinted ORP., Cambridge 1975, with new introduction by
Armstrong T. Pp. 1500.
Vol. 1 gives history, though mainly nineteenth century;
series of photographs of old Siberia.

2528. LEVIN, M.G. (ed.), Istoriko-etnograficheskii atlas
Sibiri. M.-L. 1961. Pp. 498.

2529. OKLADNIKOV, A.P. et al. (eds), Istoriia Sibiri. L. 1968-
69. 5 vols.
Vol. II, eighteenth century.

2530. SHUNKOV, V. et al. (eds), Sibir' v periode feodalizma
(XVII-XIX vv.). Novos. 1962. Pp. 255.

2531. SHUNKOV, V.I. et al., Osvoenie Sibiri v epokhu feodalizma.
XVI-XIX vv. M. 1968. Pp. 247.

2532. PREOBRAZHENSKII, A.A., Ural i zapadnaia Sibir' v kontse XVI-nachale XVIII v. M. 1972. Pp. 391.
Rev: *Ist. SSSR.*, 6 (1973), 182-5 (Gromyko, M.).

2533. MINENKO, N., Severo-zapadnaia Sibir' XVIII-pervoi polovine XIX v. Istoriko-etnograficheskii ocherk. Novos.1975. Pp. 308.

2534. IVANOV, V., Istoriko-etnograficheskoe izuchenie Iakutii XVII-XVIII vv. M. 1975. Pp. 286.

2535. SAFRONOV, F., Russkie na Severo-vostoke Azii v XVII-seredine XIX gg. M. 1978. Pp. 258.

   - social and economic

2536. DREW, R.F., 'The Emergence of an Agricultural Policy for Siberia in the XVII and XVIII Centuries', *Agricultural History*, 33 (1959), 29-32.

2537. BASHARIN, G., Istoriia agrarnykh otnoshenii v Iakutii (60-e gody XVIII-seredine XIX v.). M. 1956. Pp. 428.

2538. GROMYKO, M.M., 'Nekotorye rezul'taty zemledel'cheskogo osvoeniia zapadnoi Sibiri v XVIII v.', *Ist. SSSR.*, 2 (1965), 55-73.

2539. GROMYKO, M.M., Zapadnaia Sibir' v XVIII v. Russkoe naselenie i zemledel'cheskoe osvoenie. Novos.1965. Pp. 265.

2540. SHEPUKOVA, N., 'Podvornaia perepis' 1710 g i chislennost' russkogo krest'ianstva v Sibiri', *Ezh. A.I.* (1966), 227-234.

2541. KABUZAN, V.S., TROITSKII, S.M., 'Chislennost' i sostav gorodskogo naseleniia Sibiri v 40-80 gg. XVIII v.', in: SHUNKOV (no. 2530).

2542. GROMYKO, M., 'Sotsial'no-ekonomicheskie aspekty izucheniia genealogii neprivilegioovannykh soslovii feodal'noi Sibiri' in Pavlenko, N. (ed.), Istoriia i genealogiia (M. 1977), 197-237.

2543. PARNIKOVA, A., Rasselenie Iakutov v XVII-nachale XX vv. Iakutsk 1971. Pp. 155.

2544. KOLESNIKOV, A.D., Russkoe naselenie zapadnoi Sibiri v XVII-nachale XIX vv. Omsk 1973. Pp. 440.

2544a. SOFRONEEV, P., Iakuty v pervoi polovine XVIII veka. Iakutsk 1972. Pp. 189.

2545. OKLADNIKOV, A. (ed.), Russkoe naselenie Pomor'ia i
Sibiri. M. 1973. Pp. 449.
Essays, include Siberian nobility (Gromyko), governors
(Rafienko), Old Believers (Pokrovskii), eighteenth-
century population (Vodarskii).

2546. GORIUSHKIN, L. (ed.), Krest'ianstvo Sibiri XVIII-nachala
XX v. Klassovaia bor'ba, obshchestvennoe soznanie i kul'-
tura. Novos·1975. Pp. 217.

2547. RUSALKOVA, L., Sel'skoe khoziastvo srednego zaural'ia na
rubezhe XVIII-XIX vv. Novos.1976. Pp. 182.

2548. GORIUSHKIN, L. (ed.), Ssylka i obshchestvenno-
politicheskaia zhizn' v Sibiri (XVIII-nachalo XX v.).
Novos.1978. Pp. 332.

2549. FEDOROV, M., Pravovoe polozhenie narodov Vostochnoi
Sibiri XVII-nachalo XIX v. Iakutsk 1978. Pp. 207.

2550. KUDRIAVTSEV, F., VENDRIKH, G., Irkutsk, ocherki po istorii
goroda. Irkutsk 1971. Pp. 436.
Bibliography, pp. 430-4.

2551. IURASOVA, M., Omsk. Ocherki istorii goroda. Omsk 1972.
Pp. 314.

2552. KERMASOVA, T.I., Perm' 1723-1973. Bibliograficheskii
ukazatel'. Perm 1973. Pp. 168.

2553. GOREVA, V.V., Sverdlovsk. Ukazatel' literatury.
Sverdlovsk 1973. Pp. 278.

2554. BAKUNIN, A.V., Ocherki istorii Sverdlovska: 1723-1973.
Sverdlovsk 1973. Pp. 374.
Rev: *Vop. Ist.*, 7 (1974).

- *cultural*

2555. POSTNOV, IU. (ed.), MASLOV, D. (comp.), Russkaia
literatura Sibiri XVII v.-1970 g. Bibliograficheskii
ukazatel'. Novos.1976-7. 2 vols.
Rev: *Sovetskaia Bibliografiia* 4 (1978), 90-92.

2556. KOPYLOV, A., Kul'tura russkogo naseleniia Sibiri v
XVII-XVIII vv. Novos.1968. Pp. 168, plates.
Rev: *Vop. Ist.*, 5 (1969) (Gol'denberg, L.A.).

2557. PUBLICHNAIA NAUCHNO-TEKHNICHESKAIA BIBLIOTEKA (Novosibirsk)
Iz istorii knigi, bibliotechnogo dela i bibliografii v
Sibiri. Novosibirsk 1969. Pp. 284.

2558. KOPYLOV, A., Ocherki kul'turnoi zhizni Sibirii XVII-
nachala XIX v. Novos.1974. Pp. 251.
Chapters on enlightenment, theatre etc. in Siberia.

2559. KULKINA, E. (ed.), Problemy literatury Sibiri XVII-XX vv.
Novos. 1974. Pp. 238.

2560. POSTNOV, IU. et al. (eds), Ocherki literatury i kritiki
Sibiri XVII-XX vv. Materialy k'istorii literatury Sibiri'.
Novos. 1976. Pp. 284.

2561. MOSKOVSKII, A. (ed.), Pamiatniki istorii i kul'tury
Sibiri. Novos. 1978. Pp. 184.

2562. SOLDATOV, G., Mitropolit Filofei, v skhite Feodor.
Prosvetitel' Sibiri (1650-1727). Minneapolis 1977.
Pp. 147.

14(l) - UKRAINE

Soviet and Western Ukrainian views on Ukraine's history are
well documented (2564-70, 2579). Recent valuable studies in
political history are GAJECKY (2573) and KOHUT (2574).
DRUZHININA's studies of S. Ukraine (2580-1) continue her work
on Küchük-Kainardji (1286); the same area is covered in nos.
2583-88, 2596-9; see also 751-2. Urban history is well
served: 2589-90, 2599. Mazepa: 2605-2611.

- *general*

2563. SEMINAR IN UKRAINIAN STUDIES, HARVARD UNIVERSITY,
*Recenzija: A Review of Soviet Ukrainian Scholarly
Publications*. Cambridge, Mass. 1970-
Semi-annual. Rev: *SR.*, XXXIII, 1 (1974), 556-9.

2564. KUBIJOVYC, V. (ed.), Ukraine: A Concise Encyclopaedia.
2 vols. Toronto 1963, 1971. Pp. 1394.
This work will eventually be superseded by the projected
4 volume Encyclopedia of Ukraine (1983-).

2565. BAZHAN, M.P. et al. (eds), Soviet Ukraine. Kiev 1969.
Pp. 572, illustrations.

2566. DOROSHENKO, O., A Survey of Ukrainian History.
Edited and updated by O. GERUS. Winnipeg 1975. Pp. 873.

2567. ARMSTRONG, J., Ukrainian Nationalism. 2nd ed. N.Y. 1963.
Pp. 361.

2568. WYNAR, L.R., 'Ukrainian-Russian Confrontation in
Historiography, Michael Hrushevsky versus the Traditional
Scheme of "Russian History"', *Uk. Q.*, XXX, 1 (1974),
13-25.

2569. SAWCHAK, V., 'Ukraine Minus her Own History in the
Encyclopaedia Britannica', *Uk, Q.*, XXXII, 1 (1975),
72-77.

2570. MACKIW, TH., 'The Historical Development of the Ukraine
in the 16th-18th Centuries', *Assocn. for Advancement of
Polish Studies, Bulletin* I, 7 (1976), 1-25.
Bibliography of Ukrainian sources.

2571. NOL'DE, B., 'Essays in Russian State Law', *Annals of the
Ukrainian Acad. of Arts and Sciences in the U.S.A.*, 4, 3
(1955), 873-903.
Russian administration in the Ukraine.

2572. GAJECKY, G., 'Cossack Terminology: Suggestions for the
Study of the Hetmanate, the Ukrainian Cossack State',
Uk. Hist. (Uk. Ist.), 1-2 {45-46}, (1975), 120-7.

2573. GAJECKY, G., The Cossack Administration of the
Hetmanate. Cambridge, Mass. 1978. 2 vols. Pp. 394,395.
Rev. *RR.*, XXXIX,1(1980), 73-4. (Subtelny,O.)

2574. KOHUT, Z.E., 'The Abolition of Ukrainian Autonomy (1763-
1786): A Case Study in the Integration of a Non-Russian
Area into the Empire', Pennsylvania Ph.D., 1975.

2575. OHLOBLYN, O., 'The American Revolution and Ukrainian
Liberation Ideas during the Late Eighteenth Century',
Uk. Q., XI, (1955), 203-12

2576. OHLOBLYN, O., 'Ukrainian autonomists of the 1780's and
1790's and Count P.A. Rumiantsev-Zadunaisky', *Annals of
the Ukrainian Acad. of Arts and Sciences in the U.S.A.*,
VI (1958), nos. 3-4.

2577. SAUNDERS, D.B., 'The Political and Cultural Impact of
the Ukraine on Great Russia, c. 1775-c.1835', Oxford
D. Phil., 1979.
_____

2578. PORTAL, R., Russes et Ukrainiens. Paris 1970. Pp. 142.
_____

2579. DUBINA, K.K. et al. (eds), Istoriia Ukrainskoi SSR.
Kiev 1969. 2 vols.
Bibliography in each volume.

2580. DRUZHININA, E., Severnoe Prichernomor'e v 1775-1800 g.
M. 1959. Pp. 280.

2581. DRUZHININA, E., Iuzhnaia Ukraina v 1800-1825 gg.
M. 1970. Pp. 382.
Rev: *Vop. Ist.*, 8 (1971), 155-6 (Fedosov, V.A.).

2582. ROZNER' I.G., 'Antifeodal'nye gosudarstvennye
obrazovaniia v Rossii i na Ukraine v XVI-XVIII vv.',
Vop. Ist., 8 (1970), 42-56.

- *social and economic*

2583. POLONS'KA-VASYLENKO, N.D., 'The Settlement of the
Southern Ukraine 1750-75', *Annals of the Ukrainian
Acad. of Arts and Sciences in the U.S.A.*, IV, 4-V, 1
(Summer-Fall 1955). Pp. 350.

2584. LYNCH, D.F., 'The Conquest, Settlement and Initial
Development of New Russia (The Southern Third of the
Ukraine): 1780-1837', Yale Ph,D., 1965.

2585. PETERSON, C.B., III, 'Geographical Aspects of Foreign
Colonization in Pre-Revolutionary New Russia',
Washington, Seattle Ph.D., 1969.

2586. DURAN, J.A. Jr., 'Catherine II, Potemkin and Colonization
Policy in Southern Russia', *RR.*, 28, 1 (1969), 23-37.

2587. OHLOBLYN, O., A History of Ukrainian Industry. 3 v. Kiev
1925,1931; rep. München 1971 with new author's preface.

2588. AUERBACH, H., Die Besiedelung der Südukraine in den
Jahren 1774-1787. Wiesbaden 1965. Pp. 136.

2589. HALM, H., Gründung und erstes Jahrzehnt von Festung und
Stadt Cherson, 1778-1788. Wiesbaden 1961. Pp. 260.

2590. TRON'KO, P.T. et al. (eds), Istoriia gorodov i sel
Ukrainskoi SSR v 26 tt. Kiev 1974-. 7 vols to date.
Russian edition of 26-vol Ukrainian work, CERNOBRIVTSEV,
O.S. (ed.) (Kiev 1969-). See no. 798.

2591. BLOKH, B., 'Istoriia fabrik i zavodov Ukrainy', *Ist.
SSSR.*, 6 (1962), 140-8.

2592. BARANOVICH, A., 'Opustoshenie i vosstanovlenie
Pravoberezhnoi Ukrainy vo vtoroi polovine XVII i nachale
XVIII v.', *Ist. SSSR.*, 5 (1960), 148-158.

2593. STASHEVSKII, E., Istoriia dokapitalisticheskoi renty na
pravoberezhnoi Ukraine v XVIII-pervoi polovine XIX v.
M. 1968. Pp. 478.

2594. MARKINA, V.A., Sots'ial'naia struktura derevni
Pravobereznoi Ukrainy v XVIII-nachale XIX v.', *Ezh. A.I.*
(1966), 374-386.

2595. MARKINA, V.A., Magnatskoe pomest'e Pravoberezhnoi
Ukrainy vtoroi poloviny XVIII v. (sotsial'no-
ekonomicheskoe razvitie). Kiev 1967. Pp. 236.
Rev: *Vop. Ist.*, 12 (1968), 130-32 (Sozin, I.V.).

2596. KABUZAN, V.M., 'Krest'ianskaia kolonizatsiia Severnogo
Prichernomor'ia (Novorossii) v XVIII-pervoi polovine
XIX vv. (1719-1857)', *Ezh. A.I.* (1964), 313-24.

2597. KABUZAN, V.M., MAKHOVA, R., 'Chislennost' i udel'nii ves
ukrainskogo naseleniia na territorii SSSR v 1795-1959
gg.', *Ist. SSSR.*,1 (1965), 28-37.

2598. ZAGORUYKO, V., Po stranitsam istorii Odessy i
Odesshchiny. Odessa 1957. 2 parts.

2599. BIZER, M. (ed.), Khersonu 200 let. (1778-1978). Kiev
1978. Pp. 405.

2599a. VASIL'EV,I., Dnepropetrovsku 200 let 1776-1976. Sb. dokumentov. Kiev 1976. Pp. 511.
Discusses Ukrainian archives.

   - *cultural*

2600. ČIŽEVSKY, D., A History of Ukrainian Literature (from
the Eleventh to the End of the Nineteenth Century).
Ed. LUCKYJ, G. Littleton, Colo. 1975. Pp. 681.
Rev: *SR.*, XXXVI, 2 (1977), 355-7.

2601. DRUZHININA, E., 'Die russisch-deutschen
Wissenschaftsbeziehungen und die Erforschung der Ukraine
gegen Ende des 18. Jahrhunderts', *JbfGO.*, 10 (1967),
219-251.

2602. HOLOBUCKYJ, V., 'Güldenstädts "Reisen durch Russland"
und ihre Bedeutung für die Erforschung der
sozialökonomischen Entwicklung der linksufrigen Ukraine
im 18. Jhdt.', in: *Ost und West* (no. 1737), pp. 406-16.

2603. NEMOSHKALENKO, V.V., NOVIKOV, N.V., PELYKH, B.M.,
Akademiia Nauk Ukrainskoi SSR. Kiev 1969. Pp. 274.

2604. KIRILIUK, E. (ed.), Istoriia ukrainskoi literatury.
Kiev 1967-74. 8 vols.
In Ukrainian. Bibliographies.

   - *Mazepa*

2605. MANNING, C.A., Hetman of Ukraine - Ivan Mazepa. N.Y.
1957. Pp. 234.

2606. HOLUBNYCHY, L., 'Mazepa in Byron's poem and in history',
Uk. Q., XV, 4 (1959), 342-361.

2607. MACKIW, TH., Prince Mazepa, Hetman of Ukraine in
Contemporary English Publications, 1687-1709. Chicago
1967. Pp. 126.
Bibliography includes Mackiw's previous publications in
area.

2608. BABINSKI, H., The Mazepa Legend in European Romanticism.
N.Y. 1974. Pp. 164.
Based on Ph.D. thesis, Columbia 1970.

2609. SUBTELNY, O. (ed.), On the Eve of Poltava: The Letters
of Ivan Mazepa to Adam Sieniawski, 1704-1708. N.Y.
1975. Pp. 159.

2610. SUBTELNY, O., 'Mazepa, Peter I, and the Question of
Treason', *Harv. Uk. St.*, II, 2 (1978), 158-184.

2611. NORDMANN, C., Charles XII et l'Ukraine de Mazepa. Paris
1958. Pp. 86.

Bibliographies 2612-5; individual accounts 2616-29. NERHOOD
(2612) and CROSS (2613) give full coverage to 1970 of
English-language writing. Individual entries here cover
some recent editions of travellers' works, or accounts of
them; listing is alphabetical by traveller's name. Many of
the most interesting accounts have been reprinted: 2616,
2623, 2628. See also nos 189, 1366, 1384-89, 1406.

2612. NERHOOD, H. (comp.), To Russia and Return, An Annotated
Bibliography of Travellers' English-Language Accounts of
Russia from the Ninth Century to the Present. Columbus,
Ohio 1968. Pp. 367.

2613. CROSS, A.G., 'Travellers' Accounts of Russia in the
English Language: A Survey of Recent Editions and
Bibliographies', CanSlSt., IV, 2 (1970), 327-36.

2614. ADELUNG, Fr. von, Kritische-Literarische Uebersicht der
Reisenden in Russland bis 1700. 2 vols. St. P. 1846,
reprinted Amsterdam 1960.

2615. ZINNER, E., Sibir' v izvestiiakh zapadnoevropeiskikh
puteshestvennikov i uchenykh XVIII veka. Irkutsk 1968.
Pp. 244.

2616. BELL, J., of Antermoney, A Journey from St. Petersburg
to Pekin, 1719-1722. Ed. STEVENSON, J.L., Edinburgh
1965.
Modern edition of work first published 1763.

2617. CRACRAFT, J., 'James Brogden in Russia, 1787-1800',
SEER., XLVII, 108 (1969), 219-44.

2618. DASHWOOD, Sir Francis, 'Sir Francis Dashwood's Diary of
His Visit to St. Petersburg in 1733. Introduction and
Notes by Betty Kemp', SEER., XXXVIII, 2 (1959-60),
194-222.

2619. KIRCHNER, W. (trans. and ed.), A Siberian Journey: The
Journal of Hans Jakob Fries, 1774-76. London 1974.
Pp. 183.

2620. KRASHENINNIKOV, S.P., Explorations of Kamchatka. Report
of a Journal Made to Explore Eastern Siberia in 1735-
1741. Translated and edited by CROWNHART-VAUGHAN,
E.A.P. Portland, Oregon 1972. Pp. 375, illustrations.
Translation of Krasheninnikov's Opisanie zemli
Kamchatki. See also no. 2484.

2621. DESJARDINS, J., 'Francisco de Miranda. Diary of His
Travels Through Russia, 1786-87', M.A. thesis, North
Carolina 1973.
See also nos 1502-4

2622. PARKINSON, J., A Tour of Russia, Siberia and the Crimea, 1792-94. Ed. COLLIER, W. London 1971. Pp. 280.
Rev: *JES.*, 1 (1971), 166-74 (Cross, A.G.).

2623. PERRY, J., The State of Russia under the Present Czar. London 1716, reprinted London 1967. Pp. 280.

2624. RICHARDSON, W., Anecdotes of the Russian Empire. In a series of Letters Written a Few Years Ago From St. Petersburg. London 1784.
See nos 415 and 1803.

2625. LOEWENSON, L., 'Lady Rondeau's Letters from Russia, 1728-39', *SEER.*, XXXV (1956-7), 399-408.

2626. SEGUR, Comte de, Memoirs and Recollections of Count Louis Philippe de Ségur. London 1825-27, reprinted N.Y. 1970.
Ségur, a French diplomat, accompanied Catherine II to the Crimea in 1787. See no. 1212.

2627. LLOYD, C., ANDERSON, R. (eds), A Memoir of James Trevenen. London 1959. Pp. 280.
Siberian travels.

2628. WEBER, F., The Present State of Russia ... 1714-1720. Translated from the German. 2 vols. London 1722-23, reprinted London 1968.

2629. WINTER, E., FIGUROVSKIJ, N. (eds), D.G. Messerschmidt. Forschungsreise durch Sibirien 1720-1727. 2 Teile. Berlin 1962. Pp. 379, 196.
Rev: *ZfG.*, XI (1963), 219 (Hoffmann, P.).

This section includes both addenda, already published, to the preceding sections, and works known to be forthcoming in the near future. Arrangement is by sections as in the main body of the bibliography. Forthcoming items are marked with an asterisk.

SECTION 1

2630. THOMPSON, A., Russia/USSR: A Selective Annotated Bibliography of Books in English. Oxford 1979. Pp. 290.

2631. LIBRARY OF CONGRESS, Bibliographic Guide to Soviet and East European Studies, 1978. 3 vols. Boston 1979. Pp. 2800.
Large-scale annual project based on Library of Congress holdings. Emphasis on Soviet period.

2632. INDEX to Social Sciences and Humanities Proceedings. Philadelphia 1979-
Quarterly listing of all papers published in "proceedings".

*2633. LEWANSKI, R., Eastern Europe and Russia/Soviet Union. A Handbook of Western European Archival and Library Resources. N.Y.-Munich 1980. Pp. 380.

*2634. BROWN, J.H., GRANT, S.A. (comp. and eds), Russian Empire and Soviet Union: A Guide to Archival Sources in the United States of America. Washington, Smithsonian Institution, 1980.

2635. KOVALEVSKY, P., Zarubezhnaia Rossiia: istoriia i kul'-turno-prosvetitel'naia rabota russkogo zarubezh'ia za polveka, 1920-1970. Paris 1971. Pp. 347.
Dopolnitel'nyi vyp., Paris, 1973. Pp. 147.
Includes lists of Russian Historical Societies abroad, etc.

2636. KOSTIUSHKO, I., 'Istoriko-slavisticheskie issledovaniia SSSR (1971-78)', *Sovetskoe slavianovedenie*, 3 (1979), 87-96.

*2637. Novaia istoriia. Ukaz. lit. izdannoi v SSSR na russkom iazyke 1917-1940, 4 parts. Pt. 1: obshchii otdel.
Pervyi period novoi istorii (1640-1870). M. 1980-1986.

SECTION 2

2638. SAKHAROV, A.M., Istoriografiia istorii SSSR: dosovetskii period. M. 1978. Pp. 256.

2639. Istoriia istoricheskoi nauki v SSSR. Sovetskii period. Bibliografiia. M. 1979.

SECTION 3

2640. KALLISTOV, D.P., SMIRNOV, I.I., KOPANEV, A.E. et al., History of the USSR in 3 vols. I: From Ancient Times To The Great October Socialist Revolution. M. 1977. Pp. 376.
2nd, rev. ed. Also in French and German.

SECTION 5

2641. DE JONGE, A., Fire and Water. A Life of Peter the Great. London 1979. Pp. 279.

2642. GASIOROWSKA, X., The Image of Peter the Great in Russian Fiction. Madison 1979. Pp. 199.

*2643. MADARIAGA, I. DE, Russia In The Age of Catherine II. London 1981.

SECTION 6

*2644. PINTNER, W., ROWNEY, D. (eds), Russian Officialdom from the Seventeenth to the Twentieth Century. Chapel Hill, N. Carolina, 1980.
Important collection of essays.

2645. FRUMENKOV, G.G. et al. (eds), Iz istorii politicheskoi ssylki na Evropeiskom Severe, XVIII-nachalo XX vv. Vologda 1978. Pp. 106.

2646. RAEFF, M., 'Codification et droit en Russie impériale: quelques remarques comparatives', CMRS., XX, 1 (1979), 5-13.

2647. KAMPFER, F., Das russische Herrscherbild von den Anfängen bis zu Peter dem Grossen. Recklinghausen 1978. Pp. 281.
Based on author's 1976 Heidelberg Habilitations-schrift.

2648. CHEREPNIN, L., 'K voprosu o skladyvanii absoliutnoi monarkhii v Rossii (XVI-XVIII) vv.', in: SKAZKIN, S. (ed.), Dokumenty sovetsko-italianskoi konferentsii istorikov (1968) (M. 1970), pp. 11-61.

2649. GRIFFITHS, D.M., 'Eighteenth Century Perceptions of
      Backwardness: Projects for the Creation of a Third
      Estate in Catherinean Russia', *CanAmSlSt.*, XIII, 4
      (1979), 452-72.

2650. KAMENDROWSKY, V., 'Catherine II's *Nakaz*, State Finances
      and the *Encyclopédie*', *CanAmSlSt.*, XIII, 4 (1979),
      545-54.

2651. HITTLE, J.M., The Service City. State and Townsmen in
      Russia, 1600-1800. Cambridge, Mass.-London 1979.
      Pp. 297.

2652. RILEY, J., International Government Finance and the
      Amsterdam Capital Market, 1740-1815. Cambridge/NY.
      1980. Pp. 336.

2653. ANISIMOV, E., 'Izmeneniia v sotsial'noi strukture
      russkogo obshchestva v kontse XVII-nachale XVIII veka',
      Ist. SSSR., 5 (1979), 35-52.

2654. SMIRNOV, D.N., Ocherki zhizni i byta nizhegorodtsev XVII-
      XVIII vekov. Gor'kii 1978. 2nd ed. Pp. 343.

2655. ALEKSANDROV, V.A., 'Semeino-imushchestvennye otnosheniia
      po obychnomu pravu v russkoi krepostnoi derevne XVIII-
      nachala XIX v.', *Ist. SSSR.*, 6 (1979), 37-54.

2656. AKMANOV, I.G., Bashkirskoe vosstanie 1735-1736 gg.
      Uchebnoe posobie k spetskursu "Klassovye i
      natsional'no-osbovoditel'nye dvizheniia v Rossii v
      kontse XVII-pervoi treti XVIII v.". Ufa 1977. Pp. 84.

2657. RASKIN, D., 'Ispol'zovanie zakonodatel'nykh aktov v
      krest'ianskikh chelobitnykh serediny XVIII v.', *Ist.
      SSSR.*, 4 (1979), 179-92.

2658. RAZORENOVA, N., 'Beglye krest'iane v gorodakh Srednego
      Povolzh'ia v pervoi chetverti XVIII v.', *VMU(Ist.)*,
      4 (1979), 28-42.

*2659. ORLOV, A., Volneniia na Urale v seredine XVIII v.
      M. 1979. Pp. 264.

SECTION 8

2660. SIVACHEV, N., YAKOVLEV, N., Russia and the United
      States. (Translated by Olga Teitelbaum). Chicago 1979.
      Pp. 320.
      Written by Soviet historians for an American audience.

2661. TRASK, D. et al. (eds), The United States and Russia:
The Beginnings of Relations, 1765-1815. Govt. Publica-
tion Office, 1980.
Documents.

2662. CIESLAK, E. (ed.), Les rapports des Résidents français
à Gdansk, 1715-1796. 3 vols. Gdansk-Warsaw 1964, 1969,
1976.
Numerous Russo-Polish references.

2663. MAHRER, R., Die englisch-russischen Beziehungen
während des Österreichischen Erbfolgekrieges. Phil.
Diss. Wien 1972.

2664. CHIMITDORZHIEV, SH., Vzaimootnosheniia Mongolii i
Rossii XVII-XVIII vv. Materialy arkhivov, letopisei i
khronik. M. 1978. Pp. 215.

2665. Russko-kitaiskie otnosheniia v XVIII veke: Tom I:
1700-1725 gg. M. 1979. Pp. 1120.

SECTION 9

2666. VOLKOV, E., 'Ukazateli morskoi literatury v Rossii',
Sovetskaia Bibliografiia, 2 (1979), 40-6.

SECTION 11

*2667. FENSTER, A., Count P. I. Shuvalov: Politician and Entre-
preneur in 18th C. Russia. Newtonville 1981. Pp. 120.

2668. STRUBE DE PIERMONT, F.-H., Lettres Russiennes.
Presentées par C. Rosso. Pisa 1978. Pp. 219.
Facsimile reproduction of original (St. P. 1760), with
'Introduction', 'Notes de Catherine II, la Grande',
'Postface', 'Bibliographie'.

2669. GOL'DENBERG, L., Katorzhanin - sibirskii gubernator.
Zhizn' i trudy F.I. Soimonova. Magadan 1979. Pp. 287.

2670. KOZLOV, A. (ed.), Materialy k biografii V.N.
Tatishcheva. Sverdlovsk 1964. Pp. 110.
Based on material in Sverdlovsk oblast museum.

*2671. USHAKOVA, N., FIGUROVSKII, N., Vasilii M. Severgin
(1765-1826). M. 1980.

*2672. GRIFFITHS, D., HUDSON, H., The Rise of the Demidov
Family and the Russian Iron Industry in the 18th
Century. Newtonville 1981. Pp. 165.

Intellectual history, education, literature, science: nos.
2673-97. Art and architecture, nos. 2698-2701. Nos. 2677-80,
2682, 2683-84   are to be included in two further Special
Issues of *CanAmSlSt.*, on the eighteenth century. (The first,
on Russia and the West, was XIII, 4 (1979); contents are
listed in appropriate sections).

2673. LIKHACHEV, D.S., 'The Petrine Reforms and The Development
of Russian Culture', *CanAmSlSt.*, XIII, 1-2 (1979),
230-34.

2674. VON HERZEN, M., 'Catherine II-Editor of *Vsiakaia
Vsiachina?* A Reappraisal'. *RR.*, XXXVIII, 3 (1979),
283-98.

*2675. CROSS, A.G., The Russian Theme in English Fiction from
The Sixteenth Century to The Present. An Introductory
Survey and A Bibliography. Oxford 1980.

*2676. CROSS, A.G., 'By the Banks of The Neva'. Britons in
Eighteenth-Century Russia. Newtonville 1980-81.

*2677. OKENFUSS, M.J., 'Popular Educational Tracts in Enlighten-
ment Russia: A Preliminary Study', *CanAmSlSt.* (1980).

*2678. RANSEL, D.L., 'Ivan Betskoi and the Institutionalization
of the Enlightenment in Russia', *CanAmSlSt.* (1980)

*2679. BARTLETT, R.P., 'Culture and Enlightenment: Julius von
Canitz and the Kazan' *gimnazii* in the Eighteenth Century',
CamAmSlSt. (1980).

*2680. McARTHUR, G.H., 'Freemasonry and Enlightenment in Russia:
The Views of N.I. Novikov', *CanAmSlSt.* (1980).

*2681. CRACRAFT, J., (ed.), For God and Peter the Great. The
Works of Thomas Consett. Newtonville 1981. Pp. 400.

Reprint of Consett's history of Peter the Great, with
introductory essay by James Cracraft.

*2682. CARVER, J.S., 'A Reconsideration of Eighteenth Century
Russia's Contributions to European Science',*CanAmSlSt.*(1980)

*2683. GRIFFITHS, D., 'Soviet Views of the Russian
Enlightenment', *CanAmSlSt.* (1980).

2683a. ATKINSON, D., 'The Library of the Free Economic Society',
SR., XXXIX, 1(1980), 97-104.

*2684. GLEASON, W., 'The Two Faces of the Monarch: Legal and
Mythical Fictions in Lomonosov's Ruler Imagery',
CanAmSlSt. (1980).

*2685. DANIEL, W., 'Grigorii Teplov and the Conception of Order: The Commission on Commerce and the Role of the Merchantry in Russia', *CanAmSlSt*. (1980).

*2686. JONES, W.G., 'The Polemics of the 1769 Journals: A Reappraisal', *CanAmSlSt*. (1980).

*2687. McCONNELL, A., 'Radishchev and Classical Antiquity', *CanAmSlSt*. (1980).

*2688. RAMER, S., 'Vasili Popugaev, the Free Society of the Lovers of Literature, Sciences and the Arts, and the Enlightenment Tradition in Russia', *CanAmSlSt*. (1980).

2689. PROUST, J., 'Diderot et l'expérience russe: un exemple de pratique théorique au XVIII siècle', *Studies on Voltaire and the Eighteenth Century*, CLIV (1976), 1777-1800.
Further references in footnotes.

2690. WINTER, E., 'Petrinismus und Josefinismus. Russisch-oesterreichische Wechselbeziehungen in der Aufklärung', *ZfG.*, XXV (1977), 1046-54.

*2691. WINTER, E., 'Josefinismus and Petrinismus: Zur vergleichenden Geschichte der österreichischen und russischen Aufklärung', *CanAmSlSt*. (1980).

2692. MAIER, L.A., 'Die Krise der St. Petersburger Akademie der Wissenschaften nach der Thronbesteigung Elisabeth Petrovnas und die "Affäre Gmelin"', *JbfGO.*, XXVII, 3 (1979), 353-73.

*2693. ROBEL, G., 'Der Wandel des deutschen Sibirienbildes im 18. Jahrhundert', *CanAmSlSt*. (1980).

2694. LOSHITS, IU.M., Skovoroda. M. 1972. Pp. 223.

2695. BOBRINSKOI, P. Starchik G. Skovoroda. Zhizn' i uchenie. Madrid 1965. Pp. 77.

2696. KUZNETSOVA, I.(ed.), Liudi russkoi nauki. Ocherki o vyda-iushchikhsia deiateliakh estestvoznaniia i tekhniki. M. 1961-65. Pp. 600,579,896,778.
Short biographical accounts; good reference tool to begin in-depth studies.

2697. KASTORSKII, S.V. (ed.), Iz istorii russkikh literaturnykh otnoshenii XVIII-XX vekov. M-L. 1959. Pp.440.
Essays on various themes: Prokopovich (M. Alekseev); folklore (N.Adrianova-Perets); 'Dramatic Dictionary' of 1787 (P.Berkov); Jean de Castera and Russia (B. Tomashevskii).

2698. ARCHITECTURE OF THE RUSSIAN NORTH, Twelfth to Nineteenth
Centuries. L. 1976. Pp. 298, 212 plates.

2699. KIRICHENKO, E., Architectural Monuments of Moscow.
M. 1977. Pp. 126, 250 plates.
English and Russian text.

2700. DUNCAN, D.D., Great Treasures of the Kremlin. N.Y. 1960,
reprinted N.Y. 1980. Pp. 160.

*2701. BRUMFIELD, W., Gold in Azure. Architectural Monuments of
the Soviet Union. Boston 1980.

SECTION 13

*2702. HAUGH, R., (ed.), Encyclopaedia of Orthodox Theology and
History. Belmont, Mass. 1982+
A comprehensive on-going project with all articles in
English.

*2703. FLOROVSKY, G., Collected Works. Belmont, Mass. 8 vols.
1980+. Vols. 5-6 pub. to date. Vol. 5 has numerous
references to 18th Century.

*2704. LUPININ, N., PAHOMOV, G., (eds), The History of the
Russian Church. Belmont, Mass. 1981+
Approx. 30 vols planned including a translation of
GOLUBINSKII'S Istoriia russkoi tserkvi.

SECTION 14

*2705. LANG, D., The Last Years of the Georgian Monarchy, 1658-
1832. N.Y. 1980.

2706. WERTSMANN, V., The Russians in America. Dobbs Ferry
1977. Pp. 140.

2707. BRIGADIROV, N. (comp.), PRONSHTEIN, A. (ed.), Istoriia
Dona: ukazatel' literatury. 2 vols. Rostov 1968-9.
Vol. I: Dorevol. literatura. Vol. II: Sovetskaia
literatura.

*2708. KIRBY, S., A History of Siberia. 3 vols. London 1980.

2709. SUBTELNY,O.,' Russia and the Ukraine: The Difference that
Peter I Made', RR., XXXIX,1(1980), 1-18.

2710. GRIGOR'IAN, K. (comp.), 'Armianskaia literatura v
russkikh perevodakh', in AIBAZIAN, K.(ed.), Literaturnye sviazi. Vol 1. (Erevan 1973), pp. 252-348.

2710a. VAITKLIVICHIUS, B.(ed.), Istoriia Litovskoi SSR.
Vilnius 1978 . Pp. 679.

APPENDIX: 'The Collection of the Imperial Russian Historical
            Society' and 'The Senate Archive'

(a) Sbornik Imperatorskogo Russkogo Istoricheskogo Obshchestva.
    Abbreviated SIRIO., or Sb.RIO. 148 vols. St. P. 1866-1918.
    Reprinted, also available in microform.
    Summary cumulative index at the end of later volumes. A collec-
    tion mainly of primary sources. Particularly useful for diplo-
    matic correspondence, usually printed in the original language.
    Principal eighteenth-century materials are listed below.
    Material scattered through several or many volumes has been
    grouped together.

    - diplomatic

    1. Diplomatic correspondence of Empress Catherine II (1762-77).
       SIRIO., XLVIII (correspondence for 1762-63); LI (1763-64);
       LVII (1764-66); LXVII (1766-67); LXXXVII (1768-69); XCVII
       (1769-71); CXVIII (1772-73); CXXXV (1774-75); CXLV (1776-77).
       Partly in French. Catherine's correspondence with diplomats
       abroad.

    2. Instructions to diplomat Rehbinder from Catherine II. SIRIO.,
       III.

    3. Papers of Russian envoy IA.I. Bulgakov, 1779-98. SIRIO.,
       XLVII.

    4. Austrian diplomatic correspondence, St. Petersburg-Vienna,
       1762-76. SIRIO., XVIII (1762); XLVI (1762-63); CIX (1763-71);
       CXXV (1772-76).
       In German. Includes an account of the death of Peter III.

    5. British diplomatic correspondence, St. Petersburg-London,
       1704-76. SIRIO., XXXIX (1704-08); L (1708-11); LXI (1711-19);
       LXVI (1728-33); LXXVI (1733-36); LXXX (1736-39); LXXXV (1740-
       41); XCI (1741-42); XCIX (1742-44); CII (1744-45); CIII (1746-
       48); CX (1748-50); CXLVIII (1750-53); XII (1762-69); XIX
       (1770-76).
       In English, with Russian translation. Transcript of London
       PRO mss records, with very little omitted. Veterans of these
       PRO files can detect the faint pencil marks on the pages of
       the original marked by the nineteenth-century Russian
       copyists.

6. French diplomatic correspondence, St.Petersburg-Paris, etc.,
   1681-1772. SIRIO., XXXIV (papers for 1681-1718); XL (1719-
   23); XLIX (1722-24); LII (1723-25); LVIII (1725); LXIV (1725-
   27); LXXV (1727-30); LXXXI (1730-33); LXXXVI (1738-40); XCII
   (1740-41); XCVI (1741); C (1741-43); CV (1743-45); CXL (1762-
   65); CXLI (1766-69); CXLIII (1769-72).
   Selections from French Foreign Ministry Archive,
   Correspondence Diplomatique, Russie. In French, with Russian
   translation.

7. Polish and Saxon diplomatic correspondence, 1697-1744.
   SIRIO., XX (1697-1718; 1734-40); III (1721-31); V (1728-34);
   VI (1742-44).

8. Prussian diplomatic correspondence, early eighteenth century
   and 1763-74.   SIRIO., XV (papers of Baron Mardefeld, envoy
   under Peter I); XXII (1763-66); XXXVIII (1767-72); LXXII
   (1772-74). SIRIO., XX (correspondence of Catherine II with
   Frederick of Prussia).
   From Berlin archives. In French with Russian translation.

   - *internal affairs*

9. Peter I - 'Pis'ma, ukazy i zametki Petra I-ogo', SIRIO., XI.

10. Peter II - Codification Commission. SIRIO., II.

11. Verkhovnyi Tainyi Sovet - 'Protokoly, zhurnaly i ukazy
    Verkhovnogo Tainogo Soveta 1726-1730 gg.', SIRIO., LV (for
    1726); LVI (1726); LXIII (1727); LXIX (1727); LXXIX (1728);
    LXXXIV (1728); XCIV (1729); CI (1729-30).

12. Kabinet Ministrov - 'Bumagi Kabineta Ministrov Imp. Anny
    Ioannovny 1731-1740 gg.', SIRIO., CIV (papers for 1731-2);
    CVI (1733); CVIII (1734); CXI (1735); CXIV (1736); CXVII
    (1737); CXX (1738); CXXIV (1738); CXXVI (1739); CXXX (1739);
    CXXXVIII (1740); CXLVI (1740).

13. Konferentsiia - 'Protokoly Konferentsii pri Vysochaishem
    Dvore', SIRIO., CXXXVI (covers 1756-57).

14. Catherine II, personal and state papers, 1744-96. 'Bumagi
    imp. Ekateriny II, khraniashchiesia v Gosudarstvennom arkhive'.
    SIRIO., VII (papers for 1744-64); X (1765-71); XIII (1771-
    74); XXVII (1774-88); XLII (1789-96, 1762).

15. Commission for the Composition of a New Code of Laws.
    'Istoricheskie svedeniia o Ekaterininskoi Kommissii dlia
    Sochinenii Proekta Novogo Ulozheniia ...', SIRIO., IV, VIII,
    XIV, XXXII, XXXVI, XLIII, LXVIII, XCIII, CVII, CXV, CXXIII,
    CXXXIV, CXLIV, CXLVII.

16. Financial documents of reign of Catherine II. SIRIO., I, VI, XXVIII, XLV.

17. 'Vypiska o gos. uchrezhdeniiakh, osnovannykh imp. Ekaterinoiu II, s 1762 po 1769', SIRIO., II.

18. 'Prockt kn. M.N. Volkonskogo o luchshem uchrezdenii sudebnykh mest, podannyi imp. Ekaterine II v 1775', SIRIO., V.

19. Papers on the affair of the pretender Princess Tarakanova. SIRIO., I.

20. Papers of Ct. P.I. Panin on the Pugachev revolt. SIRIO., VI.

21. 'Vedomost' sostoiashchim v Sanktpeterburge fabrikam, manufakturam i zavodam, 1794 goda'. SIRIO., I.

- *personal papers*

22. Sheremet'ev, B.P., Fieldmarshal, 1704-18. SIRIO., XXV.

23. Shuvalov, I.I., correspondence. SIRIO., IX.

24. 'O memuarakh gertsoga Fridrikha, otsa imp. Petra III', SIRIO., I.

25. Catherine II, correspondence. SIRIO., I (with A.G. Orlov, Nassau-Siegen, Geoffrin, et al.); XVII (with Falconet - French and Russian); XV (with Grand Duke Paul and his wife); XXIII, XXXIII, XLIV (with Baron F.M. Grimm, 1774-96. In French).

26. Catherine II, 'Bumagi iz arkhiva dvortsa v g. Pavlovske, 1782', SIRIO., II.

27. Bezborodko, 'Kantsler Kn. A.A. Bezborodko v sviazi s sobytiiami ego vremeni ...' SIRIO., XXVI (covers 1746-87); XXIX (1788-99).
Biographical study.

28. Panin correspondence - N.I., P.I., N.P. Panin. SIRIO., V, IX.

29. Paul, Grand Duke SIRIO., XV, XX.

30. Repnin, Prince N.V. SIRIO., V, VI, XV, XVI, LXV.

31. Richelieu, Duc Armand-E. de, 1766-1822. French émigré who made a distinguished career in Russia. SIRIO., LIV.

15 vols, St. P. 1888-1913. Includes protocols, resolutions
and other records of the Governing Senate from the eighteenth
century. This series is quite rare. The British Library set
is incomplete. Full sets known to the compilers, outside the
Soviet Union and Helsinki, are in the Law Library, Harvard
and New York Public Library.

I   (St. P. 1888) Imennye ukazy Imperatora Pavla I.

II   (St. P. 1889) Zhurnaly i opredeleniia Pravitel'-
                      stvuiushchego Senata. Starts with 1732.
                      Incomplete records for 1732, 1735, 1737,
                      1738, 1739. Complete for 1740- early
                      1741.

III   (St. P. 1890) Zhurnaly Prav. Senata.
                      March - May 1741.

IV   (St. P. 1891) Zhurnaly prav. Senata.
                      June - September 1741.

V   (St. P. 1892) Zhurnaly Prav. Senata.
                      October - December 1741.

VI   (St. P. 1893) Zhurnaly i opredeleniia Prav. Senata.
                      1744-1746

VII   (St. P. 1895) 1. Protokoly Prav. Senata. 1747-1749.
                      2. Spisok voennym chinam pervoi poloviny
                         XVIII stoletiia.

VIII   (St. P. 1897) Protokoly Prav. Senata.
                      1750-1752.

IX   (St. P. 1901) Protokoly Prav. Senata.
                      1753-1756.

X   (St. P. 1903) 1. Protokoly Prav. Senata. 1757-1758.
                      2. Papers on the affair of Kaluga governor
                         Lopukhin.

XI   (St. P. 1904) 1. Protokoly Prav. Senata. 1759.
                      2. Ukazy i poveleniia Imperatritsy
                         Ekateriny II. 1762.
                      3. Protokoly Prav. Senata. 1760.

XII   (St. P. 1907) 1. Protokoly Prav. Senata. 1761-1763.
                      2. Ukazy i poveleniia Imperatritsy
                         Ekateriny II.
                         January - July 1763.

XIII (St. P. 1909) 1. Protokoly Prav. Senata po sekretnoi
                       ekspeditsii. 1764-1765.
                    2. Ukazy i poveleniia Imperatritsy
                       Ekateriny II.
                       July 1763 - January 1764.

XIV   (St. P. 1910) Ukazy i poveleniia Imperatritsy Ekateriny
                    II.
                    February - December 1764.

XV   (St. P. 1913) Ukazy i poveleniia Imperatritsy Ekateriny
                    II. 1765.

INDEX

(Individuals as a subject are in capital letters)

Aav, Y., 1971
Abdulaev, G., 2425-6
Abetsedarskii, L. S., 2395
Abramowitz, R., 2329
Adamshchik, A., 2401
Adams, A. E., 1362
ADELUNG, FR. von, 1777, 2614
Adrianova-Perets, N., 2119, 2697
Afferica, J., 227, 1562
Ageeva, E. E., 2449
Agzamov, F., 1938
Aizenberg, A., 1900
Akademiia Nauk, BSSR 2412
Akademiia Nauk, GrSSR 2439
Akademiia Nauk Kazakhskoi SSR 2454
Akademiia Nauk Latviiskoi SSR 2390
Akademiia Nauk Litovskoi SSR 2351
Akademiia Nauk (Biblioteka Vostochno-Sibir-
  Skogo Filiala (Irkutsk)), 2517
Akademiia Nauk SSSR 97, 1486
Akdes Nimet Kurat, 1331
Akmanov, I. G., 2656
Akopian, T., 2436
Aksakov, S. T., 670
Aksenov, A. I., 772
Alatortseva, A. I., 191
Alefirenko, P., 734
Aleksandrov, A. A., 901
Aleksandrov, V. A., 492, 725, 1027, 1418, 2655
Alekseev, B. N., 1359
Alekseev, M. P., 209, 1668-70, 1701, 1709, 1828,
  1851, 1859, 2697, 2701
Alekseeva, G. D., 191
Alekseeva, T. V., 2066, 2068, 2069, 2081, 2099
Alexander, J. T., 386, 552, 820-2, 824, 965,
  2215, 2217, 2222
Alexeiev, N., 428
Aliev, F., 1191
Alishev, S. KH., 900
Allen, R., 110
Allworth, E., 2442
Almedingen, E., 396
Alpatov, M. A., 203, 238, 1671, 2055
Alston, P. L., 1879
Amburger, E., 447, 587-8, 1017, 1093a, 1094,
  1137, 1336, 1530, 1731, 1864, 1924, 2248, 2305
Amitin-Shapiro, Z., 2448
Anderson, C. A., 963
Anderson, M. S., 249, 310, 322, 1127, 1270-1,
  1344, 1458, 1790

Anderson, P., 421
Anderson, R., 2627
Anderson, T., 273
Andolenko, S., 1299
Andreev, A. I., 303
Andreeva, N. F., 149
Andrushenko, A. I., 888
Andrusiak, N., 1318
Aniskimov, E., 1050, 2653
Annanepesov, M., 2458
ANNE (Empress), 350,363-5
Anners, E., 1320
Anschel, E., 1838
Antonova, K. A., 1117
Antropov, A. P., 2079
Anziner, H., 49
Apollova, N., 2453, 2457, 2459
Aretin, Freiherr K. O. von, 424
ARGUNOV, IVAN 2078
Arian-Baykov, I., 1983
Aristova, B., 2051a
Armbruster, D., 1953
Arminton, V., 2272
Armstrong,J., 2567
Armstrong, J. A., 456
Armstrong. T., 2512, 2527
Arsh, G. L., 1289, 1292
Artemenkov, M. N., 1010
Arjas, E., 2352
Artamonov, V., 1239
ASCH, GEORG von, 1761
Ashurkov, V., 2211
Astrōm, S. E., 1063-4
Atkin, M., 1185
Atkinson, D., 549, 2683a
Attman, A., 1108
Auerbach, H., 2588
Augustine, W. R., 510, 631
Auty, R., 283, 1597, 1914, 2041
Avakumovic, T., 2291
Avilova, N., 2044
Avrich, P., 819
Avtokratov, V. N., 1311
Avtokratova, M., 2175
Avtukhova, I., 2190
Azarenko, E. K., 1491
Azatian, A., 2456

244

CATHERINE I, 350-362
CATHERINE II, 199, 245, 455, 457, 515, 517-8, 534, 551, 638, 965, 1826, 1867, 2110, 2297, 2332, 2381-2, 2586, 2626, 2643, 2650, 2668, 2674, 2681
Cernobrivt'sev, O. S., 2590
Chambre, H., 582
Charbonneau, L, 166
CHARLES XII, 1248, 1316, 2611
CAMERON, CHARLES, 2076
Chekmenev, S. A., 752c
Chemeritskii, V., 2413
Chenakal, V. L., 1484-5, 1815, 1832-4, 2195
Chepko, V. V., 2396
Cherepnin, L., 193, 196, 213, 216, 267, 610, 612, 615, 879, 942, 1145, 1510, 2021, 2648
Cherevan, A. S., 858
Cherkasova, A. S., 992
Cherniavsky, M., 288, 2282
Chernikov, A. M., 1559
Chernov, A. V., 448, 871
Chernov, E., 2232
Chernyshev, V. I., 2047
Chevalier, B., 1476
Chew, A. F., 61
Chimitdorzhiev, S. H., 2664
Chistov, K., 1629
Chizhevskii (Tschizhewski), D., 1594, 1612, 1975, 2600
Chobanu, L., 1450
CHRISTIAN, GARVE, 1503
CHRISTIAN, GOLDBACH, 1729
CHRISTIAN, WOLFF, 1749-50
Christie, I., 112, 1347-8, 1805
Chuchmarev, V., 1756
Chugai, V., 948
CHULKOV, M., 199, 1991
Cieslak, E., 2662
Cizova, T., 503
Clardy, J., 1430, 1539
Clarkson, J., 252, 476
Clendenning, P. H., 168, 570, 577, 1070-1, 1350, 2220
Clogg, R., 1289
Close, B., 167
Cole, E. A., 1455
Colin, M., 1544
Collier, W., 2622
COMMISSION INTERNATIONALE DES ETUDES SLAVES, 1605

Confino, M., 581, 650, 677-80, 909-10, 966, 1592
Cook, M., 1266
Cooks, J. B., 2162
Cooper, B. F., 1986
Coppock, H. A., 2471
Coquin, F.-X., 521, 2514
Cornell, N. W., 643
COYER, GABRIEL-FRANCOIS, 1681
Cracraft, J., 320, 327, 358, 2246, 2260, 2307-10, 2617
Crisp, O., 258, 563, 1121
Crosby, A. W., 1078-9
Cross, A. G., 1033, 1349, 1428, 1454, 1532, 1597, 1657, 1720, 1792-6, 1977, 1809-12, 1819, 1821-3, 1863, 1869, 1918, 1954, 1955, 1988, 1990, 1994, 2165a, 2613, 2675-6
Crownhart-Vaughan, E. A. P., 2620
Crowther, P. A., 113
Crummey, R., 408, 633, 2284
Curtis, M., 363
Curtiss, J. S., 2259
Cvetkova (Tsvetkova), B., 1279

Daiches, D., 1983
Dal', V. I., 2048
Dallin, A., 549
Daniel, W. L., 512-3, 758, 2685
Daniels, R. L., 1570
Danilevskii, V. V., 1500
Danilov, V. P., 724
Danilova, I., 2082
Danilova, L., 997
DANTE, 1669
DASHKOVA, PRINCESS E. R., 1425-6
DASHWOOD, SIR FRANCIS, 2618
Davies, N., 1227
Davison, R. H., 1275
De Jonge, A., 2641
Dement'ev, A., 150
Demidov, A. N., 989
Demidova, N. F., 488, 1054, 2507
Demina, A. S., 2022
Derbov, L. A., 1522
Derevianko, A., 2486
DERZHAVIN, G. R., 1429-32
Derzhavina, O., 2165
Dergacheva-Skop, E., 2526
Desaive, D., 1281
DESNITSKII, S., 295, 504, 508, 520
Desjardins, J., 2621
Diachkov, A., 1038

Fedoseev, I., 2198
Fedoseev, P., 1506
Fedosov, I. A., 442, 1565
Fedosov, V. A., 2581
Fedotov, D., 2234
Feigina, S. A., 197, 1146
Feinshtein, S. C., 485
Fennell, J., 1614
Fenster, A., 2667
Ferguson, A., 228
Ferrier, R. W., 1088
Fessenko, T., 137
Feyl, D., 1755
Figurovskii, N. A., 1484, 1753, 2192, 2629, 2671, 2202
Filimonova, N. I., 1523
Filippov, A., 464
FILOFEI, METROPOLITAN, 2562
Fink, H., 2275
Firsov, G. G., 2186
FIRSOV, N.N., 215
Fisher, A., 1272, 1845, 2294, 2418
Fisher, R., 1406, 2317, 2466
Fitzlyon, K., 1426
Fleischhacker, H., 372, 394-5
Florinsky, M., 57, 248
Florovskii, A., 239, 1163, 1170, 1173, 1854, 1910
Florovsky, G., 2703
FONVIZIN, DENIS, 1435-6, 1596, 1758, 2026, 2696
Foote, J., 2315
FORSTER, J. R., 1771,1717
Foster, R., 823
Foust, C., 1199
Fox, F., 1075-6, 1212
Fradkina, Z., 116
FRANKLIN, BEN, 1848
Frederichson, J. W., 1077
FREE ECONOMIC SOCIETY, 581, 591-2, 626-8, 680, 738-9, 743, 1600, 1708, 1778, 1801, 2683a
Freeze, G., 2263-5
Freidenberg, M. M., 875
French, R. A., 2318
FRIES, HANS JAKOB, 2619
Froncek, T., 2054
Frumenkov, G. G., 1152, 1337, 2645
Fuchs, P., 427
Furaev, V. K., 1160
Fursenko, A., 1161

Gaddis, V. L., 1153
Gagliardo, J. G., 410
Gajecky, G., 2572-3

Galaktionov, A., 1647
Galoian, G., 1186
Galuzo, P. G., 2449
Garrard, J. G., 1595, 1991
GARVE, CHRISTIAN, 1503
Gasiorowska, X., 2642
Gastfer, M. P., 2186
Gatto, Ettorelo, 2002
Gaxotte, P., 391
Gedrimovich, G. B., 2186
Gekhtman, G., 1384
Gessen, V. IU., 854
GEOGRAFICHESKOE OBSHCHESTVO SSR, 1373
George, M. D., 2110
Georgiev, V. G., 1265
Gerasimova, IU., 31
GERMAN (The Monk), 2485
Germanis, I., 2365
Gernet, M., 539
Gerschenkron, A., 559-60, 668
Geseman, W., 554
Geyer, D., 186, 336, 431-2, 584, 786
Gibian, G., 2155
Gibson, J. R., 2476-8, 2481, 2483, 2511
GIDEON (The Hieromonk), 2485
Giesinger, A., 2343
Gilbert, D., 1153
Gilbert, M., 62, 2331
Gilissen, J., 494
Girod de l'Ain, G., 1091
Givens, R. D., 511, 642
Glasenapp, I. von, 429
Glaskow, W., 745
Gleason, A., 1667
Gleason, W., 1568, 1601, 2684
Glinka, G. L., 2527
Glinka, V., 2127
Glushkov, T., 812
GMELIN, P., 648, 2692
Goehrke, C., 265, 586, 683-4
Geodeke, H., 337
GOETHE, 177a
Gökbilgin, Ü., 1281
GOLDBACH, CHRISTIAN, 1729
Gol'denberg, L. A., 1577, 2669, 1322, 1363, 1567, 1963, 2430, 2556
Goldhagen, E., 2325
Goldmann, M., 961
Golikova, N. V., 535, 538, 743, 872, 1011-2
GOLITSYN, D. M., 362, 589, 1050
Golobutskii, V. A., 751-2,7526,859,2423 ,2602
Golovin, V., 1370
GOMM, WILLIAM, 577

247

250

251

254

257

Safronov, F., 2535
Sakharov, A. M., 202, 787, 1905, 2256, 2638
Sakharova, I., 2079
Sakol'chik, A., 2394
Sal'man, G. IA., 1356
SANCHES RIBEIRO, DR., 2219,2224
Saushkina, IU., 1380
Salmaslian, A., 2434
Samorukova, N. A., 48
Sanninskii, B., 555
Sarafian, W., 2480
Sarkisyanz, E., 2432, 2446
Saul, N. E., 1081, 1134, 1840
Saunders, D. B., 2577
Sauter, V., 1697
Savant, J., 1216
Savarenkaia, T.,
Savochkin, P., 2401
Sawchak , V., 2569
SCANDINAVIAN SLAVISTS, 80
Schakovskoy, D., 647
Scharf, C., 405
Schatoff, M., 143
Scheibert, P., 685
Schenk, H., 1741
Scherer, S. P., 2269
Schildbauer, J., 837
SCHILLER, 1620,1670,1774
SCHLÖZER, A. L. von,   1145, 1719, 1732, 1763
Schmidt, H., 1739, 1762
Schmidt, S., 366
Scholtz, B., 1899
Schop-Soler, A. M., 1243
Schreyer-Mühlpfordt, B., 1335
Schulin, E., 405
Schultheiss, TH., 75
SCHUMACHER, 1728
Schutzler, H., 839
Schwartz, H., 1195
Scott, F. D., 461
Scott, H., 1168
Scott, R., 2300
Seaman, G. R., 2134, 2138-41
Seeberg-Elverfeldt, R., 2364
Seeman, K.-D., 83
Segal, A., 2236
Segel, H., 1978, 1981
SEGUR, COMTE DE, 1212, 2626
Seiden, J., 279
Sekirinskii, S. A., 953
Selinova, T. A., 2078
Semeka, S., 2241
Semeniuk, G. I., 895
Semenova, I., 1339

Semenova, L. N., 1014, 1291
Semevskii, V. I., 686, 733a
SEMINAR IN UKRAINIAN STUDIES, HARVARD UNIVERSITY
  2563
Senkevitch, A., 2486
Senn, A. E., 73
SERAPHIM OF SAROV, 2279
Serbina, K., 721, 1000
Serman, I. Z., 1678, 2027
Sethe, P., 263
SEVERGIN, V. M., 1566, 2671
Shabaeva, M. F., 1519, 1900
Shabanova, A., 707, 865-6, 939
SHAFIROV, P. P., 199, 501
Shafranovskii, I., 1389
Shafronovskii, K., 1921
SHAKESPEARE, 1828-9, 1662
Shakinko, I. M., 1582
Shamrai, D. D., 1949-50
Shapiro, A. L., 220, 705, 877, 1358
Sharkova, I., 1111-2
Shaskol'skii, I. P., 1148
Shaw, D. J. B., 2496
Shaw, S. J., 1267
SHCHERBATOV, M. M., 199, 206, 579, 1525
  1561-5, 1592
Shchipanov, I. IA., 1628, 1632, 1649, 1652
Shchukina, E., 1037, 2126, 2131
Sheehy, E. P., 46
Shepelev, L. E., 5, 493
Shepukova, N. M., 657, 702-3, 1397, 2540
Sherman, I. L., 234
Shershavin, S., 2237
Sherter, S. R., 223
Shevchenko, Z., 2450
Shibkov, A. A., 2231
Shil'nikovskaia, V., 2108
Shimkin, D. B., 2484
Shitsgal, A., 1951
Shmeca, A., 2188
Shmidt, S., 624
Shmushkis, IA., 55
Shpak, I., 2416
Shprygova, M. R., 1842
Shtokals, I., 2200
Shtorm, G., 1556
Shtrange, M. M., 196, 1145, 1218, 1221, 1625-6
Shtykhov, G., 2397
Shukhardin, S., 2209
Shul'ga, I. G., 1022, 2401
Shunkov, V. I., 609. 787, 1306, 2530-1
Shutoi, V. E., 1323, 1328
SHUVALOV, I. I., 1306

258

259

261

Проспектъ Ораніенбаума увеселительнаго дворца Ея Императорскаго Величества
ут Финликускомъ заливѣ против Кроншата.